THE LAST DAY OF NALIBOKI

the untold story behind the massacre

MIECZYSLAW KLIMOWICZ

American Literary Press
Five Star Special Edition
Baltimore, Maryland

The Last Day of Naliboki

Copyright © 2009 Mieczyslaw Klimowicz

All rights reserved under International and Pan-American copyright conventions. No part of this book may be reproduced, stored in a retrieval system, or transmitted in any form, electronic, mechanical, or other means, now known or hereafter invented, without written permission of the publisher.
Address all inquiries to the publisher.

Library of Congress
Cataloging-in-Publication Data
ISBN-13: 978-1-934696-26-2

Library of Congress Card Catalog Number:
2008909072

Published by

American Literary Press
Five Star Special Edition

8019 Belair Road, Suite 10
Baltimore, Maryland 21236

Manufactured in the United States of America

Chapter I

THE WILDERNESS OF NALIBOKI

Rzeczpospolita Polski, that is to say, the Free State of Poland. This regime of Poland originated based upon the independence of peasants who won their struggle for freedom, and to its memory and honor Poland kept a festival on the third of May, when the constitution was consolidated, the fundamental laws and principles that normally governed the operation of Poland. After Poland was partitioned by Austria, Russia and Prussia she ceased to exist for a period of over one hundred years. The insurrections were repeatedly unsuccessful. One of the organized resistances undertaken to liberate Poland was under the leadership General Tadeusz Kosciuszko, who after the war in America decided to go back to the subjugated Poland. In Warsaw General Kosciuszko without any difficulty organized a large body of men armed for military combat, which he left there in order to arrange another army systematically in the region of Nowogrodek, northeast of Poland. With a new army, on his arrival to Warsaw he found that one day previously the entire army of Warsaw was destroyed by the Cossacks, one of a people of southern USSR famous as cavalrymen. Only for the sake of curiosity, the general decided to inspect the battlefield of the dead Polish insurgents. General Kosciuszko, in the company of fourteen cavalry officers, collided against six Cossacks, who killed all officers and took Kosciuszko, seriously wounded, captive to Russia. Consequently, in assistance to the captive insurgent made by the American president, General Kosciuszko was released from thralldom and found his refuge at Solothurn, Switzerland, where he died on October 15, 1817.

Poland endured without yielding a royal domain from the year 566 A.D., when the first king of Poland, Mieszko the First, was crowned at the ceremony in Czechoslovakia with the German alliance. The entire kingdom of Poland fundamentally was based on three dynasties, particularly Piasty, Jagieloay and Elekcyjae. That last dynasty was indeed disastrous to Poland on account of the kings being elected from foreign countries and feelings of deep reverential awe and dread; Poland struggled by veto to keep the German candidates out, but finally Germany succeeded and ruled Poland by the three Saxons, August the First, August the Second and Stanislaw August Poniatowski, in whose reign the kingdom of Poland was divided and thrown into nonexistence in the eighteenth century.

The wilderness arises from the region of Nowogrodek and embraces a large area that extends far eastward into the Russia. This Wilderness of Naliboki is surrounded by major cities, namely Nowogrodek, Grodno, Lida, Wilno, Baranowicze, Stolpce, Slonim, Iwieniec and Minsk. This Wilderness of Naliboki for Poland was a cause of honorable pride as a distinction, and it has been inside the perimeter of Polish boundary lines from the kings Miszko the First to the Stanislaw August Poniatowski. This honorable pride of wilderness was abundant of the wild kingdom inhabiting the forest and living in a state of nature. There in existence was life such as fish, amphibian, reptile, bird and mammal. But in this particular region, the major division of wildlife was mammal, because it was indispensable for the people to hunt in search of game for food. That is why, after the First World War during a widespread scarcity of food, animals like European bison became extinct in the Wilderness of Naliboki. However, there still remained wild boars, deer and hares, as well as wolves, foxes, beavers and many other creatures.

The wilderness added to its splendor an attractive and desirable variety of birds. Due to the fact that the area was extremely rich in an abundance of food, thus the great number of different kinds of birds were migrating to the same locality of habitation of the previous year. The most outstanding of migrating birds in the area was a white stork that flew from Europe 8,000 miles to winter in South Africa. These magnificent, high, two-legged birds enjoyed feeding themselves on an amphibian. They built large nests high upon the tops of trees and sometimes even on the roofs of buildings, where they laid eggs and hatched out young, and during such a process, storks clacked beautifully with their bills.

To specify the game birds, there were plenty of wild geese, ducks, pheasants, partridges and pigeons. It was well suited to one's purpose or need to obtain such easy food in the time of necessity.

Kosciusko Thaddeus, Polish Tadeusz Kosciuszko 1746-1817, Polish patriot and general born in Lithuania; fought in the American Revolution.

The Last Day of Naliboki

The wilderness was dominated by the reptile. There were some kinds of deadly poisonous snakes that could inject venom into the victim through tubular fangs. It was well known that a number of people lost their lives on account of not being cautious of the danger in the forest.

The region of wilderness is possessed of lakes, ponds, springs, streams and rivers, including the major river, Niemen, which originates in the wilderness and flows by Polish cities such as Mir, Nowogrodek and Grodna, and eventually falls into the Baltic Sea. Approximately nine miles west of Naliboki in the forest there is a lake named Kroman, from which a river used to flow into the Niemen. But soon after the First World War the Polish government had this river converted directly into a canal, used as an artificial waterway for inland transportation of the large quantity of timber to the Baltic Sea. The bodies of fresh water in the region were filled with great varieties of fish. There was a multitude of schools of fish in the canal in one place after another, where they could be easily caught by net since there were no restrictions imposed by law to use nets in fishing. Of course, one such school of fish caught in the net was enough to feed a big family or to throw a party.

The Wilderness of Naliboki was covered with inhabiting forests of all sorts of trees that grew to a considerable height. The forests were divided by square kilometers (equivalent to 0.386 square miles), and to each of the eight square kilometers there was assigned a forester who was responsible in the science of planting and managing the forest. The separation of the forest into sections was made by cutting straight lines throughout the wilderness. These lines in a miniature sense became borders to each forester, who was obligated to plough them at least twice a year for the purpose of preventing the spread of fire in the woodland. The area that was from time to time destroyed by fire, or where the trees were cut for the commercial purpose, was replaced by a young trees that were cultivated in the forester's nursery. The nursery was equipped in a number of varieties of the young cultivated trees, such as common pine, fir, oak, birch, alder, maple, ash, lime and willow, and these were transplanted in the vacant parts of woodland of the past original forest. The forester in his individual employed area had an endowment given by the Polish government that was comprised of an income and property for the permanent use of an institution. This property initially was designed and equipped for the personal business of farming, with room for the exercise of faculties for the future to enjoy and live in prosperity. Such a forester was cultivating his fields surrounding the buildings with a crop such as vegetables, grain, wheat, barley, buckwheat, Indian corn, sunflower, oats and so on. The forester's establishment contained an orchard, besides the whole area being covered with blossoms and flowers during each spring and summer, a place where the apiculture was one of well-rewarding pursuit of interest, undertaken for pleasure or business. Such a husbandry included all livestock, had a fine dairy and beef cattle, horses, hogs and sheep, and also contained poultry; generally bred were hens, geese and ducks.

On the west side of Niemen River in the zone of cities such as Mir, Nowogrodek and Lids the land was flowing with milk and honey on account of mould, which is soft, loose earth that is especially suitable for plants because it is rich in decaying organic matter. This particular kind of earth is natural and most fertile soil for the growth of crop and vegetables, and factually nowhere else was found in Poland, except a small portion in the region of the city of Toron by the river Wisla.

Because of such a rich and productive land of human habitation, the Niemen River became most famous in the public eye; thus songs were composed about the Niemen and sung throughout the country.

The people in that particular zone had a lifespan somewhat longer than average, and a notable number of them were huge, strong, able-bodied men. It was frequently said by folks that behind the river Niemen there were giants dwelling, like in legend, a manlike being of supernatural size and strength, as in Greek mythology, one of the race who warred against the gods of Olympus.

It was obvious, of course, that these giant-like men were able to consume more food than three average men, and indeed they could produce more work than three ordinary men. For example, there was Mr. Kostus, who was employed by the firm Smolaraia (a place where pitch is burnt) and whose job was grubbing up the stumps of common pine trees which contained a great deal of pitch. While he was working in the forest with the twelve other men, they had an argument about that particular work, but without any hesitation Mr. Kostus demanded a contest with them. And it came about that a contest was established between one man, namely Kostus, versus twelve working men, an event about which a bet was made, and it was understood that during the entire month they had to dig from the ground pine stumps and stack them per one cubic meter in a size required by the firm so that whichever party rooted out the most cubic meters of pine stumps shall be declared a winner and shall seize the loser's wages of the whole month. Incredibly, Mr. Kostus won this bet by gaining in the competition without a perplexing question.

Another similar incident occurred with respect to a giant-like man in 1937, when Zbyske Cyganiewicz became the world champion in wrestling and arrived from the United States of America to Poland to tour through his native country and be seen by his compatriots. Cyganiewicz was traveling in a convertible limousine through Stolpce, Naliboki and Nowogrodek. However, the highway in the forest between Naliboki and Nowogrodek was blocked when the champion arrived there by a local individual who was transporting timber and was bogged to an extent that his horses could no longer pull the load. Fortunately, on the spot there appeared to be a forester in his own district of employment who told the driver to move his horses while he lifted the rear end of timber out of a bog. At this phenomenon Cyganiewicz was astonished; he got out of his car and introduced himself to the forester. Likewise the forester made known that he was Mr. Talun and that he was seven feet four inches tall and weighed almost a quarter of a ton. Instantly, Talun was persuaded to engage in wrestling, and by amicable arrangement he joined Cyganiewicz to train in Warsaw. Soon after, both came to the United States of America before World War II, and Talun became a successful wrestler; later he appeared as Goliath in the motion picture entitled *David and Bathsheba.*

The region of Nowogradek is a part of the Wilderness of Naliboki that became especially noteworthy because of the well-known men who were born there. One such prominent man was Adam Kickiewicz, the Polish poet who wrote masterpieces such as "Pan Tadeusz," "Oda de Mlodosci" and many other poems. For the expressions used in his poems, which assured an exciting of the spirit of Polish people and an accusation of being allegedly involved in an insurrection, Adam Mickiewicz was imprisoned in Russia. Later, he was freed from confinement and lived outside of Poland in Western Europe, eventually dying in Constantinople (Istanbul).

Also, the region of Nowogrodek brought forth the invincible warrior, such as Jozef Pilsudski, who studied in Nowogrodek and following in time completed his education in Wilno. His unique idea as priority was to defeat the Russian Cossacks, then subsequently to chase out of Poland surrounding oppressors. For such a purpose Pilsudski organized large cavalries and trained them immensely to be unconquerable cavalrymen in the face of Cossacks. These cavalrymen became extremely famous and were known as Polish Legionaries. Pilsudski also made a solemn promise to each legionary that he shall grant a free piece of land of the legionary's own choosing as the most desirable place of inhabitation as a token for the Polish Legionaries, in honor for their heroism and defeat of Russian Cossacks. After the First World War, finally Poland was regained and existed under a form of government in which political power resided in all the people and was exercised by them directly or was given to elected representatives. This free form of government became under the leadership of Marshal Jozef Pilsudski.

Once again the Wilderness of Naliboki was inside the perimeter of Polish boarders, except this time no longer under a royalty, only as Rzeczpospolita Polski, that is to say, the Free State of Poland, where its subjects experienced a joy and pleasure by the freedom.

Most of the navigable rivers in Soviet Europe flow southward. The Volga and the Ural empty into the Caspian Sea; the Don into the Sea of Azov; the Dnieper and the Dniester into the Black Sea. However, the Pechora flows north into the Barents Sea; the Northern Dvina into the White Sea; the Western Dvina

Polish Ligionaries defeating Russian Cossacks in World War I.

Ligionary Jozef Lojko in WWI.

into the Gulf of Riga; and the Niemen into the Baltic Sea. On the continent of Soviet Asia navigable rivers include the Ob and the Yenisei, which flow north and northwest into the Kara Sea, and the Lena, one of the world's largest rivers, which flows into the Laptev Sea. These three rivers, frozen during the long and very severe winters, are navigable only from June to September.

The annual temperature is somewhat warmer in the west than in the east due to the higher elevation in the latter area.

In the area of Wilnus (Wilno) there are about 1,000 lakes of a surface exceeding 1 ha., with the largest lake Naroez (80.5 km.). In the south and southeastern part of Wilnus there is a rampart stretching out of a height exceeding 656 feet above sea level. Rivers and lakes of Wilnus belong to confluence of Niemen and Dzwina. The main affluent of Dzwina is Dzisna, affluent of Niemen - Mereczanka and Wilia, the largest and most important river in the land of Wilnus.

The land of Nowogrodek reaches an elevation of 1,063 feet above sea level. The main river in Nowogrodek is Niemen, into which falls larger affluents—Szezara, Berezyna, Gawja, Dzitwa, Serweez and Usza. Additionally, in the diversity of Nowogrodek's landscape there are several large lakes, Switez, Koldyczew and Kroman.

All rivers, streams, brooklets and springs in the land of Wilnus and Nowogrodek flow into the Baltic Sea from the south, east and north of the highest elevation not exceeding 1,100 feet above sea level, which is found in Baranowicze, Nieswiez, Kojdanow, Minsk, Molodeczno, Dokszyce and Glebokie. However, beyond these cities and towns, from the highest elevation water is being drained by the rivers down the slope south into the Black Sea and north into the White Sea.

In the land of Nowogrodek initially, Niemen begins to flow from the south, and in the Wilderness of Naliboki there is a sinuosity of river, which then flows westward into the Baltic Sea.

In the landscape of Wilnus and Nowogrodek there are preponderant characteristics for the areas of the global flood in the time of Noah, 2370 B.C.E.; there are forms of undulated hillocks.

When the deluge of waters occurred on the earth the waters overwhelmed the earth so greatly that all the tall mountains came to be covered. With a mighty power the water torrent had drained them off the earth, and everywhere the surface of the ground had drained dry, with a new presence of landscape such as remains now in the Wilderness of Naliboki from the time of flood.

Before the deluge of waters on the earth there was no rainfall and no seasons such as a division of the year as determined by the earth's position with respect to the sun, and as marked by the temperature, moisture and vegetation. Evaporation on the surface of the earth was the force producing a result of canopy suspended over the entire globe, which brought about and sustained a greenhouse-like condition on the planet earth. Thus, for some 44,000 years waters from the earth were ascending above the horizon to the utmost extent, and throughout the time a tropical climate by this process was maintained, when prehistorical animals remained alive.

As a logical conclusion resulting from this notable characteristic, tropical trees were found recently in the North Pole, and in addition, some paleontologists for the first time in history discovered a Woolly Mammoth in the icecap in Siberia. This large, once-very-abundant, now-extinct elephant having a thick, hairy coat and long, curved tusks was preserved in the ice with green grass in its mouth. Obviously, the creature was actively engaged feeding on a vegetable, at which time the great canopy collapsed, causing the deluge of waters on the earth. Then at that time the mammoth occurred to be frozen instantly in the ice; thus it was preserved till this day from the time of flood.

The east side of Niemen on the sinuosity of river, the force of water flow in the Wilderness of Naliboki caused discharge of a heavy sediment, such as fragmentary rocks, which became round stones, gravel, sand, clay, iron ore. However, on the western side of Niemen there has been lighter fragmentary material deposited by force of water, such as a large tract of land that once was covered with a growth of trees and underbrush.

The plants, shrubs and trees as a consequence left the land fertile and rich as black soil and deposits of peat, a substance consisting of partially carbonized vegetable material found usually in bogs. A block of this substance, pressed and dried, was used for fuel by the people residing on the west side of Niemen due to the fact that the entire area is cultivated; there is no forest. In order to obtain wood for fuel, people had to cross the river eastward to the Wilderness of Naliboki, where the land behind Niemen at the beginning was marshy, boggy and swampy. A shortcut was possible to the forest only in the winter season, when the river and boggy area was frozen solid; then there was a great rush of people to buy and transport wood for themselves from the Wilderness of Naliboki.

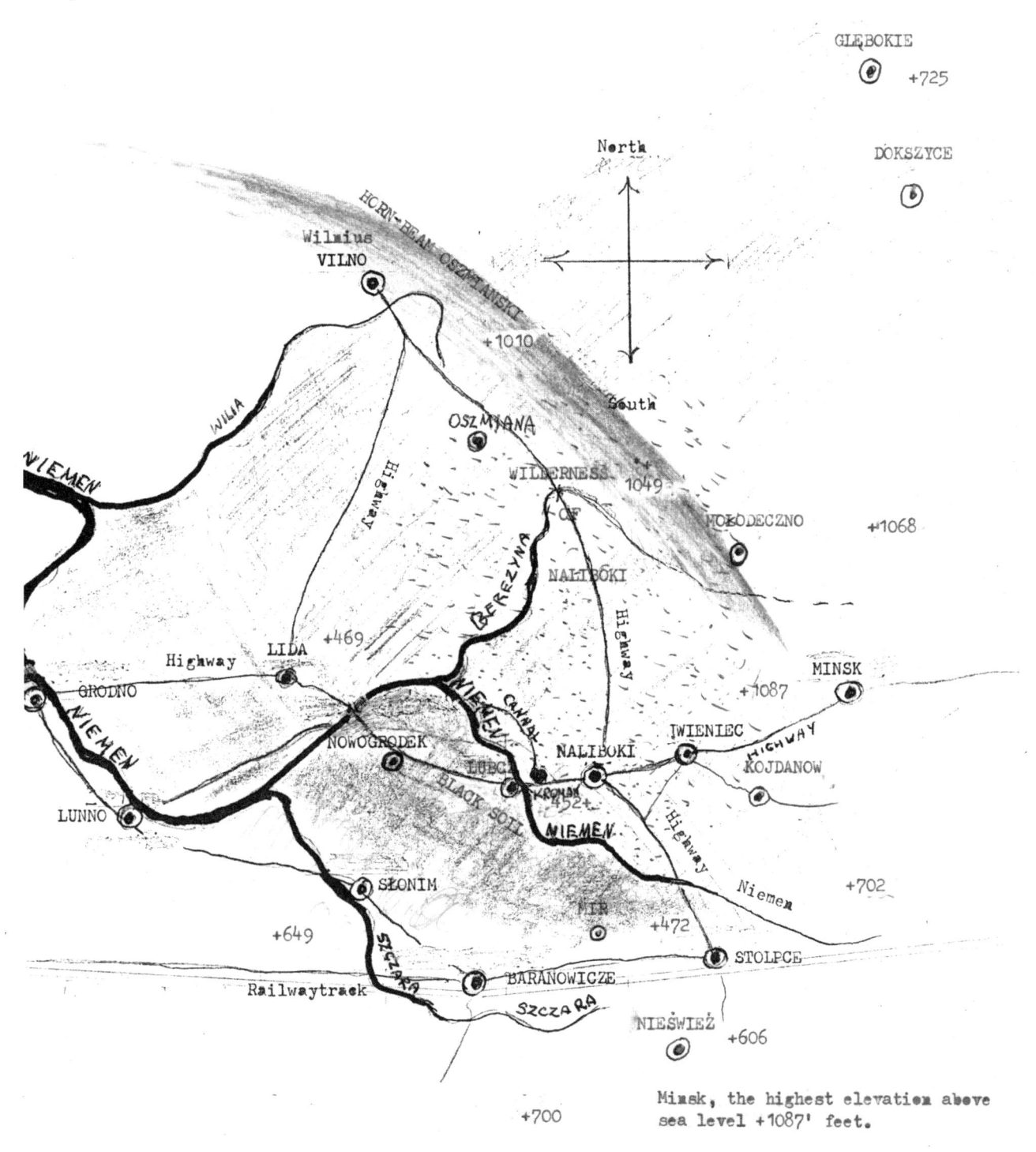

Minsk, the highest elevation above sea level +1087' feet.

Chapter II

NATURAL RESOURCES

Nature did not behave niggardly in the Wilderness of Naliboki, but rather it supplied an abundance of various resources that people desired for their needs. The most prevalent among the natural resources was agriculture, that is to say, the cultivation of the soil, breeding and rasing of livestock, poultry, fruit-culture and apiculture. The land in the region of Naliboki on the east side of the river Niemen was not as fertile as it was on the west side of the river. The soil was sandy, mixed with a decaying organic matter and with some clay, which caused the soil to be formed into small clots and by this process allowed an access of oxygen into the earth, thus vital for the roots of the growing plants. On the land in this region there was never used any fertilizer such as manure or nitrates, except dung, as animal excrement, for the growth of vegetables. All privately owned land, each owner had his land divided into sections, and every year each section was cultivated by a different crop for the purpose of protecting the plants from disease. However, as a substitute for fertilizer, people used to cultivate certain varieties of clovers, the three-leaved plant that by very nature has a tendency to absorb nitrogen from the atmosphere, and consequently it is deposited in the soil in a form of solid matter.

The country folks at the time were not scientifically minded in the field of agriculture; they were not familiar with the application of scientific principles to the cultivation of land. Rather they were governed by tradition transmitted from generation to generation, from their forefathers, who originally adopted this idea from the holy scriptures.

In spite of lacking an awareness of modern science in agriculture, the harvest was always great. People were continually and extremely busy in the mills, where wheels were turned by water from the stream, the forces of nature which men used in making a living.

There was a lot of flax cultivated by the people, from which the mucilaginous seed of flax yielded linseed oil. The hatchelled-flax was used for the linen made by a weaver's trade, which almost every housewife was familiar with. This linen was produced by skill and expertise in working with the hands, from a hatchelled-flax into a textile fabric of delicate threads spun in a spindle, to the network interwoven strands being woven in a handloom. Consequently, this constructed material had a manifold and varied types of use, finally to experience pleasure in.

The breeding and raising of sheep by some folks in the area was indeed a rewarding effort, to derive a profit from the wool, leather goods and meat. The clothes were made from the wool, leather and sheepskin for the winter, which was extremely warm and comfortable to wear.

The land in the region of Naliboki commonly was separated into certain parts owned by the individual's husbandry, in the shape of long and narrow strips. On this narrow piece of land everyone had an established farmstead next to each other, so that each strip of land beginning from the main street in town or village to the left side or right was extended a considerably long distance to the forest that surrounded the entire community. This strip of land privately owned contained in itself an arable land capable of being plowed, meadow used for grazing or for hay, and a certain part of forest from which timber was used for building and wood for fuel. In the surrounding area there was ample common ground for the grazing of domestic animals. Additionally, deep in the forest the meadows were sold by auction each year by the Polish government for the people who needed more hay for their livestock. Thus, the breeding and raising of livestock by all people was very popular in the region. Folks depended on the flesh of animals used as food, the hides from which they made leather for shoes. From NATURE they obtained the forces that enabled them to use these raw materials—the animal force for transportation, where everyone used horses of a good breed. In the winter over snow and ice a toboggan or sledge was used as a vehicle designed for carrying people or loads, such as hay and timber. Yet, in the summer horses were engaged in wagons, four-wheeled, horsedrawn vehicles that were used for carrying crops, goods, freight, etc.

Generally, domestic owls were bred of improved varieties of hens, ducks and geese. This fowl's flesh was used as food and goose feathers for feather beds and pillows.

Orchards in the region were most popular. There were great varieties of fruit trees and the produce was used for jams, juices, preserves, etc. To such an extent of being surrounded by the unlimited class of blossoms and flowers during the spring and summer in the area, therefore the apiculture was admired by most people, the raising and the care of bees. There was an abundance of desired varieties of a sweet, viscous substance made by the bees from nectar gathered from flowers. The surplus of honey was sold by wholesale in Warsaw to the government, which made an effort to encourage and give assistance for the people to be progressive in the production of honey and to extend the apiculture for the benefit of the forest.

Before the First World War, on the southeast side of town in Naliboki on the site of common land, there was established the world-famous glassworks, where the glass was manufactured as a material used in glassware, decoration, crystal, chandelier, etc. These articles made of glass were sold worldwide, thus the glassworks of Naliboki became well known. However, after the First World War, the time when Poland was regained, this glassworks unfortunately for some reason ceased to exist. Yet, after such a long time elapsed, there was an article written about Naliboki's glasswork in 1960—it is in the Roman Catholic literature describing a fine work of art, which was read in Baltimore, Maryland, by an individual named Bronislawa Kiczula, the former resident of Naliboki, who was born there in 1892.

However, after the disappearance of the glassworks, that common ground was used for the grazing of domestic animals. But the only trace of it was left when the shepherds gazed on a sunny day into the molten glassy images that were popping out of the sand after heavy rain.

In 1937 in the original site where the glassworks used to be there was placed a large sawmill, an establishment for sawing planks with a steam-powered machine. The timber that was sawed into boards, planks, etc., at specified lengths was used for marketing, and its profit was disposed for the public welfare, such as to build or improve social buildings and the church in Naliboki. This huge steam-driven machine at the same time was engaged to move a huge dynamo, a generator for the conversion of mechanical energy into electrical energy, which was indispensable in lighting the town of Naliboki for the first time in history. At last the lamps and hanging lamps became obsolete, when naphtha used to be as a fuel, a volatile, colorless petroleum distillate intermediate between gasoline and benzene. This type of substance was obtained from the local natural source, as from pitch. Naphtha was produced by distillation in Smolarnia, located in the forest about three miles west of Naliboki. Smolarnia is the place where pitch was burnt from pine stems and from extraction of the resinous sap of pines. This crude material of pitch was refined to improve precise alterations and by boiling down tar from the residues of distilled turpentine, so that by this process a different class of product or by-product was obtained, such as benzene, gasoline, naphtha, naphthalene, ether, oil, grease, bitumen, etc.

In this region there was a large, as sediment, mass of clay—a fine-grained variously colored earth, plastic when wet, used in the making of bricks, tiles and pottery. Southward from the town center, approximately two miles in the forest, there was a brick kiln built by the community in 1937, a structure in which bricks are burned or baked. There was a molded block of clay baked in various shapes and sizes, used for building. Tiles were made out of a thin piece of baked clay, used for covering roofs, and ornaments and many other things. These materials made in the brick kiln were sold in the large cities, and the profit was used by the community for the improvement of town.

There were some individuals who were experts at making earthenware and porcelain vessels on a horizontal rotating disk used by potters for holding and manipulating prepared clay; then finally a molded ware from clay was hardened by intense heat. These artistic varieties of earthenware tastefully executed were displayed weekly in the market by a potter's family, where the merchandise was finally sold.

During three seasons in the year—spring, summer and autumn—people were very busy in their own occupations. They all made their livings being principally self-employed. In the fields they were spreading dung for planting potatoes, ploughing, sowing and harrowing, then throughout the time they were hay making and gathering a ripened crop of grain and fruit. Then later there was a thrashing of wheat, grain, corn and flax. Following in time there was picking potatoes and vegetables, the division of nature that includes all organisms classified as plants. Without going into specific details, simply everyone was productively engaged by making a living from the natural resources. However, the winter was a time suitable for relaxation and to take it easy. But there was a great opportunity to earn some handy cash from the government by working in the forest because the Polish government conducted a sale of timber on the international market at the Baltic Sea. Trees in the forest were cut down by the local workers at full length or cut into sections according to specification after being stripped of the branches. Anyone who was interested was engaged in the operation of cutting and transporting this timber from the woodland to the nearest point of the canal or river Niemen. Large and full-length logs were loaded onto the two-section sledge and fitted with swivels for the timber to rotate independently during the operation of hauling over snow and ice. At arrival to its destination, the timber was dumped into the water to remain suspended and be carried along to the sea. The recompense for such service was calculated based on volume. So much was paid out per cubic meter of timber being hauled. This money earned was well suited to one's needs, and in particular to pay one's taxes, spend as commodity, and perhaps to have a social gathering for pleasure or entertainment.

However, in the forest after cutting a timber down and hauling, there was left quite a remnant that needed to be disposed of in order to have this land cultivated for its wood. The leftover large pieces of wood were cleaned of their branches and sold as combustible matter used as a source of heat energy or to feed a fire. Of course, the branches were stacked in a pile and consumed by fire so that the area where the trees used to grow became clean and neat, pleasing in appearance for the new and young trees to flourish.

Timber required by the local people as being suitable for building or structural purposes was available for everyone to be purchased from the government. Out of this timber from the surrounding forest people used to build for themselves homes to live in, barns for storing hay and stabling livestock, and buildings for storing grain. In the whole region there was a common design, made with skill, as a work of art, to the structures people composed of logs. These logs were shaven and trimmed flat-face on the inside of the building, or both the flat face inside and outside. The structural wall that was flat on the inside was suitable for plaster work or paperhanging, but an outside flat surface was made just for painting, thus towns such as Naliboki and all villages or hamlets in the surrounding area were constructed mainly out of logs, but some buildings were built with stone, brick and clay.

An apparatus for producing heat and cooking, stoves were built in the houses. These stoves and glazed-tile stoves were constructed out of brick and clay. The main stove normally was heated once a day, in which most cooking and baking for the day was done. Additionally, there was a small type of stove with a cook chamber built in, by the main stove, which imparted extra warmth and gave an opportunity to fry something or boil for the daily needs.

For the winter season everyone had double windows installed in their homes because the northeast of Poland was extremely cold. This region had a relatively low temperature, reaching up to 40°C or over during some winters. Generally, the ground was covered by snow in December and it remained on the ground till the end of March. But the folks were well prepared for such a season; they were dressed in warm suits made out of wool and sheepskin. The horses with bells and decoration were employed in the domestic state as a draft of sledgers for riding whenever it was absolutely needed for one to accomplish a certain result or pleasure. The area was enclosed with varieties of beautiful trees, which purified the air in all seasons, that quality of a substance that renders it perceptible to the sense of pleasant smell, as of incense. The environment, in abundance of blossoms and flowers throughout the time of spring and summer, was a place of great beauty and delight, a place of a gratifying odor, as in paradise that ascribes as belonging to and resulting from the natural resources of mother nature.

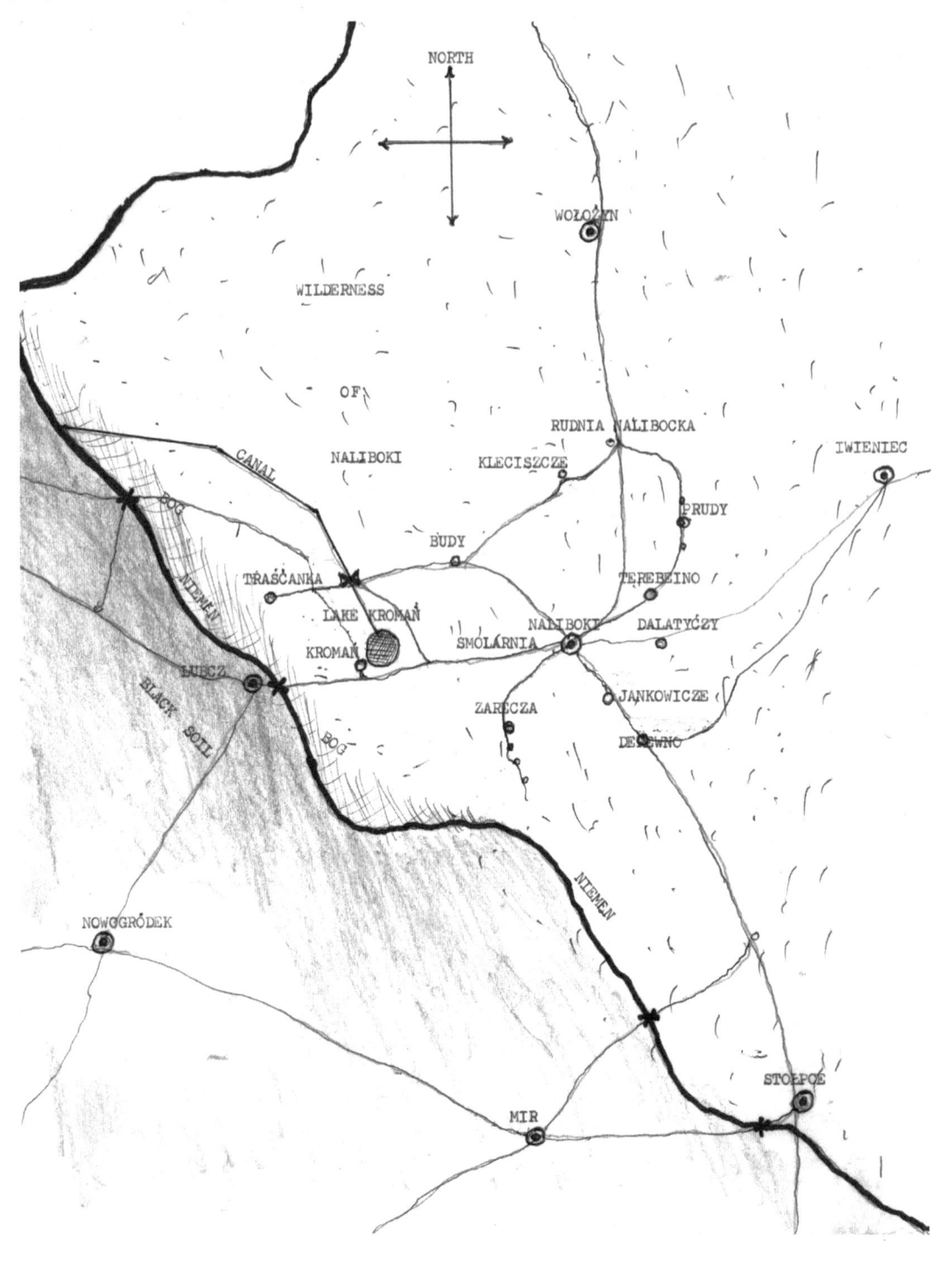

Chapter III

THE PARISH OF NALIBOKI

It has been well observed and said by the old men in the region that the Parish of Naliboki was established in the time of the Jagielo Dynasty, approximately four centuries ago. The church itself was a wooden structure built on the summit of a hill in a Gothic style of architecture used in Europe from 1200 to 1500 A.D., characterized by pointed arches, ribbed vaulting and flying buttresses. An accidental excavation in the churchyard in 1936 uncovered underground tombs of buried priests, about whom the signs indicated they were buried there some 300 to 400 years ago. In a tomb, vault-like grave, a body of a clergyman was placed in a recumbent position and it remained aggregated, giving an impression as if he were buried yesterday, but when touched the whole image dropped down and passed from sight. These priests, especially consecrated to the service of divinity and serving as mediators between the divinity and the worshipers, were pertaining to the Roman Catholic Church from its beginning when this particular church was established. Thus, there was no sign of being any other domination in the region, not even a Russian Orthodox Church, which is prevalent among the people in general. In fact, the Parish of Naliboki was completely under dogma of the Roman Catholic Church throughout its existence, under which many generations lived and worshipped as man's relationship with the powers and principles of the universe, especially with deities from the time when Poland was christened by means of the first king Mieszko in 966 A.D.

This church possessed the qualities and presented an appearance of beauty in form and grace. The large, long windows had fittings of panes of glass in various colors resembling holy figures, and similar paintings were painted on the walls and ceiling, designating religious worship. The high altar in the front and on each side of the church had banners and portable altars that were carried in a procession; they were truly magnificent. In the middle there was a huge chandelier presenting an extraordinarily imposing appearance, and above in the rear there was permanently located a powerful organ with a place for the chorus. The steeple with a huge bell was built high, which caused a loud sound at regular intervals, announcing that something was going to take place.

On the north side of the church there was a parsonage, a clergyman's dwelling, and it was a free official residence provided by the church. The parsonage consisted of landed estate with a farmstead, where the land was cultivated and livestock bred and all other attention given by men and women employed there permanently.

On the south side of the church was a cemetery enclosed by a thick, tall wall built from stones. The main entrance to the cemetery was from the churchyard, with an iron gate fastened to the pillars of stone. Inside the cemetery the graves were marked by tombstones of different sizes, iron crosses and wooden crosses. This place inside the walls was consecrated, and it was forbidden by the church to bury non-Catholics, children born unbaptized and suicides. These unfortunately were buried behind the walls of the cemetery. Tombstones there indicated that some people were buried near the beginning of the eighteenth century.

At the main entrance on the right side by the wall there is buried Kazimierz Klimowicz, who died in 1900 at the age of thirty-eight, and his wife Elisabeth Klimowicz, who died in 1932 at the age of seventy-five. Kazimierz Klimowicz was employed as an organist by the church and was given authority from the official source to issue birth certificates, death certificates and marriage lines. He was engaged by the church in 1880. At home he worked in his clinic as a family doctor who was also familiar with standard formulas and methods for the preparation of medicines, drugs and other remedial substances. He was a dedicated doctor to the people. He took good care of the sick and saved the lives of many people in the region without exception, whether they could meet the expense or not. He had gracious and noble qualities. He was kind with a conscience and mercy toward fellow creatures. He died of leukemia. His funeral was of a great crowd gathered closely together in a deep mourn and manifestations of grief.

Kazimierz left his wife and five children. Two grown sons, Edward and Edmund, were students in the university in Russia. Later, after the Russian revolution, they were exterminated by the Soviets on account of their education acquired in the czar's regime, by means of which they were regarded as a threat to the Union of Soviet Socialist Republics. The two teenage daughters, Bronislawa and Orszula, were at home with the baby brother, Wilhelm, whom the dying father Kazimierz requested to have put on his chest before he died. Orszula subsequently became married to Von Metro Majer, who was born in Berlin, Germany. After the First World War they lived in the city Vilno, the place where they were actually married. Von Metro Majer sent a letter to her mother requesting that Orszula should he permitted to go to Vilno to continue with her education. However, since mother knew that Vilno was famous for its pedagogy, she did let Orszula go. After some time they moved to Lithuania with two children, son and daughter, where Von Metro Majer became the prime minister of Lithuania. Finally Elizabeth Klimowicz was left with the two children at home, Bronislawa and Wilhelm. This particular residence later was divided equally in two parts between sister and brother. It was located at Pilsudski Street, about a quarter-mile from the church.

Kazimierz Klimowicz had three brothers, Peter, Benedict and Jacob, and two sisters, Orszula and Alzusia. Peter Klimowicz was a doctor, a licensed practitioner of medicine and surgery. He lived in his own large and impressive house in downtown Naliboki. He had two children, son Eugenjusz and daughter Wierka. The son was legitimate, but daughter was of the maidservant. Jacob Klimowicz was a farmer and lived on the other side of river Niemen between Lida and Nowogrodek. Benedict Klimowicz was an organist and virtuoso, a master of technique as a skilled musician who played the violin, and also he was an expert performer on the piano. Benedict was a skillful tuner of church organs and skillful in constructing his own violins. Alzusia was unmarried with a daughter, Regina, and they lived together with Orszula on their own estate in Naliboki.

The Parish of Naliboki embraced a considerable extent of the inhabited area, namely villages such as Derewno, Jankowicze, Dalatyczy and Terebejno, hamlets such as Budy, Kroman and Trascianka, and many other little villages. This inhabited region consisted of approximate 50,000 people, including Jewish race, White-Russian and Lithuanian. The main residence of Jewish people was located in the center of town, and they were all of the Hebrew religion. These Jews in Naliboki had their own established synagogue in which they met for Jewish worship and religious instruction in the ancient Semitic language of the Israelites as used in much of the Old Testament. They also used the modern Hebrew language, which is the official language of the Republic of Israel. But daily in their practical lives they spoke Yiddish, a Germanic language derived from the middle high German spoken in the Rhineland in the thirteenth and fourteenth centuries, now spoken primarily by Jews in Eastern Europe and by Jewish immigrants from that region in other parts of the world. It contains elements of Hebrew and the Slovic languages, and is written in Hebrew characters.

The Lithuanian people were mingled with the Polish, and some were intermarried but of the same religion, so that they were hardly noticed in a social life of the parish. However, the people of Lithuania spoke a Polish language from long ago, since Poland and Lithuania were united during the Jagielo Dynasty in the fifteenth century.

The White-Russian people in the area were all of the Roman Catholic religion and they also spoke the Polish language, but at home in their own private conversation they used a White-Russian language that was sustained among all people in the region as the native language. This Byelorussian language bears resemblance to the Russian language, with its own existing alphabet originating from the Russian system of symbols representing the sounds of speech.

Notwithstanding the fact that the people in this community were of different constituting nationalities and different languages, they lived together in unity and harmony under the condition of being free from a variety or diversity in one locality and subject to the same laws, having common interests and common participation. This society in general was devoid of any grave offense against morality or social order; that is to say, anything done contrary to justice, honesty, modesty or good morals was unknown. People were acquainted with nature and thus feared God. That is why under the circumstances it would be very strange, for instance, for one to hear about dissolution of a marriage, whether it be by legal process or by accepted custom in that region.

In town and out of town on the highways there were small chapels for the purpose of worship and to observe as a festival with rejoicing during the march in procession. They were decorated with flowers and lit with candles on such an event. On Corpus Christi Day and Whitsun Tide the church itself was embellished with beautiful flowers, candlelights and magnificent chandeliers were clustered with light, shining bright. On All Saints Day and All Souls Day, November first and second, days of commemoration on which intercession is made for the souls of all the faithful departed, throughout the night the churchyard and entire cemetery were made bright by innumerable candles burning; really it was something to behold. On Easter, a Christian festival commemorating the resurrection of Christ the Sunday immediately after the first full moon that occurs on or after March 21, the sound of organ and chorus was spread far and wide throughout the town when mass was performed. Great crowds gathered always to keep the religious holiday.

The Christmas holiday, December 25, was the time to celebrate the memory of the birth of Christ Jesus. Children exhibited restlessness, anxiety and tension before the approaching catechism. It was a short manual giving, in the form of questions and answers, an outline of the principles of the Roman Catholic creed. This oral examination by questions and answers was catechized by the priest at people's homes. After a catechism the priest presents the parents with wafers of different colors, which are small, flat disks of unleavened bread stamped with a cross or holy image being already consecrated for use on Christmas Eve. In the surrounding of the natural home, dear because of personal relationships and feelings of comfort and security, beautifully decorated Christmas trees with ornaments and lights, then there was the occasion of partaking in a meal that consisted of twelve particular kinds of prepared food. These dishes of delicious food prescribed a period for fasting that one had to persevere in, fourteen days before Christmas.

Toward the east from the church down the hill was a wooded area, and on the bottom a lowland with a stream and bridge erected across to afford passage for the people moving on foot. Toward the left side there was a lake and main street leading to the church from the town center. Toward the right side there was a tillable land of some thousands of acres stretching toward the east to the forest, and from the bridge up on the opposite hill there was established a castle from long ago, the fortified availing of a certain nobleman, "Ciechanowicz." The yard of this dwelling was extremely large, containing approximately twenty to thirty acres, and around on all sides there were stables set apart for lodging and feeding horses or cattle. This place very great in size was known as "MAJATEK," meaning the property of fortune. More distant ahead there was a north-south highway guiding from Naliboki southward to Stolpce, and another road from the east was connected to the highway leading to the neighboring town

Iwieniec. This road from Iwieniec, with a left turn on the way to Stolpce, was a very exciting route once a year during the international motorcar race. On the north side in the corner of this junction there was established an elementary school of the Parish of Naliboki. On the street from the school to the town square on the right side there was a large and impressive house of Dr. Peter Klimowicz, which also maintained a cooperative store, being the only one in town of the Polish folks. From the center square to the right on Vilno Street toward the east was a Jewish community that consisted of all sorts of stores and craft, especially handwork; loosely, art. Onward at the end of the Jewish community on the left side of the street there was a post office, and next to it was a government building containing a public welfare, court, tax office, police station and jail. The chief person of Naliboki was the bailiff, a subordinate magistrate with jurisdiction limited to this district and these functions. The court trials were executed once a month. Judges and lawyers were appointed for such trials from Iwieniec, Stolpce or Baranowicze. The environment was virtually of a peaceful nature, therefore the offenses were classified as misdemeanors, infractions or petty offenses, and these were lower than felonies and generally were punishable by fine or imprisonment other than in penitentiary.

Next to the government building there was a hall, a building with a large room used for public business and entertainment, and next to it there was a library, a commercial establishment that rented a great variety of books. On the other side of the street toward the south on the common ground there was a Turkish bath, a bathing establishment where sweating is induced by exposure to high temperatures in a room heated by steam, followed by washing, massage and beating the bodies with twigs for one especially to reach the top shelf, to be eventually well treated by steam. This side in particular was a common ground used for a kermess or fair, a periodic and usually competitive exhibit of agricultural products, pottery and fancywork; the place was a gathering of buyers and sellers. This location was also set apart specifically each year for the merry-go-round, a revolving platform fitted with wooden horses and seats on which people, especially children, ride for amusement and pleasure. There was always a large gathering of people and children at this carousel, with music and pleasant diversion.

The Jewish community was made up of approximately five hundred people in the Parish of Naliboki. The main group of them was located close together, constituting the center of town. Their dwellings were constructed principally from bricks and the fronts of them were shaped into various shops, such as a mercer's shop, grocery, hardware, butcher, pharmacy, forge and so on. Their stores were always filled completely with merchandise. They were well organized and a hard-working people and also easy with mutual agreements between customers to buy or sell goods. It was on all occasions declared that one could have a better bargain in the Jewish store than one could have in the Polish.

On the north side of the street there were narrow strips of land joined together, stretching northward and nearly half a mile long, which comprised about the same dimension in width and was made in a shape of square considered as having formed a distinct part of a whole. This open area of Jewish property was beautifully fenced of a high structure, about seven feet tall. Inside of the enclosure there was a magnificent orchard containing all sorts of fruit trees. In the midst of the Jewish community there was a permanent synagogue, the place of meeting or assemblage for religious instruction, observances and Jewish worship. Their adoration was given to the Almighty God, Jehovah, normally on the seventh or last day of the week, that is, on Saturday. Meanwhile, on Sunday the Roman Catholic Church performed service of the eucharistic liturgy, consisting of various prayers and ritual ceremonies and regarded as a commemoration of repetition of Christ's sacrifice on the cross. However, with such diversity in worship between two different groups of people of a separate creed or doctrine, there was no distinction found in the Parish of Naliboki; thus, all persons were regarded equal. All groups of people lived together in peace and a state of order, agreement and aesthetically pleasing relationships among the elements of a whole on account of the Free State of Poland and its constitutional law, which, concerning the effect of statutes or practices that confer particular privileges on a class arbitrarily selected from a large number of persons, everyone stood in the same relation to the privileges granted and no reasonable distinction could be found.

It has been always maintained by the influential senior member of a respectable family among the Polish people to regard Jews with high esteem and admiration on account of their ancestors. Because their forefathers constituted the great nation of Israel, whose patriarch was Jacob, the leader of a nation who ruled by paternal right, and the twelve sons of Jacob, considered as the progenitors of the tribes of Israel. This holy nation chosen by the Almighty God, whose name is Jehovah, brought forth great prophets who foretold the preordained ordering of events beforehand with divine inspiration as a medium between God and man. The last of all, foretold by the Hebrew prophets, was the deliverer of Israel, namely Jesus of Nazareth, regarded as fulfilling the prophecy. His name Christ bears the name of Christianity, affirming the divinity of Christ. The civilized humans derived and are related to his doctrine; thus, now they are characterized by a high level of intellectual, social and cultural development.

From this point of view, one should be in fact contented and must rejoice on account of the barbarous era that now is of the past and remains history, because there should not be around any more uncivilized people, primitive, lacking in refinement, coarse, cruel, brutal, rude or foreign, those which might be something unfamiliar about them or strange. After all, we are the people of the twenty-first century, of high theoretical knowledge of industry and the industrial arts, of science and the power of true and right discernment, a high degree of learning and a wise saying. That is why the parochial church in Naliboki sustained the people in a state of civilization, brought them out of savagery long ago, and they became refined and enlightened. The expression "parochial church" has various significations. It is applied sometimes to a select body of Christians, forming a local spiritual association, and sometimes to the building in which the public worship of the inhabitants of a parish is celebrated. But the true legal notion of a parochial church is a consecrated place, having attached to it the rights of burial and the administration of the sacraments, which was continuous, uninterrupted, so persistently repeated at short intervals as to constitute virtually an unbroken series from the time of the Jagielo Dynasty, four to five centuries ago.

In this sense, meaning or signification, where the diversity of civilian people resided together in the Parish of Naliboki with an equal entitlement to protection from the government and with a conscience doctrine, in the way just indicated, they all were law-abiding citizens and God-fearing people. They had an occupancy of their dwellings and they toiled with the sweat on their foreheads.

Passing the government building eastward on Vilno Street there was a great number of houses on both sides. On the left side there was a dwelling of Jozef Koscukiewicz, who lived with his beautiful wife Gabriela, maiden name Klimowicz, and two children. Farther on there was a dwelling of a Jewish blacksmith, one who worked iron on an anvil and used a forge. Next to him there was a vacant land with silver birch trees growing alongside pavement. This land was cultivated and conformed to an absolute standard of excellence for the future dwellings of proprietors Bronislawa and Wilhelm Klimowicz, who were residing at Pilsudski Street. Vilno Street northwestward merged into the road and branched off to the north directly to Vilno. On the road eastward about two miles from Naliboki there was the village Terebejno, and farther on the road there were hamlets within the boundary line of the Parish of Naliboki. However, in the village Terebejno there lived a modest man with his wife and children whose name was SZABUNIA. This character, Szabunia, was totally unnoticed by the community and was unknown by the people as a whole. He did not take any part in the social activities, nor did he attend the church at any time. The people from the hamlets beyond Terebejno attended the church every Sunday. Some of them used a transport of four-wheeled horsedrawn vehicles, but most of them walked to the church, and usually in the warm summer days they used to take the Sunday shoes off their feet and walk barefooted, then they washed their feet at the lake and entered the church neat. Between the town and Terebejno there was a place partly inhabited called Maczylin, in which from the Terebejno road across Vilno Road there was a strip of land running northward into the forest. This land was the property of Wilhelm Klimowicz and consisted of tillable land, meadow and forest, with a concept of supreme perfection for a place of residence that never came to pass. In this locality was a residence of Bailiff Korzenko, who lived with his wife, three sons and daughter. He was an agent appointed by the government to superintend the Parish of Naliboki, to collect fines, taxes, inspect the buildings, order repairs, cut down trees, impound cattle, take an account of wastes, spoils, and misdemeanors in the woods and lands, and do other acts for the government's interest.

From the town square westward there was Nowogrodek Street, which was about two miles long and was inhabited exclusively by members of the parish with names such as Baszuro families, Korzenko, Wolan, Korzuszko, Jesc, Szarrzanowicz, Zielonko, Dubicki, Lukaszewicz, Konowal, Grygorcewicz, Klimowicz, Radziwill and so on. The Baszuro family was located next to the town square with a blacksmith shop. Farther there were other families and subsequently the Wolan families, with their dwellings located on both sides of the street, whose strip of land actually was stretched southward up to Pilsudski Street, on which there was the residence built and occupied by the late Mr. and Mrs. Kazimierz, Elizabeth Klimowicz, by maiden name Wolan. On the Wolan's property there was established a small chapel (chapelet) which was used during processions on a day designated as a religious festival. Among such families living on the street sloping down there were Alfons Klimowicz and his wife and child. Next in place on the right side of the street there was a dwelling of Benedict Klimowicz; brother of the late Kazimierz Klimowicz, he lived with his two sisters, Orszula and Alzusia, who was with her daughter Regina; they were both spinsters. But most of his life Benedict spent working in the large cities in Poland as an organist and tuner of organs. Next to Benedict's property lived relatives Wladyslaw Klimowicz and his wife and three sons, Ben, Eugene and Michael. On the south side of the street there was a residence of the Radziwill family. Jan Radziwill lived with his mother, but his only brother was enlisted in a military service and he never lived at home. In this place lived also a widower, Szarzanowicz, with two sons, Frank and Leon. Frank was pious, actuated by reverence for a supreme being, but his brother Leon was contrary in character; he had the qualities of the devil and became notorious from his very youth in the Parish of Naliboki. Farther up the hill on the south side of the street there was a mansion built with bricks and flat roof by a certain father and three sons who lived there. These men of one family were the civil engineers, professionals trained to design, build and maintain public works, as schools, churches, buildings, etc. This Nowogrodek Street from the square of town about two miles stretched westward and was completely inhabited on both sides of the street, which was constructed of cobblestone, and along at certain intervals there were located chapelets. This street ended in the forest, in which the road was constructed out of pine trees during the First World War across the entire forest. Along this wooden road and in the forest there were a lot of small graveyards of dead soldiers buried from the czar's military forces. The graves used to be marked with wooden crosses that originated from the Russian Orthodox Church, where one extra beam across is inserted in a diagonal line. These Russian crosses underwent decay and most of them became decomposed. Near the graveyards there were piles of rotten shoes, cans and rifle ammunition.

From the town square there was Pilsudski Street leading southwest to the church. On the corner of the north side there was a residence of a Jewish family, Skniut, an old couple who lived with two bachelor sons, and opposite there lived another Jewish family, Srol, a married couple with two adolescent sons. Next to them there was a large and impressive house belonging to the Lawon family, who lived with only an adolescent daughter Elizabeth. Part of this house was perpetually rented to a doctor of medicine as his residence, and some portion of it was used as an infirmary, a place for the treatment of the sick. Doctors used to change the place of practice and a new doctor was appointed for a post or duty at this particular residence. Farther along the street there was a new house built for the executive personnel of government who lived there with his beautiful wife and two adolescent sons. Next to the Skniut family there was a residence of Baszuro family, Witold and Mania Baszuro with three children, Jadwiga, Teresa and Stanislaw. Baszuro family was neighbor to Bronislawa and Wilhelm Klimowicz. Bronislawa was

Wilhelm's sister, a marriageable young lady who lived in a place of residence inherited from her parents, Kazimierz and Elizabeth Klimowicz. She had converted her father's clinic into the art and practice of cooking after her acquisition of knowledge and skills in the formal schooling in an institution of learning at Minsk. She was an outstanding professional female cook. She was familiar with a great number of different cakes, pastries, custards, tarts, pies, etc., and such as confits, jams, candied fruits and seasoning beverages. Her savory dinners were served only by appointment to the eminent and distinguished people such as priests, judges, lawyers, doctors, engineers, etc. This residence consisted of a double dwelling that was divided in the will and shared between brother and sister. Her brother Wilhelm occupied the other half of the dwelling and subsequently became married to Jozefa Lojko, daughter of Orszula and Franciszek Lojko, who lived at the time in the west end of town, Naliboki, Nowogrodek Street. Following in time her parents moved from Nowogrodek Street to the outlying district by the forest with their son Jozef. Jozef Lojko apparently was a valiant Polish legionary in the First World War who fought against in a physical combat with the Russian Cossacks. As a token for his heroism and defeat of Russian Cossacks, he was granted a free piece of land of his own choosing made by the solemn promise of Marshal Jozef Pilsudski. In the northwest outskirts of town he built himself a superb husbandry that was surrounded by an arable land, meadow, pond and pine-tree forest. Jozef subsequently became married, had four children and lived with his parents. His brother Michael Lojko had a similar established husbandry behind the cemetery in a place remote from the center of town. From the town square Pilsudski Street led to the church, and beyond there was a fork road branching into two separately continued roads, one to the right leading west by which road Michael Lojko was residing, and the other road to the left leading to several hamlets that were between three and eight kilometers from Naliboki. These hamlets were also in the boundary of the Parish of Naliboki. Michael Lojko was an official appointed by the government to carry out the functions of an administrator in Naliboki. He was married and had three children. His oldest brother Waclaw Lojko was a forester and lived on the government property at the place known as "TRASCIANKA," which was about three kilometers from "KROMAN," the residence of the chief forester with the lake Kroman, from which a canal was connected to the river Niemen. Waclaw was married and had three children, Jania, Czeslaw, and Henry. The youngest brother, Boleslaw, was a student in seminary of theology. He was applying the mind in acquiring the knowledge of a priest. But before consecrated to the service of a divinity as a clergyman in the second order of the ministry, ranking next below a bishop, and having authority to administer the sacraments, he changed his mind and instead entered the university to study law.

From the town square southward on Stolpce Street next to the mansion of Dr. Peter Klimowicz there was the residence of Lady Makarewicz, who remained unmarried and lived with her son Arkadjusz. Lady Makarewicz was a sister to Alesia Makarewicz, who was a maidservant of Dr. Peter Klimowicz. She remained also unmarried and lived with her daughter Wierka in the mansion. Dr. Peter Klimowicz was married to Mania and they had a son, Eugenjusz, who was a student in university, but Wierka and Arkadjusz were also his children out of wedlock. Next to Lady Makarewicz there was a residence of Guminski, who was married with two children. Guminski came to Naliboki as a schoolmaster from his place of origin, Poznan, a city located by the German border on the west side of Poland. On the west side of the street there was a residence of the Poplawski family. They had a large, beautiful orchard that was frequently in the summer season taken on lease by a Jewish businessman. Next, on the east side of the street there was a large grounds on which an elementary school was situated, and opposite along the street there were buildings set apart for lodging and feeding horses or cattle belonging to Ciechanowicz castle, known as "MAJATEK." This fortified dwelling of a noble in feudal times was a place of refuge and stronghold that was built upon the hill in the time close to the existing church, some four hundred years ago, or probably even before the church, when Poland was ruled by principalities under the PIASTY DYNASTY in the twelfth century.

Jozefa Lojko, as yet a maiden, in the company of two other girls, was compelled to go beyond the river Niemen in order to trade in some gold pieces for salt. This sodium chloride, a compound found in sea water and as a mineral, used as a seasoning and as a preservative, was scarce at the end of First World War, after which a great famine followed—a widespread scarcity of food was everywhere. In the course of their search for salt they stumbled upon the Polish armed forces, where they were examined formally by questioning and accused of espionage, the securing of secret information. The defendants were transported by rail to the city Cracow, and there they were held in confinement. Jozefa's brother Jozef was notified by his parents that his sister was arrested for being a spy by the Polish military and she was now in a prison at Cracow. Jozef, while he was at a place occupied by the detachment of Polish legionaries, left for Cracow. As a Polish legionary, he had the power to govern or the right to command and to enforce obedience. He had his sister Jozefa and her two friends released at once, and subsequently they arrived safely back home.

1. Piotr Klimowicz; 2. Mania Klimowicz; 3. Aleksandrja Makarewicz; 4. Elżbieta Klimowicz; 5. Kazimierz Klimowicz; 6. Benedikt Klimowicz; 7. Łojko; 8. Maria Klimowicz; 9. Orszula Klimowicz; 10. Alżusia Klimowicz; 11. Jakub Klimowicz.

The picture taken by photography in 1903.

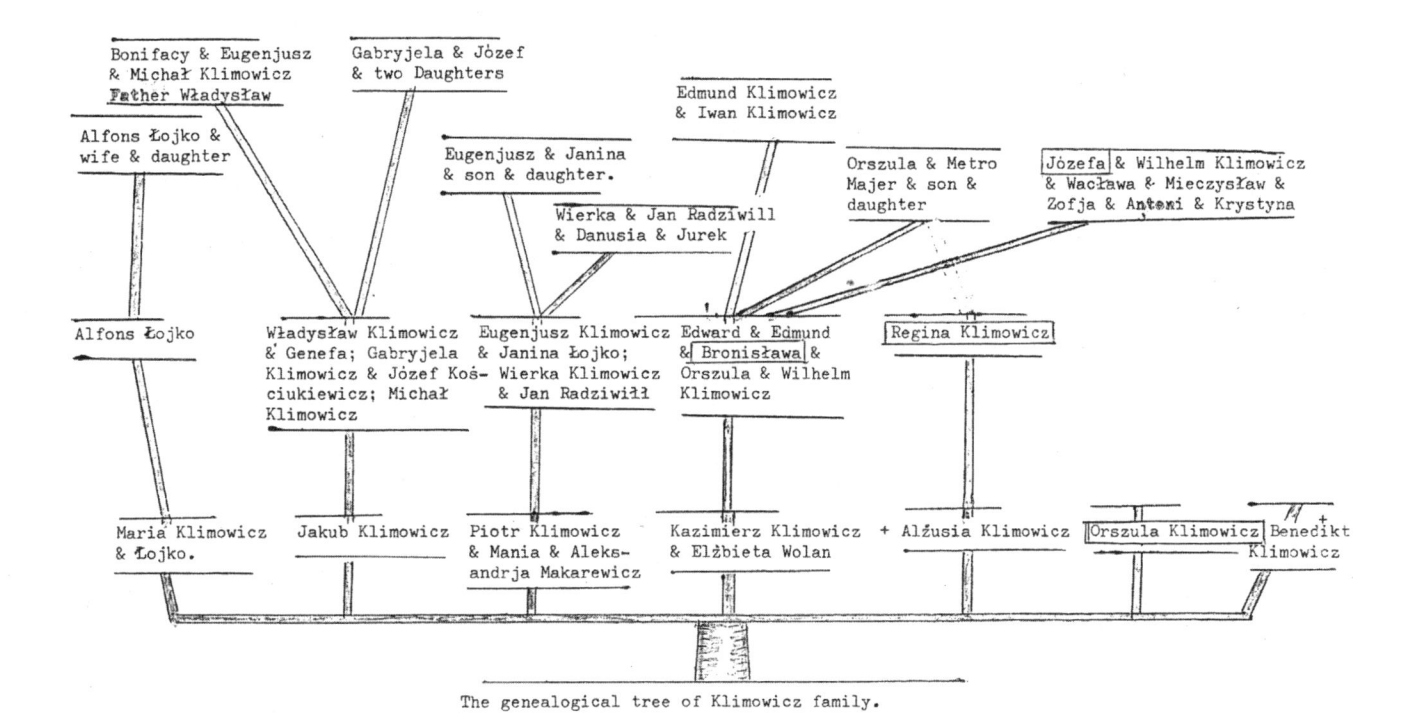

The Last Day of Naliboki

Klimowicz family tree (top):

- Bonifacy & Eugenjusz & Michał Klimowicz Father Władysław
- Alfons Łojko & wife & daughter
- Gabryjela & Józef & two Daughters
- Eugenjusz & Janina & son & daughter.
- Wierka & Jan Radziwill & Danusia & Jurek
- Edmund Klimowicz & Iwan Klimowicz
- Orszula & Metro Majer & son & daughter
- Józefa & Wilhelm Klimowicz & Wacława & Mieczysław & Zofja & Antoni & Krystyna

- Alfons Łojko
- Władysław Klimowicz & Genefa; Gabryjela Klimowicz & Józef Kościukiewicz; Michał Klimowicz
- Eugenjusz Klimowicz & Janina Łojko; Wierka Klimowicz & Jan Radziwiłł
- Edward & Edmund & Bronisława & Orszula & Wilhelm Klimowicz
- Regina Klimowicz

- Maria Klimowicz & Łojko.
- Jakub Klimowicz
- Piotr Klimowicz & Mania & Aleksandrja Makarewicz
- Kazimierz Klimowicz & Elżbieta Wolan
- + Alżusia Klimowicz
- Orszula Klimowicz
- Benedikt Klimowicz

The genealogical tree of Klimowicz family.

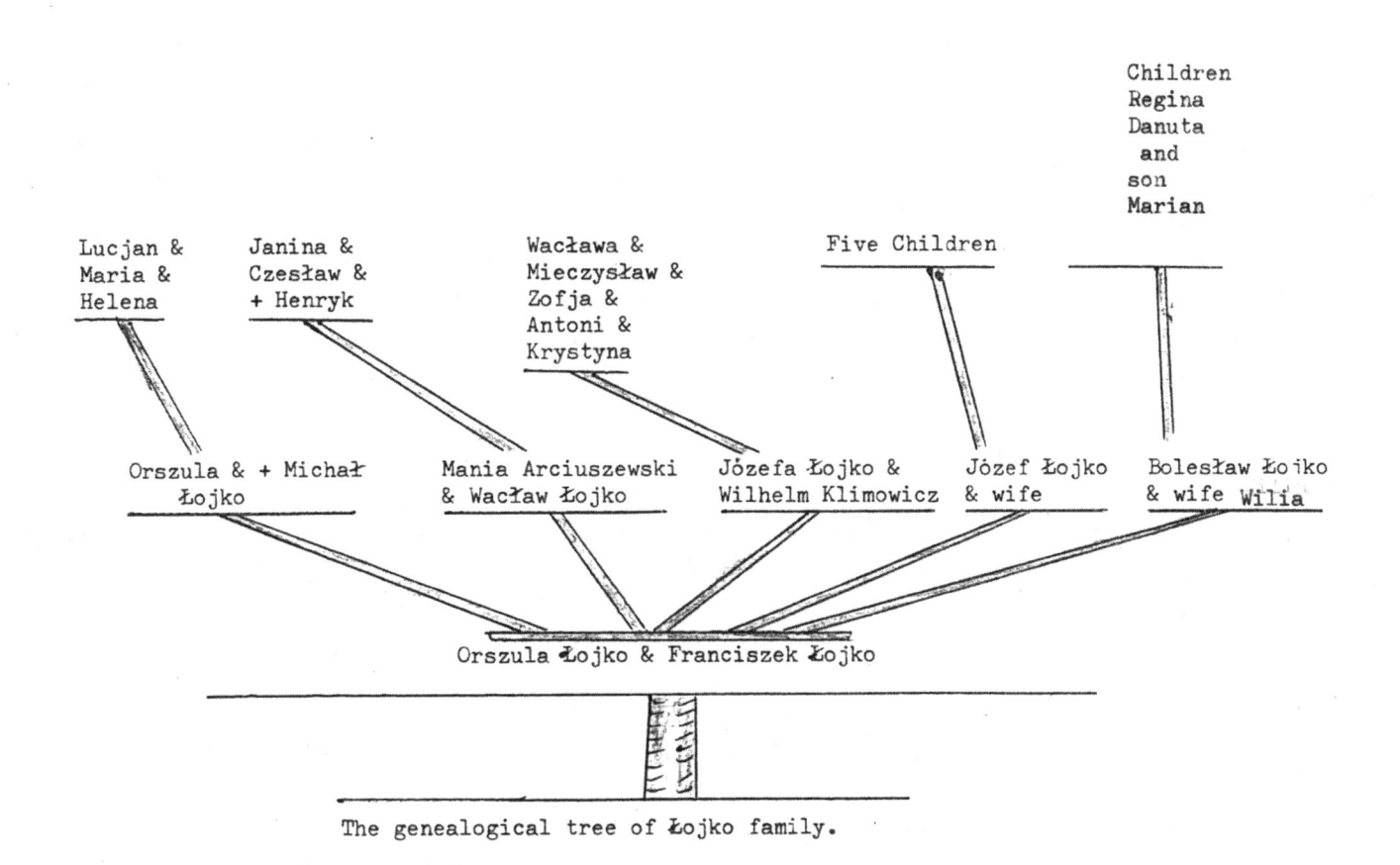

Łojko family tree (bottom):

Children Regina Danuta and son Marian

- Lucjan & Maria & Helena
- Janina & Czesław & + Henryk
- Wacława & Mieczysław & Zofja & Antoni & Krystyna
- Five Children

- Orszula & + Michał Łojko
- Mania Arciuszewski & Wacław Łojko
- Józefa Łojko & Wilhelm Klimowicz
- Józef Łojko & wife
- Bolesław Łojko & wife Wilia

Orszula Łojko & Franciszek Łojko

The genealogical tree of Łojko family.

```
                    Waclawa, Mieczyslaw,
                    Zofja, Antoni,&
                    Krystyna.
                       Parents
                 Jozefa & Wilhelm Klimowicz

Stefania & Anna Wolan
                                         Son & daughter
                                            Parents
                                       Orszula & Metro Majer

                        Ivan Klimowicz
                         father Edmund
 + Edward & wife                                    Two sons &
   & two daughters                                   daughter


                        Edward & Edmund &          Marylka & Franciszek
                        Bronisława & Orszula            Wolan
 +Edward Wolan &        & Wilhelm Klimowicz
 + Kazimierz Wolan


     Edmund Wolan        Elżbieta Wolan         Józef Wolan
```

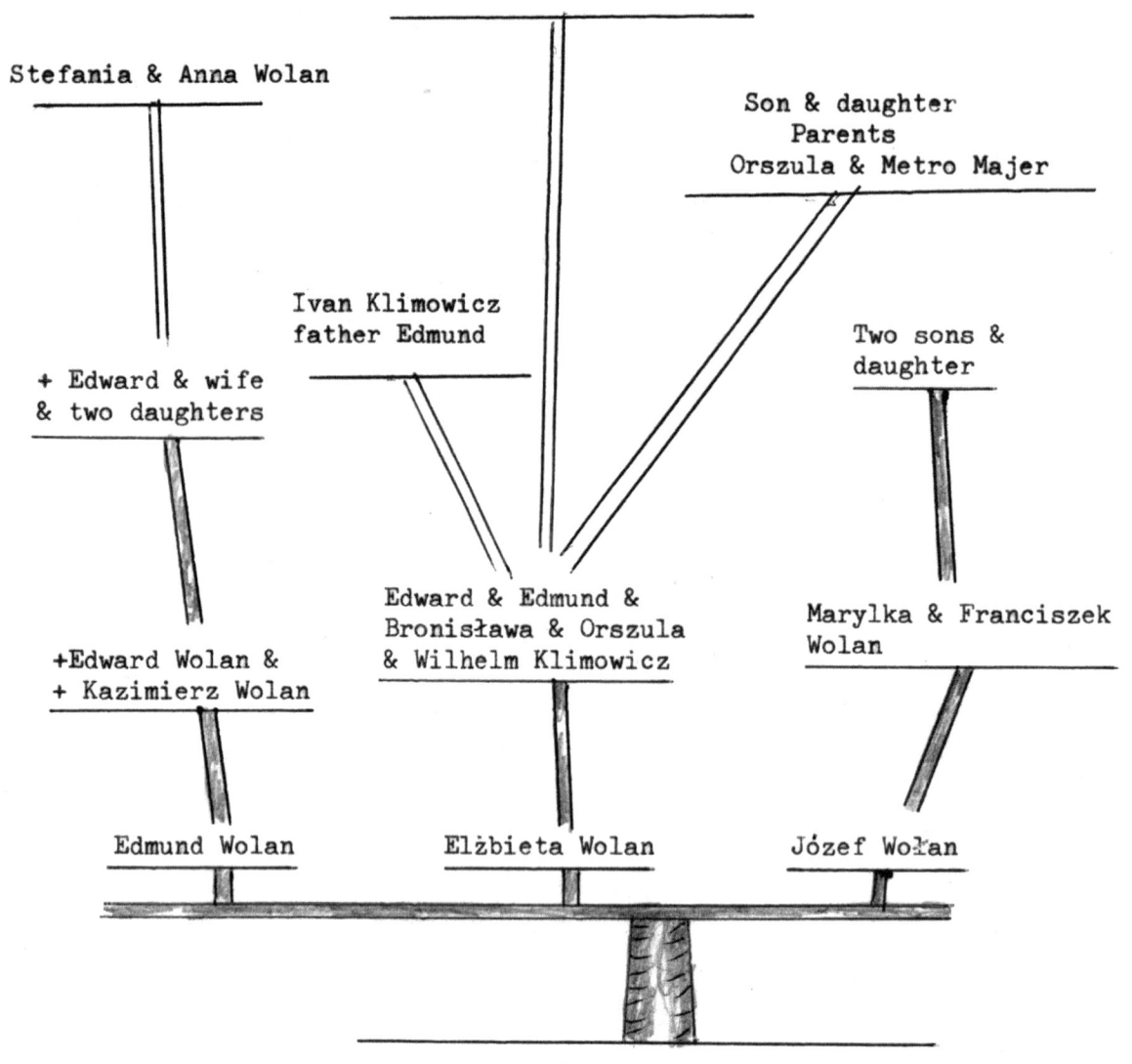

The genealogical tree of Wolan family.

+ War Victims

Following in time Jozefa Lojko became married to Wilhelm Klimowicz, and they resided at Pilsudski Street within a little distance from the elementary school and church. Her youngest brother Boleslaw lived under her protection to frequent school in rudimentary stage until he finished, and then he went to continue his studies in the city of Nowogrodek. His place of abode was then taken by the oldest daughter, Jania of Jozef's brother Waclaw, who was a forester and lived about sixteen kilometers from town in Trascianka. Likewise, Jania was under the Klimowicz family's protection while she attended elementary school. In the intervening time they began to have their own children, and the first-born was a girl named Waclawa. Subsequently I was born and was known by the name Mieczyslaw. Coming directly after in time my baby sister was born and her name was Zofia.

To act as a godfather to Waclawa, my sister, was our uncle Boleslaw, and my godfather was his brother Jozef. In my childhood I underwent severe illness of a whooping cough and I would have died in my parents' opinion if it were not for grandfather's brother, Dr. Peter Klimowicz, who really saved my life. Later, at the age of five, I was deceived by my friend, Arkadjusz Makarewicz, through unfortunate occurrence involving injury. Being three years older, he presented to me for acceptance certain poppy seeds in exchange for the cake I was eating, which I took and consumed without discretion. Unfortunately this particular poppy was grown wild and it was exceedingly poisonous; taken internally by an organism, it acts chemically upon the tissues in such a way as to harm or destroy. This poisonous hemlock locally was known as "szalejnik," which signifies madness, fury, frenzy and folly. It creates a state of extreme excitement or agitation suggestive of or bordering on delirium or insanity and manifesting severe mental disorder. It had also an effect of swollen belly to an extent of bursting. Being under such a predicament, an embarrassing and dangerous situation, Dr. Klimowicz without delay had to perform a clyster by washing out the bowels of its poison, by means of which my father's uncle saved my life for the second time.

Shortly after my restoration from sickness I remember Dr. Peter Klimowicz unexpectedly died from influenza. He left his wife Mania and son Eugenjusz. They both remained close with our family in existence together.

Throughout the time of religious holidays almost every time at our home there was a family re-union. All our relatives were gathered in such an important event to be present in the church for the rites, ceremonial forms, prayers, confessions and communion. The mass, in the Roman Catholic Church the eucharistic liturgy, consists of various prayers and ritual ceremonies and is regarded as a commemoration or repetition of Christ's sacrifice on the cross. A celebration of this liturgy is accompanied with a musical setting for some of the fixed portions of liturgy. This commemoration of the divine service on Sunday was scheduled at 9:00 a.m. for the children, and for the adults at noon. Of course, the mass appointed for mature people was with a sermon. At the conclusion of mass this unusual pipe organ, a musical instrument consisting of a collection of pipes and reeds made to sound by means of compressed air controlled by one or more keyboards and by various knobs used to vary registration, was giving forth musical sounds extremely loud when the doors were opened and the people started walking out. During such religious holidays outside in the churchyard and on the both sides of the street there were tables containing an abundance of various merchandise, things glittering and sparkling brilliantly. There were jewels, articles for personal adornment, especially some made out of gems and precious metal, and various religious articles such as crosses, rosaries, pictures and many other similar things. There was also a refreshment of food and drink such as sandwiches, soft drinks, ice cream and kernel, which was most popular in this part of the country. This kernel of gourd or pumpkin, the entire contents of a seed within its seating, is an edible part of a nut and it was desired to a very special extent by all children.

Relatives who had been separated from each other for some period of time were cohered again. From the university arrived Eugenjusz Klimowicz, Boleslaw Lojko and his niece Jania Lojko, from Trascianka her father Waclaw Lojko with his wife Mania and sons, Henry and Czeslaw, and from the remote place of town arrived Jozef Lojko with his wife and children, and of course, the parents, Orszula and Franciszek Lojko, who were residing with Jozef. Mania Klimowicz, Wierka Makarewicz, Alfons Klimowicz, Benedict Klimowicz, his two sisters Orszula and Alzusia and her daughter Regina Klimowicz and friends and neighbors were also present.

For a sumptuous feast the magnificent food was prepared under the supervision of skilled expert chef Bronislawa Klimowicz. This cuisine had great varieties of delicious food, from a crawfish to a decoratively fried goose or young pig, and again from rich and costly cakes to marzipans, and for refreshment when one is affected with thirst a collection of diverse beverages was readily available, some seasoned with juices and other various ingredients. Following in time there was a musical performance, singing and dancing. The music was entertained by the skillful accordionist Wilhelm Klimowicz and his uncle Benedict Klimowicz on the violin, and to play a musical accompaniment on a guitar was Eugenjusz Klimowicz.

My grandfather Franciszek Lojko was familiar with the holy scripture, the books of the Old and New Testaments, including often the Apocrypha. Obviously, he must have read a great deal of it and learned by means of study. At such a family reunion he had a convenient time of expressing a favorable opinion about a discourse based on text of the Bible, which was delivered as part of church service by the priest intended for the pulpit. An examination of the fearless and courageous faith of the judges should stir in our hearts a like faith, grandfather said. No wonder they are mentioned with such glowing approval at Hebrews 11:32-34. They were fighters in vindication of the true God's name, but not in their own strength. They knew the source of their power, God's spirit, and they humbly acknowledged it. Likewise, we today can take up "the sword of the spirit," God's Word, confident that he will empower us as he did Barak, Gideon, Jephthan, Samson and the others. Yes, we can be as strong spiritually as Samson was physically in overcoming mighty obstacles if we will but pray to true God and lean upon him so as to have his spirit. Grandfather was talking further about Jerusalem, that she has forgotten her first love. She has left true God, the source of living waters, and prostituted herself with strange gods. Jerusalem irreformable and doomed, how true God illustrated his determination to bring to ruin the pride of Judah and the abundant pride of Jerusalem. Grandfather was warning in some degree our group of people the district in which they live, speaking of a similar judgment, a disaster or misfortune regarded as inflicted by God the Almighty on account of their sinful deeds.

The elementary school in the Parish of Naliboki gave a course of education to seven years, and pupils usually entered at about seven years of age. The formal schooling in this institution of learning was simple and rudimentary based upon the fundamental subjects such as geography, history, nature, Polish language, geometry, arithmetic and religion. Of course, the Roman Catholic religion was lectured by a clergyman from the parish, during which the Jewish pupils were excused from this obligation to which naturally all other pupils present were subjected. Each class in the entire school in front of the room on the wall had a cross bearing an effigy of Christ crucified, to which Catholic pupils directed their prayers and songs before commencing learning and again; the same ceremony was repeated at the end of class. The group of pupils under each teacher in school, those that were pursuing daily study together, in the morning they orderly sang the following song:

> When the morning rising dawn,
> To You the earth, to You the sea,
> To You every living thing is singing,
> Be praised God the Almighty.
>
> And a man with immensity,
> Strewed with Your gifts,
> You who created him and saved him,
> Why should he not praise You.

This elementary school was established under the condition of methodical, proper and harmonious arrangements made for the benefit of pupils to be under discipline, which involved training of the mental, moral and physical powers; thus they were all subjected to the rule. Any violation of established rule, neglect of duty, the standards of good society, either by commission or omission, was punishable by submission to inflicted pain, to hold a pupil within limits or to force to end attendance at a school. The school afforded wider scope for the exercise of faculties in the scout, where the boys and girls put into action what they had learned in theory in order to gain skill and facility by practice. This scout was free to participate for anyone in school, which was a cultural tradition of the Polish national heritage. However, the Jewish boys and girls declined participation in the scout at school in Naliboki, as they were also exempt from the subject of Roman Catholic religion in the classes. It was therefore evident that the Jewish youths had much to learn in their own field of activity. No wonder they were capable of speaking fluently many languages and as a pupils in school they were productive with the outcome of an action by minimum wasted effort.

In spite of order and discipline in the school, there were some individuals who were bullies, swaggering, quarrelsome, usually cowardly persons who terrorized weaker ones. Such ignorant, unenlightened ones were at every time severely punished. Those ones frequently attacked with violence the Jewish boys in obscure places having little or no light in hidden and remote locations.

Nevertheless, it was a good thing for a Christian in the Parish of Naliboki to show proper respect for the government and appreciation for the beneficial services it was performing. We all had good reason to be glad because the government under which we lived provided roads for travel, schools for our education, fire protection and food inspection. Courts of law and protection against crime were also of great value. In these and other matters the superior authorities employed themselves to be the country's public servants who rendered services that resulted in benefit to the people. That is why we were paying taxes, on account of our conscience, for they were the country's public servants, constantly serving this very purpose. We rendered to all their dues, to him who called for the tax, the tax; to him who called for the tribute, the tribute. These matters were constantly expressed and spoken of to all the people concerned at the church by the priest in his common Sunday discourse based on a passage or text of the Bible.

Naliboki's Catholic church of St. Bartholomew built in Gothic architecture 1630 C.E.

Chapter IV

MODERNIZATION

In the 1930s the people in Naliboki were living like in many other places throughout the world; they resembled the manners or style of early times, which was simple and crude. To a certain degree throughout the time the people already underwent cultural development, social, customs, belief as a doctrine, folkways, but they were yet lacking in material development that was essential to keep up with the modern times. It was necessary that anything composed or constructed, anything used in creating or developing something was up to date and reflected light so as to appear of a different color from a different point of view. However, by means of transportation there were still admired horses, which were employed in the domestic state as a draft or for riding, when at the same time in the celestial regions there were heavier-than-air, powered flying craft having fixed wings, and in the 1920s there were balloons inflated with gas lighter-than-air and designed to rise and float in the atmosphere, having a car or basket attached for carrying passengers. Also there were airships lighter than air, powered flying craft and zeppelins, large dirigibles having rigid, cigar-shaped bodies. The name was taken after Count Ferdinand von Zeppelin, 1838-1917, the German general and aviator who designed it. On the ground in this region, of course, agricultural machinery was not established yet as a new element, nor was mechanical transportation, although the people here were familiarized with automobiles. They had watched frequent international motorcar races passing through Naliboki, but nobody in town possessed an automobile or motorbike, and yet there were already qualified mechanics in town wait for a modern day of favorable occasion.

There was a considerable number of individuals who were skilled and talented of remarkable ability. For example, there was a certain youth living in Maczylin with an extraordinary mind; he decided to construct himself a bicycle, which at its completion the whole structure, position and arrangement of parts was made out of wood. When his task voluntarily undertaken was completed, he made an examination for the purpose of proving or disproving some matter in doubt. So, he was riding this bicycle along Vilno Road and unexpectedly he passed a Palatine who was riding in his automobile. The Palatine became astonished at what he just perceived; he stopped his car and made a swift business transaction with the youth. He took the wooden bicycle with him in the car and then he sent a brand new bicycle from a store for the boy, which he received. Afterward this minor episode was incredible and became well known in the area.

The population in this specified area was rapidly growing in number, and therefore the parish needed an ecclesiastic of high rank to direct the priests and people to that which ultimately constituted an advance in excellence and superiority. So, for this particular advantage there was designated a certain prelate whose name was Bajko. He arrived to Naliboki on his powerful motorbike in the summer of 1935 with a loud roar and cloud of dust behind him. Folks were amazed when they heard the loud noise of a motorbike with a man on it clothed in green overalls who was moving with considerable speed toward the church. It appeared to be very strange, because it was impossible for one to think in those days that the high priest would ride such a powerful motorbike; besides, there were no motorbikes anywhere in the area. But as a matter of fact this particular prelate, Bajko, was unusual of extraordinary intelligence surpassing that of most intellectually superior individuals. He certainly had an outstanding gift for some specialized activities which were unique, being the only one of its kind and different to his actual profession, the act of binding oneself to a religious order and the condition of being so bound. On the first Sunday after his arrival to Naliboki, Prelate Bajko delivered a powerful sermon as a part of church service. All people were moved by it and became exceedingly excited and impelled to some immediate action. The prelate in his speech of a solemn kind, as a formal exhortation at once directed the people's attention to the urgency of modernizing Naliboki on account of its famous name, "The Wilderness of Naliboki," following upon the fact that Poland had two wildernesses only—the other one was known as the Wilderness of Bialowierz. However, the town indicated a decisive change in a specified condition was to some extent critical and that it was the right time to accept or adapt modern ways and ideas. Obviously, such a modernization project required a large sum of money or its equivalent accumulated for this specific purpose. So the money was piled up soon by the process of collecting and, of course, any individuals who donated one hundred zloty or more, their names and the amount of donation were announced from the pulpit each Sunday in the church. The members of the parish felt a strong sense of what was right and as a consequence they were accompanied by marks of honor. The main course of action in improvement first was to build a new church and to install electric energy for the community. Without procrastination, Prelate Bajko caused to be delivered a generator for the conversion of mechanical energy into electrical energy and fixed it in position for the service in personage. In town there were qualified, professional electricians who as a matter of fact designed and installed an electrical apparatus, and thus had the church and its area lit by electrical power intended to be used for a short time until the whole town determined to be lit by the similar source. When the beginning of success was made, later eventually in proportion to the prelate's plan, he purchased a huge machine for the sawmill, powered by steam, which was established for sowing logs or timber into boards, planks, etc., of specified lengths, and by means of which he had a large generator affixed to it. Of course, then his idea supplied an adequate demand of electrical energy to everyone in town. Now not only the church and its area but all streets and the entire town's dwellings were lit by a new energy, forming an essential quality of power to produce an effect differing from the ordinary illuminating oil that existed so long, pertaining to former times.

Now a new church was a chief course of action in order to provide the space equal to what was required for the community that was growing in number. Alongside the existing old church there was a long narrow excavation in the ground prepared to be a foundation for the proposed new church. This was the time when burial chambers were found of priests buried in the churchyard some four centuries ago. Soon after, the foundation was laid and the construction of the new church began under supervision and skill of a certain local individual with his three sons who were actually civil engineers. In this construction they used very recently made bricks in the brick-kiln, which was set up by Prelate Bajko intentionally for the completion of the church. The lumber from the sawmill, which was also established elegantly by the prelate, was used as building material in the church project. The mortar for bricklaying was used from the natural resources in its surroundings devised by fabrication of a mixture of lime, clay, sand and water. These materials when joined as a single body bind bricks together. The lime and clay sediments were abundantly deposited underground in the entire region and were easily obtainable to be used for a building purpose or any practical advantage. Many of the people in the district participated in constructing the new church out of bricks and mortar and other available materials used that were a source of wealth provided by nature in that province.

The modernizer Prelate Bajko was very much concerned about the construction of new roads in the region in order to establish a method of regular public transportation connected to the surrounding cities. The route taken in traveling from Naliboki to Stolpce became under construction without lapse of time. Large stones were broken by sledge of specified size and laid closely together on the prepared surface that served as foundation, which was marked in a straight line with a long narrow excavation in the ground on both sides and a certain width of edge of highway. Then the gravel from broken stones was distributed over the surface in a thin layer in order to cover all spaces between stones to have the exterior face finally smooth and even. The appearance of this new road was a bowlike curve, so that the water after a heavy rainfall would flow off gradually into the trenches on both sides of the highway, and of course its shoulders were landscaped with covered grass and planted trees. Telegraph posts bearing the weight of numerous wires were stretched along the highway on one side from Naliboki to Stolpce and eastward on the road to Iwieniec. This telegraph communication device was preserved and kept in proper condition at all times. The construction of bridges was necessary to undertake—that could not be locally denied—on account of old and unsafe structures erected across a waterway, ravine road, etc., to afford trustworthy passage. Naturally, for such a job there was assigned a qualified bridge engineer, Mr. Korzenko, who was actually constructing bridges in the entire area of the Wilderness of Naliboki. Mr. Korzenko frequently experienced pleasure in dining at the Bronislawa's restaurant, and soon he conceived a love for her. He enjoyed in her restaurant good food and drink, and as a result Mr. Korzenko began to have regular appointments with this most desirable member of the opposite sex.

The prelate had purchased a luxurious bus that was engaged to provide transportation to Stolpce each morning and in the latter part of the day, then the first part of night it came back home to be garaged and serviced by the local mechanic. This type of transportation by luxurious bus from Naliboki to Stolpce was something characteristic of modern times; it was quick, convenient and well suited to one's needs. Regional people traveled for pleasure, something that gives a feeling of enjoyment, and the same for business, a proper interest or concern, and others for emergency, a sudden and unexpected turn of events that called for immediate action.

The population living in the Wilderness of Naliboki—Puszcza Nalibocka, the largest complex of forest in the palatine of Nowogrodek, about 240,000 ha. or 592,200 acres—realized that characteristic of the most recent period of development was essential in order to dwell comfortably in a free state of human society already characterized by a high level of intellectual, social and cultural development, when the countries and peoples considered to have reached this stage. But above all, the Parish of Naliboki was morally obligated with its effort to Prelate Bajko for his modern ideas which made all things possible and capable of being done to current standards.

Out of red bricks the new church structure was shaping itself in the similar Gothic style as the existing church that was built in 1630 A.D., but much greater in dimension, as length, breadth and height. The manner of construction was most progressive toward its completion in the year 1939. Only the exterior upper covering of the church was left unfinished, and the representation of inside the church, such as decorating and furnishing. But unfortunately, the outburst of the Second World War in the latter part of 1939 caused to withhold completion of this most desirable project. Since this new construction was situated upon the summit of a hill that actually was the highest spot in the area, the top of the new church became a strategic point and was used in battles between hostile armies. One being on the top of the church structure could see distantly and extensively everywhere, so that even the illuminant city of Nowogrodek at night was clearly seen over the line of the apparent meeting of the sky with the top of the forest that grew so tall on the ground.

From the very presence and influence of Prelate Bajko the Parish of Naliboki began to take and follow as a course of action the characteristics of modern times. Subsequently, they felt morally excellent, honorable and worthy to such a cause, because they all hoped to live in an improved and better condition of recent times. They complied to the fullest extent with law and regulation, such as a rule or an order having force of law issued by the executive authority of government. By way of illustration, the government ordered that all private fences in Naliboki erected of stakes or iron as an enclosure be painted white. As it might be expected, the streets of this considerable collection of dwellings presented an appearance of beauty when in fact something like this was done ostensibly for public good.

The people did act indeed, in accordance with the government's direction authoritatively given in all aspects of a problem. They did pay taxes, repaired buildings, trimmed the trees, kept lawns clean from wastes, etc., and above all they refrained from crime and thus dwelled happily in the public order and tranquility from the time when Poland reemerged as an independent nation after World War I in 1918.

In the fourteenth century when Poland's Queen Jadwiga was married to the Grand Duke of Lithuania, it helped create a new power in Europe. Successful wars and treaties expanded the boarders of the unified nations from the Baltic to the Black Sea at the end of the fifteenth century. During that time Naliboki was just a good manor house of the Dukes Radziwill. When the church was built in 1630, Naliboki was developed more fully to the form of a parish. Formerly here existed Steelworks with a smelting furnace in which the fire was intensified by an air blast, and of course a glassworks. Here was manufactured crystals and beautiful hilts for the swords from polished stone. During the period between 1918 to 1939 Naliboki in conformity with fact was blooming and growing as if to time indefinite. By the year 1939 the Parish of Naliboki was inhabited approximately by 50,000 people, mainly Polish nationality, and of course there was a certain percentage of mixed nationality such as Lithuanian, Byelorussian and Jewish. Essentially the people of the Parish of Naliboki adopted modern ways and ideas of the genius Prelate Bajko, and in that following way of manner Naliboki became modernized.

A long time ago Naliboki was fortunate to have steel production. The iron ore for the blast furnace was obtainable in overflowing supply from Rudnia Nalibocka, about sixteen kilometers north of Naliboki. But on account of lacking some essential transportation for the ready sale of merchandise, Naliboki was gradually falling behind its competitor, namely Minsk. No wonder that Minsk today is the biggest manufacturer of steel cord in Europe. Other products such as angle pieces, discs, channels, reinforcement, wire rods and castings are also in great demand among the works customers. All the products meet international standards. But not only in production of steel, yet in many other products Minsk prosperously advanced, such as rubber products for cars, tractors and agricultural machinery. Special transport vehicles for the consignment of large freights and major individual items with loads from 40 to 200 tons and transportation of assembled technological equipment. Also Minsk worsted wool mills, Minsk watch factory and timber mills.

However, now before World War II Naliboki was making its own progress in advancement to what was peculiar to modern times, but unfortunately dreadful war interrupted forever a journey to desired outcome for all of something attempted.

About 75 kilometers, or 46.6 miles, east of Naliboki is the relative position of Minsk, the capital city of Byelorus SSR, the city of 1.3 million inhabitants. There are mass graves of about 250,000 persons murdered by NKVD during the years 1937 to '41. NKVD stands for the People's Commissariat of Internal Affairs (1935 to 1946; since 1946 MWD, the Ministry of Internal Affairs), equivalent to German Gestapo.

Besides, to place this city in opposition so as to set off differences, Naliboki during the period of 1939 to '43 became totally a bloody battlefield where the entire town was finally annihilated. Here, partisans of the Union of Soviet Socialist Republics fought in battle with German forces. The German forces in their attempt to capture, fought with the Soviet partisans. On the other hand, Naliboki's guerrilla remained in combat between hostile armies; they fought both the Soviet oppressors and German invaders. The Wilderness of Naliboki was filled with a swarm of Soviet partisans, and in addition there was a large concentration of Polish underground troops, an adversary to Soviet partisans because they fought for the Free State of Poland.

The Last Day of Naliboki

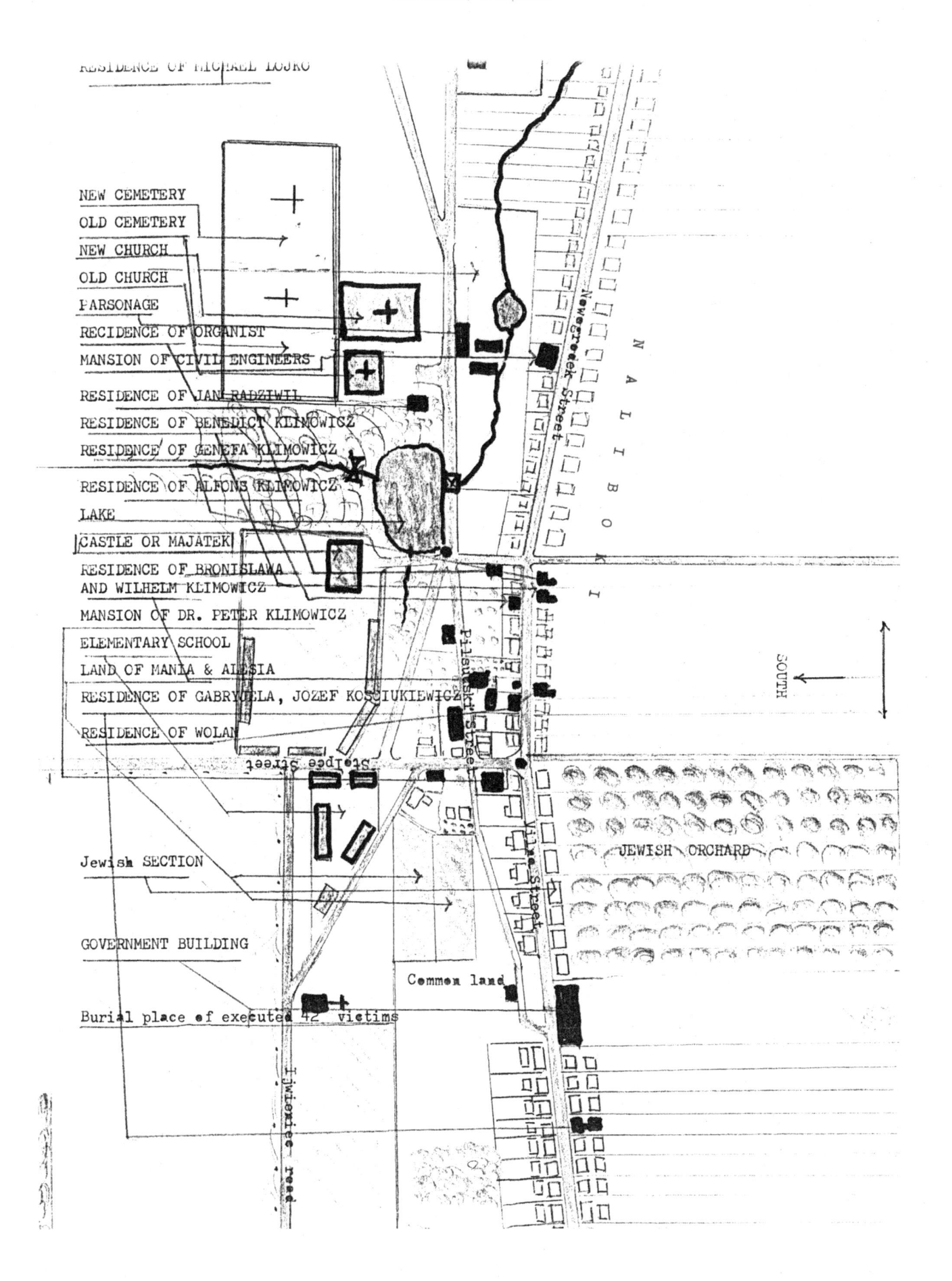

- RESIDENCE OF MICHAEL LOJKO
- NEW CEMETERY
- OLD CEMETERY
- NEW CHURCH
- OLD CHURCH
- PARSONAGE
- RECIDENCE OF ORGANIST
- MANSION OF CIVIL ENGINEERS
- RESIDENCE OF JAN RADZIWIL
- RESIDENCE OF BENEDICT KLIMOWICZ
- RESIDENCE OF GENEFA KLIMOWICZ
- RESIDENCE OF ALFONS KLIMOWICZ
- LAKE
- CASTLE OR MAJATEK
- RESIDENCE OF BRONISLAWA AND WILHELM KLIMOWICZ
- MANSION OF DR. PETER KLIMOWICZ
- ELEMENTARY SCHOOL
- LAND OF MANIA & ALESIA
- RESIDENCE OF GABRYELA, JOZEF KOSCIUKIEWICZ
- RESIDENCE OF WOLAN
- Jewish SECTION
- GOVERNMENT BUILDING
- Burial place of executed 42 victims

Newcreek Street

NALIBOKI

Pilsutski Street

Stoupee Street

Vilna Street

JEWISH ORCHARD

Common land

Iwieniec road

SOUTH

The manor house of the Dukes Radziwils built in the fifteenth century, subsequently known as the Majatek of Ciechanowicz.

Chapter V

PEACE AND PROSPERITY

The people in the Wilderness of Naliboki endured under severe trial and prolonged stress of the First World War and immediately in close succession they had to put up with the notorious bandits that were at large for some time in the wilderness. These outlaws used to attack violently by force with intent to commit robbery or murder on anyone who was traveling on the highways through an uninhabited region. As a result of the bandits' criminal actions, many people were brutally killed in cold blood in their own territory. These brigands became a menace to society, endangering the lives of law-abiding citizens who were entitled to protection from the government, which was not in the state of war at that time. A decisive movement toward this end was undertaken by urgent enlistment of a great number of able-bodied men to the police force in the surrounding cities and towns.

It was incredible that among those bandits there was entangled even a certain ''ZNACHOR,'' originally from Warsaw, whom Doctor Wilczur portrayed in the most prominent Polish motion picture made before the Second World War. Znachor in Polish pertains to a quack, a pretender to medical knowledge or skill. Dr. Wilczur actually was adroit in surgery and as such was most famous in the country. He was robbed and left for dead. After he came back to life again, he wandered from Warsaw to our part of the country in a state of total loss of memory and became known as Znachor when he subsequently began skillful treatment by operative procedures involving bodily injuries, deformities and diseased conditions.

This disturbing trend of violence, robbery and murder by the evil men who caused suffering and misfortune overpowered the Wilderness of Naliboki and had to be stopped once and for all. To this end the terminal point of determination was taken in order to wipe out a dreadful crime from the state of human society, characterized by a high level of intellectual, social and cultural development.

However, it came about that Znachor was captured in the company of bandits and eventually was released. From this time on, as his memory was raising to a more desirable condition, he drifted steadily toward Warsaw along with his amazing ability of healing the sick. Subsequently, when Znachor reached his homestead, his children were grown up and his wife deceased. As they recognized themselves in the cemetery at the grave of their loved one, Znachor realized that he actually was Dr. Wilczur.

My father, yet a single man, was enlisted to perform a duties of law and order in the company of other engaged men in Naliboki. Their task was to seek out in an attempt to capture the outlaws in their concealed places of cover in the district of Naliboki.

Many more bandits were apprehended and taken into custody to stand the examination before a court of the facts to determine their guilt or innocence. The greater part of alleged bandits were found guilty and sentenced to long-term imprisonment, and some to death. In order to perform an execution of convicted bandits sentenced to death the policemen had to cast lots to determine who would carry into effect the judgment of the court that punishment was death by hanging. Nevertheless, there was an option for the ones who were destined to execute, and in the event they declined or simply were unable to inflict death upon a human being they had to resign their position from the police force without any obligation. As it actually happened, my father was destined to perform this execution, and therefore he chose to resign.

Following in time, while the bandits were still at large in the wilderness, my father was traveling from Nowogrodek back home to Naliboki in the coldest season of the year. He had a forceful and efficient horse, Arabian breed, engaged in a sledge that had a railing made of wood resting on supports around the sledge used as guards to carry goods or passengers. This horse was easily activated into a sudden gallop intelligibly by a sharp and sudden pull on the halter. Father was traveling quietly through the uninhabited region during daytime and it was already getting dusky; a certain strange man was standing in the middle of the highway, and when the hackney transportation drew near he broke into the sledge by his own force and in a lying position he expressed his own amusement with scoffing laughter. At this moment father began to take the slack of leather straps easy, and as soon as he had done so he pulled the halter suddenly in a strong manner, which caused the horse into a quick-tempered gallop. The uninvited individual rolled off the sledge and held on by the guard railing with his hands while his body was dragged. Father struck his hands with the handle of a whip until he had to let go. The bandit became angry and cried out, "You have recognized me, son of a bitch," and further he expressed himself in a euphemism for many offensive epithets.

According to the truth of what was averred, the bandits were driven out from the wilderness by force, which all resulted in due course of time. So by the time father was married in 1925 and I was born in 1929, the Wilderness of Naliboki was free from danger, and there was no one exposed to evil, injury or loss. The public harmonious arrangement of things over tranquillity had effective power of governing influence and control throughout all parts of territory. It came to pass that there was no agitated feeling aroused by awareness of actual or threatening danger, trouble, dread or terror. People began to travel everywhere in a free manner throughout the wilderness; thus they enjoyed gathering common edible forest mushrooms, various berries, fishing and seasonal hunting. The act of starting business took place. Various jobs sponsored by the government were undertaken by people in the forest. Citizens collectively with skill were engaged to act under lawful authority in performance of duties, such as foresters who were provided with weapons so that the entire wilderness was so secured as to render loss, escape or failure impossible. However, possession of firearms was forbidden by law extending throughout the nation.

Finally the peaceful conditions prevailed over the entire free State of Poland. The dreadful crime nationwide had diminished, and particularly in my place of birth crime was not perceived by the ear. For the assurance, intended to give confidence Ignacy Moscicki, President of the free State of Poland (Rzeczpospolita Polski), INTENTIONALLY made a tour in 1929 into the most affected areas by the bandits. He gave a speech to the people in Naliboki, and on his way to Nowogrodek he interrupted a journey in Kroman at the beautiful lake. Here the president planted a young linden tree in honor of peace and prosperity, which is striking roots there until this very day.

On the nineteen degree T-junction, the place where roads come together from Iwieniec west to Stolpce south right behind the elementary school, there were apple trees growing. So, as we traveled through that place, father directed my attention to those apple trees on which the bandits were hanged before I was born. After that, whenever I passed through that place in my childhood, I was terrified because I could not help myself imagining dead bodies hanging on those trees, but I did not admit to anyone that I was afraid. Besides, this location was much celebrated when the cars sped from Iwieniec to Stolpce in the international motorcar race.

In the warmest season of the year the old folks, mainly from the Parish of Naliboki, made a pilgrimage to a shrine or some most sacred place in Wilno. Each year people used to make a journey on foot, and fortunately they all came back home safe. There was no fear anymore of threatening danger in the entire land of Wilno and Nowogrodek.

But unfortunately in the year 1934 my sister Zosia at the age of four was taken ill and, after one week of sickness, she died. My parents put her body in the grave in a new separate section of the consecrated cemetery. It was expressed by the relatives at that time that if Dr. Peter Klimowicz was still alive possibly Zosia would not have died. In this particular time my brother Antoni was born and he, like the rest of us, was christened at the church in Naliboki. Shortly after the procession was held for the final disposal of the body of my dead sister, the Christian baptismal ceremony of an infant took place. Customarily such an event was observed as a festival with rejoicing in the company of relatives and friends, but unfortunately on this occasion a formal social entertainment of guests was indeed modest in order to excite admiration.

It was most important for any Polish citizen who loved his country and zealously guarded its welfare, especially a defender of popular liberty, to appreciate the fact that from the public order and tranquillity standpoint there was no organized crime, no riot or public disorder, no violence or murder under the leadership of Marshal Jozef Pilsudski. He certainly knew how to conduct the war and preserve the peace. As a unique patriot, he had his own plans and made his own decisions. Pilsudski did not trust anyone, nor did he place confident reliance on the integrity, honesty or justice of another. In the beginning he had his opposition exiled, among which there were outstanding individuals such as General Helerczyk and General Sikorski, but even these were by no means a match to his quality or characteristics; therefore, Jozef Pilsudski was admired not only in Poland, but also abroad in the foreign lands among Polish people, where he was perpetually loud by a clergymen at the pulpit during a sermon. On account of a frequent emphasis of very special affection and deep appreciation for the leadership of Jozef Pilsudski, some veterans from General Helerczyk's army became annoyed. That is why it was observed in Baltimore, Maryland, in the church that once such a veteran made a remark to the Catholic priest while he was conducting a sermon by saying, "Pilsudski, Pilsudski, Pilsudski, but what about Helerczyk, is he worth nothing?" However, it happened to be an unusual experience for the people in the church, because as a rule no one is allow to speak when the priest delivers a sermon.

My Aunt Bronislawa and father, that is, sister and brother, were constantly receiving letters and parcels of gifts from my Aunt Orszula, who lived with her husband and two children in Lithuania. She also enclosed from time to time her family's photographs. The son and daughter were both students in a university. The whole family photographed beautifully. They had an appearance indicating all aspects of health, happiness and prosperity, following upon the fact that Uncle Metro Majer was the prime minister of Lithuania; thus they were at a peak of success, which resulted by some favorable circumstances. My father, I noticed, was very proud of his brother-in-law and his family. His two brothers, highly educated, lived in Russia, but unfortunately he had no news from them. Father and Aunt Bronislawa talked a lot about their brothers, and they were worried because they knew nothing about them, nor did they know what could have happened to them in Russia. Being troubled in mind respecting this uncertain matter, their hopeful attitude to be reunited was frustrated indeed on account of the fact that Jozeph Stalin inspired hate and horror because of cruelty and his wickedness nationwide. However, at this point in time nobody knew what Stalin was up to in his country.

My mother's brother Waclaw from Trascianka and his children Janie and Qzeslaw were under our parents' guardianship while they attended elementary school at Naliboki. So we all lived together as one large family.

Uncle Waclaw had under his supervision eight square kilometers of forest adjoined to the lake known as Kroman, including the residence of the chief forester, which was comprised of several dwellings. The location of Kroman was only three kilometers south of Trascianka, from which lake an artificial waterway for land navigation flowed north to the river Niemen.

Uncle Waclaw's own husbandry comprised of arable land, meadow, a large house of two apartments, storage, barns, stables and beehives in the orchard. This husbandry was extended around by the most beautiful pine-trees forest. He had country servants who took care of the farming business such as the cultivation of land and breeding domestic animals and fowl. His store was filled with different comestible. He was well equipped and had a prosperous, happy family life. In his woodland worked Mr. Kostus, whose job was to grub up the stumps of common pine trees ready for the place where pitch was extracted by heat in Smolarnia, which was located east of Kroman about five kilometers on the highway to Naliboki. This considerable tract of land between Trascianka and Naliboki is a part of the Wilderness of Naliboki.

Every Sunday we all looked forward to seeing Uncle Waclaw, Mania and their son Heniek, but they were not always able to come to Naliboki together. Nevertheless, whoever arrived from Trascianka, Uncle Waclaw thought as a rule that it was his turn to treat us the best he knew how. Besides, Janka and Czeslaw had to be equipped with necessary things for the elementary school, such as clothes, books, writing books, and so on. In addition to that they were amply furnished with victuals, food that was prepared with care and wisdom in the management of Uncle's resources. To take advantage of an opportunity, we all went to the church, and after that we had festive entertainment as usual.

Mr. Kostus was in his late twenties, unmarried, and was as if from the Nephilim, so we became in our own eyes like grasshoppers, and the same way in his eyes. He was huge and because of his gigantic size he was proud to profess that at night he was devoid of fear, and so Uncle believed him. That is why he always used to come to Uncle's place of residence from the forest late at evening to pass the night.

But the fear was experienced by Mr. Kostus one Sunday when Aunt Mania drove by hackney coach to Naliboki to the church, and afterwards, being delayed at our residence, she was late riding back home. Uncle Waclaw, troubled in mind respecting his wife, decided to walk with his son Heniek so far as the Glass Bridge, a distance of one kilometer in order to meet her. Because of a multitude of mosquitoes in the wilderness, the female having a long proboscis capable of puncturing the skin of man and animals for extracting blood, Uncle put his child on his shoulders and covered him with a white sheet he took from the bed. In such a fashion he walked toward the Glass Bridge, and he scared the life out of Mr. Kostus when he approached the Glass Bridge from the opposite direction. He then made a sudden left turn and started running in such a manner that both feet were off the ground for a portion of each step toward Kroman. However, some weeks later Mr. Kostus by his own admission conceded that this was a first time in his entire life he has actually seen a ghost, a disembodied spirit of unusually large size, which appeared on the Glass Bridge, and that he was terrified.

A long time ago the Glass Bridge received its descriptive name instead of or in addition to its actual name after an incident of a certain descendant of the Hebrew people, a merchant transporting a wagon full of glassware from Naliboki's glassworks, actually lost his entire load of glassware on the bridge in a collision. However, this bridge over a canal was constructed completely out of solid wood, and that is why people always wondered why on earth it was called the Glass Bridge.

It was common, widespread knowledge that the dwelling where the chief forester resided at Kroman was haunted; supposedly it was visited regularly almost every night by a ghost. On account of repeatedly recurring to the mind a haunting tune of apparition in this particular house, a great number of chief foresters were reassigned for different posts, but only one of them persevered permanently because he claimed he was able to endure this unusual terrifying occurrence. The arrangement of rooms inside this dwelling was as follows: At the main entrance in the house on the left side there was a large kitchen, and on the right side there was a living room, but in between there was a long corridor, and on each side doors leading to a great number of rooms. So precisely at twelve o'clock at night while the chief forester was laying down in bed he began to hear footsteps in the kitchen, following to the living room, then the opening door to the corridor, and systematically carried out with organized regularity, each door to all rooms was opened and shut till lastly his bedroom door was opened with a sudden current of air, and then a coverlet from the bed was cast aside onto the floor. During the time when the chief forester was laying uncovered on the bed his door closed, and then he heard all doors closing and footsteps leading to an exit in the same manner as the ghost had entered the house.

This haunting recollection of a ghost in the house of the chief forester was investigated and consecrated by a Catholic priest, but it did not put an end to the animating spirit. For years the chief forester lived in his haunted house to which he got accustomed, and he claimed that there was no use to express feelings of dissatisfaction because after all, the ghost was not causing any harm.

My parents were well acquainted with Mr. Kostus and the chief forester from Kroman, of course, through Uncle Waclaw. Mr. Kostus often came to town on weekends to visit some Jewish stores in order to be furnished with what was needed for his job in the forest, and then he called upon us to pass the night. For the last meal of the day he ate his own food—one loaf of a rounded mass of bread baked in a single piece in one hand and a large piece of salami in another hand, and for an uncomfortable feeling of dryness in the throat and mouth, accompanied by an increasingly urgent desire for liquids, he drank a couple gallons of beer. Finally, when he lay down on the floor to rest, his body was stretched from one end to the other end of the room because he was so big and yet magnanimous. Mr. Kostus, a gentle and kind person of good family and good breeding, manifested generosity in forgiving insults or even injuries.

The chief forester, when he occasionally was in town on some business, made a brief visit at our residence. During his short stay in the company of my parents he told them in detail about his haunting experience and actual participation with an apparition in the house he resided. In spite of such a terrifying experience of being haunted by a ghost in the large house living on his own, he declared positively that this phenomenon did not bother him in the slightest degree. But as I was influenced to hear his story, it scared the living life out of me and it caused me continually to remember this house at Kroman notwithstanding the fact that I never happened to be there yet. However, the chief forester was a unique and remarkable individual. He even took a bath regularly in Lake Kroman during the coldest season of the year as long as ice could be broken in order to have free and easy access to the water.

Mr. Korzenko, an engineer, was engaged in courtship with Aunt Bronislawa already for some period of time. Their nonmarriageable romance at first was characterized by high ideals of purity and devotion with intensified affection. Their love affair gave an impression of being perpetual until her mother Elizabet absolutely forbade them to be joined as husband and wife in matrimony. In an exclamation of regret and sorrow Mr. Korzenko made the matter worse because from this point of view he increased his drinking ability, and in due time he became an alcoholic. In the meantime my grandmother passed away in 1932 and my aunt became crushed in spirit by grief with the feeling of resentment arising from a sense of having been wronged by her own mother. Since then she repeatedly reminded herself of mother's culpability, how she had spoiled her lifetime and designated her destiny to remain living apart from others.

Grandmother was buried together with my grandfather, Kazimierz Klimowicz. Since then as far as I remember I never saw Aunt Bronislawa go to church because of her anger and ill will in view of fancied wrong. However, she continued working in her restaurant in order to keep away from vexation by occupying her mind with cooking and baking extremely tasty cakes, pastries, cookies and so on. Her cousins, Wierka and Gabriela Klimowicz, frequently visited her to acquire knowledge through practice as to how to bake delicious cakes and pastries. This particular baking was really taking place always on a full scale for the Christmas or Easter Holidays. Gabriela, of course, was just married to Jozef Kosciukiewicz, but Wierka Klimowicz was a maiden. She was a young and most beautiful girl of an average height with a physique of perfect structure, having all the qualities requisite to its nature, with long blonde hair and dark blue eyes. She was of a strong personality and moral force. She also had a good reputation as a businesswoman selling merchandise in her own store, known as a cooperative, a business enterprise organized by a group for its common economic benefit, set up in her own dwelling place, the mansion of her late father Dr. Peter Klimowicz. This (spoldzielnia) cooperative was the only one of its kind and stood alone as a Polish business among great varieties of Jewish stores in Naliboki.

But there was still a certain young man with a noble name, descended from dukes who originally were the founders of Naliboki in the fourteenth century, when Poland's Queen Jadwiga was married to the Grand Duke Jagielo of Lithuania—it helped create a new power in Europe. Successful wars and treaties expanded the borders of the unified nation from the Baltic to the Black Sea by the end of the fifteenth century. During those days Naliboki happened to be just a good manor house of the Dukes Radziwill. This good manor house, or a landed estate to us, was known as "Majatek," and its proprietor was Mr. Ciechanowicz. It is probable that one of the daughters of Duke Radziwill married Mr. Ciechanowicz and thus he became a sole owner of the Dukes Radziwill's domain in Naliboki. However, this present Mr. Jan Radziwill existed without ruling power or wealth; he lived with his mother in a little house on the street Poplawski. His brother Jozef Radziwill remained always in the military service. Their mother Mrs. Radziwill, a tall lady, was regarded as our best neighbor and friend, and she often used to come to our house to visit. Her husband was never mentioned briefly or otherwise as I recall, so it seemed apparent that he died long before my time. Mr. Jan Radziwill was a young man, about six fee four inches tall, and he suddenly fell in love with Wierka. He kept following her no matter where she went because of being enthusiastic; he was crazy about her. He was inspired by her beauty and possessed by her spirit; her characteristic temper, mood and state of mind had the power to enchant him. The accumulated variety of whatever had been actually met with or engaged in the force of her presence, Jan could not enjoy a satisfying life even one minute without her. She unknowingly kept in an active force his dynamic energy. That is why, because of Jan's persistence and his stubbornness in the period of courting and wooing, Wierka was terrified. She began to hide from Jan in various places. Sometimes she used to hide in our residence, where she thought she was savingly concealed, but unfortunately Jan found her. Then they both walked on a recessed space at the entrance of a building at night and he commenced the act of uttering in a poetic manner about the stars in the open air with the serenade of love. At the same time he embraced her gently and hugged her affectionately.

Jan was an extremely talented individual. He had ability to write poetry and was skillful in sculpture, in the art of fashioning figures of wood, clay, plastic, metal or stone. This Mr. Jan Radziwill subsequently became acquainted with her half brother, student Eugenjusz Klimowicz, and thereafter they came about to be lasting mutual friends.

Mrs. Radziwill and her son Jan Radziwill.

My mother professionally was a skilled tailor and was familiar with weaving, which she usually underwent in the winter after she had made her texture from the cultivated flax, an annual plant that yields the fiber used in making linen. She used to fashioned a certain style or mode of dress on the material, then cut it with sharp scissors ready for the sewing machine. This type of work she carried through to completion on order for the people in town or private need. Apart from her profession, mother kept her duties of housekeeping in the best interest and welfare for the family. Father, however, had a Russian education before World War I, and during the war he was mobilized to the czar's army. Immediately after the czar's defeat in October 1918 he found his way home successfully, when at last Poland reemerged as an independent nation, and the Bolsheviks, political radicals, started to rule Russia. Subsequently, father became a farmer just like most folks in Naliboki. As a farmer, he also had proficient skill and expertness in working as a butcher. He used to slaughter and dress animals for market or domestic use privately for the people in town.

Both mother and father, similar to all citizens in the Wilderness of Naliboki, occupied themselves with the cultivation of the ground and gathering in the harvest as a main resource to support life. In the spring, the season in which all vegetation starts anew, they actively engaged in planting bulbs and sowing seeds. Following in time, father had to mow, cure, gather and store the hay for the cattle and horses as winter feed. After his own meadows were mowed manually by scythe, he went then to Trascianka with his friend Antony Szarzanowicz for a few weeks to make hay-ricks, so that in the winter the hay could be transported home by sledge when the ground was frozen by cold. The meadows were located on the east side of the canal in Uncle Waclaw's forestry, which afforded the opportunity for father and his friend to gain advantage. In order to be able to work there by the canal for some time, first they had to construct a shelter from inclement weather. This shelter they usually used to build swiftly. The frame was made of round and upright pieces of wood cut from the forest, then it was covered with the straw permitting no water to enter or pass through. This impermeable shelter to provide protection from inclement weather was design to accommodate comfortably at least two persons. In front of the shelter they built as part of the structure an open fire, on which they prepared their own food for eating. Early in the morning they mowed the grass while it still contained dew because it was easier to work with the scythe. Then after midday they turned over the swaths to dry. Dry hay they piled up together in one place, forming a large heap or stack. These stacks or hay-ricks were left there in the forest for the winter to be transported in the coldest season of the year.

Just before August the act of gathering and collecting a ripened crop of grain fruit and vegetables began. Father mowed by scythe the barley, oats, buckwheat and millet. Mother tied the sheaves, fastened with the same plant, the ends of which were drawn into a knot. Subsequently, they arranged the sheaves into piles or cocks to allow this crop to dry adequately before it was removed from the field and stored in the barn ready for thrashing. Following this procedure, in August a harvest of rye and wheat had begun. This rye in Europe is an extensively cultivated cereal plant bearing seeds on a single ear and is primarily used for bread and rye vodka. Likewise, a wheat similar to rye only more refined, this grain of a cereal grass, is widely cultivated in Europe and provides a fine flour used for white bread, cakes, pastries and so on. The plant producing this grain bears at its summit a dense spike called the ear or head, sometimes with awns (bearded wheat) and sometimes without awns (beardless or bald wheat). So the wheat and rye was a special job for women to cut by sickle because its unspoiled straw was used for covering roofs and other numerous useful needs. That is why this particular crop of grain usually was thrashed with a flail manually by hard-working men. At such a harvest parents always had someone hired to help them complete this task of thrashing as soon as possible to store the grain and make flour. Of course, after gathering the ripened crop of grain, a harvest at home was celebrated as a festival, with rejoicing by all participants.

Such a crop of grain, namely as oats, buckwheat, barley, millet, corn, rye and wheat, had significant usefulness as a particular kind of nourishment. For example, the oats were used as an oatmeal, a cereal food made from the cooked meal of oats, also a meal in itself, or the oat gruel prepared of leaven with crushed poppy and honey. The buckwheat was used as kasha, whole or granulated into a small grain or particle, tiny pellets commonly known as buckwheat kernels. It was generally used as a hot cereal, or kasha prepared with pork or beef, which was mostly desired by the Polish or Russian army. The buckwheat flour was used for pancakes at breakfast time, a thin, flat cake made from batter and fried in a pan or baked on a griddle.

Comestibles, linen, cloth, a woven, knitted, or felted fabric of wool, cotton, leather such as animal skin usually with the hair removed and prepared for use by tanning, and of course many other products were created with exchangeable value here by physical power and ingenuity from that which was resorted to for aid and support of prosperous living conditions in the Wilderness of Naliboki. This was in fact a period of rising prosperity for the people before and during 1934, the time when an economic setback in commercial and industrial activity had its critical effect upon the nations worldwide. Hence, Naliboki was blooming and growing as if forever on the furthermost end of Europe.

My uncle, Michal Lojko, mother's oldest brother who formerly was in Naliboki, a subordinate magistrate with jurisdiction limited to the district of Stolpce, purchased a square piece of land approximately forty acres in size for his homestead located westward from the church about one kilometer. His husbandry was newly established. He lived there successfully with his wife Orszula and three children, Helena, Lucjan and Marysia, about two kilometers from our residence.

My grandfather's brother Benedikt Klimowicz in his early fifties had his residence by the junction of Poplawski Street, which led southward to the church. His husbandry was established on the long strip of land subjoined with another strip of land belonging to his nephew, my father's first cousin Wladyslaw Klimowicz, his sister Gabryjela Klimowicz. Wladyslaw lived with his wife and three sons. However, Benedikt was living there with his two sisters and niece, Segina. He also had a large plot of land located eastward not far behind Uncle Michal's husbandry. But neither he nor his sisters were ever interested in the cultivation of land, except that he enjoyed planting an orchard and had pleasure in grafting different varieties of fruit trees. Besides, most of his time was dedicated to his professional duty since he was a prominent organist and an expert in tuning up organs to a standard pitch. He used to work mainly in a large cities, and he came back home only on vacations and holidays, with lots of gifts and elegantly dressed in an expensive suit of clothes, like his favorite fur coats in the winter time. Because he was sensible of honor and personal elation, folks at home had a feeling of resentment and discontent over Benedikt's superior attainments. Therefore, they held preconceived, irrational opinions, and because of dislike they nicknamed him a senseless Benedikt. Of course, knowing the reality of who these folks actually were, Benedikt was at his liberty to irritate them moreso. He was odious toward unreasonable people, not only at home but also in the cities of his employment. Once, for instance, he was working in the city of Bialystok for an extremely stingy priest who promised him an increase in salary for being productive. But as Benedikt expected, his increase never came about. Then finally he packed his suitcases and decided to surprise the priest. As usual, he attended the mass and performed his duty, but at the end of the mass, instead of a common church holy song he played polka. The priest then in his exasperation ran after Benedikt through the crowd with a candle extinguisher in his hand, but unfortunately his organist passed from sight and vanished.

One block east from Benedikt's residence was the most important concentration of control in the central authority of town. Here was also a tract of land having established boundaries lawfully acquired and held by descendants of the Hebrew people. Their section of fertile land contained approximately 500 acres. Naturally, on the north side of the street Wilno the land was enclosed with a fence as one separate part of many owners combined. On this enclosed land in company with each other they had planted a most beautiful orchard, yet their land behind the orchard was far-reaching into the forest, but it was hilly and sandy, which served no purpose.

Benedikt usually expressed an admiration for the Hebrew people and enjoyed spending a lot of time with them doing business or playing for them Jewish music on the piano or violin, whether it be classic or popular music. The aggregate of Benedikt's experiences and education represented that he was well-acquainted with Jewish customs, religion and holidays such as Hanukkah, a Jewish festival lasting eight days from Kislev 25 (early December) in memory of the rededication of the temple at Jerusalem under the Macabees in 164 B.C.; Passover, then Rosh Hashana, the Jewish New Year, celebrated in September or early October; Sukkoth, the feast of Tabernacles, a Jewish holiday beginning on the fifteenth of Tishri (late September-October), originally a harvest festival; and Yom Kippur, the Jewish Day of Atonement, the tenth of Tishri (September-October), marked by continuous prayer and fasting for twenty-four hours from sundown on the evening previous. This entire body of human beings living in the same town of Naliboki had a fond attachment and kind feelings toward Benedikt. To alleviate anxiety he was invited by them to be present in some important events to perform pieces of music for their enjoyment and diversion in search for pleasure from the philosophy that stresses the active role of the will rather than of reason in confronting problems posed by a hostile world.

Remaining in uninterrupted peace, public order and tranquility, yet there was something considered as terrible as death, not by intentional killing of one human being by another, but rather this hostile power was expected to strike one by natural causes, accidents or unforeseen occurrences that happened to be inevitable. In this comparatively large community we all observed quite regularly common funerals since our family resided next to the church. The Christians' dead souls, which constitute the divine principle of life in man that once was a living person, were buried in the Catholic consecrated cemetery with the hope that these dead souls are subject to the rising again of all the dead at the day of judgment according to the promise of God the Almighty. Of all those dead and living Christian souls, the records of identity were kept in the church of Naliboki and also in archives at palatinate, Nowogrodek, Wilno and Warsaw. The dead souls, however, of the Hebrew people were buried in the Jewish cemetery at Iwieniec; they had their records of identity kept there and likewise in archives at those important cities.

Our neighbor Mr. Hirsh lived on the corner next to Baszuro's residence and opposite Walun's large house where the doctors had their clinic. Mr. Hirsh was an elderly person who lived with his wife and two sons of middle age, unmarried. This honorable family conducted business transactions with livestock intended for maintaining their existence. Parents in this matter had various details of trade with Mr. Hirsh who satisfied them fully with what they desired. Mr. Hirsh and his family were socially acceptable in conduct with the highest respect in the neighborhood, where all the people considered themselves to be equal because no distinction could be found. Yes, it was indeed a gratifying feeling of delight for one to grow with vigor and to bloom toward maturity in such an extremely pleasing vicinity.

An intensely sad disaster took place in "Zascianek Nalibocki," meaning, a collection of frontier dwellings forming a community, or downright, a "Settlement of Naliboki," which was located on the west side of town. There a house was consumed by fire with four children in it, ranging from three to nine years of age. Their parents took the chance and went to another town on business, but on their arrival the same day they found the loss of their children and property.

Another tragedy embodied human life of the entire family of six persons in the remote place of town, when they all ate mushrooms for the last meal of the day and went to sleep. Again, a formal examination by the local authority revealed that the mushrooms consumed by the victims were certain poisonous varieties loosely called toadstools, which resembled some fleshy, rapidly growing, umbrella-shaped fungi, especially the common edible forest mushroom.

A certain family traveling through the wilderness were devoured by a pack of wolves in autumn during their mating season. It was disclosed in the local newspaper that only some bones of the horse and people were left behind as evidence of the most unusual tragedy.

Three individuals on the highway to Iwieniec found shelter under a large tree during a rainstorm.

They were struck by a sudden flash of light caused by the discharge of atmospheric electricity between electrified regions of a cloud, and between a cloud and the earth. Certain travelers quickly buried these unfortunate ones in the ground for the earth to free an electrical charge from their bodies. One person was revived but two other failed to regain consciousness.

Mr. Walun with his wife and child Elizabeth resided in one of the apartments of their own multiple-dwelling building. His close relatives resided southward from town center at the brick kiln, where there was an actual structure in which bricks were burned or baked for the construction of a new church in Naliboki. Mr. Walun and Mrs. Walun were loving and kind neighbors. Elizabeth used to come to our house repeatedly. We all as children together used to play games.

Mr. Baszuro with his wife Mania and three children, Stanislaw, Jadwiga and Teresa, as well as his mother, resided between Mr. Hirsh's real estate and ours on the north side of the street Pilsudski. Mr. Baszuro's sister was married and resided in Stolpce. Her husband worked in the city as a chief of police and her older sister was living with them in Stolpce, but sometimes she stayed with her brother Witold Baszuro in Naliboki; she was a spinster. Witold had the exclusive title to the fine piece of land with a pine-trees forest behind the cemetery adjoining the land of Ciechanowicz. It was Witold's concept and standard of supreme perfection to build his husbandry on such a land. So Witold with his wife Mania decided to save as much money as possible by avoiding waste and being most economical in a new adopted way of life. From this point on, Baszuro's family commenced to live their life in a poor state by indulging in fasting to time indefinite. Because of having a fixed purpose concerning a new business of farming, they became insufficiently supplied with domestic necessities. Their sacrifice led to self-inflicted destitution where they had to entreat earnestly with some strange explanations in order to borrow something. Mania came over to our house repeatedly borrowing things such as sugar, salt, matches to light the fire and so on, but my parents knew exactly why they were always short of things.

Wladyslaw was a favorable friend, first cousin to my father. He used to make casual visits at our home, usually in the evening, and then as they began to talk, he stayed through the whole night. Father had an ability to counsel any defendant summoning him to appear in court and to write a preliminary version of skillful negotiation of an official document, as evidence offered by the accused to defeat civil or criminal charges. As he was in the process of engaging in legal actions, father was extremely successful, in that way a number of people endeavored to inquire in order to obtain legal aid, to whom of course he gave assistance always when time was permissible. Father was also an artist in telling endless stories intended to entertain. His stories provoked laughter and were most amusing, and others tended to excite horror and fear. When father really became engaged in telling Uncle Wladyslaw his stories I concealed myself under the table in order to hear the stories, but alas soon after I fell asleep. They both drank vodka, ate snacks, a slight, hurried usual Polish meal, and they smoked cigarettes and played cards during the whole night. While they were playing cards, father would talk about a certain group of men in the heart of Naliboki who once played cards just like them. During their game of cards they began to say how spooky it must be at the cemetery, especially in the middle of the night. However, one member of the group emphatically declared that no apparition could possibly haunt him at that cemetery in the night or by any other means, besides, he asserted that in fact there is nothing spooky about, nor is there such a thing as ghosts. At that instant the companions of the group laid a large sum of money on the table by placing a bet. The brave gambler also laid his money on the table to cover their bet, and went on his way to the cemetery precisely at midnight. Shortly afterward he came back and brought with him a wooden cross as proof that he pulled from a grave. His companions were astonished at this piece of action, and they told him just to return the cross and put it in the same position as he found it, then to come back to collect his reward from the table for his elegant achievement. But this brave, intrepid, unshaken-by-fear man, when he bent down to insert this wooden cross into its place, at the same time he caught a corner of his long overcoat, which he firmly pressed together into the ground. Now, when he start rising from the bent position, he felt as if some force was pulling him to the grave. So the more he rose, he felt, the stronger he was pulled in the direction of the source of force which he most probably imagined. As a result, he died of tremendous shock on that grave, where in the morning his companions found him expired from a sudden and severe agitation of the mind.

Another episode that was related was when a certain farmer from Naliboki decided to go see the city of Minsk and possibly there to do some business. This was an event that took place during the czar's period. As it happened, this individual was a vigorous person and appeared to be distinguished, as with a noble face. But as a stranger in the city, he was easily noticed in the crowd. So unfortunately, he was kidnapped by some swindlers, bamboozling persons, hoodwinks of Minsk. They had categorically made clear to him that his life was worth nothing, that they were going to kill him unless he did exactly as they told him. They dressed him in an officer's clothing to have a commanding appearance as a general of the army and they dressed themselves as a group of officers who were ready to assist the general in purchasing a woven, knitted, or felted fabric of wool, cotton, such as textile fabrics of the best quality essential for army use. Then they ordered him to just to say one word, which translated means beautiful, fine, splendid, excellent, and to say it only when he was approached. They put him into a limousine and arrived at the largest store in Minsk. As they walked into the store with the "general," they placed him in a seat as if it were a chair of authority for a superior officer in the middle of the store. At that time, they requested the owner of the store to show them his best merchandise of textile materials. As the rollers of material were passed over to the officers by attendants, the officers presented the same to their general for approval and asked him what he thought about the quality of the material. At each such occasion, the general answered, "excellent!" The swindlers of Minsk loaded their limousine with the most expensive textile fabric and told the owner that they did not bring enough cash with them because they did not expect to purchase so much material, but not to worry, they declared, they would allow the general to remain behind in the store, and after they unloaded the merchandise in the military camp, they would be back with a large sum of money to pay for the goods. This in all would take them one hour, they said. Of course, the storekeeper gladly agreed to their terms without any hesitation. Consequently, the swindlers left. However, shortly after one hour passed the emotionally troubled storekeeper gazed at the general with wonder, so as to convey a specific feeling or some meaning, then immediately afterward he told the general, "Pardon me, General. It seems to me that your officers violated their promise." The general answered, "excellent!" Subsequently, an official civil force was called to the scene of the crime. After police investigation, it was revealed that the general was an impostor and as such he was a victim subjected to suffering.

Such and great many similar episodes were told by my father not only to Wladyslaw but to other relatives, like his brother Alfons, Benedikt, Eugenjusz, Edward Wolan, Jozef Lojko and his brother Waclaw. To a very special extent these were characters full of humor on account of dominant peace and prosperity. Of a like kind an assemblage of people were made quite frequently, where everybody experienced joy and pleasure in funny stories, songs, music, dance, the steps of a waltz or tango, and at the same time they all enjoyed good food and drink. Because in the life of our community time was never an object; for this reason such social gathering for entertainment was continued for days at a time or even for weeks.

Wladyslfiw's older brother Michal was a bachelor who emigrated to the USA and he started living a regular life in the New York City. Alfons on the other hand at this time was in the period of courting and wooing.

Our real estate was established on the plot of land given as natural endowment to my grandmother by her Volan family. It lied adjacent to the street Pilsudski, but the rest of Wolan's land extended through the street Nowogrodek and far beyond northward. Between these two streets adjoining our property was Wolan's orchard, and this land was divided in two long strips between two brothers of my grandmother.

The elder brother was deceased and his successor was his son, Edward Wolan, proprietor of the real estate adjoined to our residence. Edward's uncle had his dwelling established on the other strip of land on the south side of Nowogrodek Street, where next to his residence on his brother's land was a "Kaplica," a small chapel or chapelet. But on the north side of the street was the dwelling of Edward, who lived with his mother and younger brother, who was at this time a student in the university. Their uncle living next door across the street was the best watchmaker in town. His son was the chief officer of a prison in Baranowicze, married to Marylka, who with Józef Lojko became my godparents. Marylka Wolan had three children, one girl and two boys, and her father-in-law was a widower who was always very busy repairing clocks and watches. On their strip of land next to our property was the dwelling of our neighbor Witold Baszuro. He felt he was crumpled and squeezed, as it were, therefore his mind was made up to build himself a new place on the land with plenty of room behind the cemetery. But he had to save a lot of money for this project before his dream could be materialized.

My father decided to increase the size of his property by purchasing a small portion of land from Edward. Edward without hesitation agreed to sell to us about half an acre of his orchard, which we all thought was extremely kind of him. Uncle Waclaw for a present gave father a large beehive, which he transported home from Trascianka by four-wheeled horsedrawn vehicle. The beehive was so large and heavy that it took Mr. Walun, Witold, Edward and father to lift it off the wagon and place it in the orchard. This hive of bees next year was expected to leave the parent stock at one time, to take new lodgings, accompanied by a new queen bee, and in this way the beehives would be multiplied in reproduction. Mother regarding this idea was very excited and exceedingly pleased because she loved honey for cooking and the beeswax to make candles for light or church.

"Zaduszny Dzien," All Saints Day, November 1, is a church festival commemorating all saints and martyrs; following that, All Souls' Day ecclesiastical, November 2, is a day of commemoration on which intercession is made for the souls of all the faithful departed. The act of interceding or prayer on behalf of all the departed souls is made on these two days. The cemetery of the Parish of Naliboki was bright at night like a magnitude of stars in the sky. Everyone was celebrating the memory of loved ones by lighting candles on the graves of departed relatives. At night during those important two days when I looked through the window in the church's direction, it was a strange sight that caused chills throughout my body, as in a horror story or movie. The cemetery and streets continuously were crowded with people, and the bells of the church were ringing. Indeed, the commemoration of All Saints Day and All Souls' Day was something to remember for a lifetime.

Subsequently, in December was Advent, the two-weeks fast season prior to the birth of Christ. These two weeks in truth were a crucial test for the children because they had to abstain from certain foods in the observance of religious duty imposed by the doctrine and practice of the Roman Catholic churches.

In the course of fasting, a priest visited people's homes to catechized children and to instruct in the principles of Christianity by asking questions and discussing the answers. Then the priest placed some wafers on the table essential for Christmas, a small flat disk of unleavened bread stamped with a cross or the letters IHS, and in various arrangement of colors used for Christmas Eve, the evening meal before Christmas Day. This evening meal on Christmas Eve was composed of twelve fasting dishes. Children were always cautioned by parents not to eat too much of the first dishes because they would not be able to eat or even taste the last ones that would be placed on the table. As usual, it was very difficult for the children to heed the parents' warning on account of being deprived of food during two weeks of fasting, and now at last so much food to eat. Who could resist such a temptation?

This particular preparation of food that amounted to twelve dishes was usually created by mothers from prescribed kinds of food in observance of a religious duty. Following such as sour Polish soup, salty herrings prepared with onions and tomatoes, boiling potatoes, fried fish or river crawfish, sauerkraut seasoned in oil, vegetable salad served with a dressing, sometimes mixed with chopped fish, also, a similar dish made with fruit, pearl barley with poppy sauce prepared with honey, unleavened bread baked in small round shapes topped with poppy sauce, gruel prepared of leaven and honey, whortleberry jello, a European variety of blueberry-flavored gelatin dessert and a compote, fruit stewed or preserved in syrup.

However, for Christmas Day and up to New Years Day food was prepared more luscious to the taste with an excess of fats, a flavoring composed of valuable ingredients. On such an occasion the home was filled with various cakes and cookies baked at our home, and various roast meats, smoked or fried, such as roast leg of pork, lamb and beef, turkey or goose decorated with sour apples, smoked ham and fried steak and various Polish sausages and salamis, including fruit and berry juices and beverages, all in plentiful supply.

During this holiday my parents received a great deal of Christmas cards from relatives and friends. Father and Aunt Bronislawa were delighted to receive a complimentary message from their sister Orszula, her husband Von Metro Majer and children residing in Lithuania. They all together were growing impatient to hear from two brothers, Edward and Edmund, who lived in Russia, but unfortunately there was no news from them. Reciprocally, my parents were as usual actively engaged in preparing Christmas and New Years' cards for all those admired friends and relatives.

On Christmas Day the church was filled with a great crowd of people, and during the mass a chorus performed by a group of singers, accompanied by church organs, sang in a joyous strain Christmas carols that reverberated sound waves throughout the entire horizon in the Parish of Naliboki. Being present in such a magnificent surrounding, one could imagine that it was heaven on earth with an endless flourish and tranquillity.

In the year 1935 during January and February it was a convenient time for father to be engaged in a transportation of timber from the forest, commonly known as "Wozka," where the growing trees were cut and hauled to the nearest waterway, a river or canal, by means of a two-section sledge fitted with swivels for the load to rotate independently during the hauling process over snow or ice. Initially the timber was pulled along by horse to a convenient place where father with his technical ability was able to load the timber on the sledge and then travel with it to the waterway. These series of continuous actions that brought about this particular result were repeated throughout the day so many times depending upon the distance traveled. However, at the end of the day the horses left for the night in a stable set apart for lodging and feeding and men withdrew for rest in the forestry house. When the labor imposed by authority during the winter season was completed, father came back home, and we all were extremely glad to see him safe again. After a while, as usual, my parents went to Nowogrodek for a day to visit stores in order to purchase some goods, and we kids were left in the care of Aunt Bronislawa. When our parents returned from their long journey they found us children as always well behaved and they were pleased to have the various domestic affairs in order. Then we all were delighted with our parents' excellent choices of valuable merchandise, such as clothes, shoes, jewels and souvenirs.

As most people in the community, mother throughout the winter season was occupied with the spindle, making the thread by means of the slender rod in a spinning wheel containing a spool or bobbin on which the thread is twisted and wound, then finally it was used in weaving textures to produce woven fabrics. The thread mainly was made of flax and wool obtained from the natural resources by skill and ingenuity in meeting a requisite situation. The woven produce of a textile made of flax was unrolled from its cylinder on the ground in spring to be bleached or whitened by the sun. Then the linen made of flax was ready for doing a tailors' work, from which mother used to make garments, shirts, blouses, dresses, slacks, tablecloths, etc.

Apart from Aunt Bronislawa there was also Mania Klimowicz who had a special relevance with the family circle. Her late husband Dr. Peter Klimowicz devised his real estate by dividing into equal parts a grant in perpetuity to his wife Mania and his mistress Alesia Makarewicz, who unlawfully cohabited with him over an extended period of time. Initially she was the head of a staff of servants working for

Dr. Klimowicz. Now she was left with her daughter Wierka, and Mania with her son Eugenjusz, to be successors in interest, and of course in the future they would be entitled to hereditary right. Father's uncle Peter Klimowicz was the lessor and father became the lessee to whom the tenement and land was conveyed to farm out for life in consideration of rent to be paid one third of crop to Mania and Alesia. So by inherent nature this family circle was joined together permanently by legal, social and blood relations. Father cultivated the land with the help of all members of the family, who participated with a strong feeling of happiness. Throughout the winter season Mania experienced joy working with mother. While she was spinning or weaving to an advanced hour at night, Mania was knitting to form gloves, socks and garments, as a sweater or pullover, by interlocking loops of a single yarn or thread of wool by means of needles. These fabrics she was knitting specially for her son Eugenjusz, who at this time was acquiring knowledge at the institution for higher instruction that includes one or more colleges for graduate or professional study, as well as a grants master's and doctor's degree. At the same time when they performed their functions near the lamp in which naphta was burning through a wick to produce light, they were conversing on various subjects. During such winter evening's activity, usually there was an assemblage of people among whom there were relatives, neighbors and dear friends of the family. The frequent visitors were Orszula, Alzusia, and Regina Klimowicz, Wierka and Gabriela, the neighbors Mania Baszuro, Mrs. Radziwill, and friends, Miss Katlarycha, sister, a head nurse in the ward of a hospital and her associate Taciana, and a Jewish lady who was an official having charge of a post office. Sister Katlarycha was developed and informed by education under the regime of the former emperor of Russia. She, with her associate Taciana, fled from Russian Revolution, the conflict (1917-1922) beginning in a Petrograd uprising on March 12, 1917, that resulted in a provisional moderate government and the abdication of Nicholas II. On November 6, the Bolsheviks under Lenin overthrew this government (the October Revolution), and in December, 1922, united the soviet states in the Union of Soviet Socialist Republics under Communist (Bolshevik) control. They both consequently found a refuge near the border of two adjoining countries, and following in time they started living a regular, orderly life in Naliboki,

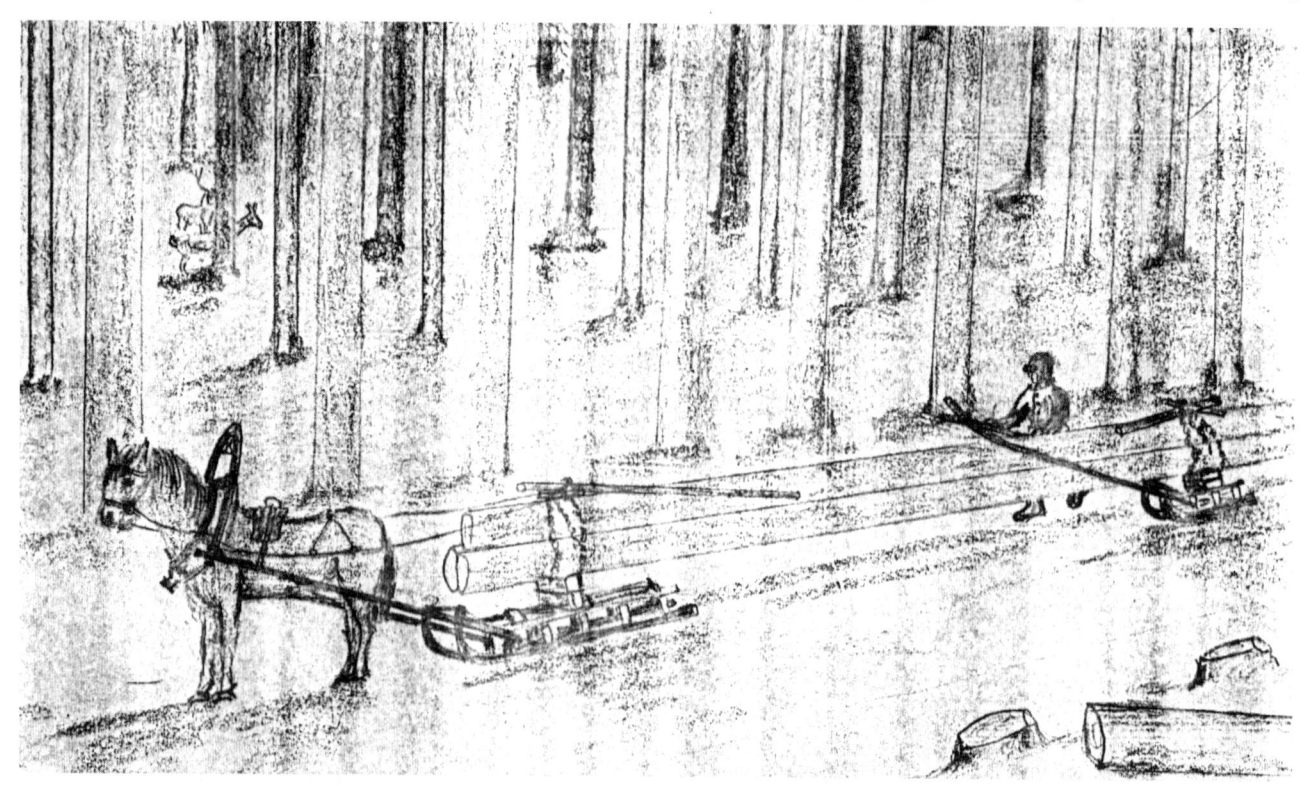

"Wozka," the transportation of timber to the waterway destined for the international market from the Wilderness of Naliboki. Here were various trees harvest such as common pine, fir, oak, birch and ash.

1. Dr. Piotr Klimowicz; 2. Mania Klimowicz; 3. their son, Eugenjusz Klimowicz

especially after a period of wondering as one who flees from a radical invasion, persecution and political danger. Katlarycha and Taciana resided together as a body of women united by some bond of fellowship but not by blood as sisters. Sister Katlarycha, rather advanced in age, visited our home mainly in a professional capacity, having important consequences of essential need for medical emergency. On the other hand, Taciana made social visits, inclined to seek company by affording occasion for agreeable conversation and friendliness. For their thoughtful and kind treatment and solicitude toward the family, mother became obligated to provide them with milk, butter, cheese and other farm produce they required. Concerning this reward, mother had me deliver these victuals to them frequently to a considerable extent, except for during Taciana's visitation, when she was obliged to carry things home.

The Jewish lady was a spinster educated in Poland. She was assigned for postal duty in Naliboki and held a function here as the postmaster. Her immediate relatives lived in Palestine, a territory on the eastern coast of the Mediterranean, the country of the Jews. She was extremely intelligent and possessed psychic powers pertaining to mental phenomena that appear to be independent of normal sensory stimuli, as clairvoyance, telepathy, and extrasensory perception. She presented an appearance of beauty and she visited mother frequently to chat and occasionally to offer her postal service. Reciprocally, mother sent me or my sister Waclawa to deliver to the lady milk, butter or sometimes the young of domestic fowl, but in return we were bestowed with matzoth, halvah or apples in the winter season, which was certainly most desirable by children. Of course, the matzoth was a large, flat piece of unleavened bread, traditionally eaten during Passover, and halvah, a nourishing sesame confection made of the following ingredients: crushed sesame, glucose, sugar, partially hydrogenated vegetable oil (cottonseed, soya), cocoa, chocolate, dried egg albumen, natural and artificial flavors. The apples, which were rarely found on the market in Naliboki, were kept intact by the lady's own effort throughout the winter season.

Mrs. Radziwi was a woman who had lost her husband by death and had not remarried. Her husband was descended lineally from Dukes Radziwill, those original ones who long ago established Naliboki. In European countries Radziwills had a title of nobility ranking immediately below a prince and above a marquis, with exclusive right of possessing wealth or estate, such as an estate in lands, tenements and hereditaments. But unfortunately, after so many generations Mrs. Radziwill in Naliboki was left without the title and hereditaments, things capable of being inherited, be it corporeal or incorporeal, real, personal or mixed, and including not only certain furniture, which by custom may descend to the heir together with the land. She lived with her two sons in a little house on Pulawski Street with a view of the lake, Majatek, and church. The common people in Naliboki, as opposed to the nobility, found no distinguishing superiority or preeminence in Mrs. Radziwill's characteristic that distinguished one individual from another. Her ex-noble name having hereditary title, rank and privileges, was no longer different than her next door neighbor Mr. Szarzanowicz or Mr. Korzenko. So unnoticeably she intermingled in the community and lived a normal life according to an established order. She was our good neighbor and had our high regard and appreciation of worth.

My grandfather Kazimierz Klimowicz and his brother Peter Klimowicz were the only doctors in the Parish of Naliboki who worked in the science of the preservation and restoration of health and of treating disease. When Grandfather died his two sons, Edward and Edmund, were students in the university in Russia, but my father was just a baby at home with two sisters, Bronislawa and Orszula. Peter Klimowicz then became his substitute parent, and later gave him the rights, privileges and duties of heir, a right to all lands, tenements and hereditaments that belonged to him or of which he was seized. Thus from the early period of life between childhood and manhood father was obligated to cultivate the land to support the combined family, since another potential male, Eugenjusz, was yet just a school boy. After the death of Peter Klimowicz, whom my father knew in the way he was raised as his father, or Eugenjusz and Wierka as his brother and sister, my father continued to be the head of the combined family by means of furnishing subsistence. Later, of course, during the intermission of the course of studies and exercises in an educational institution, Eugenjusz helped father in the business of operating the farm. In like manner, all members of the family were honestly engaged working together in maintaining one's existence.

On the authority of mother's assertion, father particularly fancied big women, and she implicated his favorite was no other than Alesia, who, being of a fine figure, weighed abound two hundred pounds. Her physique represented likeness, as in painting or sculpture, but mother weighed only one hundred and twenty pounds. So she was fearful and suspicious of being displaced by a rival in affection when father was thrashing grain with Alesia. Mother, in the recklessness growing out of despair, needed someone to keep an eye on him. Mania was well suited to mother's purpose, conducive to her comfort since Alesia had already been her rival and lived near the same stream, as it were. That is why Alesia became her husband's mistress. In this way, Mania was extremely pleased to oblige mother with any information concerning father's infatuation that she was able to observe in her residence, which was divided between her and Alesia. Mother was grateful for her affectionate kindnesses and therefore they spent a lot of time in companionship, whereas Alesia visited our home occasionally, only in urgent need or requirement. Other than that, with father she was most friendly and pleasant, exactly what was mostly confusing mother. A state of jealousy and strong surge of feeling, marked by an impulse to outward expression often accompanied by complex bodily reactions, led to a dispute and eventually to conflict that was normal in the average marriage.

Ensuing was the constitution of a religious order, Lent, the period of forty days, excluding Sundays, from Ash Wednesday to Easter, observed annually as a season of fasting, penitence and self-denial. In ecclesiastical law, the quadragesimal fast has been complied with by the Catholic people here since the year 1630 when the Roman Catholic Church was built in Naliboki. This penitent body of human beings, having the same history, culture and traditions and speaking the same language, transmitted for acceptance doctrines down through successive generations. During this season of fasting all Christian believers collectively participated in devotion to God and his worship as demonstrated by their obedience and good works. Rosary prayers and litanies, a liturgical form of prayer consisting of a series of supplications said by the clergy, to which the congregation repeats a fixed response, were conducted daily in the church. Sad songs were sung to remember Christ's torment and his sacrifice for the world, songs such as this one, for example (translated):

> People my people, what did I do to you, or of what I was guilty?
> I have freed you from the house of Pharaoh,
> and you have prepared a cross on my shoulder.

Palm Sunday, the Sunday before Easter, being the last Sunday in Lent and the first in Holy Week, is named for Christ's' triumphal entry into Jerusalem, when palm branches were strewn before him. At the beginning of Lent palm branches were gathered by people and placed in jars of water at their homes. On Palm Sunday, already germinated palm branches were decorated for the church to be consecrated by the priest during the mass. After the mass people brought the palm branches home to remind everyone that in one week it will be Easter.

Subsequently every family living together was making preparations, getting ready for the Easter. Abundantly supplied food, luscious to the taste with an excess of fats, was brought together from various sources. On the authority of traditional practices, boiled eggs were brilliantly colored or decorated with paint. These eggs, bread and other desired comestibles people took to the church on Easter Sunday in order to be consecrated by the priest during the mass. After the mass a festivity began at home. A ceremonial dinner followed by prayers was started with consecrated eggs and bread. Then a sumptuous feast was in progress, by means of which the previous forty days of fast was forgotten. Nowogrodek Street was overcrowded with men and boys engaged in a competition against one another by striking the small end of an egg—one that brakes must be turned over and hit again at the larger end—if it breaks then the owner of that egg loses. If the large end of the egg dose not brake, then the opponent turns his egg and if it breaks, he loses. The eggs for this purpose were tested for a strong outer coat by skillful individuals who knocked the egg at their teeth and by its sound recognized the strength of the egg. This game involved an act of bluffing, whereby one could convince another to swap eggs and then strike them. Of course, in such a contest struggling against one another everyone had an equal chance to win a great deal of eggs, often being hard boiled. Lastly, the eggs that had both ends broken were used in another game. People at the same time were engaged in rolling these eggs down off a board, and whoever's egg collided with another was the winner and took all eggs from the field. Thus, Easter Sunday was the most exciting day of the year in Naliboki, especially for the youngsters; it was something to remember.

Pilsudski Street from the east toward the west on the north side originated with Mr. Michal Machlis, the Jewish family's residence, followed by Witold Baszuro and our family, Klimowicz. Behind our residence there was an orchard leading northward to its proprietor, Mr. Jesc's residence on Nowogrodek Street next to the chapelet. Starting from the Mr. Jesc's orchard there was a large, old orchard called Poplawski, but Mr. Poplawski really did not exist; it was only his name that remained. This orchard extended to Poplawski Street, which led to Majatek of Ciechanowicz, and, of course, straight to the church. On both sides of this street there was a boggy land that was abundant in an amphibian life, which was indispensable to serve as food for the storks migrated there. Every spring on their arrival to our region, the storks built their nests high on top of the trees that grew on the both sides of Poplawski Street near the lake starting from the Pillar of Saint John. This tall structure with a sculpture of Saint John was erected specifically for worship by people in the Parish of Naliboki in 1630, the time when the church was built. Normally all inhabitants paid obeisance when passing by the Pillar of Saint John by various means, where

Nowogrodek Street heading west.

Pilsudski Street leading from the town square to the church.

some would bow or take their hats off, and others would make the sign of the cross or say, "praised be, Jesus Christ! For the ages of ages. Amen." Beneath the tower an area was enclosed by a cast-iron fence, and inside the enclosure folks cultivated beautiful flowers. Usually during a procession a complete but temporary stop was made and the priest conducted a brief service before advancing forward. On the other side of Poplawski Street opposite the lake a creek flowed westward from the lake. In this creek my friend Arkadjusz Makarewicz and I used to fish by hand, catching pike with reference to its pointed snout and most slippery leach. However, interestingly enough, having the attention involved in regard to the most fertile land behind the river Niemen, here too a particular kind of earth was found, namely a black soil on this small patch of ground. Next to it there was a parsonage combined with the husbandry and its attendance. Beyond that the road to the west led to Zascianki, that is the far end of Naliboki, but to the south it led to Zarecze and to a number of other remote, similar, small villages. On the north side of the road to Zascianki, behind the parsonage, there was a husbandry of my uncle Michal Lojko.

The corner house, where Stolpce Street and Pilsudski Street meet on the southern side, was the residence of the Jewish family, Mr. and Mrs. Srul, with two sons who were my age. We used to attend the same class in school and play together subsequently. Next there was a large residence that was the property of Mr. and Mrs. Lawon and their daughter Elizabet. Incessantly a part of this residence was occupied by doctors. Adjoined to Mr. Lawon's property was an orchard stretching all the way to the school street, with its edifice facing Stolpce Street, and this was the residence where our friends Sister Katlarycha and Taciana lived. Farther ahead on the remaining isosceles shape of ground a new house was built facing the Pilsudski Street for the "Wojt Gminy," the chairman who presided over the entire community of Naliboki in the interest of government. This position was formerly occupied my uncle, Michal Lojko, but now a new Wojt was assigned by the government who happened to be a former member of the armed forces and became an invalid during the war when he lost his leg. He commenced to live in this new house and worked for the government in the "gmina," the community building. But for his sport and pleasure he frequently enjoyed fishing in the lake with an angling rod. This small lake did contain a plentiful supply of bleaks and a great deal of pikes. There are two springs flowing into the lake, one from the east between school street and "Majatek," the stronghold of Ciechanowicz, and the other in a depression of the earth's surface by the cemetery. These flowing springs from under ground are significant for they convey some covert meaning that reflects upon the deluge, the flood in the time of Noah. Before the flood, in all probability, these springs that join together at the lake, one from the east and the other from the south, originally were rivers that were covered with fragmentary material deposited by water, and as a consequence the valleys where the rivers existed became covered physically and appeared to be hills that consist of clay on the bottom and sand on top, a hard, granular rock material finer than gravel and coarser than dust. But the surface of the hills were covered with round stones of different sizes, from under which now springs flowed, thus creating a lake that before the deluge probably never existed because the landscape originally was different. Therefore there is black soil behind the lake such as is found relatively on the large scale on the other side of river Niemen; all this came about as a result of the global flood in the time of Noah, 2370 B.C.E.. However, the spring water by the Pillar of Saint John was amazing to drink, wash hair, undergo cooking and make tea, coffee or a similar beverage. The water in the spring was ice cold during the mid-summer, but in the coldest season of the year this water never froze. On the contrary, the spring water was full of steam, the form of vapor ascended above the spring.

Directly from Pilsudski Street and straight through the crossroads the lane confined between the cast-iron fence and lake led up to Majatek of Ciechanowicz, located about 100 to 200 feet or more above lake level. On the other side of the lake there was a steep bank, and on this slope of land at the edge of the water large trees grew, such as oak, linden, birch and alder. Of course, on top of the flat expanse there was a continuous stone structure designed to enclose an area of the church and cemetery. There were cast-iron gates, and old cast-iron crosses and fences enclosed the graves, which indicates that once there was an abundance of cast iron in Naliboki when a blast furnace was in operation, which existed before our presence. Before the entrance to the church there was a belfry, the part of a tower or steeple containing the bell, and on the left side of the belfry there was the residence of the organist, who lived with his wife and two adult sons. His sons were away from home somewhere in some university. But they were home on vacation during Christmas holidays when they both performed beautifully in figure skating on the frozen lake. Beyond the consecrated ground westward there was a horizon of the apparent meeting of the sky with the cultivated land, but southward there were fields used for pasture or for crops, and very close leading to the forest there was the parcel of land belonging to Mr. Witold Baszuro. On the southern side of the cemetery there were slopes leading down into the valley, through which a spring flowed. This was the only location of Naliboki's skiing resort, where every winter adults and children frequented for pleasurable exercise. In an elevated land there were some pastures where my neighbor, Stanislaw Baszuro, herded his cattle, but his parents never allowed me to join him with our cattle despite the fact that they were borrowing something from us all the time. Stanislaw wished for me to keep company with him because he was unfrequented by human beings and induced by loneliness, yet nothing he could do would convince his parents to change their minds.

The holidays and observances, the act of observing a law of constitution that was consolidated on the third of May to be the element of independence of the Polish peasants who won their struggle among the gentry. Thus Poland annually celebrated a ceremony to uphold the fundamental laws and principles that normally governed the operation of the free state of Poland. So every year people in Naliboki were engaged in this gladness arid rejoicing. The youth marched commencing from school through the school street on their way to church for the eucharistic liturgy that consisted of various prayers and ritual ceremonies and was regarded as a commemoration of Christ's sacrifice on the cross. After such a mass, these children marched orderly from the church through Pilsudski Street to the town square, each one carrying a flag, a piece of cloth or bunting, usually oblong, bearing devices in white and red colors to designate the Polish nation. At the town square there were adults with the faculty of expressing thoughts and emotions by spoken words, the youth likewise proclaimed a poetry of outstanding Polish poets who had the power of artistic expression such as Adam Asnyk, Adam Mickiewicz and many others. Then they all marched together to school southward through the Stolpce street where they finally were dismissed for the rest of the day. Inspired by pride and as they marched they sung a song (translated):

> Welcome the May of dawn,
> Honour to our Polish country,
> Welcome May, the third May,
> Among Polish people it is blissful paradise (with repetition, and so on)

On the occasion of "Zielone Swiatki," that is Whitsuntide, Whitsunday, Whitmonday and Whit-Tuesday, Naliboki externally became decorated with the green foliage of growing plants. Holy pictures were hung on the walls outside the houses and embellished around with garland, a wreath of flowers, leaves, vines and many other beautiful growing plants. The sidewalks and footwalks were decorated with broad, lobed leaves of the plane tree. Then people marched in procession from the church, some of them carrying up in front holy flags and portable altars. The priest made a stop at the column of Saint John to perform a quick sacred service, and immediately afterward moved with the procession toward town square through Nowogrodek Street westward, where he made a similar stops at each chapelet starting from one that was built on the property of the Wolan family. Subsequently returning from "Zascianki," the Settlements, at the far end of Naliboki, this procession went back to the church through Poplawski

Street. Finally in observance of Whitsunday the sacred service in church came to an end. The relatives were reunited at such occasion and everyone was entertained at dinner. It was most exciting and enjoyable at Whitsuntide for everybody in the vicinity of Naliboki.

The holy day of the sea. In the fourteenth century, when Poland's Queen Jadwiga was married to the Grand Duke of Lithuania, it helped create a new power in Europe. Successful wars and treaties expanded the borders of the unified nations from the Baltic to the Black Sea by the end of the fifteenth century. At that time Poland had no cause to adore or to render divine honors to the sea, because accessibility to it was great. But when Poland reemerged as an independent nation in 1918 after being partitioned by three nations over a period of 146 years, Poland had narrow access to the sea, characterized by small resources at two cities of customary entry and exit for ships of commerce, namely port Gdynia and Gdansk. This limited access to the Baltic Sea for the Polish nation was extremely precious and important for survival. So in order to cherish and to hold dear as a real possession based on past achievements, the holiday of the sea was consecrated. Thus Polish people nationwide celebrated and commemorated the day of the sea. On such a day in Naliboki a large platform above the lake was constructed, upon which a company of persons organized to play musical instruments were located and a gathering of people performed the steps of a waltz, tango or polka. Then a great number of rowboats on the lake were available for exercise. Around the lake and on every street there was a multitude of people from the Wilderness of Naliboki. There were kiosks everywhere selling presents or temporary necessities. Folks acquired jewelry, souvenirs and, of course, snacks, soft drinks and ice cream.

From Iwieniec right through Naliboki on the way to Stolpce was the racecourse of the annual international European motorcar race. There was given notice of the approach of automobiles on a particular day and time. People from Naliboki were curious and excited by its strangeness because at this time a common transportation was known only to be drawn by horses. So the folks gathered together to see this unusual motorcar race at Iwieniec Road, behind the school on the cultivating land of Ciechanowicz owned by Majatek. And as they intensely watched the cars speeding, they saw some even catching fire, becoming totally ineffective and useless. It was indeed a most frightening experience and exciting phenomenon to observe. Besides, the weather was beautiful at this fine race as the day was filled with the light and warmth of the sun. Of course, afterward long conversations continued as people made remarks about certain motorists they thought performed in a most excellent way. However, every motorist was easily identified in regard to his nationality by his flag and the name of his country that was written on his automobile. Indeed, by inherent nature our people were more concerned about their own flag, and that is where braggartism occurred for those striving against others for the prize.

Highly esteemed because of uncommonness was the visit of the smallest man on earth, who arrived to Naliboki in his limousine. He was of Irish descent and was twenty inches in height. In the town center he rode in a four-wheeled cat-drawn vehicle, dressed in fur coat with a bowler hat, smoking a cigar.

A carrousel returned every year to Naliboki to receive and care for guests in town. This merry-go-round was erected on the common ground by the gmina, the municipal building next to the Jewish proprietor Mr. Brocha's Turkish bath. The ground was also used periodically for the kermess, a competitive exhibit and sale of agricultural products, machinery, fancy work, pottery and livestock. The carrousel amusement for the children and young people was in progress during several weeks. Every participant had an enjoyable experience and excellent time. The extent of common ground was called "Wygon," the pasture where people's domestic animals grazed. My parents sent me there to herd the cattle and that is where I tended the flock most of the time. My friend Arkadjusz frequently joined me to play games there, or perhaps to make something, such as to wreathe garlands, twist together a basket or bast shoes, which we made from a bark of linden tree. Of course, the baskets to gather potatoes from the field were made from the roots of the common pine, pinus sylvestris, but the frame itself was constructed from the furze, a spiny evergreen shrub of the bean family, having many branches and yellow flowers, also called gorse, whin. For the same purpose we could also use the stem of a hazelnut tree because it is an elastic cane that bends easily without breaking.

As we both experienced joy and pleasure in games and making things, now and then there was an act of sneaking upon us by Leon Szarzanowicz, the only evil one in the Parish of Naliboki. He was about fourteen years of age, morally bad, wicked, causing injury or any other undesirable result. Arkadjusz was ten years old, three years older than I. This Leon was a tormentor, and after subjecting us to excruciating physical and mental suffering he left us in pain and fear, usually accompanied by tears. Arkadjusz told his mother about him, who expressed feelings of dissatisfaction to young Leon, but in reply he knocked her teeth out. Such an act of evil disconcerted the entire neighborhood—people were shocked and felt great sorrow for lady Makarewicz, yet there were no legal charges filed against Leon for the assault of the mother of my friend Arkadjusz.

As time went by, one day Janka came home late from school; she was terrified and crying. Father became affected with anxiety and endeavored to find out what really happened. But as a matter of fact, this beautiful girl was attacked and threatened with rape by some hoodlum, a young street rowdy who was inclined to create disturbances and disorder. Immediately, father guessed that it was no one else but Leon. So he went outside and found him in the street; then Leon began to run. Father chased him and when he caught him he gave him a good flogging. The next day Leon's father, who was well-disposed to my father, came to our house. He did not complain that my father punished his son, but rather he was sorry for himself that he had such a spoiled male child and there was nothing he could do about it to convert him to be as his brother Frank.

In the village Terebejno lived Szabunia, who actually was a Soviet spy but nobody knew this. He observed stealthily and with hostile intent concerning all people in the Parish of Naliboki in the interest of the Union of Socialist Republics. Here lived also a madwoman known by her Christian name as crazy Orszula from Terebejno. She was well built, of average height, middle-aged, and always carried with herself a handbag loaded with round stones for personal protection. When she went by, kids would notice her and instantly start calling to her, "Hello, crazy Orszula." She would launch through the air by means of a sudden whirling of the arm a stone at them, and all the kids would scatter in different directions. Sometimes she would stay for some reason too long in Naliboki, and when it was getting dark she came to our house asking mother to pass the night, and in return she promised that she would help mother to do some work in the morning. However, in the morning she was never there to help as promised because she had moved out secretly earlier.

The fiance Korzenko continuously made visits to his beloved Bronislawa at her residence. But his romantic persistence began to be a burdensome for Bronislawa since he became an alcoholic, having a diseased condition resulting from the excessive use of alcoholic beverages. He had a side effect, a secondary injurious effect, as of a drug. This injurious effect as a consequence impaired the mind and thus changed his character by overindulgence. He seemed to be getting increasingly aggressive and of violent disposition, especially toward Bronislawa. In such a frame of diseased mind, Korzenko began to use force of assault and battery as never before on his victim Bronislawa, who was unnecessarily subjected to suffering. This commotion disturbed my father very much, but there was nothing he could do to change the course of circumstance because of the fact that it would not be even right to intervene by taking a part in the personal affairs of his sister. Subsequently to and because of Korzenko's engineering bridges work he was compelled to become sober, and soon after he left to his position of employment. Except that after his departure unfortunately Bronislawa was left behind with multiple bruises on her face and entire body. She was deterred by fear and shame from going out, and it caused her to be in seclusion for several weeks. She never expressed her true feelings about her courtship to anyone, and therefore it was generally understood that she loved him very much, and for that reason she was destitute of power to terminate this kind of courtship.

A love affair intermediate in relation to Jan Radziwill and Wierka was gradually causing to a mutually strong ardor. Wierka had seemed to be untamable, but now on the contrary she happened to be as a matter of fact more intimate, characterized by pronounced closeness of friendship. No longer did she have to run away and hide herself from Jan; besides, he was crazy about her to the extent of his powers to worship the ground she walked on. When she came to our residence again, not to hide from Jan but to learn about the formula of ingredients for baking delicious cakes and pastries for Christmas, she was happy and contented as never before. Now it was easily perceived that their love had a uniting force to be betrothed. Obviously, it was time for them to be engaged to be married and live together happily ever after.

A "Spoldzielnia," a so-called cooperative or business enterprise, was established at the late Dr. Peter Klimowicz's residence and was managed by Wierka. Under such peaceful and prosperous circumstances affecting the existence of all people in general, which was a cause of hopeful expectation to grow to material well-being, every Jewish business in Naliboki including Wierka's cooperative was successfully flourishing and moving with sweeping motions. One could very much appreciate the sale of fine woollen or any other fabric from Mr. Szymanowski's store. Again, one could very much appreciate extremely pleasant to the taste cakes and pastries in Mr. Chaim's bakery. There were many other excellent business experts of the Hebrew origin in Naliboki such as Mr. Chaim, who lived behind the school: Mr. Michal Machlis, who lived near our residence behind the Baszuro family, Mr. Kwartacz, son-in-law Mr. Rozowski, Mr. Wajner, Mr. Sklut, Mr. Ela Kagan, Mr. Nachama Graf, son of Szmuil, Mr. Czorny Isko, a fine businessman with a large store, Mr. Sanagoga, son-in-law of Mr. Menusz, Mr. Here, who lived by the municipal building (gmina), Mr. Bluma Isko, Mr. Isko the blacksmith, and Mr. Brocha, the owner of the Turkish-bath. These are only a few people of Hebrew origin I bring back to memory who enjoyed happy lives in Naliboki.

Ulica Stolpecka, Stolpce Street

Ulica Wilenska, Wilno Street, the center of shopping in the Naliboki Jewish section.

Stolpce Street and town square indicates the late Dr. Peter Klimowicz's residence, which presently was a cooperative of Naliboki, and next to it was a tavern of Mr. Skniut, where beverages and snacks were served.

Commencing from the town square eastward on both sides of Wilno Street was an exclusively Jewish section, and here was the shopping center of Naliboki. On the right side of street, the last building at the far end on the common ground was a Turkish bath of Mr. Brocha, and next to it there was an empty space of common ground reserved for the market and merry-go-round, but in between there was a (gmina) municipal building and next to it there was a town hall; then there was the fire station, which was equipped with a siren that often used as a warning signal for awareness of danger. On the left side north of the street opposite the municipal building there was a police station with the place of confinement. However, farther ahead eastward this street continued to be inhabited by Polish people on both sides of the street for nearly half of a mile, except that at the end of it on the north side was a residence and blacksmith business of Mr. Isko. Mr. Isko's property was attached to the plot of land of my father and his sister Bronislawa Klimowicz, and this section was called Plac. From this Plac northward the point set for a journey's end to Wilno commenced through the towns Klieciszcze, Rudnia Nalibocka, Wolozyn and Oszmiana. However, westward to Nowogrodek led through Kroman, Szczorce, Korelicze, Zajeziorze and Wolkowicze, or through Lubcz to Nowogrodek. Then from Naliboki southward to Stolpce the road led through Derewno, Ml. Lumiernowszczyzna and Siemienczyce. Eastward, of course, the road to Minsk guided through Prudy, Rudnia Pilanska, Dzierzynowo, Kamien, Iwieniec, Drenzaly and Wiertniki, but after World War I free entrance to Minsk was closed up to the time of 1959, due to the fact that Poland reemerged as an independent nation and during that period she exercised her domain under one government, that of the Free State of Poland.

The plot of land in Plac was left in will by parents and shared by equal proportion between brother and sister. Wilhelm's half size of land was situated next to Mr. Isko, but the other equal part of land belonging to Bronislawa neighbored a certain Polish widow resident living with her two children. This Polish resident often expressed her feelings of dissatisfaction toward my aunt in reference to her own boundary. She claimed that Bronislawa moved her boundary and thus obtained in a surreptitious manner her land. Of course, such a usurpation alleged by the neighbor to Bronislawa was absurd and ridiculous. I remember as a child when my parents worked there in the field and I was invited often to the aunt's neighbor's house to play with her children. The neighbor appeared to be very nice. This lady with the spirit of being hospitable always treated me with food and drink. Nevertheless, she actually had filed a complaint in the court of law against my aunt, who had no alternative but to hire a surveyor in order to obtain some necessary material evidence that would have an effective influence on the issue for the defense as a reason why the plaintiff should not recover what she seeks. So, as the session in court was open for the transaction of judicial business, the counsel for the plaintiff stated its complaint. Then the counsel for the defendant denied the plaintiff's allegation and presented the court the conviction of the mind of a judge by exhibiting evidence of the reality of the fact alleged. Of course, the judge then dismissed this action without any further consideration. Subsequently, the frustrated woman openly expressed her idea about Bronislawa before a group of persons, saying that it was no wonder she became a prevailing party, since all bureaucracy and high officials dined in her restaurant, and that furthermore she would not be surprised that they also had sex with her. When Bronislawa heard of this story spread as a rumor, she stuffed her abdomen in vertebrates with a pillow, and one Sunday she occupied a bench on the porch in such a position for the woman to see clearly her advanced stage of pregnancy when she was passing by on her way to the church with a crowd.

Consequently, in the church the woman destitute of necessaries of life had an auricular confession, penance and communion. However, throughout this sacramental rite involving contrition, confession of sins to a priest, the acceptance of penalties and absolution, she realized how much wrong she caused intentionally in the presence of her neighbor, Bronislawa. Finally, a few weeks later, she came to Bronislawa's residence to beg her disposition to forgive. She said, "Fani Bronislawa, oh please forgive me and do accept my humble apology, an explanation expressing regret for my error and offense."

Immediately Bronislawa answered, "Dear Pani, neighbor, your apology is absolutely worthy of acceptance. Please, just do occupy a chair by the table. Without delay I shall prepare a meal and drink. We shall drink together the health of by a toast."

So, an unexpected party took place where everyone present burst out laughing to the extent of making public order and tranquillity in this flourishing good year, a year that was absent of ruthless crime, an act or omission in violation of public law. People in the Parish of Naliboki all applied their ability and effort to the cultivation of land, and of course they worked hard from sunrise to sunset. It was only the Sunday, their day of worship and rest. The domestic animals, poultry and the cultivated produce of the land in the mind of all people was the first right established on emergency or need. In these circumstances and conditions the peace and prosperity could not be prevented from happening.

Yes, indeed it was a great advantage of peace and prosperity, except from the worst enemy, death, which nobody can escape. Such an enemy in a particular way affects the whole nation's expectancy of the future and directs a different course of destiny. From this point of view the year 1935 happened to be overshadowed by deep mourning and sorrow, because the Free State of Poland was put in jeopardy, for its deliverer and sovereign leader, Marshal Jozef Pilsudski, had died on the twelfth day of May.

Pilsudski was born near Wilno in Poland, once Lithuania, on December 5, 1867. He was educated in Wilno and at the University of Kharkov in Russia. He was exiled to Siberia because he was interested in Polish independence, and after five years he was released and returned to Wilno, where he joined a Polish political party that sought independence for Poland from Russia. In 1894 he began to publish *Robotnik* (*The Workman*), a revolutionary journal. The Russian government tried to arrest him but Pilsudski escaped to Austria and then to England, devoting his time for the Polish cause as he traveled. He returned to Poland and established residence in Lodz, where he was arrested for printing *Robotnik* and confined in St. Petersburg. He escaped to England, then returned to Poland again in 1902 and began to organize a secret Polish army. During World War I Pilsudski with his army fought against the Russians, but after the Central Powers overran Poland, Pilsudski resigned his command in protest against German and Austrian interference in Polish affairs. The Germans as a result arrested him in 1917 and imprisoned him in Magdeburg, where he shared his cell with Adolf Hitler, subsequent notorious leader or dictator of the Third Reich. After a year Pilsudski was released from prison because of the German revolution and returned to Warsaw, where he immediately reorganized the total military land forces of the Polish country and used them to speed the evacuation of German troops from Poland. Under the first Polish premier, Ignacy Paderewski, a government was established, but due to disagreements in the government he shortly after resigned and a succession of unstable cabinets under unsure premiers followed. However, during this crucial period Pilsudski remained at the head of the army and opened an offensive against the Russians. In Warsaw with assistance from General Maxime Weygand of France, Pilsudski made his ultimate move and defeated the Russians decisively. Nevertheless, political conflict and chaos existed from 1919 until 1926, when Pilsudski used the army to effect a coup d'etat and assumed control of the government. From May 1926 until his death in 1935, Pilsudski in his position as minister of war and head of the army completely exercised control over Poland.

Notwithstanding the fact that among some Polish people Pilsudski was unpopular, but those were only losers and collaborators. They used foreign ideas rather than their own in the interest of Poland. Thus Pilsudski had no alternative but to exile them. Yes, when Pilsudski died it was then brought forward for consideration by the people of honest disposition that Poland died also. Expressive of mourning spirit embraced the nation and particularly the people of Naliboki. Everyone being manifested with grief wore black dresses or ribbons on their arms. For self sacrifice and complacency of penance people from Naliboki made a pilgrimage, advancing on foot to Wilno, where Pilsudski's heart was buried in the grave with his mother, but his body was buried in Warsaw.

Now General Edward Rydz-Smigly became marshal and subsequently the political stability of Poland began to deteriorate. The foreign policy of a state without natural frontiers and situated between two such powers as Germany and the Soviet Union would have been difficult even with stable internal political conditions. Yet with Marshal Jozef Pilsudski there was hope because he had absolute watchful regard for his country without relation to or dependence on other things or persons. The Foreign Minister, Jozef Beck, being of German descent, became free to view Nazi expansion in the company with Hitler.

Undoubtedly, Pilsudski was one of the greatest rulers in Polish history and somewhat equivalent to Jan Sobiski, who was born August 17, 1624, at Olesko Castle near Zolkiew in southeastern Poland. He was educated in Krakow, and in 1647 joined the Polish forces fighting against Russian Cossack encroachments. In 1665 he was made virtual commander-in-chief of the Polish armies, and in this capacity defeated invading Tatars. Turks invaded Poland, and Sobieski defeated the Turks at Cochim on November 10, 1673. As a result, Sobieski was elected king and crowned February 14, 1676, after which he left Krakow to renew his campaign against the Turks. To help bring order out of chaos, to make the country strong and to establish the monarchy firmly in control, like Pilsudski, Sobieski hoped to set himself up as the absolute ruler of Poland. But in this he was opposed by France and Austria, which preferred to keep Poland weak. Yet, Sobieski saved Austria from a powerful effort of Turkish invasion, defeating the Turks on September 12, 1683, and he also liberated Hungary from Turkish rule. Finally, Sobieski drove the Turks from Europe as he planned, and thus future Turkish advances into Europe were halted permanently. Sobieski, again like Pilsudski, was engaged in speciality training of his armies into Polish Hussars, members of a cavalry regiment distinguished by brilliant dress uniforms, gallantry, valor and skill in arms, who really portrayed the personal bravery and technique of Polish Legionaries. The remainder of Sobieski's life, however, was embittered by court intrigues and political and social chaos due to obstruction through foreign interference in Polish internal affairs. These two Polish men, the most powerful leaders, set up in history a prosperous precedent, an instance capable of being used as a guide or standard in evaluating future actions that are contrary to one who loves his country, zealously guards its welfare and is, of course, a defender of popular liberty. What really helped both these great Polish rulers be free from external authority or influence was the fact that they were born in Poland, but one in the midst of Lithuanian people and the other in the midst of Ukrainian people were compelled to use their minds to form unique and honest ideas in the best interest of their country.

During Sobieski's lifespan it is appropriate to say that Naliboki in Poland already was firmly established, having had its origin from Dukes Radziwill in the fourteenth century when Jadwiga was elected queen in 1384 and married Jagiello, Grand Duke of Lithuania, in 1386. She was the youngest daughter of Louis I the Great, king of Hungary, who was nephew of Casimir III the Great, the ruler from 1333 to 1370. Jadwiga was sixteen years of age when she became married, and she died one year just before the closing of fourteenth century. However, even beyond the reign of Casimir III the Great, that is to say, during the dynasty of Piast before the time of Dukes Radziwill, the Wilderness of Naliboki remained within the jurisdiction of the rulers of Poland. In 1650 a wooden church presenting an appearance of beauty was built in Naliboki. Here the process of manufacturing crystals and hilts for swords from the polished stone began in full progress, which, of course, Polish Hussars used in battle against Tatars, Cossacks and Turks. Here again, the blast furnace extracted steel from iron ore through fire intensified by an air blast that was sufficient to produce arms ready for battle against invading hostile armed forces. Nonetheless, as time went by Naliboki in the year 1935 was 90 percent inhabited by Polish population, notwithstanding the fact that the east region was surrounded by a majority of Byelorussian people and the north by the greater part of Lithuanian people.

Now, as the year 1936 progressed, the people in Naliboki and surrounding areas were preoccupied so, as it occurs in the ordinary course of events, in supporting their existence. The spare and available time in winter was used by most people in transportation of timber from the forest to the nearest waterway, which was floating in the river Niemen to the Baltic Sea for the international market. When the spring arrived, folks became busy as usual in the field with plantation and the act of cultivating the ground. Then, of course, followed the act of gathering a ripened crop of grain, fruit, vegetables, flax, etc.

Prelate Bajko made his announcement on the pulpit concerning the excavation of ground for the foundation of a new church, building a new brick kiln and installation of a large dynamo, a generator for the conversion of mechanical energy into electrical energy. This dynamo was delivered to Naliboki and installed at the parsonage on the north side of the church. The church site, including the central part of Naliboki, was illuminated. So, as it was announced by Prelate Bajko, without lapse in time the whole project became to be in progress. Folks began working according to a detailed and timed plan. Fortunately, our residence was electrically wired for the distribution of electric power because an insulated electrical conductor passed through Pilsudski Street into the center of town from the power house at the parsonage. Thus, all houses and streets received electrical light so far as the cable was able to reach.

From Nowogrodek a new doctor came to replace another doctor. He occupied Mr. Walon's dwelling opposite our residence, and at this location he established his medical practice. This doctor, being in the early period of life, was single and pleasing in appearance. His young nephew used to come from behind the river Niemen and remained temporarily as a guest with the doctor at some indeterminate time.

Wojt, the chairman presiding over the community building, resigned his position in Naliboki and a new Wojt Gminy was assigned for this particular function. This new chairman was also an invalid, person and veteran, disabled by injury to his leg in war. He lamed as he walked on his right leg. He was married to a very beautiful lady and they had two infant sons, Ziutek and Zygmund. They, of course, occupied a new residence that was built for the former Wojt on Pilsudski Street near the lake. As time went by, Ziutek and Zygmund became my good friends. They were impatiently desirous to learn from me whatever I was doing, for example, cutting and chopping wood, forming the gear of a draft horse and attaching it to a wheeled vehicle, plow or harrow, using a scythe to cut grass, feeding livestock, and whatever else was necessary to accomplish on the farm, about which they were manifesting intense eagerness. Subsequently, their parents and doctor came to be associates of our parents, and also they were good neighbors.

The romance intermediate in relation to Jan Radziwill and Wierka Klimowicz at this point was characterized by high ideals of purity and devotion and became a strong ardor in affairs of love. Together they both understood and fully appreciated that it was time to get married, and of course they decided that the wedding ceremony ought to be performed without delay. Subsequently to and because of a brief rehearsal at the church they were joined in wedlock. Their fabulous wedding was observed as a festival, with rejoicing at the late Dr. Peter Klimowicz's residence. For this noteworthy occasion there was present the bride's half brother, Eugenjusz Klimowicz, from the university of Wilno, and also from Wilno the theological seminary, Boleslaw Lojko, and of course their companions. On the other hand, the bridegroom's brother from the military forces, Jozef Radziwill, and their mother Radziwill, Vierka's mother Alesia, her sister Natasza, Mania, mother of Eugenjusz, our parents, Wladyslaw Klimowicz, his sister, Gabriela Kosciukiwicz and her husband Jozef, and all relatives and close friends mutually experienced pleasure in this astounding mirth.

After the wedding Jan Radziwill resided with his wife Vierka at her own dwelling, where she worked and controlled her business. Jan was engaged in the cultivation of land with my father, who at last found steady relief, since Eugenjusz was his only provisional assistant. Now they both spent time working together during farming season in cultivation, harvest and thrashing. After agricultural tasks were accomplished they indulged themselves in leisure time, available for recreation and relaxation.

For a while I nagged my father to make me skis for sliding over snow on slopes behind the cemetery where everybody experienced the joy of skiing, but father was always putting it off because he claimed he was too busy. However, Jan was artistic in sculpture, fashioning figures of wood, clay, metal or stone. So, in the meantime when they were drinking alcoholic liquors, father mentioned to Jan that I was repeatedly urging him to make skis, which usually were made of ash, a tree of the olive family with light, tough, elastic wood. Jan told my father not to worry, "I shall make him skis easily which undoubtedly he will enjoy in the winter season." So, as it was promised, without lapse of time Jan made me the most beautiful skis, classified according to my size. I cherished the skis and was proud to slide over the snow on slopes with other kids, where I certainly developed an ability and technique in this sport.

Just like Boleslaw, the godfather of my firstborn sister, Waclawa, who on arrival from Wilno treated her with gifts, but while in his youth he was a member of our family during his school period in Naliboki. Janka likewise had graduated from the educational institution in Naliboki, and now her parents from Trascianka sent her to Nowogrodek for higher education, where consequently she became a law student. After her departure indeed it was a sad moment for all of us. It was most difficult to say goodbye. Everyone present had tears in their the eyes from the emotional distress.

Now only Janka's brother, Czeslaw, was left with us, and he was going to school in the same class with Waclawa. It was the year in which I started school in the first grade, a level of progress in school, as it constituted a year's work, and if successful a pupil after seven such years would be granted a diploma by this educational institution at Naliboki. However, before my school attendance, my uncle, Waclaw, decided to take me with him to Trascianka at his woodland. Here I experienced joy and pleasure during several weeks of vacation at such a magnificent place. Uncle showed me around his property and subsequently, in order to impress me with wonder, I was engaged with him to extract honey from the beehives. During the course of operation to obtain this sweet, viscous substance made by bees from nectar gathered from flowers, my uncle told me to eat as much honey as I liked. So, I ate and ate to my full satisfaction as never before. But at night it made me very sick, and while I was sleeping through the severe perspiration honey came out on top of the skin of my body. As a result I became affected with disease for a short while. After my restoration from sickness, I learned that it is not wise to eat too much honey, and so it was noticed by all our relatives who had a pleasant diversion and amusement on account of my dreadful experience.

The chief forester from Kroman used to come to our house frequently to get his linen that was always prepared for him by my mother. My parents were concerned about the ghost that haunted his residence, so when they asked him in reference to this unusual occurrence, he said that there had been no change regarding this phenomenon—the ghost continue to reappear time and time again. But undisturbed Chief Forester claimed again that such a phantom did not bother him in the least. Nevertheless, I was terrified being solely a listener, and just making sense of the things they were saying was enough for the hair on my head to stand on end.

It was common knowledge among people in the Wilderness of Naliboki that there were some individuals possessing psychic power, sensitive to extrasensory phenomena, able to cure most unusual diseases or unwholesome conditions in the human body. Such a person of local note was well known, a spinster living with her married brother, Mr. Kanowal, in Maczylin, about three kilometers east of Naliboki. Their husbandry neighbored our long strip of land. During the time when my parents were working in the field I saw a four-wheeled horsedrawn vehicle arrive in a hurry to Mr. Kanowal's courtyard with a man bitten by a poisonous snake. Immediately, this dexterous lady with mental adroitness, after she cleaned herself from dirty work on the farm and was marked by neatness and orderly disposition, commenced a peculiar ritual performance over the stricken victim, who was almost unconscious. In pursuit of her repeated walk around the injured and repeated utterance, the victim was revived. Then the lady Kanowal said to the folks, "Please take him home and let him rest a while; he is going to be all right." Yet, in spite of the fact that some people were skeptical, this man became fully recovered from the deadly venom and came back to Miss Kanowal offering her a reward. As we observed from a distance this unusual occurrence, later I listened to my parents' conversation about the doctrine that denies either our knowledge or the existence of a reality beyond phenomena.

Eastward from Maczylin over the horizon was easily seen the village of Terebejno, approximately one mile away. However, northward our strip of land cut through the road leading to Kleciszcze and finally it was terminated at the skirt of woods. The road to Terebejno from Naliboki afterwards led through a number of small villages and at last to Rudnia Nalibocka. In the village of Terebejno lived not only Mr. Szabunia and a mad woman, Orszula, but also an old man 105 years of age who had the ability to foretell the future as by divine influence, and particular the fate to which Naliboki was destined. This distinguished old man with uncomplaining endurance entirely from matchsticks constructed a portable altar for use during a procession. On completion of this structure of wood he became penitent and carried the altar on his shoulders bare footed in winter through the snow from his residence to the church in Naliboki. His altar, a magnificent work of art, was consecrated and placed with others sideways in the church, readily attracting everyone's attention during the mass. The 105-year-old man instantly became worthy of admiration in the Parish of Naliboki. People everywhere arose with curiosity because of the unusualness and remarkable disposition of this human being. Rumors were spread that this old man foretold future events, but because of the present peace and prosperity in the country not many people in general had really a keen interest in what he had to say. Nevertheless, my parents in the company of relatives seriously discussed this subject, what the future held for us, and because they felt that it was impossible for peace and prosperity to continue to time indefinite, they were eager for information from this inspired predictor. So, in order for this particular knowledge to be attained it was unanimously put forward for acceptance to invite this man at some proper occasion for a party, a social gathering for pleasure and entertainment, where he would be comfortable and be treated as a most important guest. Yet this idea was put quietly to rest, and as time elapsed everyone in the family forgot to talk about the future problem any more; rather they were pursuing the current flow of an actual set of circumstances.

Bronislawa was an outstanding chef and gourmet, a fastidious devotee of good food and drink. As usual, she was actively engaged in the preparation of most delicious food in her kitchen intended for distinguished guests whose seat in her restaurant was reserved in advance. During the intervening time her fiance, Korzenko, already nicknamed "Mazdzer" in Byelorussian language, meaning a shipwrecked person, grew to be a fat man due to the fact that he was a gourmand; he was taking hearty pleasure in eating and drinking alcoholic beverages. It was no doubt that at this point in time he was suffering from alcoholism. During his inebriation he became a rude and violent character to the extent that Bronislawa had to run away and hide from him. She blamed her mother, who forbade her to marry Korzenko, for this adversity because if she was married to him he would never be an alcoholic, she believed. Therefore, on account of her mother's prevention however, Bronislawa had a premonition of something evil and harmful in her love affair, and in fact it came to be so. Of course, in this matter her brother, Wilhelm, lacked the necessary power to help her, and because of it there was nothing he could do but just be silent.

Bronislawa, in the extreme state of being frustrated, renounced going to church by reason of her mother's wrong, which she knew was impossible to amend because her mother no longer was in force to supply fully what she desired or ever needed. And yet, on the other hand, probably she could not see what her mother was able to recognized about Korzenko since she fell deeply in love with him. That is why she was left unconvinced that their fate was in doubt. Blinded by love, Bronislawa concealed reality from the truth, and in this way she was hurt in conformity with the fact of an outcome. By inherent nature, her mother's love for her child instinctively was protecting Bronislawa from her folly. Just like with her sister, Orszula, mother forbade her to marry a certain Von Metro Majer, who seemed to her a very strange man, born in Berlin of German nationality and being totally unfamiliar. It was quite natural that her mother had an agitated feeling aroused by awareness of threatening danger to her beloved daughter, and of course she acted defensively. But in spite of her mother's effort to stop any close union, Orszula became united in matrimony and lived attended with good fortune.

In the occasional course of remembrance about Orszula and talk concerning her family having reached a high degree of worldly prosperity, my father and Aunt Bronislawa became affected by great sorrow when they received a very sad message from Lithuania informing them that Orszula's husband, the President of Lithuania, had been assassinated. Because of this terrible tragedy all relatives assembled at our residence to pay their respects and to express compassion for the sorrow caused by losing their brother-in-law, beloved husband of their sister. The relatives began to talk about the Lithuanian utter disorder and confusion taking place in the country.

It was immediately evident to every inhabitant of the country that when Poland was partitioned in the last half of the eighteenth century, almost all of Lithuania passed into Russian hands and the country disappeared as a national unit. Hopes were that either Napoleon or, later, Alexander I would reestablish Lithuania, but they failed. Only because of World War I and the downfall of Russia was the long-desired independence regained. In 1917 Antanas Smetona was chosen president of a Lithuanian diet, and in 1918 a German prince was elected king. With the utter ruin of Germany in November 1918 the election was cancelled, a parliament assembled, and the first republican government was formed, with Professor Augustians Voldemaras as premier. Germans and Russian Bolshevists striving to control the country were driven out by force. But during the following years Lithuania was recognized by Russia, Germany and other world powers, including the United States. Organizing their country, the Lithuanians distributed the large estates among the landless peasants, secured foreign loans, introduced a stable currency, and furthered the cooperative movement. In 1922 a democratic constitution was adopted. A university was founded at Kaunas, and education was extended and supplemented by a system of parochial schools for national minorities. In the 1950s compulsory education to the age of sixteen was instituted.

The international problems, combined with religious issues resulting from the parochial school system and with corruption among officials, weakened the existing regime. Party politics hindered the progress of the country. In 1926 the government was overthrown, and with the help of young army officers Voldemaras was brought back to power. But Voldemaras was forced out of office in 1929 by President Smetona, who set up a new government under his brother-in-law Tubelis. This government dissolved Fascist organizations and provided for local representative bodies, but retained many totalitarian features and battled against peasant risings and workers' strikes.

Additional difficulties arose with Hitler coming to power in Germany in 1933. Internal discord increased, a coup of Voldemaras and some military groups was barely suppressed in 1934, and international crises multiplied. Thus internal national chaos embraced the country, and subsequently Von Metro Majer was assassinated in 1936.

However, in spite of the Lithuanian national chaos, the members of the family continued discussing current world news and shocking headlines in the local newspaper. Constant articles in the newspapers summarized the Japanese invasion of China. When, at the dawn of the 1930s, China seemed to be on the way to developing a stable, unified government and to freedom from the galling restrictions on her sovereignty, which had earlier been wrested from her, Japan's action brought a prolonged and disastrous reverse. In September 1931 the Japanese army, on a slight pretext, launched an attack in Manchuria. Within a few weeks the existing Chinese regime in that area was eliminated. Early in 1932 fighting broke out in Shanghai as a result of the Chinese anti-Japanese boycott, and much destruction was wrought in that commercial metropolis before temporary peace was restored. Japan, censured by world opinion through the League of Nations, defied it, withdrew from the League, and as rapidly as she dared, advanced her control across Inner Mongolia and in the northeast of China proper. What at first appeared a minor incident developed into full-scale, although undeclared, war. Much of the most severe fighting was in the lower part of the Yangtze Valley, in and around Shanghai and between Shanghai and Nanking. At the time in 1936, most of China's air force and best armies were destroyed. Nanking fell among an excessive indulgence of rape and slaughter of defenseless civilians.

At the same time the people in the Parish of Naliboki were indeed shocked to read about the Italian conquest of Abyssinia, known as Ethiopia, an empire in northeastern Africa consisting of the former kingdoms of Amhara, Gojjam, Shoa and Tigre and including the territories of the Danakil, Somalis, Gurages, Sidamos and Gallas.

Meanwhile, the quest for imperial glory and the humiliating memory of Aduwa gave to Mussolini and his fascist regime an excuse for again invading Abyssinia. As regent, Ras Tafari strove for admission to the League of Nations as protection against the continued pressure of Great Britain, France and Italy for concessions that might lead to limitations on the freedom and sovereignty of his country. Admission to the League was unanimously voted on September 23, 1923. Five years later a twenty-year treaty of friendship was signed with Italy. But the peace these acts seemed to portend did not last. The feeling toward Italy, none too good at any time, was made less friendly by frontier and diplomatic incidents magnified in Italy out of all proportion to their real importance.

A frontier clash on December 5, 1934, at Walwal near the ill-defined frontier of Abyssinia and Italian Somaliland was referred to the League of Nations for an opinion as to responsibility, but the decision rendered nine months later in September 1935 held that neither state was responsible. In the meantime, negotiations with Italy were without positive results and the League of Nations, to which the quarrel had again been referred, offered no help or solution. Finally, as the result of a conference between Great Britain, France and Italy, proposals were formulated as a basis for settlement. Abyssinia agreed to open negotiations, but Italy, which had been assembling large forces of men and munitions in Italian Somaliland and Eritrea, refused. On October 3, 1935, without any formal declaration of war, the Italians invaded Abyssinia. In spite of the fact that Abyssinia had delayed mobilization until the Italians moved, its poorly armed and equipped troops were able to slow initial Italian advances. Abyssinians as a matter of fact fought with bows and arrows against Italian machine guns.

On November 18, 1935, the League of Nations invoked a scheme of economic and financial sanctions against Italy, having previously adopted a resolution in favor of coal, oil and steel sanctions. Sabre rattling by Hitler and Mussolini kept the nations of Western Europe in a constant state of uncertainty, and no nation wanted to become involved in commitments elsewhere that might compromise its actions at home.

The Italian troops, commanded by Marshal Pietro Badoglio, entered Addis Ababa on May 5, 1936, but Emperor Haile Selassie had already left for England, which he had chosen as a place of refuge. Abyssinia was formally attached to Italy on May 9, 1936, and on June 1 the king of Italy was proclaimed emperor, and Abyssinia, combined with Eritrea and Italian Semaliland, was named Italian East Africa.

In view of the Lithuanian national chaos, the Japanese invasion of China and Italy's conquest of Abyssinia, paranoia began to haunt my father's mind, and thus his outlook on future peace and prosperity was indistinct from this time on. He often continued political discussions with our neighbor Witold Baszuro, who was concerned because his sacrifice to save sums of money for a new husbandry would be in vain if world conditions unfolded to full extent. Witold was worried about the realities of war, which possibly could jeopardize his existing conditions; for this reason he would come to our house to obtain information with respect to political developments affecting various nations. So, they both continued discussing at each occasion for quite a long while about the international political affairs that began to be evident were at the threshold to utter threats against the global public order and tranquillity.

On the ground of a picture that portrays a now-mundane political system, my father felt that his infliction was increased due to an unfortunate reiterated death in the family. This time, his beloved first cousin and dear friend Wladyslaw Klimowicz, with whom he was in constant association, became ill and after two weeks died of pneumonia, a disease of bacterial or viral origin occurring in many forms as bronchial pneumonia or lobar pneumonia. The doctors afforded no ground for hope to regain health from such a disease, and Wladyslaw, at the age of thirty-five, departed suddenly from his wife Genefa and three sons, Boniutek, Gienek and Michal. Father became saddened by the unexpected deprivation of his beloved cousin and perceptive of the fact that their worthy companionship was cut off perpetually.

My second cousins Boniutek and Gienek and I pursued study together in the same class and under the same teachers in school. We played all sorts of games and acted in accordance with what was expected. Our most favorable sports to play were volleyball and kwadrant (quadrant), which is something similar to American baseball, a game played with a wooden bat and a soft ball, instead of hard, by two teams of nine players each, one team being at bat and the other in the field alternately. The object of the game was to make as many runs as possible within nine innings of play. Of course, a soft ball was adopted to keep participants from danger and unnecessary harm. The volleyball we played on school grounds, but the quadrant we played on the common ground (wygon), and preferably on the Poplawski ground right on the west side of our residence just behind Mr. Jesc's orchard. My grandparents told me that the Poplawski ground a long while ago was a magnificent orchard of tall trees where every year storks built nests for the hatching of their eggs and the rearing of their young, but the plantation of fruit trees, the few that still were there, were extremely old and Mr. Poplawski himself was long ago deceased. Our team, a set of players competing in the games of quadrant or volleyball, was always the same. It was made up with the following players: Boniutek, Gienek, the three sons of my father's friend Antoni Szarzanowicz, Janek, Michal, Olek, including my friend Arkadjusz Makarewicz, and two Hebrew brothers, the sons of Mr. Srol, Chaim and Joska, who were my schoolmates. Together as a team apart from that mentioned, we experienced enjoyment in swimming, diving and fishing in the lake or river by the Poplawski ground. In the winter season we had the pleasure in skating over ice on the same lake and skiing over snow-covered inclines behind the cemetery where everyone was engaged in this sport of gliding and ski jumping.

With the exception that for most of the time I was engaged with Arkadjusz. He purposely led me to catch fish or gather sorrel, an herb with acidic leaves used in salads, but here locally people used to make soup by boiling this vegetable in water with meat, eggs, etc., and served it hot or cold. This fish and sorrel were most desired by Hebrew neighbors, for whom Arkadjusz's mother, Natasza Makarewicz, worked. She acquired by experience their Hebrew language and taught her son to sing beautiful Hebrew songs, for he was gifted with an excellent voice. When we brought the very best quality of fish and sorrel to these Hebrew people, they always made a request for Arkadjusz to sing their songs in Hebrew, which is a Northwest Semitic language. Hebrew was not different from the language spoken by the Canaanite inhabitants of ancient Palestine and adjacent areas, and, indeed, the Hebrews called their language "the speech of Canaan." Later, when the principal body of Hebrews was in the Kingdom of Judah, they called their language "Judean." However, Arkadjusz learned to sing an indefinite number of Jewish folk songs, both religious and secular, that were used in many regions of the vast Russian territory. These folk songs were published in great quantities by the most outstanding composers active in this field, including Joseph Achron, Michael Genessin, Alexander Krein, Moses Milner, Solomon Rosowsky, Lazare Saminsky and Jacob Weinberg. Of course, some of them accompanied by good fortune emigrated eventually either to Palestine or to the United States and played an important part in shaping the course of music of the fundamental ideology of the society, which emphasized the musical value of the Jewish national idioms. Nonetheless, our local Jews who expressed a desire for Arkadjusz to sing were astonished at the timbre of his voice and the amazing quality of Jewish folk songs created by the most outstanding composers. They gladly then paid us more than the fish and sorrel were worth and rewarded Arkadjusz generously with sums of money and gifts.

Unfortunately, Arkadjusz was accident prone, that is to say, mentally predisposed to sudden disaster. When we played on the common ground, while I herded the cattle, he went to a strange horse that was grazing nearby and began to smooth it along its surface calmly and evenly, starting from the front and moving to the rear. As he did that, the horse without warning struck Arkadjusz in his jaw with his hoofs, knocking him unconscious. I cried because I thought he was dead. Immediately, he was taken to the clinic where he naturally remained for some time. Again after his long recovery we went fishing in the river, but having no luck, on the way home Arkadjusz began to run with a knife in his hand pointing upwards. As he ran in such a fashion, he tripped and fell on the bridge opposite our residence with the knife sticking in his throat. As in his previous condition, he was rushed into the clinic, with my parents' assumption that this time Arkadjusz would probably suffer death indubitably. Yet, he was restored to health after a while, and our association continued such as occurs in the ordinary course of events.

During the intervening time, Alfons Toiko announced the act of betrothing a certain beautiful sweetheart named Jadwiga. At this occasion there was a formal gathering of guests in accordance with the habitual practice of a community. Alfons was a young fellow in his twenties who already completed his service in the Polish army and thus was considered to have reached his maturity.

In spite of everything, this community in the Wilderness of Naliboki still moved with the sweeping motions of flourishing prosperity exclusively determined by the peace that had predominant control for the people to enjoy life under the Free State of Poland. Of course, in these neighboring places collectively there had been no report of serious unnatural crimes or disasters other than misdemeanors, infractions or petty offenses, crimes for which the maximum punishment is generally a fine or a short term in a house of correction. A court proceeding according to the course of the common law of the nation and governed by its rules and principles, as contrasted with a "court equity (q.v.)," was held in the summer season at Naliboki. The term "equity" denotes the spirit and habit of fairness and justness, which would regulate the intercourse of men with men. At such occasions, that portion of the courthouse in which the actual proceedings took place in the municipal building (gmina), the public now and then was amused at an outcome of judicial examination and determination of issues between parties to action. Often plaintiffs and defendants were portrayers of a clown or professional buffoon, like in a circus rather than court.

In such an environment, the prelate Bajko was steadily moving along with his progress of modernizing Naliboki, and also he decided to organize a new church choir. This choir was characterized by a good selection of young men and women with natural ability. Of course, the youth church choir was conducted by our organist through its routine of regular weekly rehearsals. But when the work was repeated three times each week it required a person with an insatiable love of music to achieve and maintain the high standards. Our organist was such a person. This dedication was illustrated by his frequent appearances to conduct this choir in Naliboki's church. The young members in the choir with fine voices were such ones as Jan Radziwill, Wierka, Alfons Klimowicz, Jadwiga, Jozef Kosciukiewicz, Gabryjela, Regina Klimowicz, Edward Wolan, Marylka Wolan, Franciszek Arciuszewski and many other distinct entities.

However, a similar choir in Naliboki was filled with the sound of timbre five decades ago when my grandfather Dr. Kazimierz Klimowicz, an organist, had the task of guiding an organized body of singers. His performance in that period was often recalled by my Aunt Bronislawa, who was able to remember, in addition to what she saw, that which she learned from her mother. Unfortunately, my father, Wilhelm Klimowicz, did not know anything about his father because he was just a baby when his father died, whose last request was to put the baby on his chest while he was suffering the pain of death.

After the usual act of gathering a ripened crop of grain, fruit and vegetables came the thrashing and preservation of food for future consumption, as by boiling with sugar or by salting. Fruit that has been cooked, usually with sugar, preparation of meat and bacon, the salted and dried or smoked back and sides of the hog, making sauerkraut in the barrel, a keg of herrings, a pipe of wine or barrel of pickled cucumbers, and pickled or dried mushrooms, this conservation of food from harvest was a common effort made by every household in this community. All members dwelling as a unit under one roof equally performed their task in the preservation of food for future consumption during the autumn season, and as soon as this job was done the Christmas holiday was near. Parents underwent the process of decorating and painting the interior of the house for this special religious observance. Finally, an evergreen tree was decorated with ornaments and lights for Christmas.

At this point in time, family members that were engaged actively in some employment far from home had an interlude of several weeks from customary duties for recreation and rest; they were reunited again after separation. My father's uncle, Benedikt Klimowicz, employed as an organist, arrived home dressed in an expensive soft, fine, fur coat. He always furnished me with gifts and money at his presence. Father's first cousin, Wolan, the chief officer of a prison in Baranowicze, arrived home to his immediate family, his wife Marylka, three children and his father, the watchmaker. Our neighbor Witold's two sisters from Stolpce came to reunite with their mother, Mrs. Baszuro, at his residence. The older sister was a spinster but the other was married to a police officer who had steady employment in the city of Stolpce, and they had just become parents of a baby boy. Apart from many of those who were working away from home in Naliboki, there was also a considerable number of students from Naliboki at the large cities in institutions for higher education. Those ones too had vacation and were inclined to go home for Christmas.

My uncle, Boleslaw Lojko, arrived from the seminary of theology from Vilno. He usually stayed with my godfather Jozef because his parents resided at his magnificent new husbandry that was built in a remote location north of Zascianki, the west far end of Naliboki. This location of fine woodland was granted by Marshal Jozef Pilsudski for his bravery in combat against the Russian Cossacks in liberation of Poland. Our grandparents were most desirous for their youngest son, Boleslaw, to be a priest. Particularly, the grandmother saved all her money for her favorite son's education and remained in expectation impatiently to see Boleslaw come home one day in a cassock dressed as a priest.

The Last Day of Naliboki

Eugenjusz Klimowicz also came back home on his vacation from the university to celebrate Christmas with his mother, Mania, and to enjoy his reunion with all his relatives throughout the time of holiday.

Usually, everyone that made this journey home through some distance had a different story to tell about their adventure, and with some individuals there were quite thrilling experiences. For example, an indigenous young student, Stanislaw Arciuszewski was learning in college at Nowogrodek. He decided to make a journey on foot back home for the Christmas holiday season simply because he was unable to meet the expense of transportation. In his pocket he had only a fifty groszy (cents). Of course, in the middle part of December the weather was cold, and the young student was slim and gentle. He started to walk the approximately fifty kilometers to Naliboki. After his best endeavors, he commenced getting weary and discontented and began to look for a ride to his destination. And, as a luck happened, there was a certain Byelorussian peasant riding along in his hackney coach in the same direction as the student was walking. So he asked the peasant, "Sir, please, be so kind as to give me a lift."

The peasant replied in a coarse tone of voice, "Get in!"

The young student quickly entered his hackney coach and felt very pleased to be relieved from walking because now he assumed that he could refresh himself. But subsequently the peasant had to cross a river to get on the other side, and as he was driving across he stopped his horse right in the middle of it. He looked at the student and told him to pay him one zlot (one dollar). However, the student replied and said, "But, sir, I do not have a dollar on me; I have just a 50 cents. Please, take this 50 cents."

But the peasant said, "I demand one dollar of you. If you cannot pay me this amount, then get off my wagon now."

Obviously the water was extremely cold, and the student, who had a pen knife in his pocket, had no alternative but to jump on the horse's back. As soon as he did that, he swiftly cut the harness loose with his sharp knife and was borne along by a horse on the other side. At once he got off and left the horse there, and began to make his journey on foot again. As he advanced he passed a few hamlets, and by the time mentioned, there was the apparent daily descent of the sun below the horizon. He thought that if he were able to reach another hamlet before dark he would be compelled to look for a place to pass the night. Subsequently, when he arrived to a little village, he came to a certain house and knocked at the door. When a lady answered, the young student asked her if she kindly could let him pass the night because he was indigent and traveling from his educational institution back home for Christmas. The lady presented an opportunity for the student to stay overnight and told him that unfortunately he would have to sleep on a bench at the glazed tile stove because there was no extra bed available. Naturally, the young student was delighted and expressed gratitude to the lady. Conveniently as it was, she had a supper made ready and asked him if he would like to have a meal before turning in. He gladly accepted her hospitable invitation and enjoyed his meal. But before going to sleep, he noticed that the lady was troubled emotionally for some reason. When he asked her what was wrong, she told him that her husband had gone to do some business far away and by now he should be home. "I do not know what has happened to him, why he is so late."

At this particular point the student started exercising his mental capacities and forming ideas as he lay on the bench, asking himself, *Would that be by any chance her husband whose harness I have ruined by cutting it with my knife?* So help me God, this is true. While the student was engaged in thought he fell into a light, brief sleep. And so the time rapidly passed till about eleven o'clock when the peasant, a rustic, clownish person, arrived into his courtyard with malediction and execrative loud expressions. As he entered the house he was turbulent and confused, but when he saw a boy sleeping on the bench by the stove, his face dramatically changed and in a soft voice he asked his wife who it was. She said, "A certain student traveling asked me to pass the night."

The boor villager then woke him up and told him to sit at the table, that he was going to eat his supper in his company and after, he said, "I am going to ask you some questions in order to see what you have learned in your college." The student tried to explain that he already ate his supper, but the peasant invalidated his claim and ordered him to eat with him again. In spite of overwhelming fear, the student thought himself, *What could such a rustic man as he ask me that I shall not be able to answer*. So, during the time that he was eating, he grew to be satisfied with things as they were. But things turned out to be unexpected.

The peasant understood Polish but could only speak Byelorussian. Likewise, the student understood Byelorussian, but he used Polish words in communicating among the people in this particular area. In these circumstances on the ground of mutual comprehension the challenge had begun. The peasant demanded defiantly of the student a question by pointing to a cat lying under the bench by the stove, and he said, "What is that?"

The student replied promptly, "That is a cat."

At this moment the peasant gave him a box on the ear. Then he asked him again, "What is that?"

The student had thought that perhaps it was a tomcat, but he learned that it was in fact a female animal. So he said, "It is a female cat."

At that the boor gave him another box on the ear, and he said, "According to our manners, it is CHYSTADOM, which in slang means a creature that keeps the house clean. Then he showed him a vessel in which naphta is burned through a wick to produce light, and he said, "What is that?"

The student cautiously answered, "It is a lamp."

At this instant, the boor gave him a box on the ear and asked him again. "What is that?"

The student thought that it could not be anything other than light. So he replied, "It is a light."

The boor then struck him with his hand in his face a second time and said, "According to our manners, it is KRASIDLO, which in slang means brightness that emits or reflects much light. Finally, the peasant brought him into the vestibule and showed him a low story beneath the roof of a building, and asked him, "What is that?"

The student frighteningly replied, "It is an attic."

At that the boor gave him a box on the ear, and asked him again, "What is that?"

The student then cautiously answered, "It is a garret."

The boor struck him again and said, "It is not a garret; according to our manners it is VYSADO, which in slang means height, a lofty or high place. Now, he said, "Go to sleep, and in the morning I am going to ask you some more questions in order to see what you have learned in your college."

As a direct result of the injury inflicted to the slim and gentle student by the peasant, one with a tough constitution and unmanageably rough disposition, having a heavyweight body and resembling a large dwelling, the student's delicate cheeks were read as a beet-root and swollen badly in size. As he lay down on the bench by the stove, he could not think about enduring another such treatment in the morning. His imagination and fear of reality kept him from falling asleep, but the boor on the other hand was weary and exhausted through an incident, namely a piece of action in the river that he underwent. That is why he fell rapidly under a spell of deep sleep. Consequently, when he became dormant the young student knocked on his window and with a sudden and loud outcry uttered, "Master, master of the house, get up! Your CHISTADOM took KRASIDO and set a fire to your VYSADO. And at this particular point in time the student swiftly fled from danger in the direction of his original desired destination.

During Advent, the season prior to Christmas, usually adolescents were well rehearsed to perform a play and sing carols. They portrayed in their act characters such as the three wise kings, shepherds, old Jews with long beards, the devil and so on. The best actor coming into view to play the role of a devil was Jan Szarzanowicz. He was most talented and had a suitable feature, a distinctive part of the face, dark eyes and jet black hair. He was brisk and comparatively smaller in size than an average adolescent. Thus, he played his role extremely well and was renowned in Naliboki. Such a group of actors performed in the evening from door to door at their best. They were suitably dressed and ornamented, and they carried a large colorful star illuminated inside with a candle. For their outstanding performance the inhabitants rewarded them with all sorts of gifts and money, which is called KOLENDY, or Christmas box. That is why Jan was nicknamed in a popular local Byelorussian expression a little devil, and he was the older son of my father's friend, Antoni Szarzanowicz.

Customarily, at the same time the priest was expected to visit every household to catechize children and deliver a wafer, a small flat disk of unleavened bread stamped with a cross or the letters IBS used to initiate an evening meal on Christmas Eve. It was also expected according to the habitual practice of the community to make a substantial donation toward the church. Under these circumstances the children were shuddered in advance from a short manual giving in the form of questions an outline of the principles of a religious creed, and on the other hand the parents were embarrassed because it was difficult for them to decide the actual measure of donation that should be made. However, once it all came about in the immediate vicinity of a person of superior rank, having authority to administer the sacraments, the excitement was diminished and the termination of catechism was free from anxiety and adequate to what was required in this situation for all concerned.

It was a glorious Christmas Day. The stretch of inland natural scenery was ornamented with a thick layer of snow. The low temperature caused the lake to turn to ice, and its surface was continuously even and transparent, admitting the passage of light and permitting a clear view of fish moving below. Above the lake a steep hill overgrown with various trees increased in beauty on account of the coldest season of the year, among which the steeples rising above the tower of the church were visible in a blue sky on such a delightful day. The people from the south and north, from the east and west tended toward the church on foot, but ones from the remote places traveled in their sledge vehicles, having horses decorated with cup-shaped metallic instruments that gave forth a ringing sound when shaken. When as many people as possible had filled the church by midday, the mass began. Benedikt Klimowicz was asked courteously to be present in the church to perform his part on the organs, while a duly authorized organist was going to lead the choir during the course of mass. The choir through its routine of regular weekly rehearsals and guided by a person with an insatiable love of music sang magnificently the songs of joy. The keys of organs that were touched by Benedikt's fingers created music that resounded the exposed surface of the hill upon which the consecrated church of his forefathers stood for centuries. The church inside was embellished and illuminated by means of candles and with the use of electricity thanks to Prelate Bajko. The walls and ceiling had large holy figures in beautiful colors that were painted by outstanding artists long ago. In front above the altar on the wall there was God the Father in the shape of an old man, a large comparison in color painted with a magnitude of angels. The aroma of incense perfumed the entire church and produced a pleasant fragrance to make one feel as if being in heaven. Such an inexplicably wonderful feeling I have had in my childhood while being there during this heavenly surrounding on Christmas Day as my father held my hand. After the mass, everyone came home to celebrate this marvelous day by means of a sumptuous feast followed by games, skiing and relaxation, during which time I have watched through our window excellent figure skating on the lake performed by two sons of the organist who came home on vacation from the university. These young men were hardly known here by anyone except their immediate family because they briefly visited home only and most of the time they were absent.

The winter season in the year 1937 was normal and relatively moderate in regard to temperature. My mother at home was engaged in tailoring women's outer garments, which were made to order from a new fabric of the customer's own choice. Father, on the other hand, decided to make some extra cash and left us for a month or so to go with his friend Antoni Szarzanowicz to the forest to transport timber to the waterway. Of course, once they drove the distant journey to where the job was, they had to lodge at the nearest forestry, and in this way they continued working until their task was completed, which they had contracted and was legally binding. In the end they were fully paid for the services rendered and arrived back home safely.

After considerable time of relaxation at home, father had a fixed purpose to go to his uncle, Jakub Klimowicz, who was residing trans-river Niemen near the city of Nowogrodek. In company with his friend Antoni they left for Nowogrodek, and when they arrived they had a very good time while visiting Jakub. Consequently, Jakub with his friends invited father and Antoni for a drink in his favorite tavern in Nowogrodek. When they arrived, they started drinking liquor there. Father, already being intoxicated, began a conversation with some strangers in this particular tavern. But by their accent he realized that they were inhabitants of Lithuania. So, in his present mood of brave disposition being under the alcoholic influence, he said to them, "You are Lithuanians, are you not?" They answered yes. Then my father said to them, "You are the ones who assassinated my brother-in-law."

They asked him, "Who was your brother-in-law?"

Father replied, "He was your president, Metro Majer, whom you murdered last year."

At this particular point in time they began to look for an opportunity to kill father also, but noticing the situation his partners in time pulled him out to a place free from danger. Afterwards when father arrived home and was possessed by properly controlled faculties, he realized how foolish he was, and had it not been for his uncle and friends, how easily he could have lost his life. However, such an outcome could have been expected to occur in his intoxicating state because his character could not hold what was really on his sober mind. The things that were hurting him most, he always spoke them out only under the influence of alcohol no matter the consequence. Yet, later he looked back on it with a feeling of distress and sorrow; on the other hand, he could not remember what he was saying or doing while he was drunk.

Under the influence of alcohol father's character happened to be entirely changed. His integrity and moral force was diminished obliviously; thus he became suspicious, endowed with imagination that there is something wrong without proof or clear evidence. He was violent toward mother and several times he beat her up, leaving an injury caused by bruising on her body and face. This he let himself do because he was inebriated and thought that his wife was not true to her marriage vows. I remember the grandparents came to our house to see how badly their daughter was bruised and to talk some sense into their son-in-law. But my father was ashamed and very sorry for what he had done, which he claimed he hardly could remember about such a horrible piece of action. Of course, the best solution concerning this difficulty was for my father to stop drinking vodka, a strong alcoholic liquor originally made in Russia from the fermented mash of wheat. On this account before my mother and grandparents he made a solemn affirmation with an appeal to God that he would definitely quit the practice of drinking alcoholic liquor to excess. Afterward father endeavored to use his will power to regulate and direct his personal behavior in an orderly manner.

Our neighbor and friend Jozef Farbotko, whose husbandry adjoined the late Dr. Peter Klimowicz's land and who associated often with my father, was the most violent person in the neighborhood when under the influence of alcohol. Sometimes it took a several men to hold him down; indeed he was a dangerous individual when he was drunk. But unfortunately a tragic death of his dear brother by suicide was the main reason for Jozef to change his mind concerning past actions. He became a nice, respectable person and kept himself back from drinking alcohol. Jozef was working in the construction of macadam, which was a new road built from the town square southward to Stolpce. Due to broken stones that had to be used in macadamizing the road, Jozef superbly had developed his muscles and therefore was a very strong man. Once he demonstrated his strength when my father was loading a wagon with grain to be taken to the mill. All bystanders were overwhelmed by wonder and surprise to see the way Jozef handled the large, heavy weight of sacks of grain by loading them on the wagon, yet he was shorter than my father. As a kid I enjoyed watching Jozef at his work, the way he broke stones to build his muscles.

During the progress of macadam Prelate Bajko made an arrangement for a new luxurious bus to be taken from Naliboki to Stolpce. This route was established permanently from the day the bus was delivered to Naliboki. A local individual with twofold qualifications as driver and mechanic was appointed for this assignment. The daily departure from Naliboki to Stolpce took place in the morning, but in the evening the bus arrived and was stored, serviced and repaired if needed. Before departure, the bus was parked on Stolpce Street opposite the residence of the late Dr. Peter Klimowicz. The bus driver was naturally attracted to the children and used to invite us kids to have a ride on this most luxurious bus, from the bus stop to the garage when its obligatory service was brought to completion.

Prelate Bajko, in his vigorous and effective force, did not waste any time; he had also made arrangements for a huge steam engine to be delivered to Naliboki, which was placed on the common ground where long ago a glassworks used to be. This particular location was chosen to establish a large sawmill for sawing logs with power-driven machinery. It adjoined westward to the property of Jozef Farbotko and southward to the land of the late Dr. Peter Klimowicz, which presently was cultivated by my father. In addition to the huge steam engine there was attached a much bigger dynamo than was installed already in full service at the parsonage. Without delay this new dynamo was put to service, and as a result of it the whole town of Naliboki received a current of energy. At the same time the sawmill became to the fullest extent operational, the brick kiln Prelate Bajko established behind the school in the forest was producing daily a large amount of bricks. The construction of a new church began to be in full progress. The civil engineers, a father with two sons, who were building the church also started to build a brick mansion with a flat roof for themselves in the middle of town on Nowogrodek Street about one kilometer west of the Jewish center.

In the vicinity of the brick kiln there was a forester dwelling under care and wisdom in the management of his own resources, who was appointed to take charge of the forest by the authority of government. His son was pursuing study in school with me in the first grade. Precisely at the age of eight he killed his father, an unfortunate tragedy that happened accidentally at home. His father, after he made his usual round of inspection in the forest, came home fatigued as a result of physical and mental exertion. He placed his rifle in a horizontal position on the bed in one of his bedrooms and went to another bedroom to lay down and rest. Soon after that his son came to the bedroom and started playing with the rifle. Consequently the rifle went off, and as it fired the bullet went directly through the wooden wall and hit the father as he was resting, which resulted in fatal death. This disastrous news shocked the entire community of Naliboki. In school I had shivers and a prickling sensation in my skin when I looked at this boy and thought to myself that he was the one who killed his own father. It was indeed the most terrifying occurrence of an incidental circumstance I have experienced in my life, knowing that a boy of my age became the killer of his own father.

In the early season of spring father was loading a wagon with dung and transporting this animal excrement to Maczylin about three kilometers from home. This dung we unloaded from the wagon into about a dozen piles in the open field. When this process finally was completed, our whole family went there for a day to spread that manure and to plant potatoes. Father engaged the horse into a plow and made a long furrow in which we laid potato seeds approximately twelve inches apart and raked manure on top of it. Then he plowed over it, and in a third furrow we planted seeds again, and continued this method of operation until the job was done. When the potatoes began to put forth shoots, father had to harrow the potato field for leveling plowed ground. Lastly when the potato plants appeared in the rows, father used an implement powered by horse to heap up the potato plants with soil for protection.

I was impatiently desirous of doing all things on the farm, such as loading dung on the wagon from the stable, driving a horse, harrowing, earthing potatoes, and above all to plow. But my father was apprehensive because I was yet too small; he did not let me plow or even earth potatoes, although I was capable of doing many other jobs at home and in the field. Therefore I cried and was full of tears when we planted potatoes, begging father to let me plow. Feeling sorry for me, he promised that next year that I would be somewhat taller and consequently would be able to hold the handles of a plow better. So in an expectation of his promise I was looking forward to the next year in order to be able to plow and to use an implement earthing potatoes.

As we transported dung to Maczylin from home, we crossed over the common ground, passing by the municipal building, and we traveled through the PLAC (PLATZ) where father's cousin Gabriela lived in a remarkable new unfinished house her husband Jozef was building by using material such as timber, straw and clay. Father used to stop by there and came to visit her in order to converse in a gossipy manner while I was let to play with her two daughters who were much younger than I. Jozef always was happy and funny. That is why father had an idea concerning which he told him over and over again that Jozef could become beyond question a well-known actor in comedies.

As the picture (right) indicates, the road to the left northward leads to Maczylin. The people's strips of land in Maczylin beyond commence from the highway and then cross the road that leads to Vilno up to the forest. The highway straight eastward beyond Maczylin leads to the village of Terebejno. Our

Wierka and Jan Radziwill with their baby Kanusia.

To the left is Maczylin and straight ahead is the village of Terebejno.

strip of land, however, was situated behind the residence of Mr. Kanawal, which is seen in the picture as the last buildings on the right side of the road next to the forest. In line with the strip of land deep in the forest there was also our meadow. In the valley beyond the stream on the right side of the highway in one of those dwellings there lived Mr. Grygorcewicz with his beautiful wife, daughter and three sons. Mr. Grygorcewicz was a bailiff working for the government. He also collected taxes, but for delinquent payers he had power to impound their assets, which he was often compelled to exercise.

Jan Radziwill and Wierka, harmoniously joined together in love, now became delightful parents of a little baby girl named Danusia. Danusia brought to them inexpressible joy and a uniting force to hold them together incessantly. It promoted great pleasure indeed for one to see them being so immensely happy. Surely, this couple measured up to a standard for other neighbors who were vivacious under the mode of divine peace and prosperity where the happiness is dominant. The statement of relative likeness in this case can be compared to the principle of fire, which is represented in the triangle, bound by three corners that symbolize three essential elements, namely oxygen, combustion and material. By removing anyone of these three elements, it will extinguish the fire. Likewise, by removing any one of those elements, whether it be peace, prosperity or happiness, it will destroy a means of supporting one's existence, that is to say, livelihood.

Alfons Klimowicz also became father to a baby girl. He lived with his wife and baby on Nowogrodek Street between the town square and the Poplawski Street near the residence of Jan Radziwill's mother, that is, on the south side of the street.

At this time Korzenko was still visiting Bronislawa, but unfortunately was affected with an alcoholic drink now more than ever. Bronislawa at this point found herself in the state of uneasy feeling, knowing that something bad could happen, trying to avoid him at all costs and remain concealed. His character had completely changed on account of intoxication, and thus he became extremely abusive.

In June as usual father and Antoni Szarzanowicz prepared themselves to do some haymaking in a tract of grassland by the canal in Trascianka. When they got ready, father went to the common grazing land to put his horse in harness, but among all the horses grazing there he could not find his, which was brown with a long black tail. After two days he still could not find his horse, but on the third day during the night it rained, and when he came to the pasture ground he could not believe his eyes. Because he was standing right by his horse, which was painted white with lime and its tail had been cut off and was losing blood. The rain washed off the lime and therefore he recognized his horse. Then father wondered, who could do such a thing? Of course, it came to his mind, no one else than the wicked one, Leon Szarzanowicz. As it luckily happened, not far ahead toward the municipal building there was a merry-go-round revolving with wooden horses on which children were riding for amusement. When father got closer, he noticed that Leon was riding there also. So father asked the owner of the carousel how long the boy had been riding here. The owner answered, all day. Consequently, after a thorough investigation concerning this action, father learned that Leon had made a deal with the owner of the carousel. The deal was that Leon had promised to supply him with a sufficient amount of horse tail essential for his wooden horses, for which Leon was granted a free ride all day on his carousel. These findings no doubt upset my father very much and it made him move with unrestrained anger to beat Leon hard with a strap again.

In the first part of June Father finally with his friend set out for Trascianka. On arrival there, they constructed a shelter on the east side of the canal and started cutting the grass. At sunset they came to the shelter to prepare the last meal of the day. Suddenly, they heard an unusual human voice on the other side of an artificial waterway, where along the side there was a footpath mainly made by wild animals in this Wilderness of Naliboki. No humans, especially at this hour when it was growing dusky, could be expected there. Yet, when they both had a good look, they really got scared. Indeed, they saw a middle-aged woman jogging nude along on the footpath, with very long hair and with her hands removing the leaves from branches of shrubs and putting them in her mouth, which she was masticating just like chewing gum. At the same time she was also uttering unfamiliar words, repeatedly saying, "ERE MENE NA ROBILO." Father said he became so afraid that he had to grab an ax for protection. But as innocent as it may sound, this nude woman jogged along the footpath southward throughout the wilderness without even an act of noticing them on the other side of the canal. However, after a fortnight when father with his friend Antoni arrived home from the haymaking, we read an article in the local newspaper about this naked woman. Apparently she had escaped from an asylum in Lubcz and was recaptured in Mir, a woman of Jewish nationality. It was reported that she was found unharmed, and that was an incredible phenomenon, because she was exposed to danger of all sorts of wild predators in the wilderness through which she advanced barefoot and naked, a journey of approximately one hundred kilometers.

Father did a lot of business with Jewish people, namely Mr. Chaim, Mr. Machlis, Mr. Sanagoga, Mr. Here and many others. Mr. Chaim and Mr. Sanagoga often used to hire a four-wheeled horse-drawn vehicle for carrying goods necessary for their stores from the city, Stolpce. Sometimes they kept our horse for their need as long as a week or so. But this time Mr. Sanagoga returned from Stolpce after two days. He told my parents the most dreadful news that there was a city massacre. The night before he arrived to Stolpce, all the people there were filled with extreme terror. A great number of policemen one night were murdered by members of the Russian Communist Party. They had clandestinely crossed the frontier line during the night and they knew exactly where to find each member of the police force in Stolpce. Some policemen were found and killed even in the houses of their fiancees. Soon the story about this malicious and intentional murder appeared in the local newspapers, which shocked the people despairingly because there was nothing anybody could do about it.

Now the war seemed more imminent since Germany and Japan were linked in the Anti-Comintern

Pact, which Italy joined also in this year 1937. Comintern was an international organization formed in 1919 for extending the scope of Marxist socialism, which happened to be at the peak of success in Russia. Thus hostility toward Russia was the prime idea of Hitler's foreign policy. All Nazi propaganda against Communism and the Soviet Union continued to be in progress, not to mention the internal German National persecution of Jews, which remained top secret. In spite of the fact that nobody knew about the holocaust in Germany at this time, Jews themselves in Poland were aware of this fact because it was passed through to them by their relatives living in Germany. Sudden fear caused by awareness of danger urged irresistibly many Jews to flee from Poland to Palestine. Some Jewish families in Naliboki, including Mr. Iskol with his family, emigrated to Palestine that year. He was Naliboki's most prominent blacksmith. That is why the people kept saying in reference to his emigration that Mr. Iskol ran away to Palestine; that is to say, ran away from some danger, but what danger nobody knew. So it was a complete mystery. The question was, why were Jews all of a sudden fleeing to the Holy Land?

The regathering of Jews, the twelve tribes of Israel in Palestine, was foretold by the prophet Ezekiel, who stated that God, the God of Israel, would collect Jews and gather them from the lands among which they had been scattered and that God would give them the soil of Israel. When they arrived there, they would remove all disgusting things and God would give them one heart, and a new spirit to come to life in order that they may walk in his own statutes and keep his own judicial decisions and actually carry them out, so that they may really become his people and he himself may become their God. And Gog will be bound to come up against my people Israel, said God, like clouds to cover the land, and in the final part of the days it would occur, that is, in the time of the end. The nations in the four corners of the earth, or the world powers, with its leader Gog will bring the last hostile attack upon the Kingdom of God. Therefore, Ezekiel's prophecy reveals that this attack is what triggers the complete wiping out of Satanic forces by means of God's awesome power.

At this particular time it was noticed that the Jewish people rapidly returning to Palestine from all European countries including USSR, which was most unusual because their compatriot Karl Heinrich Marx happened to be the inventor of Communism. Lenin, or Vladimir Ilyich Lenin, studied with extreme effort and concentration the works of Karl Marx and his friend Friedrich Engels. Consequently, on November 20, 1922, at the plenary meeting of Moscow the Soviet delivered his last speech, which he ended with the words: "Out of Russia of the New Economic Policy will emerge a Socialist Russia." After his death on January 27, 1924, Lenin became a national Soviet shrine. Now under Stalin's guidance and leadership of the Union of Soviet Socialist Republics, many Jews in Russia were high officials of the Communist Party who embraced power and security for the Jewish group in USSR Yet in spite of this fact they were relinquishing a claim of their own making and even from Russia were emigrating to Palestine. That is why the gentiles thought that the God of Israel would execute his judgments upon the nations in the four corners of the earth and the end of the world was near. Nevertheless, the Jews knew different. They had learned that Hitler's entire policy was Anti-Judaic and Anti-Communistic, which is a theory of social change advocating a classless society, public ownership of almost all productive property, and the sharing of the products of labor, and was created by a Jew. However, concerning the Anti-Judaic knowledge they did not have the courage to reveal to the gentiles on account of prejudicial opinion that were held against their nation.

It was most important that immediately they learned the fact that in Germany Hitler already had started the genocidal course of action, which was the systematic extermination of the entire population of the Jewish race.

Now, such an inaccurate interpretation of Ezikiel's prophecy was made by the majority of Bible readers, including my grandfather. Here, however, a correct interpretation concerning the Gog is evidently cryptic or symbolic, not being that of any known human king or leader. Both names, "Gog and Magog," are shown to apply to "those nations in the four corners of the earth" that allow themselves to be misled by Satan after he is released from the symbolic "abyss." Since other texts show that the millennial rule of Christ brings an end to national rule and divisions, it would appear that such "nations" are the product of rebellion against his earthwide dominion. They advance "over the breadth of the earth to encircle" the camp of the holy ones and the beloved city. This comes after the millennial rule over earth by Christ Jesus has reached its completion.

The use of the names "Gog and Magog" evidently serve to emphasize certain similarities in this postmillennial situation with that of the earlier assault (prior to Satan's being abyssed). Among these similarities is that, both in Ezekiel and Revelation, the opposers are numerous (those in Revelation being of an indefinite number, "as the sand of the sea"), the attack is the result of a widespread conspiracy, and it is directed against God's servants in a state of great prosperity. So the use of "Gog and Magog" to describe those led into a postmillennial rebellion is very fitting. Their end is absolute destruction. - Rev. 20: 9, 10, 14.

Nonetheless, people such as my grandfather understood in accordance to their own way of thinking about the significance of the sacred and inspired writings in God's word, the Bible, thus they were not far off from the rational perception accompanied by feeling that something wrong was about to manifest. Yet they did not know the fact that the Second World War was at the threshold, concerning which Jesus said to his disciples, "For nation will rise against nation and kingdom against kingdom, and there will be food shortages and earthquakes in one place after another. All these things are a beginning of pangs of distress. Then people will deliver you up to tribulation and will kill you, and you will be objects of hatred by all the nations on account of my name. Then, also, many will be stumbled and will betray one another. And many false prophets will arise and mislead many, and because of the increasing of lawlessness the love of the greater number will cool off. But he that has endured to the end is the one that will be saved. And this good news of the kingdom will be preached in all the inhabited earth for a witness to all the nations, and then the end will come."

John's vision depicted a war in heaven in which Michael (Jesus Christ), immediately after the "birth of the male child" who was to rule the nations with a rod of iron, led the armies in heaven in a war against the dragon, Satan, the outcome of which was the hurling of the devil and his angels to the earth. A loud voice in heaven then announced, "Now has come to pass the salvation and the power and the Kingdom of our God and the authority of his Christ." This brought relief and joy to the angels, but presaged troubles, including wars, for the earth, as the declaration continued: "Woe for the people, because the devil was come down to you, having great anger, knowing he has a short period of time."

From the time of the hurling of the devil and his demons to the earth, we had World War I in 1914, after which now another war seemed to be inevitable.

Based upon the people's keen observation it was easily recognizable that now more than ever radical political changes started taking place in the world. Our people in Naliboki began to wonder why there was so much distress in the earth, why the world was so unsettled, why, with all our peacemaking agencies, did the fear of war hunt the people, and why, with the many scientific advances and inventions for enjoyable living, did most people not get the benefits of them and living conditions became more difficult.

Since such is the case when a threat to our peace and security is palpably true, people here started pouring to the church to such an extent that there was no room inside the church, and still the great crowd was piled up outside the churchyard. The new church, however, already had walls formed almost half way up. There was always much more people when Prelate Bajko was celebrating the divine service. Indeed, he had an extraordinary intelligence surpassing that of most intellectually superior individuals, a person who exerted a strong influence over others. He was a wonderful lover of wisdom. When Bajko delivered his discourse based on a text of the Bible, the people in his parish were amazed. His pulpit had to be placed outside by the exit of the church so that everyone could hear his sermon. I remember that when other priests officiated, the elderly ones failed to keep their participation for they were falling in a state of sleep, which was contrary in Prelate Bajko's situation at his divine service. Concerning the fear of war, Prelate Bajko advocated urgently that we all must repent and be more prayerful; we must keep on asking God's forgiveness and asking him to bring us not into temptation, but to deliver us from the wicked one.

On one of such Sunday after the divine service when people started to go out from the church my sister Waclawa found a man's wallet crammed with money but without personal papers. At home she told our parents that she had found money in the church. Father then ascertained the total, which was ten thousand Polish "zloty," equal in value to one hundred sixty-six head of cattle, or ten European tons of sugar obtained from the juice of the sugar beet in Poland. Under this factor, for a moment my parents did not know what to do with the money. However, as soon as they calmed down they decided to take the money to the church and to hand it over to Prelate Bajko. And that is what they did. Prelate Bajko in its stead during his sermon announced to the people that someone had lost his money which was found on the church ground. The one who had lost it should please go to the residence of Mr. Wilhelm Klimowicz.

It was not long until a certain individual came to our house and made his acquaintance face to face with our parents. He said that he was a sole proprietor of the mill in which grain was ground at Dalaticzy, a village that was the first one from Naliboki on the road to Iwieniec. Then he said that he was the one who lost 10,000 zloty. Naturally there was no doubt in my parents' minds that his claim was genuine, and at this moment they directed him to Prelate Bajko. But as a token, a reward was given in partial fulfillment of this obligation; he made a promise to my father that he would grind our grain free of charge for life. And so it came about that from this time on father had his grain ground without making equivalent return for his service in accordance to assurance given that he would perform this specified act. Father used to take me to the mill, and after some time he would send me alone to this mill. When I arrived there, the owner had his men sent to do the job and took me to the waiting room, where I slept during the night. Because the mill was always engaged fully, usually at daybreak the owner put me on the wagon and sent me home with a full load of flour and coarsely crushed grain.

Because of the uncertain future, father now more than ever was extremely curious to find out what that old man from Terebejno had to say regarding this present perplexing situation for which it was difficult to work out the correct explanation and precisely what the future held for us. Since by now he became well-known as an inspired predictor, in order to invite this old man to the house father proposed to the relatives to cause a social gathering for entertainment concerning this remarkable purpose. Eventually all relatives, friends and neighbors came to be present at the party in our house on a Sunday when this old man was walking home from the church, passing by our house. My father and grandfather came close to him and asked him courteously to be present at this party, which he had no idea was prepared specially for him. But surprisingly enough, the old man was pleased to accept our invitation. So he came into the house and saw indeed a party with lots of food, drink and people. While everybody was in the process of eating and drinking, grandfather approached him privately and said to him, "We heard that you, sir, can foretell the future. So, please, would you tell us what will be in time to come from your point of view, since there is already so much distress in the earth at this present time?"

Then he said, "The things that I am able to tell you, you may not believe me, and yet even I myself because of my age may not live long enough to see its fulfillment in order to remind you I told you so. Nonetheless, I am going to tell you that you may know and remember me:

"First, here shall be a persecution where one citizen shall turn against another.

"Then, a great number of people shall see the sign, in one place, and after in another.

"Two fires shall swipe the town, but the last one shall give an ultimate blow.

"Very cruel men shall occupy those two locations where the signs originally occurred. These men possessed by demons shall absorb a great number of people, so that they shall become alike, and soon after, these men shall cause to determine the last day of Naliboki.

"After those signs, the column (SLUP) of St. John shall be defiled and the church shall become like a stable set apart for lodging horses, and this shall be caused by impious, ungodly men who shall arrive here first in the furnaces; these shall shake the ground and shall bring terror to entire region.

"Then many people shall be seized and carried away. Naliboki shall become a capital place of corpses.

"And all these things which must come to pass shall be executed in the range of the devil's number."

After he finished saying these things the party was over. Our relatives, I noticed, were stunned, as in a state of deep preoccupation or absence of mind. So I gazed at the face of my father and then at the faces of my uncles. Their faces were sad; nobody was saying anything. I only imagined that Uncle Waclaw was opulent; therefore he had a good reason to worry. Likewise, Uncle Jozef and Michal had a brand new husbandry built that presented an appearance of beauty.

Consequently, the old man got up from his chair with his hat in his hands and said, "Now, gentlemen, I must go home, and I thank you very much for behaving in a kind and generous manner toward the guests. It was indeed, a warm reception."

Then father said, "Oh, sir, please, you do not have to walk. I shall give you a ride home."

"Not likely," said he. "In the first place I came on foot to the church, and in the same usual way I intend to get home."

Yet his refusal to ride home was not acceptable in my father's mind because to begin with he invited him, and above all he procrastinated his journey home. Therefore, he felt, he was under obligation. In that case, he had to approach him in accordance with reason and to argue logically. Father said, "You see, sir, I have to settle a business transaction with my neighbor, Mr. Kanowal, in Maczylin. So I must go there now anyway."

"Well then," he said, "in that case I shall ride with you."

As soon as father put the harness on the horse, they left for Terebejno. When father came back home I asked him what the old man meant by saying that ungodly men shall arrive to Naliboki in the furnaces. Because I did not understand, for example, how our furnace, which did not have wheels and in fact was attached to the house, could move. Father replied, saying, "I do not know, my son, what he meant by this remark."

Presently, Witold Baszuro was visiting father more than ever to discuss the fear of war and particularly this prediction of the old man, because according to him it did not measure up to his expectations. By now he had saved a great deal of money for his new husbandry that he intended to build behind the cemetery, and the old man's theory was contradictory to his personal desired end. So he argued with my father incessantly, pretending that it could not be true what the old man had predicted.

During the intervening time, Elizabeth, Elzbieta Walon, who was living opposite our residence, suddenly became ill, and also a girl of the same age in the Grygorcewicz family, whose dwelling was on the corner of Stolpce Street and Nowogrodek Street. This family was relative to the bailiff, Mr. Grygorcewicz. We used to play together and were in the same class in school together. It was not long, about a period of two weeks, when these two beautiful girls suffered death. Mr. Walon, by the loss of his only child eight years old, was driven into despair. Because of this tragedy, he abandon hope that there is a God almighty, able to do all things. He said, "If there was such God, he would not take my only child." As a result of his loss, indeed, he was on the verge of losing his mind; even all the neighbors felt extremely bad about it. Elizabeth's coffin was placed in an empty room facing our window. During the day and night there was a candle giving off light placed on her coffin where her body was laid.

Soon after Elizabeth's burial, one night when I turned my eyes to the direction of Mr. Walon's window where the coffin was placed in that room, I saw a candle was still emitting light and burning. It scared me and I told my parents to look and to figure out why that candle was still burning. After father's full investigation, however, he learned that in that empty room there was no coffin, and no candle was supposed to be burning. Yet, in spite of father's conviction, the candle at night kept on glowing for some time, and there was no explanation to clarify the reason.

At the death of these two young girls, the bells in the church tower above were gave forth a ringing sound, loud as thunder and longer than usual. All people in the Parish of Naliboki became aware of some sense that a human life had been embodied in a tragic event. Consequently, more people than in an ordinary manner came to the church on Sunday in order to be informed what really happened. I was there with my parents seated on a bench next to the portable altar that an old man from Terebejno had made out of a match sticks. With this altar there was placed a standard of white silk, upon which there was an image of Mary, Mother of God. It was a large and very beautiful picture in chromatic colors. It appeared to be a real person. I could not take my eyes off it because of its divine influence operating in man.

Chapter VI

POLISH YOUTH

In 1935 Marshal Jozef Pilsudski left Poland with an armament consisting of 250 small tanks and about same amount of airplanes, heavy artillery mobiled by horse power, cavalry and infantry being all that was adequate for any need in those days. However, during his absence Poland failed to strive against her neighbors for superiority and thus remained in a state of cessation.

The current ruler of Poland, Marshal Edward Smigly-Rydz was contrary to that of the king, Casimir III the Great, who ruled Poland from 1333 thirty-three years, during the dynasty of Piast. He was son of Ladislas Lokietek, the last of the House of Piast. During his reign the royal power was increased and the nation was consolidated by reorganization of administration and justice by promulgation in 1347 of a code of laws known as the Statutes of Wislica. But one of his main actions that contributed to a change in Polish history was indeed the fact that he had found Poland built of wood and he left his country built of stone, unlike Smigly-Rydz, who was disinclined to act due to his ill health and left Poland in the state he found it, built of wood as it were.

Now in 1938, Colonel Jozef Beck, the minister of foreign affairs, being of German ancestral derivation, could be compared as similar to Stanislaw August Poniatowski because after John Sobieski's death in 1696 the Polish throne was occupied for seven decades by foreigners in the persons of the German elector of Saxony. During that period of time Saxons entirely ruined the country, which led to three partitions of Poland. The first partition took place after eight years during Poniatowski's reign, and at the final partition, which caused the extinction of Poland in 1795, the king resigned on account of the fact that his job was well done as a Saxon. It was, however, immediately evident that the evil force behind that effect was the LIBERUM VETO, but who was the actual agent that throughout the period of 123 years of foreign domination soaked the country's soil in Polish blood by useless insurrections? This one yet remained to be identified.

Likewise, since history repeated itself, Jozef Beck adopted Hitler's policy in order to soak the country's soil in the blood of Polish Jews. By pleasing his friend Hitler, he introduced to Poland a new organization that was called "MLODA POLSKA," concerning which Polish people knew nothing. But Mloda Polska, or Young Poland organization, sounded most desirable, so many young men in Naliboki like elsewhere in the country joined voluntarily for some unknown end. They were given dark blue uniforms to wear and were trained to march, etc., but when these members of the Young Poland organization became qualified the power and authority was invested with them. Unfortunately, by the time they realized that this power and authority was designed solely against Jews, it was too late to withdraw from this evil and morally corrupt organization.

They were moved to exercise their power and authority over Jews in Naliboki in such a manner that when they marched through their section they splashed Jewish doors with red paint and wrote slogans such as "Begone with the Jews and Communism." These members of Mloda Polska also distributed pamphlets spreading propaganda against the Jews and the Soviet Union. A booklet I remember issued was entitled

"LEPIEJ ZYC W POLSKIM WIEZIENIU NIZ W SOWIECKIM RAJU," which means, "it is better to live in the Polish prison than in Soviet's paradise." Inside this booklet there were caricatures of Jewish businessmen seated on sacks of gold, claiming Jews were parasites and a menace to Polish society.

This organization of Mloda Polska was in fact equivalent to "Hitler's Junger" or "Deutsche Junger" in Germany, designed solely for the same purpose, supposedly to protect the Nazi regime from the Jews and Communism, and to carry out the intentional genocide with respect to the Jewish national group. It is therefore proper to call this organization in the English language the Polish Youth.

This was in the beginning of 1938, when Jozef Beck established the Polish Youth Organization in the Free State of Poland, the act of baseness, vileness and moral turpitude that persecuted unjustly our citizens, Hebrew neighbors. Indeed, this evil force acted contrary to our legislative policies and purposes already declared by the legislative body or such as are devolved upon it by the organic law of its existence.

There was a large group of men from Naliboki who joined the Polish Youth Organization, among whom was Jan Radziwill, Alfons Lojko and Jozef Kosciukiewicz as participants in this abominable devil's work. They were conned into this shameful and disgraceful organization, but by the time they realized what it was truly for it was too late for anyone to make a withdrawal. Of course, if anyone would try to quit, he could be then charged with desertion and treason, a betrayal of allegiance that might be punishable by death. So, they were trapped and had no right, power or liberty of choosing, but just to go along with it and pretend they were Polish Youth in the blue uniforms marching through Naliboki.

Our friend, a Jewish lady, the manager of the post office, finally came to us to tell my parents that she had arrangements made to emigrate to Palestine. Being a psychic, one who is sensitive to extrasensory phenomena, she told my mother that it was terrible for the Jews now to suffer persecution in Poland. However, she said it would not take long to thwart an opponent's action and turn the situation to his disadvantage. Soon it would be that the Jews would wash our feet in water to purify them from defilement and guilt, and our people would drink this water. Shortly after this lady emigrated to Palestine. My parents were sad losing such a remarkable friend and neighbor, but for her it meant surviving, the optimum regarding which at this particular time we had no comprehension.

One Sunday in early spring Prelate Bajko announced from the pulpit during his sermon that the money gathered from people's donations for building a new church was stolen from the altar sometime that week. Alarmed, people of the parish became ashamed of their own community, not knowing who could be responsible for such an evil deed. However, this unprecedented act upset the progression of, and thus interrupted the construction of, this vital new church. Everyone in Naliboki endeavored to figure out who actually did the stealing, but their efforts were of no avail. My father suspected Leon, yet without proof or clear evidence, he said, before you want to judge someone, first you must judge yourself.

One Monday just before my exam to pass from the second to the third class in school, I came to school, except our teacher was absent and our class was moved to the third class, which as a result became crowded. As usual we commenced the class with prayer and song, "Kiedy ranne wstaja zorze," when the morning rising dawn. We all were standing and facing our teacher, who was standing by the desk, behind which there was a blackboard and the wall upon which was a cross bearing an effigy of Christ crucified. As soon as we finished praying and singing, the teacher told us to sit down, and then we followed a regular course of instruction. Subsequently, the classroom suddenly became bright. Someone in the classroom uttered with a shout, "Cud! A miracle!" Another pupil uttered a piercing cry, as of surprise, "Mother of God?" The teacher became troubled emotionally, I noticed. Some pupils had fallen on their bent knees; other pupils stood up. The door opened. The teachers, caretaker and other pupils from different grades came into our classroom with a feeling of mingled surprise and curiosity. Many claimed that they perceived with their own eyes Mary, the Mother of God, with a bright light all around her. Yet, I was looking intensely, but could see nothing on the wall where the vision occurred, except that the wall was somewhat brighter than it was supposed to be.

This event in school, which appeared to be neither a part nor result of any known natural law or agency, was therefore often attributed to a supernatural source and became widely known throughout the Parish of Naliboki. The people began to talk about it and tried to make application to it. Therefore, there was widely spread gossip that the Sibylline Books contained a prediction made under divine influence and direction for our time. Sibyl, named by the Greeks and Romans, was a prophetess that was inspired by Apollo or by some other deity. But there were several sibyls in antiquity, of whom one, Herophile, prophesied the Trojan War. However, the Sibylline Books supposedly contained prophecies for our present time also, and that is why people in Naliboki gobbled a great deal about it. They endeavored to compare it to the current affairs of the world. Then they switched their opinions toward Nostradamus, who was born at St. Remi in Provence on December 13, 1503, of Jewish descent and became most famous professing to foretell the future and interpret the influence of the heavenly bodies upon the destinies of men. So, people tried to fit his predictions to nowadays to perceive what would happen in the near future.

Due to the severe persecution, a cruel disposition with respect to Jews because of race was taking place in the large cities in Poland. So, on account of mercilessness and inhumanity, my granduncle Benedikt chose to quit his job as an organist in one such city and came home for good. Yet he found that even at his birthplace this Polish Youth Organization was at large indeed, but at least not as severe as elsewhere. Here, although a ten-o'clock curfew at night was imposed upon the Jews, no Jew was ever flogged and no willful and malicious destruction of property occurred, except that some of their doors and gates were splashed with red paint, a color resembling that of blood. Nevertheless, in the eyes of great uncle the whole concept of this machination set up against the Jewish nation, or for that matter any other nation, was abominable and not scriptural. Therefore, he claimed that anyone relating to or derived from Christ or his doctrine could not be a participant in such an organization.

My great uncle Benedikt made his home in Naliboki permanently, and he lived here with his two adorable sisters and niece, namely Orszula, Alzusia and Regina. He enjoyed very much working in his orchard, which he had planted several years previously. He made some experiments in grafting to obtain different varieties of fruit on the same single tree. He experienced pleasure in making new violins, by spending considerable time in the forest looking for the Picea-excelsa most suitable to form a sounding box of this seasoned wood. At home, he played violin and piano, and in the church he tuned the organ and from time to time played on Sunday during the mass, helping an organist who was here regularly employed. When he played a musical setting for some of the fixed portions of liturgy and sung in reply to the officiating priest the words of scriptures, he knew them by heart. And indeed it was of a nature to excite wonder. Frequently he was invited by the Jewish friends to perform on his violin their classical music. He also enjoyed to play the same at our home, which father admired since he was a musician himself, but was more familiar with the Russian music than Jewish.

Mother's youngest brother, Boleslaw Lojko had completed his seminary of theology and was granted to be a Roman Catholic priest. He was allowed to wear a cassock, a close-fitting vestment, usually black, reaching to the feet, and worn by priests. He had a picture taken in Wilno and sent it to his parents, which we all admired to see him being a priest, except the fact that in his letter he wrote that he was not going to take vows and enter the religious order. Instead, he had decided to devote his life to incessant erudition, and in this way he began to study the law. He did not even bother to come home that year to spend his vacation, knowing his parents would be disappointed in their expectations. As he thought to keep everything free from agitation and for the sake of serenity, Uncle Boleslaw chose to stay in Wilno, and as it happened, we never saw him again in Naliboki.

Eugenjusz Klimowicz arrived home for his vacation from university in Warsaw. After a few days of rest his friends gathered together outside his house with Eugenjusz in a beautiful evening for entertainment and to welcome guests. There was conversation and laughter, and of course they all were singing some pleasant Polish songs. Eugenjusz brought his guitar out and they sang with an accompaniment.

Boleslaw Lojko finished his theological seminary at Wilno in 1938.

The sound of their voices and the guitar filled the gratifying environment. The neighbors came out onto their porches to relax and listen to the most enchanting melodies.

Father as usual made his way to cut the grass for hay in the meadow located next to the common ground in low land. From this meadow one could easily observe over the land of Ciechanowicz the people who traveled on the road to Iwieniec. As father commenced to mow the grass by scythe, Jan Radziwill and Eugenjusz came also with their scythes to help. But during their work they were chatting and laughing. And it was not long till Benedikt came to see what they all were doing. The day was gorgeous, filled with the light and warmth of the sun. So they all gathered together and sat down on the grass. Father lit his cigarette, but none of the others smoked because they did not approve of bad addictive habits. However,

Eugenjusz Klimowicz at home on his vacation from the university in 1938.

they began to have a serious political conversation regarding activities of those engaged in controlling or seeking to control a government. In this respect Eugenjusz reassured that Beck would fail to achieve his power over Poland because of his obvious tyrannized policy joined with that of Hitler, which stood contrary to the nature of national conception. He said, "Throughout history we struggled to obtain the power of the will to follow the dictates of its unrestricted choice, and to direct the external acts of the individual without restraint, coercion or control from other persons." His motion was seconded unanimously and Benedikt asserted that the fact was so. Then they changed the subject and started talking concerning Wierka, since she was in the state of being pregnant and about to give birth to another new baby. Radziwill was delightful in expectation of this marvelous occasion, and of course at the fact that his beloved Wierka was feeling very well at her pregnancy. Consequently, by sunset the meadow was cut down completely and they all separated home. But a few days after a baby boy was born; the parturition was easy and both Wierka and Jan were extremely happy.

Every time Korzenko's engineering construction of bridges was near Naliboki he was a more frequent visitor to fiancee Bronislawa. At first, he conducted himself in a proper manner, but after a while, when he undertook heavy drinking of an alcoholic beverage, he began to be most vituperative, to the extent that Bronislawa was compelled to keep herself out of sight. One particular time she sneaked to our house and came to hide behind the stove, where I was playing with the firewood that was kept very dry to start the fire in the stove in order to prepare food. When Korzenko entered our house, my aunt became terrified and she moved farther behind me to hide on this elevated warm place. Yet as he appeared by the stove facing us, he spotted her hiding behind me, and he kept calling her to come down, but because she was not coming down he took a piece of firewood and threw it at her. Unfortunately, he missed and instead hit me in my forehead. As a result, blood covered my face and I began to scream. Suddenly father walked into the house, and when he saw my face covered with blood he grabbed Korzenko and punched him with all the way outside. He continued doing so throughout the yard and then on the street till he beat him unconscious. Finally, he rolled him off the street and down into a ditch, where Korzenko could remain for a while. Now, father came back to the house to get his instrument that he used to slaughter pigs, intending to go finish him off there. Of course, mother and Bronislawa, noticing his intention, began begging, saying, "Please, Wilhelm, think about us and children. By this act of yours, they surely will become orphans, and we all shall see you no more. He is not worth it." Mother said, "Please do not go," and at the same time with tears and lamentation we all held him down. In the meantime father calmed down, took a seat and lit his cigarette.

For curiosity, a while later mother took a pail to fetch water from the spring that flowed to the lake, and as she passed by that ditch she noticed that Korzenko was not there. As it happened, from this time on Korzenko was never seen again. But concerning my forehead, a blood vessel was cut above the eyebrow and therefore I was covered with blood; other than that, the injury had been minor, and family suggested that I was just lucky.

Now, throughout the summer season we had planned a movement of troops in large-scale tactical exercises simulating war; it was concentrated in the eastern part of country at the Polish-Russian border. This large organized body of men armed for military action on land moved through Naliboki during several weeks. Among this army there was infantry, cavalry, artillery and all other heavy equipment mobilized by horse power. The soldiers stopped only at lunch hour or supper time to have a meal, and immediately they moved on as the convoy followed behind. Watching them passing through, some elders in Naliboki kept repeating, "Well, it is a shame." Some asked why. "Because they should be passing through like this not now, but last year. Then at least they would prevent the Bolshevik's massacre in Stolpce."

Many have asked why all of a sudden maneuvers had to take place at the eastern border? But soon it became crystal clear. Notwithstanding the fact that based upon the recent anti-Communist propaganda and the reality that Beck and Hitler had intentions to wage war against USSR, therefore it was essential to maneuver Polish troops in that order, which were temporarily equipped only for tactical exercises, not for actual war against the Soviet Union. For such a purpose, however, measures had been taken by Hitler in advance in order to face the USSR with the modern arms of his own standard of supreme perfection.

At the end of July usually every year the weather promises to be fair. Some people would begin to examine their standing crops in the fields to see if they were ready for harvest, others prepared themselves to gather a ripened crop of grain. Generally speaking, at this particular time one could see that there were many people getting busy in the land, and as the days went by a considerable extent of harvesting work had already been done. One could see some fields covered with standing sheaves of wheat or rye that were drying up and becoming available to be stored in the people's barns.

Suddenly, on the first day in August, a rumor was spread throughout the Parish of Naliboki that the Virgin Mary had appeared to the certain number of people who were working in their wheat field by the forest in Maczylin. Of course, the people started to behave without equivocation or subtlety, pouring in great numbers to Maczylin with eager expectation to see the miracle because of the anxiety people felt that something evil of the political system was about to be manifested. Everyone was tense and

In Maczylin at the entrance of the forest the Virgin Mary appeared repeatedly the first week of August 1938.

in an emotional state characterized by fear and apprehension with apparent change because the world happened to be so unsettled, therefore they were desperate for relief with the intervention of something supernatural. Besides, anything miraculous is so marvelous and extraordinary that it is usually attributed to divine agency, provided one has the faith, and one will continue hoping even when it may be in vain. Subsequently, the people gathered together on this site of an event that appeared to be neither a part nor result of any known natural law or agency, and therefore was often attributed to a supernatural source, where many individuals beheld the wonderful Virgin Mary. Yet, a large number of persons did look intensely, but saw nothing. However, those to whom the Virgin Mary appeared described the vision by saying merely that there was a great light in contrast with the forest, in which the Virgin Mary was standing with her hands crossed together and her head sloped downward in a humbled and sorrowful inclination with tears in her eyes. The vision was clearly perceived by the eye to whom it was destined to appear, and as a matter of fact each and every one gave an identical picture by means of words.

In the course of this wonderful miracle our family came to Maczylin in order to cut the rye with a sickle. Our rye and wheat was growing by the forest on the left side of the road, a few strips of land away from the place where the miracle had occurred. While mother and her friends were cutting the rye and father was tying and piling up the sheaves in fifteens, I suddenly noticed that a lot of people kept rushing on the other side of the road. When I told my parents to see what was happening, we all went over the stubble field with anticipation to see the miracle. Some individuals knelt down with an utterance that causes wonder. "It's a miracle!" they noticed. But as I stood there among others and gazed, I saw nothing except an unusual brightness that shone against the forest northward. Yet, I thought that it was just a reflection from the sun, shining directly on the trees, but again I was not sure about it. However, not one person from our group was able to see the Virgin Mary as we all expected, notwithstanding the fact that this sign kept appearing during the first week in August 1938 exclusively.

By inherent nature, after that week people spent a great deal of time talking about this miracle. Many, of course, professed they saw the Virgin Mary, and all those gave an identical description. Among those were father's two first cousins, Edward Wolan and his brother, Benedikt Klimowicz; moreover there were Mr. Kostus, our organist, Prelate Bajko, Leon and a great number of other persons. Prelate Bajko repeatedly made reference to the event each Sunday during his sermon, and after it became known widely as "The Miracle of Maczylin." But how far it was spread or if it was ever reported to the Vatican by Prelate Bajko, no one will ever know.

Leon told his father that he too saw the Virgin Mary in Maczylin, and that being in direct contact with the vision, he said, caused him to experience a torment within himself that was difficult to endure. Then he said, "I cannot help, it father, I must confess my terrible sin and repent for what I have done, which I promise I shall do it no more. I am the one who stole that money from the altar in our church and hid it in the old tree outside the house."

His father said, "Son, go and bring this money into the house."

Leon at once climbed the tree and brought the money home and placed it on the table. After his father examined the contents of the box carefully for defects and found none, he told Leon, "Son, take this money with you and first go to the priest to have a confession in church, and after your confession give this box with the money to the priest." As a result, from this time on Leon had changed and became a new person, and he was harmoniously joined with all the people in the Parish of Naliboki.

This fundamental record of events that led to "The Last Day of Naliboki" rests on the plain truth, which in the proceeding chapters will appear to be stranger than fiction.

The foreign policy of Colonel Jozef Beck led him to take part with Hitler in the partitioning of Czechoslovakia in September 1938 in order to obtain Teschen. Under these circumstances, the government was unable then to prevent Poland from becoming the next partner of Nazi rapacity. It seemed at the time that Jozef Beck was the only figure who was causing Poland to be assimilated by Hitler. With respect to Teschen, he tried to convince the nation that it was Polish territory to begin with. Nevertheless, the Polish people refused to approve his idea of usurping part of their country by habitual aggressive action. In spite of national disagreement with Beck's policy, he pursued with Hitler to wage war against the Soviet Union, in return for which Poland would receive dominion over the Ukraine. But, because the Polish nonaggression pact was extended in June 1934 for ten mere years with the Soviet Union, and the alliance with France was regarded as the cornerstone of Polish diplomacy, the majority having the most power in the Free State of Poland (Rzecz Pospolita Polski) endeavored at any cost to preserve the peace. Hence, Polish leaders in the government, including the Cabinet, categorically contradicted Beck's plan of action. Obviously, Polish disapprobation caused Hitler to fly through the ceiling.

The nation as a whole felt guilty of having committed a moral offence against Czechoslovakia. Since Poland received her Christianity through the first king Mieszko during his reign from 960 to 992 C.E., there was never any hostility between two countries; thus we regarded Czechoslovaks as our neighbor and cousins based too on the similarity of language. Now, as it turn out to be after a millennium of affinity, Jozef Beck, a German descendant, spoiled Poland's useful relationship with its ally. Just like one who would give a bad nut to an elephant, whom then he never forget. Therefore one cannot be surprised that one day Czechoslovakia return the same deed to Poland.

During Maczylin's apparition in August, Edward Wolan incidentally became acquainted with a local young beautiful lady there because he claimed to have an experience of seeing the Virgin Mary in her sad state accompanied by tears.Consequently, both found themselves suitable to each other and continued the act of courting and wooing until the autumn season, when they decided to get married. The celebration of their marriage took place in Edward's residence, which was easily seen from our back window behind the existing chapelet, and actually was on the other side of Nowogrodek Street. Here, on the Sunday after the ceremony in church, the wedded couple in the company of a great number of people observed their happy event. There was lots of food, drink, music and dance, and the wedding lasted through the whole night; not till morning did our family return home. My parents talked about the bride and said that she brought her dowry to her husband from Maczylin, and that the act of endowing was well proportioned.

In close succession after Wolan's wedding, Christmas was approaching. Aunt Bronislawa's two cousins, Wierka Radziwill and Gabryjela Kosciukiewicz spent weeks in advance with her to acquire a knowledge of how to bake a great variety of delicious pastries and cakes. In the end, the whole residence became odiferous with those baking cakes extremely pleasant to the taste. Obviously, my mother too was involved with them in the first-rate preparation for the Christmas holidays. Finally, when Christmas arrived, together with the whole family I felt an instance of happiness like being actually in heaven. I was so excessively affected by emotion that I burst out in tears. Then father said, "Mietek, what is the matter, why are you crying?"

I replied, "Dad, because I am so happy that we all are together, and I cannot bear the thought that one day we shall be set asunder by an unforeseen occurrence or even death."

Chapter VII

THE YEAR 1939

Up to this time, due to the lack of a suitable and appropriate leader for this particular climax situation, Poland was left vulnerable. The people in Naliboki were saying, "If only Jozef Pilsudski remained in power, he would certainly be able to regulate and direct the European organized system of governments in order to cause the cessation of war." Perhaps by some antagonists he was called a socialist, but in his country he did not exercised the doctrines of those advocating this system. The Polish Republic (Rzeczpospolita Polski) was proclaimed on November 3, 1918, at Warsaw, and on November 18 a provisional government was formed with Jozef Pilsudski and Jedrzei Maraczewski as chief of state and premier, respectively. In spite of chaos and political confusion in the government, Marshal Pilsudski was the most powerful leader in the history of Poland. He successfully emerged from the trials of a most difficult and perplexing plight during the World War I. Subsequently in his government, for the sake of peace and prosperity, he was forced to put some opposed individuals in exile. Again, for that reason by some persons he was called a virtual dictator, but surprisingly enough, neither this nor that he was. In 1934 he agreed to a ten-year nonaggression pact with Nazi Germany in order to have easy access to use the left wing of the party, led by captain Ernst Röhm, head of the Brown Shirts, to an absolute removal of Adolf Hitler from power. Consequently united with Germany, Pilsudski then would cause two countries to advance against the Soviet Union to eliminate Communism in order to maintain the global peace. This would entirely change the course of history. Then there would be no World War II, no wholesale destruction and tremendous loss of life, no cold war, and no armamentary and planetary race that forced the world to economic decay and death of many by starvation.

Under such peaceful conditions an earthling man would have to be contented with the natural disasters in the future. Alas, it would be to the contrary of Jesus the Messiah's prophecy relating to his second presence, concerning which he foretold that in the last generation nation will rise against nation and kingdom against kingdom, meaning an inevitable destination of world wars that will be directed by a god of this system of things, Satan. Therefore, Pilsudski, like many other world leaders all along who endeavored to maintain the peace, unfortunately had to suffer timely death because he was standing in his way, in resistance to his machinations.

In this case, in order to please Satan, the devil subsequently, Adolf Hitler and Hermann Göring, with the assistance of the Elite Guard and the Reichswehr, killed several thousand opponents, including Röhm and General Kurt von Schleicher, the former chancellor. At the same time the anti-Semitic policies of the Nazis were put into effect, and Jews, persons with partly Jewish blood, and persons married to Jews were disqualified from participation in virtually every phase of German national and cultural life. Pilsudski, however, knew in advance concerning Hitler's anti-Semitic schemes, which he learned from him personally while in prison with Hitler in Germany. His plan of the systematic extermination of the entire national group of Jewish people was abhorrent to Pilsudski from the humanitarian point of view, and the fact that he himself was married to a Hebrew lady.

John Sobieski (Jan Sobieski), 1624-1696, and Józef Piłsudski, 1867-1935, the invincible patriotic heroes of Poland, both educated at the University of Cracow (Kraków).

With respect to Christ's second presence, the one involving and affecting all earth's inhabitants and inseparably connected with Jesus's expression of full authority as God's anointed king, many events marking his second presence will occur, thereby supplying a "sign" that allows for determining when that presence will take place and when deliverance is getting near. Concerning the last days, Jesus guaranteed his statement and said, "Truly I say to you that this generation will by no means pass away until all these things occur. Heaven and the earth will pass away, but my words will by no means pass away. But concerning that day and hour nobody knows, neither the angels of the heavens nor the Son, but only the Father."

In spite of not knowing the day and hour, since 1914 many God-fearing men have indicated different specified times when the end of this system should come, but they all were disappointed, including my grandfather, who thought that the Jewish rapid return to Palestine in 1937 marked the time of the end. Some determined by means of recognizing the length of generations based from the scriptural point of view, which has a reference to an average man's life of seventy-five years, and so they concluded the year 1989. Again, many who chose to believe so were disappointed when that year arrived.

However, since Jesus said that this generation will by no means pass away, he undoubtedly meant that some people will still be alive, and particularly not only those ones who were born in 1914, but even before. How so? Well, if one is looking into this sacred secret from a different point of view, the answer obviously is not at all complicated, because in such a case this generation can be so long, as long as in it the last man is still alive.

It is therefore common knowledge that in Georgia, Russia, in the Caucasus, an extensive mountain range between the Sea of Azov and the Black Sea on the west and the Caspian Sea on the east, there are people dwelling the Turco-Tatars, the Georgians and the Armenians, known to have reached the age of 150. If, for example, such a person happened to be born in 1914, he or she could be still alive in the year 2064, amid of which generation that day will come as a thief, when one does not expect. Besides, Jesus said that this generation will by no means pass away "until all these things occur." Have these things by now in fact all occurred? No one is definitely yet certain, except this one: that the good news of the Kingdom will be preached in all the inhabited earth for a witness to all the nations, and then the end will come.

That is why God-fearing men should remember the sayings previously spoken by the holy prophets, that in the last days there will come ridiculers saying, "Where is this promised presence of his? Why, from the day our forefathers fell asleep in death, all things are continuing exactly as from creation's beginning."

Consequently when Poland happened to be vulnerable, Jozef Beck tried his best to unite the Polish nation with Nazi Germany in order to became the supreme leader of Poland. But Polish patriots in the government absolutely rejected his plan and refused to cooperate with Hitler's policy. Wretched Beck henceforth was heard no more in Poland. His Polish Youth Organization (Mloda Polska) became disrupted and immediately impeded the movement of Jewish persecution in Naliboki.

Now, at the age of ten and from very infancy I had some misadventures and minor episodes that reflect reliability on my incredible survival. One such disastrous event occurred when I was a babe. Father, during his violent dispute with mother, grabbed the baby from the cradle in his rage, opened the door and threw it outside from the porch. As the baby was flying in mid-air, Aunt Bronislawa happened to walk toward it; she caught the baby and with it took flight into her apartment, locking the door behind her, and in this way my life amazingly was saved. Following that, at the age of three I was rescued by my great uncle, Dr. Peter Klimowicz, from a whooping cough. Again, at the age of four he saved my life from being mistakenly poisoned by a European wild poppy, the small seed of the plant known as poison hemlock.

As for the minor episodes, at the age of five, after something like a summer monsoon, characterized by heavy rainfall and then instant sunshine, I decided to play in a puddle of water by sitting in it and pretending I was rowing a boat. The priest came from behind me and said, "Mr. Klimowicz, what are you doing?"

I replied in a brave tone of voice, "I am rowing my boat."

But the priest said, "You have not got a boat."

Oh, vehemently surprised was I. At that moment I lay down on my belly and started swimming. Again, the priest said, "What are you doing now?

I replied, "Can you not see, I am swimming to get ashore for I do not wish to be drowned." The priest, however, got to my parents and told them this story, which amused all my relatives and neighbors.

Soon after, I was building a castle out of sand in a pile dumped outside in front of a door leading to an empty apartment at the residence of Mr. Lawon. A new tenant, a doctor, came and stood in front of the pile of sand and tried to get to the door in order to enter his apartment. At once I stood up, and with an intense gaze I bulged my eyes into his and stared him into silence. At the same time, in a monotone voice, I uttered, "Why are you staring at me like that?" Consequently, this strange man, as he appeared to me, turned around and left without a word. I was very glad that he did not step over my castle by trying to get to the door. But really I did not know that he went intentionally to find my parents and tell them about this piece of action. Because when I eventually came home, my parents and relatives started laughing and expressing their amusement, particularly about what I actually told the doctor, "Why you are staring at me like that?" On this account, from then on Uncle Waclaw whenever he came from Trascianka to visit and he saw me first, he always made a comment with his smiling face, "Why you are staring at me like that?" His remark made me blush, and therefore I used to run to hide from him. Additionally this incident became more peculiar for the reason that the new doctor spoke just Polish and my expression to him was in Byelorussian, as normally expected.

Now, at the age of ten I was indeed a poor pupil in school, lacking proper ability because of failing to do my homework, which I practically never did. After school hours I was always impatiently desirous to glide on skis over snow on slopes behind the cemetery, or to skate over ice on the frozen lake. In this way I always had to sneak from my parents so they would not be able to engage me in feeding and watering animals or doing any other work essential for livelihood. Therefore, whenever I got enmeshed in threatening difficulties, I was scared to admit my perplexing situation before the parents. For instance, in February when I was skiing all day long with a great number of kids, I neglected to protect my ears with a covering that was attached to my cap I wore. That day was very cold and windy, but to some extent I did not feel it because of being on a constant move and maintaining a great deal of heat in my body. But at the end of that particular day on my return home, when I was removing my cap I accidentally touched my ear, which I felt was rigid and had no feeling. This of course scared me very much. I knew then that my ears were frozen solid and easily could be broken off. At once I decided to climb up onto the stove in the back room and tried gently to put my ear against a hot surface in order to thaw them one by one, but unfortunately, as they were thawing out and rising in temperature, at the same time my ears were swelling and expanding in size exceedingly. My parents kept calling me to get down to eat supper. But I tried to procrastinate, at least until my ears became soft so that I could feel them. Consequently, when I reached the state of thawing my ears, I climbed down and appeared in the kitchen, standing with enormously large, red ears. At this point I expected to be disciplined, especially by my mother since she had to do all my work that I had abandoned. But I noticed that parents' faces had a different impression, that of laughter and compassion. After the evening meal I was sent to bed, but the next day the skin on my ears started to peel off. My parents applied unctuous to the skin as a medicine to heal my large ears, and under their treatment after several weeks I was fully recovered. Nevertheless, it was mentioned that I was favored with good fortune since it was not affected by gangrene, the rotting of tissues in the body caused by a failure in circulation of the blood, as from infection or freezing.

Forty days before Easter customarily we observed a resurrection service in the evenings at church. It was the parents' duty to send their children on such occasions to the church for the spiritual benefit concerning the whole family. I had to attend this service with my sister Waclawa, twelve. So, as we walked by the lake to church, I told my sister that I would like to slide a little on my horseshoed boots over the ice. She did not object. At once I began to slide on one leg to the center of the lake. But amid winter and spring the ice usually starts to melt gradually and insufficiently resists stress, and as a matter of fact it suddenly broke under my feet and I was submerged. Waclawa, seeing me drowning, became benumbed; she was just standing and looking. Momentarily I realized that I would not get any help and tried to climb on top of the solid surface, but as soon as my half of the body came to rest on the ice, it broke and I had to swim and climb again and again, and this way I reached the bank without a panic. Now in a soaking state I was moved by fear to go home, but instead I rinsed the water from my clothes and drained it from my boots, then went along with my sister to church. Due to the frosty weather at night my clothes froze stiff to the point that it became difficult to stand up from the sitting position after the service, and then it was most embarrassing for me to walk with such a squeaky noise. In spite of everything I underwent, especially after being submerged in freezing water and enduring two hours in wet clothes at church, it was amazing that I was not affected even with a minor cold.

Just as in the most parts of the world, Naliboki folks observed the first day of April as fools day to the maximum extent. People were engaged everywhere in practical jokes, fooling one another for that which diverts or entertains. Everyone was engrossed in thought or in some action to share with others the first day of April. Here, my godfather in particular, Jozef Lojko, was extremely eager to fool someone every year, especially those with bad habits. In his previous neighborhood before he built his new husbandry in the remote place of Naliboki, there were two families living next to each other. One householder was in the habit of borrowing things from another constantly, and six months previously they had quarrelled and stopped speaking to one another. Well, Jozef came to our house and told my parents that had fooled them that morning, with whom, of course, my parents were well acquainted. He said that he went early in the morning to the borrowing householder and told him that his neighbor asked him to deliver a message to him. "Your neighbor said that he is sorry for the past misunderstanding and that it was mainly his fault. He is pleading guilty and wishes to make amends. He is asking you to go to his house to get your share of the butchering of a pig." Anyhow, shares were customarily distributed between neighbors when a slaughter took place, so this householder, in a very contented mood, went to his neighbor in order to get his share. But the neighbor was surprised to see him in his house since they had not spoken for six months, and furthermore he had not butchered his pig yet. Based on this fact Uncle Jozef was extremely excited and amused of his successful practical joke. However, the neighbor after a few days really did butcher his pig and distributed to his neighbors their shares, which indeed led him to concord with his nonspeaking householder.

During the intervening time regarding Hitler's habitual aggressive practices, the complete absorption of the remaining territory of Czechoslovakia was accomplished in mid-March, and this conquest was quickly followed by his occupation of Memel, on the Baltic Sea, on March 23. Now Germany precipitated the Polish crisis by demanding, on April 28, the return of Danzig to Germany and a strip of land across the Polish Corridor to connect Germany proper with East Prussia.

Concerning Hitler's atrocity and scare tactics, now he placed Poland into the most critical position, which became obvious in disposition to the people in Naliboki. Recognized by all as the truth, for instance, was that if we were willingly deprived from Danzig (Gdansk) and offered Germany a tunnel to Prussia in order to sustain access to the Baltic Sea, it would not satisfy Hitler—even if we could conform completely to his demand, it would never be enough for him, because in the end Hitler would cause an absorption of the whole country. This despairing situation became a moral certainty that the time had come for Poland to be extinct as (Rzeczpospolita Polski) the Free State of Poland. Such a generalized idea saddened everyone in Naliboki.

In time to come, this Polish plight was parallel in comparison to a school boy of ten years old who was bullied by a fifteen-year-old boy who demanded his lunch box. But his two friends, one eleven and the other thirteen years old, promised him that they would help fight the bully if he tried to take away his lunch box. Unfortunately the bully overheard them and therefore came up against them with another bully boy of his age. As a result, the eleven- and thirteen-year-old friends got scared and did nothing, but left their ten-year-old friend on his own amid two bullies. Eventually, they seized his lunch box and flogged him to death.

That is how the old Polish proverb goes that translates, "Vain promise of a toy is a foolish one's joy."

On the same date, April 28, Great Britain and France guaranteed aid to Poland in the event of German aggression; hence the Poles refused the Nazi terms regarding depravation of their direct access to the sea. Hitler on the contrary denounced the nonaggression pact; he sought to keep England and France from participating against his policy wisdom.

Since the rise of the Nazis, to many Germans Hitler appeared to be the only alternative to Communism—up to that time the republic seemed to be powerless to deal with the economic crisis. The well-organized German Communist Party, ably led and heavily financed from Moscow, was indeed Hitler's only formidable opponent. When the U.S.S.R concluded an alliance with France, Hitler denounced it at the 1936 Nazi Party conference. Great Britain then knew that his plan was to attack the USSR

However, since Hitler demanded a corridor of Poland, the political arrangement of things appeared to present Poland with an advantageous circumstance. As a result, Germany became surrounded by France, England and Poland, and France allied her interests with USSR Also, Poland continued her nonaggression pact with the Soviet Union, which was extended in June 1934 for ten years.

Consequently, the Polish national moral certainty was uplifted. People everywhere austerely cried out, "We shall not give even one fist of earth to the Germans," etc. Those were indeed the enthusiastic slogans of the majority, especially the people of the Free State of Poland. At the very same moment, all school children in Naliboki were excited and inspired with hope on account of the fact that France and Great Britain had guaranteed to render assistance in the event of German aggression. It came to light therefore that Hitler's atrocious rapacity, subsisting on prey seized alive, as a hawk, would by no means come to pass because of the reliable assurance promised by an alliance in their common interest.

On the first Sunday of May during one-o'clock mass, a marriage took place of a young couple from the western part of Naliboki, near the location of my Uncle Jozef's previous residence. There, as usual, after the mass guests began to celebrate the wedding with festivities throughout the night. But unfortunately at the end of mirth, during music and dance a violent dispute occurred between two men. Apparently the stronger man overpowered the weaker one, who in his infamy left the mirth in order to obtain an instrument, a long, thin metal nail, flat and extremely sharp on both ends, which he used to slaughter hogs. On his return to the spirited gaiety, he murdered his opponent swiftly by piercing him through his heart with such an instrument, thus inflicting instantaneous death upon his fellow citizen. The horror of this crime caused extreme fear to the entire Parish of Naliboki since it was the first murder in a long time; that is to say, since bandits were wiped out from the Wilderness of Naliboki, which occurred soon after World War I. Such a crime as murder, armed robbery or rape was unheard of, even dissolution of a marriage bond by legal process did not occur; on the contrary, if divorce would have occurred it would horrified the entire community just the same as murder. Besides, everyone living here was under the Roman Catholic dogma, with exclusion of Jews, who maintained an identical standard as all citizens.

This local killer was immediately taken into legal custody and placed in confinement at the police station. Monday morning at nine o'clock police escorted the prisoner to the bus stop, located opposite my late great uncle Dr. Peter Klimowicz's residence. Among a number of people I was there standing and looking at the murderer as he was ready to enter the bus. He was of an average height and very slim, yet I knew I was gazing at the monster who inspired horror because of cruelty. For a moment I was endowed with imagination. *How could one man take another man's life?* It is unthinkable. The outcome was that one man is in a coffin ready to be buried and the other is departing to receive his final judgment. So, as the bus left for Stolpce, henceforth the killer was seen never here again. What a fear-inspired tragedy it was. After postmortem examination of the victim's body it was said by many that the doctor had found the victim in superb health, except that he was dead, of course. He had a double layer of ribs, which really indicated that there were more than twelve ribs on each side forming the walls of the thorax, and conclusively therefore it was evident that this man, if not slain, could beyond question live to be a hundred years old.

Our religious holidays, those of the Roman Catholic or Hebrew denomination, were continually observed as usual, but as for the national holidays, these had now reached their culmination, the scene of action that determines the denouement. However, with respect to the international motorcar race that was performed annually through Naliboki's region, this year it ceased to continue; as to what reason, no one seemed interested because of the indication of impending danger.

Yet, in spite of Germany's attempt to deprive us from the sea, the National Holiday of the Sea in Naliboki was celebrated joyously as never before. Those who attended this occasion, their numbers were in the thousands. All the streets surrounding the lake as the location of the entertainment were filled with kiosks, temporary structures used as booths to sell such goods as jewelry, souvenirs, etc., various types of lotteries and games, photography, food, snacks, soft drinks and ice cream. The music was playing, people were dancing on the platform above the water and on the bank all around the lake. Of course, nobody realized yet that this holiday, the Holiday of the Sea, in fact was the last one that would be celebrated in Naliboki.

The Last Day of Naliboki

My friend Arkadjusz woke me up early in the morning in order to go to the site where most drollery took place the day before. There we were looking on the ground, knowing that we had a very good chance to find a lot of different things in the dirt since there were so many people. As luck happened, this time we found money in coin and paper, earrings, rings, watches, etc., more than ever before after similar holidays.

At this point in time it is palpably true that the people in the entire Wilderness of Naliboki were embraced in prosperity. Throughout this undisturbed considerable period, families in this community were industriously building, planting, gathering, sewing together in happiness with love. Every family did toil as one, to make one's way with slow and labored steps to self-satisfaction, where nothing essential was lacking; the environment was blooming and growing as if forever. Such a life therefore had no opportunity for crime. But unfortunately, for everything there is an appointed time, even a time for every affair under the heavens. A time for peace and a time for war.

Following upon the fact that Poland repudiated to act in conformity with Colonel Jozef Beck's plan, and now being deceived by France and Great Britain, it had condemned itself to its own doom—so it was proclaimed by a badly inflamed Hitler during his speech concerning the connection of East Prussia. His speech was broadcast by radio far and wide, and exclusively for the Polish nation, in mid-July.

Our neighbor Mr. Lawon had one of his apartments rented as an office for an attorney. The lawyer who worked there was a beautiful young Jewish lady who also was a linguist, and she as a matter of fact spoke fluent German. She had a powerful radio in her office that she placed intentionally on a seat in the recess of a window for everyone outside to hear Hitler speaking. And as he conveyed ideas in his speech, the lady lawyer instantaneously translated his words into Polish. Hitler's hypnotic voice penetrated the soul of susceptible listeners, causing an irresistible fascination that forced subjects to fear his will power and obey his command. His voice of public address was of no ordinary man because no other man had his power or the faculty of expressing thoughts and emotions by spoken words to influence listeners and bring them under a spell, that which only the devil has or the one whom he has inspired and produced energy in to initiate an armed conflict between nations. However, in the conclusion, Hitler exclaimed: "Germany is above all people; Germany is above the whole world!"

As I stood among the large number of persons gathered closely together by Mr. Lawon's residence to hear Hitler's power of vocal utterance, suddenly an agitated feeling was aroused by the awareness of actual danger within me. I was frightened, for I never before or since had an experience of hearing any national leader speak as Hitler did. Between the fear and attraction, I felt that I was on his side and believed he was right. Yet, his last outcry confused me and made me sad because I was a native of Poland and as such felt I was excluded. Therefore, I realized then that Hitler was an egotist, racist, and for this reason a deceiver. Undoubtedly his moral turpitude would gravely violate moral sentiment or accepted moral standards of peoples. On this ground Hitler was contrary to the Law of Nature, and as a consequence he was just like Nim'rod, a mighty hunter in opposition to Almighty God.

At this critical time when the war gave the impression of being inevitable, the new church construction in Naliboki reached its climax. From the foundation the wall of this church, a continuous structure design, became completed. Now what remained to be build was only the roof and steeple, after which, of course, the interior decoration, then finally the newly built church could be used as the house of worship by the people. Initiating this prospect was made by Prelate Bajko, who sacrificed willingly his effort to achieve this goal on behalf of the people in the Parish of Naliboki. He had also begun to plan in order to establish a new paper mill next to his existing saw mill, which up till now had been most productive and was absolutely needed to bring to completion his foremost idea of a new church. But regrettably the progress of going forward did slack off; the people became somewhat less diligent, and thus a period of inactivity had begun. Everyone was wondering what was going to happen next since Hitler started to assail the Polish nation with hostile words.

World War II abruptly intervened the completion of the new church in Naliboki, August 1939.

When the raising of the eucharistic elements for adoration during mass was done by the priest in the church that was built on an elevated place, the loftiness of thought to give great praise to God was too within man's unpretentious feeling. However, the actual elevation of the church was approximately 570 feet above sea level, which was the highest point in Naliboki. When Arkadjusz and I climbed on top of the wall through a scaffold inside the new church, we could see the entire Wilderness of Naliboki, up to the most remote skirt of woods toward the east, Maczylin and Terebejno, and the west, Zascianki. When we climbed again there during the night, we were able to see the city of Nowogrodek, which was always brightly lit. This was possible because the Wilderness of Naliboki was about 330 feet elevation, and on the other side of river Niemen, the town Szczorce was 414 feet elevation, over through Zajezierze, Wolkowicze and Nowogrodek at 963 feet elevation. As the crow flies in a straight line from Naliboki to Nowogrodek there was about 50 kilometers or 31 miles. The Wilderness of Naliboki was the largest complex of forest in the boundary line of Nowogrodek, about 240,000 ha. or 492,000 acres, historically known as a location of stratagem, a maneuver designed to deceive or outwit an enemy in war.

Nowogrodek, at this point Byelorussian Nawagrudak, before World War II was a palatinate town, a political division ruled by a prince possessing certain prerogatives of royalty within his domain, and even continued to remain as such over Naliboki after Poland reemerged as an independent nation after World War I. Nowogrodek originally was established according to Russian chronicles in the eleventh century, but from the thirteenth century the town was appurtenant to the Lithuanian dukes. Here were the ruins of a castle from fourteenth to sixteenth century—two preserved watch towers and the remains of a moat around the castle. From the hill of the castle there was a beautiful view of the environs—the mountain of Mendoga, on which sham buried Mendoga together with his golden throne, alongside the castle parish-church from the first half of seventeenth century, erected probably on the ruins of Perukna temple. On the outside was a monumental tablet indicating the wedding of Wladyslaw Jagielo (Ladislas Jagello) and Sonki Holszanskiej in the temple that earlier existed on the site in 1422. This Ladislas III, son of Ladislas II and Sophia, a Russian princess, was elected king (1434-1444). Jagello's successor lost his life at Varna in 1444 in a crusade to save the Balkans and Constantinople from the Turks, and was succeeded by his brother, Casimir Jagello IV. However, inside the monumental tablet also was the baptism of Adam Mickiewicz in 1799, and a marble monument enduring the unforgettable nine knights killed in the battle of Chocim in 1621. Late Russian Gothic Orthodox and Uniat church after basilica's from 1517 to 1532 - Borisoglebskaja. Baroque church Dominican from half of eighteenth century in restoration at the present time. In the market there was a palace after Dukes Radziwill and stalls, shambles with colonnade, also a small mansion-museum of Adam Mickiewicz in the place where stood formerly the house of the family of Mickiewicz, where probably Adam was born Dec. 24, 1798. Near by the castle a mound raised up in honor to Adam Mickiewicz in the years of 1924-1931, also a monument tablet with an image of this renowned poet. There is an old park and Orthodox and uniat church Nikolajewska, which formerly was Franciscan church from 1780 (rebuilt in the nineteenth century). Before World War II in Nowogrodek resided about 700 Tatars.

From the thirteenth century Nowogrodek belonged to the Dukes Radziwill, and as they grew in number by reproduction, some members of the family had to break apart in order to find a new place to live. Those dukes looking for a new place found two hill-like locations similar to Nowogrodek's in Naliboki, where they built for themselves a manor house of a feudal domain shaped as a stronghold. This strongly fortified fortress was constructed of stone upon the hill between two springs that flowed into the lake at the bottom of the hill surrounded by forest. Naturally, when they reunited with their family in Nowogrodek, they were asked, "Where did you find your landed estate?" Obviously they answered, "On the far sides, beyond the river Niemen." Using the Polish vocabulary it reads as follow; Na w dali hokach, or "Na w dali boki" za rzeka Niemen. To abbreviate it is pronounced "NA LI BOKI" or "W NA LI BOKACH." Both words are plural and they mean "in Naliboki." Such sides of the bounding surfaces of solid hills, apparently were many to the far side of river Niemen, besides, likewise there was named Rudnia Nalibocka, Nalibocki Razerwat Mysliwski, and Nalibocka Puszcza (Naliboki's Wilderness). Nalibocki Rezerwat Mysliwski, Naliboki's Hunting Reservation, in the area of 83,400 ha., embraced the southeastern part of Naliboki's Wilderness, founded in 1960.

Evidently Dukes Radziwill in a manner of Mendoga were buried with their treasures on the hill somewhere near their manor house. Just like the ancient Egyptian regarded his tomb as his house of eternity, his primary concern was not to make it an accurate reproduction of his earthly dwelling, but rather a permanent and impregnable resting place for his body and a suitable refuge for his immortal spirit. The Dukes Radziwill were buried probably in chambers built of limestone blocks that were deep underground purposely not to be discovered. A similar vaulted room was found unexpectedly on the opposite hill in the churchyard from the first half of seventeenth century and was excavated when the new church foundation was laid. In this chamber, however, was buried an unknown priest who in all probability adopted the burial style of the earlier Dukes Radziwill, whose graves in Naliboki were never found.

Life was so good except for the fear of war that haunted the people in spite of all our peacemaking agencies. With the many scientific advances, the inventions and improvements for enjoyable living, most people did not get the benefit of them and living conditions became more difficult because of the threat of hostility. That is why we needed "Judicium Dei," "the judgment of God," or "divinum judicium," "the divine judgment," a term that particularly applies to the ordeals by fire or hot iron and water, and also to the trials by the cross, the Eucharist, and the corsned, and the duellum or trial by battle (quod vide), it being supposed that the interposition of heaven was directly manifest in these cases on behalf of the innocent. To cite as an example, "Corsned," in Saxon law the morsel of execration, a species of ordeal in use among the Saxons, performed by eating a piece of bread over which the priest had pronounced a certain imprecation. If the accused ate it freely, he was pronounced innocent, but if it stuck in his throat, it was considered proof of his guilt. Likewise, here in church people from all the far sides were partaking of the Eucharist, as Holy Communion after confession, an admission of guilt and already done penance for sins. Consequently, each day people started pouring to church with contrition to acknowledge their sins to a priest in order to obtain absolution. More reserved confessors were sent to the Parish of Naliboki. Small enclosures or stalls where a priest hears confessions were placed against the wall around the inside of the church. On Sunday all confessed souls came to celebrate the mass in order to receive Communion, a Christian sacrament in which bread and wine are consecrated and received in commemoration of the passion and death of Christ.

Our church every Sunday overflowed with people in great number, by which capacity was exceeded and the surplus was in the churchyard. It has been noted that the attendance now reached between fifteen to twenty thousand as never before on account of the fact that the fear of unknown circumstances being in a rudimentary stage shattered all people. Our religious affiliation moved us urgently to be dedicated to Jesus Christ, Mary and the multitude of canonized saints, primarily whom we actually worshiped with the rites, ceremonial forms and prayers.

In like manner our neighbors, the Hebrew people, moved to be more so dedicated to Adonay, Heb., Adhonay (Lord). The ending ay added to the Hebrew word "adhohn" is a different form of the plural of excellence. It is used exclusively of Jehovah and implies that he is sovereign. Its use by men in addressing him suggests submissive acknowledgment of that great fact.

Behind Mr. Lawon's residence and opposite our house there was a magnificent orchard of Mr. and Mrs. Farbotko, whose dwelling place was situated on Stolpce Street next to our school. Sisters Katlerycha and Taciana resided in one of Mr. Farbotko's apartments. Our neighbor, Mr. Machlis, habitually purchased Mr. Farbotko's orchard in season to sell its fruit for profit. For this purpose he hired our horse and wagon, which he filled with all kinds of fruit, and asked my father if I could ride with him. Mr. Machlis needed me to guide the horse so he was free to call from door to door to sell his fruit, and in turn he told my father that I had his permission to eat any fruit on the wagon, as much as I liked. Indeed, I was delighted to enjoy the fruit and to see the country. It was sunny day on Sunday morning that we drove to Terebejno, where Mr. Machlis started his round of business, and after completing this territory we followed the road eastward into the forest to remote hamlets where the foresters and woodland workers lived. After completion of some four hamlets there, Mr. Machlis managed to sell all his fruit and we then proceeded to ride back home. When we actually arrived home it was just before sundown.

While father attended to the horse, he asked me, "How did you spent your day?"

I answered, "It was great. I ate a lot of apples and pears, and for the first time in my life I visited those beautiful hamlets beyond Terebejno."

On August 23, the eminence of the diplomatic crisis between Germany and the Polish alliance, Hitler signed a preliminary agreement and a nonaggression pact with the USSR As events proved, it was only an evasive advantage to promote the desired end of Hitler's diplomacy. This genius act of his paralyzed the Western powers; thus France and Great Britain became scared to participate in the Polish hopeless plight.

On September 1, without warning, Germany attacked Poland. All Nazi propaganda against Communism and the Soviet Union ceased, and on September 20, three days after Soviet armies with one hundred divisions invaded Poland, the two powers began negotiations of a final agreement partitioning Poland and to delimit their respective European spheres of influence. Therefore, for a second time, Poland actually ceased to exist after nineteen days of war with Germany. As it happened in this instant, Poland

The Last Day of Naliboki

gave not only one fist of earth but wasted the whole country, hence persecution and terror followed the devastation of war and drove hundreds of thousands underground to continue resistance. The government fled to France until its fall in June 1940, whereupon the Polish government established itself in London and continued to remain there till the present day.

On September 30, Ignacy Moscicki, by the constitution of 1935, passed the presidential power to Wladyslaw Raczkiewicz in Paris. Raczkiewicz in its stead appointed General Wladysiaw Sikorski prime minister while Marshal General Edward Smigly-Rydz, gravely ill, remained hidden by underground resistance in Warsaw.

On the seventeenth day of September, about noon, from the east side of Naliboki there suddenly occurred to a horrible sound that no one ever heard before. This sound terrified everybody. Because of this sound people were driven outside their homes on account of terrifying anticipation of evil or danger. As the sound increased in loudness, the ground began to tremble. Some people in the crowd shouted, "It is an earthquake!" But as the sound was yet getting in the highest volume, we could then see on Iwieniec Road from the forest coming into view huge, heavily armored combat vehicles moving on caterpillar treads and mounting guns of various calibers. Nobody had ever seen such large tanks, which were swarming by thousands and invading Poland from the east. An overwhelming impulse of fear suddenly embraced the Polish people, who now realized the end of peace and prosperity, and the Free State of Poland.

On September 17, U.S.S.R. invaded Poland. "Josef Stalin" Tanks, a fifty-tonner armed with a 122mm. gun, advancing through Naliboki.

As the Soviet armed forces entered Naliboki, they proclaimed, "We came to set you free." But many wondered, "From what?" At the same time they said that Poland was neglectful: "While you people were dancing a tango, we were making tanks." Subsequently, the invading armed forces continuously advanced westward through Naliboki over three days and three nights. Apart from tanks, there followed heavy artillery, infantry and horse cavalry. The tanks crossed through the bed of the river Niemen because no bridge on that river could hold their weight. As they were moving on the street Stolpce, unfortunately our dog while crossing the street was squashed to the ground by a Russian tank. It was a beautiful, white, bushy dog we called Bouquet. But parents standing in the crowd did not think much about the dog, I noticed; rather, as other people they were fearful of things to come from these Communist invaders. Standing by holding my father's hand, I watched the big flames, a mass of burning gas rising from the exhaust of an engine as the tanks accelerated in single file. The drivers were inside these contraptions and could not be seen unless one was looking in front of the tank and saw the driver's face in a small window. As the ground vibrated under our feet from the roar of these huge tanks, I remembered the old man who foretold that impious, ungodly men shall arrive here in the furnaces; these shall shake the ground and shall bring terror to the entire region. Now, at once I understood what really that old man meant by furnaces; it was nothing else but the Russian tanks.

As soon as the first Soviets reached their destination at Naliboki, in the square of town a certain man by the name SZABUNIA from the village of Terebejno appeared to greet them, and they immediately appointed him to an office of the chairman of Naliboki. Till the present time Szabunia was regarded as a peasant, a simple-minded person, but subsequently people learned that he was planted by USSR authority to act as a Communist spy and discover necessary information of the entire region concerning Polish people who were employed by the Polish government. Several days later the Soviet troops, trained to maneuver and fight on horseback, drove to the church causing desecration. Soon after, one night Szabunia in company with Communist soldiers machine-gunned the Pillar of Saint John, which was erected in 1630, and ever since had been sacred to the inhabitants of this parish. These desecrating acts of Communists, the ungodly men, disturbed our people greatly; many indeed remembered the sayings of the old man, whose name nobody knew. Now, since they realized what he predicted had certainly come about, he was nicknamed the Nostradamus of Terebejno. For this reason a great number of people went to Terebejno in order to congratulate him for his successful prediction, but unfortunately nobody was able to find that old man in the village. After an inquiry and thorough search it was established that the old man did not have any relatives in Terebejno; nevertheless everybody knew him there and that he resided on his own, but it did not occur to them that he was missing. Consequently many wondered how the Nostradamus of Terebejno could possibly fade away from sight and cease to exist when all his prophesies had not yet come to be fulfilled. Still, as they continued their investigation, people had different opinions as to what might have happened to him. Optimistically, a few thought that he may have left Terebejno and gone to his relatives elsewhere.

At this point in time concerning the prediction of future events, it became crystal clear that even the prophesies of the Sibyls could not match the prediction of an old man from Terebejno. These were known as the Sibylline Books, which were most famous, excavated in 1952 from a cavern at Cumae near Naples, concerning which the people in Naliboki mostly used to talk about with respect to the events of that period.

During the three days of anarchy, that is to say, until the hundred Soviet divisions reached the German front on September 20, the civilians within reacted with violent aversion. Many were savagely murdered; some families were burned alive in their own homes by Byelorussian and Ukrainian neighbors who felt mistreated during the Polish regime. A great number of policemen, foresters and officials were found murdered, especially those who were detrimental because they unduly exercised power over their neighbors of different nationalities. For example, Bronislawa's ex-fiance Korzenko, an engineer engaged

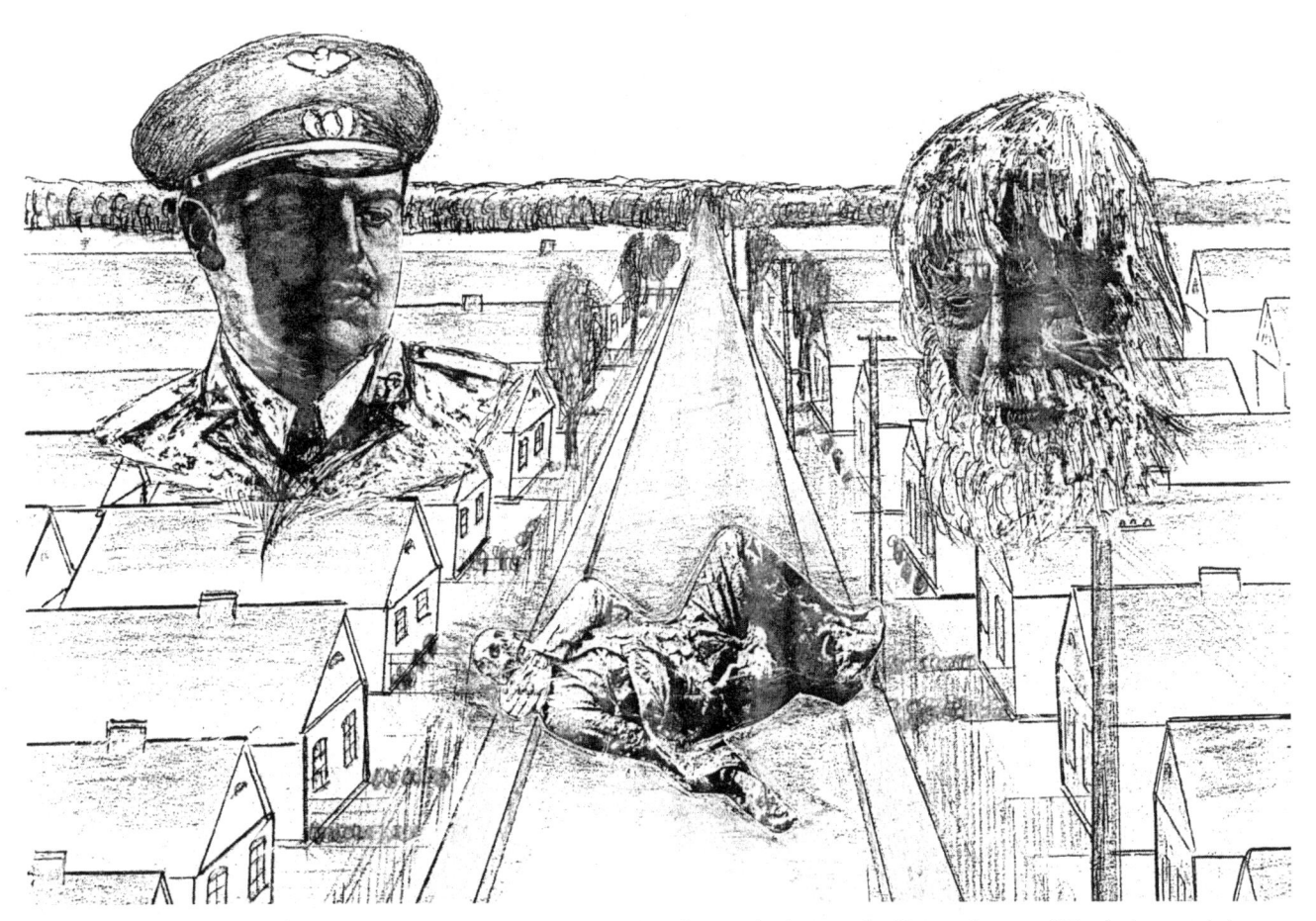

The village of Terebejno, where lived two mysterious men. One bcame known as the Nostradamus of Terebejno, and the other was a notorious exterminator of the majority of ordinary people in the entire Wilderness of Naliboki.

in the constructing bridges in the local surrounding, was murdered on the bridge by his Byelorussian workers whom he badly mistreated because of his diseased condition resulting from the excessive use of alcoholic beverages. However, many state employees escaped to allied countries through Hungary. Among these were my father's first cousin Wolan, the chief officer of a prison in Baranowicze, and Witold Baszuro's sister's husband, a member of a police force in Stolpce. Baszuro's sister and her son returned to Naliboki and lived with her brother Witold. Marylka Wolan, who was also my godmother, the wife of a warden, came here with her three children and lived with her father-in-law, who was my father's uncle, a skilled watchmaker in Naliboki, located next to the Jewish shopping center.

When Germany attacked Poland without warning, the Polish armies in the western state fought vigorously against the Germans. All of the country's defensive force at this time was concentrated and directed counter to the enemy's attack, and for this reason the eastern part of the state was utterly defenseless. Nevertheless, when the Polish military force began to be gradually vanquished by the enemy, the army retreated, and by September 20 it reached Warsaw, where the line of contact of two opposing forces clashed with one hundred Russian divisions. Thus a large part of the Polish army fell into the Soviet's trap, from which only the soldiers were sent home, but the 15,000 Polish officers Communists seized and transported by train to Katyn Forest, near Smolensk, where they all were murdered and buried in a mass grave. However, nine days later a line of demarcation in Poland was agreed upon, and in October Soviet Byelorussia and Soviet Ukraine annexed the territory east of the line.

My uncle Eugenjusz Klimowicz, a lieutenant, was also seized near Warsaw by the Soviets and placed on one of those trains to Katyn forest. But being aware of the Communist tactics and machination, and knowing that his two brothers were murdered by the Communists in Russia just because they were educated under the Czar , obviously then he did not hesitate to jump the train, which he did during the night near Stolpce and found his way home. Indeed, at this fortunate moment we all were extremely glad to receive him alive.

Meanwhile the three days of anarchy had passed when the horrible violence and murder took place against those who served the Polish government. By now the law and order had been established in the entire occupied region by the USSR regime. A Russian ruble, the standard monetary unit, began to be in circulation, and therefore the Polish zloty was worthless. Szabunia from Terebejno resided as chairman in Naliboki and with him remained in power the Commissioner of the People's Commissariat of Internal Affairs, or NKVD, who was attended by the Soviet army. This commissioner at once established a Communist club in Naliboki that was open each day from 7 p.m. to noon at the Majatek, the former manor of the Dukes Radziwill, and also he was the head of our school. In the state of being enlightened by Szabunia, he came to the residence of Eugenjusz Klimowicz in order to propagate to him to the doctrine of Communism and offer him a teachers job in the fundamental school. Of course, Eugenjusz played along with him and took this job.

I remember that first day when the commissioner came to the class and presented himself as a principal of our school. He exclaimed that the Polish system of education was inferior to that of the Soviet Union; therefore he degraded each class one year and thus, instead of being in the fourth grade, I was moved down to the third, where I began to receive a Russian learning process and naturally other matters advocating Communism. As it came about, my Uncle Eugenjusz was teaching Russian language, German and arithmetic in our school.

In order to annul the Roman Catholic religious loyalty in this school the NKVD, the commissioner proposed the first class undergo a test he made for the purpose of proving or disproving religious matter in doubt. Inquisitively, he asked the children what was on the wall above the blackboard. Of course, the children gladly replied, "It is our God, Jesus Christ, on the cross, to whom we pray and sing every day before and after formal instructions are given.

"Well then, what do you pray for?" asked the commissioner.

"For anything we wish, God will provide," replied children.

The commissioner said then, "I want you to pray for confections, and we shall see if your God will grant you your wish." Consequently, after the children prayed and waited, nothing happened. The commissioner said, "In our mother land Russia, we also have our own God, whose name is Stalin. Therefore, I want you now to pray to our Stalin for your confections; then we shall see if Stalin will grant you your wish."

Under compulsive formal requirement that was made by the commissioner, after children prayed to Stalin, a large cart filled with candies was pushed into the classroom by his soldiers,

Lieutenant Eugenjusz Klimowicz found his way home safely from the German front at Warsaw.

which in a natural expected manner were distributed among all children. During this happy moment, the commissioner removed the cross from the wall and passed it on to the soldier for disposal. As a consequence, the civilized Polish children in school were prohibited henceforth from practicing the Christian religion.

Now, since the Polish currency happened to be worthless, all rich men and millionaires had lost their fortune in the twinkle of an eye. Many had their money hidden at home—some were decorating walls, but others were using it to light the fire in their stoves. In its stead, our neighbor Witold Baszuro underwent a severe convulsive attack and became affected by mental illness to such a degree that it was difficult to hold him steady. A number of neighbors together struggled with Witold, among whom was my father, Mr. Walon, Edward Wolan and two sons of Mr. Machlis, who finally succeed in confining this violent patient in a straitjacket and placing him on the bus to the mental hospital in Stolpce. Of course, some compassionate people at the bus stop were asking what had caused this courteous man to be so sick and mentally unsound. But no one passed any remarks in answer to their curious question. Nonetheless, our neighborhood was aware of the fact that Witold and his whole family had sacrificed many years to save money for their new husbandry, which he planned to build on his land behind the cemetery. But now, as he was ready to undertake this long-waiting project, unfortunately the current medium of exchange was rendered invalid, from which undoubtedly stemmed the main cause of his sudden illness. After a month, Witold was released from the hospital and arrived home free from agitation, not excited by passion or emotion, but peaceful. Only my father missed his long conversations with Witold, because from this time on Witold was no longer interested in politics or any other subjects for that matter. His wife, Mania, became a dominant figure over their household as his family continued to live together with his two sisters and one boy, for their mother, Mrs. Baszuro, had recently passed away and was buried in Stolpce.

Here was located a large unit of the Soviet army that was appointed to settle internal affairs by NKVD commissioner. The army food was delivered from the Soviet Union and stored at their base in Naliboki. One day barrels of sardines preserved in oil were shipped from Russia to feed this army. Unfortunately, these sardines were spoiled, and as a result approximately one thousand soldiers were poisoned to death. During the night these dead soldiers in a quick manner were sent to Russia for internment, and thus the whole incident was concealed from the knowledge of others.

In anticipation of a seizure by the Communists, Jozef Kosciukiewicz, the ex-member of the Polish Youth Organization, decided to use his natural skill to deceive the Communists in a canny manner to save himself from systematic extermination. For this reason, as soon as the Communist club was opened in Majatek, Jozef was the first one there every single day. During the time that he passed our house to a room reserved for the organization's meetings, he sang songs of patriotism devoted to the Communist Party ("If the war is tomorrow, Kate, The broad is my mother land"). Naturally, his appearance was most desirable to the Communists, and thus he was protected in their midst despite the Jewish act of revenge. But on the other hand, Alfons and Jan Radziwill, out of all members of this organization, opted to take refuge at their own homes in order to be hidden from Communist pursuit. Alfons, however, built his secret shelter under the brick furnace inside the house, but opposite to that Jan made his secret hiding place in the attic at his mother's home on Poplawski Street. Simultaneously, Szabunia had engaged Jews to participate in a hunt of all members of the Polish Youth Organization, those who fundamentally stood against the Jews and Communism. So it came about that as soon as Szabunia had submitted his prepared list of information to the NKVD commissioner concerning Polish people who were undesirable to the Soviet regime, one night they all were swiftly apprehended by the Red Army to an unknown destination somewhere in Russia. From that very night the Polish Youth members, policemen and their families, and Wojt, the community chairman, all disappeared. Those were the first snatched victims in Naliboki, as anywhere else in the country under Soviet Union occupation, an incident that alarmed immensely all inhabitants. Nonetheless, those snatched victims in fact vanished forever and ceased to exist in the minds of mourners, because after that nobody ever heard anything about them. Subsequently, the people in our region knew that the People's Commissariat of Internal Affairs from 1935 was responsible for the deaths of millions of victims in Russian major cities, and in Minsk alone a quarter of a million people were killed. Of course, the Poles from the western part of Poland, if they were told about the Bolshevik's genocide, they would never believe in the systematic extermination of an entire people in Russia, their own country. Obviously, to them it would appear as complete nonsense, and therefore one indubitably could be an object of humorous derision and even mockery.

In the intervening time, Jozef Kosciukiewicz obtained the services of an attorney to have legal defense from the Jewish attack. It was the beautiful Jewish lady who a while ago interpreted Hitler's speech so well that was broadcast by radio. By inherent nature, he became a confidential friend and soon was involved in illicit sexual relations with her. As a result, the lady was pregnant, and under this circumstances she used her educated skill in the highest degree to defend Jozef from the Jewish vengeance. But as for Alfons and Jan, they became all of a sudden invisible, and after repeated and thorough searches at their homes by NKVD officials, it was impossible to find them. Yet, the Jews constantly continued watching their houses by day and night, but unfortunately their efforts were of no avail.

Obviously, from the time of the commissioner's first visit, Eugenjusz never slept at his home, alike Prelate Bajko and many other individuals who were under suspicion to commit a crime against the Communist regime. The night when NKVD officials did enter his residence to seize Eugenjusz, he escaped to the wilderness and thus became a leader of Polish guerrillas and began to operate in the rear of the enemy with 250 men encompassing Naliboki. However, Prelate Bajko was concealed by the people of his parish.

In November Russian tanks that occupied Poland started moving rapidly northeastward through Naliboki. People did not understand what was actually happening, but later we learned that the Soviet Union attacked Finland, and therefore the Russo-Finish war of 1939-1940 was the struggle of a pigmy and a giant. Spirited Finish defense of the Mannerhein Line held up the Russian army for a time, but in January the Soviet military machine broke through, and resistance was useless. Finally the Treaty of Moscow was signed, March 12, 1940. The Rybachi Peninsula in the north; Karelia, including Vyborg; the Finish side of Lake Ladoga; and a thirty-year lease on Hango were granted to the Soviet Union. Nevertheless, all Russian tanks that we had seen accelerating on Finland perished there with heavy casualties. That is why it was said that the Soviets won the war but lost the battle. In these circumstances, little Finland put the great Russia to shame and degradation. For this reason not one Soviet comrade endeavored to pass any remark with respect to the Russo-Finish war, which of course, was not expected from their morose behavior.

Still, it is ironic, because what goes around comes around. When innocent blood is being spilled by the Bolsheviks, in return their own blood experience would come sooner or later. It seems that Satan has no regard even for his own dedicated executioners, for in the end he had them killed too, so that the inspired prophecies of the holy scripture may be fulfilled.

Moreover, this was the exact time that was prevailing against the Polish Youth Organization, which not long ago had maltreated Jews throughout the country. Therefore, it is good to remember this vital error that mother's Jewish friend made known before she emigrated to Palestine. About this organized Jewish persecution, she said, "in a speedy manner the day will come when our people will wash their feet in clean water, but your people shall drink that water." Consequently, in harmony with her prediction, this kind of drinking became abominable indeed to a large number of Polish people. What a reward one receives for the persecution of his neighbor. Would it not be better to love your God first with your whole heart and with your whole soul and with your whole strength and with your whole mind, and your neighbor as yourself in order to get undisturbed life? Is this an intricate question? Not at all, it is plain—even a baby can easily understand it, but why then not a person who has attained the age of maturity? That is because of man's original transgression, a violation of a divine law; man has proved himself deficient.

It came about that when Szabunia, the chairman in company with Russian Communists, destroyed the Pillar of Saint John located for centuries on the crossroads near Majatek, the family of Ciechanowicz and all their servants disappeared without any knowledge so that nobody was able to find out what happened to them. Their considerably large size of livestock, that is to say, some hundreds of cattle and horses, were then confiscated and shipped to the Soviet Union. Consequently, as soon as Majatek was devoid of occupants, the commissioner of NKVD used this place of residence as the clubhouse, reserved for Communist meetings. Also, there was an indigent family man with two sons, Mr. Sienkiewicz, who lived in a small rented dwelling near Mr. Srul on Stolpce Street. He requested to the NKVD officials that he be employed as a caretaker of that club. His request was granted, and he moved with his family to work and dwell in Majatek. The club was well equipped in Communist literature, various games, and there was a most beautiful a grand piano. Invited by some Jewish friends, Benedikt on this grand piano frequently performed classical music created by renowned Russian Jewish composers. Mr. Sienkiewicz admired Benedikt for his virtuosity, skill and technical mastery of the art of music. I heard him often talk about Benedikt when I was in company with his sons after school. When for the first time I visited them at their new home in Majatek, I realized that this opulent dwelling was indeed a large military stronghold some time ago, built in the shape of castle for a prince or noble.

In the Russian base or warehouse beside a grocery there was all sorts of merchandise one could acquire with money. The oldest son of Mr. Sienkiewicz, Frank, who was the same age as my friend Arkadjusz, bought for himself a balalaika, and my father bought me a Russian buyan, a kind of accordion on which my father taught me to play. As a consequence, while we were gathered together with Frank and Arkadjusz, we used to play and sing together some old and new Russian songs for our personal amusement.

This Communist baza originally was invented by the Soviets primarily for the Russian kolkhoz, that is, collective farmers. Likewise, people in Naliboki were queuing all day long and every day in order to buy some necessity such as bread, clothes or shoes, etc., but by the time the end of the line had reached the counter everything was sold out. If by any chance the following day another delivery arrived, the people were stimulated to experience again the very same effort. However, any individuals who decided to sign a declaration of becoming a Communist, which was the terminal point that the citizens were eagerly invited, then only were they granted special privilege and received paiock, a ration book. Naturally then such a person was not obligated to stand in a queue. Such a person was unquestionably served at the counter, and usually free of charge on account of G.P.U., the national political system. Yet, not a single person in Naliboki had signed such a contract with the Bolshevik Communist party, and therefore all had to make earnest effort and suffer without yielding in spite of difficulties.

At this particular moment in time about 95 percent of people in our community were able to support themselves without aid or cooperation from others. But nonetheless many came to the warehouse merely for inquisitiveness, to test the quality of a foreign product or to taste some Russian foodstuffs. Apart from that, the most inexpensive brand of tobacco was called Koreshkey, stalks from tobacco leaves chopped in small pieces, prepared for smoking in a Russian newspaper tube or pipe. Of course, this habitual way of smoking in the Soviet Union at this time was common, but here it was something new for the folks to try. As the matter of fact, a great crowd was always gathered by the warehouse. Among other people, Mr. Kostus and some female were spotted there. At that time, my parents were talking about him, and I overheard Mother tell my father that not long ago Mr. Kostus got married to a woman of an average build and height from Naliboki and that they were presently dwelling in the forest, a place called Budy, which was about three miles northeastward from Trascianka. Additionally mother said, "This is what my brother Waclaw told me about Mr. Kostus when he brought us honey from Trascianka when you, Wilhelm, were absent. But in the meantime, I just forgot to tell you about this incident." Later, I saw Mr. Kostus and his wife walking in the Jewish shopping center, and his wife reached just up to his waist line.

    A little village, Budy was the central location of the chief foresters administration northeast from Trascianka, and from there three miles south was a hamlet, Kroman, the head office of the chief forester, at Kroman Lake, which had an area of 227.24 acres. This, of course, was a dominant part of the Wilderness of Naliboki, constituting an area of 592,800 acres, which combined together with the Wilderness of Niemen (Puszcza Zaniemienska) and the Russian Wilderness (Puszcza Ruska) comprised the territory of Nowogrodek, the domain over which a sovereign state exercised jurisdiction (Tereny Ziemi Nowogrddzkiej). However, from September 1939 to June 1941 existed here a Polish partisan detachment of major Dabrowski, who fought with Soviets to the time of German invasion in 1941 and was able yet to set off firearms against retreating troops of the Red Army. Naturally, Lieutenant Klimowicz at the same time was at large in the surrounding of Naliboki with his unit to protect his own and all men's kin from the Communist's elimination, to them a suspicious and objectionable element. Since the day he was forced to flee into the wilderness our consanguinity had no idea of his whereabouts, which happened to be in their best interest because of the fear of interrogation and, worst of all, surreptitious abduction during the night by the People's Commissariat of Internal Affairs. For this reason, Lieutenant Klimowicz remained secretly hidden and exhibited superior abilities to direct guerrilla movement opposing an occupying power.

Chapter VIII

THE SOVIET UNION OCCUPATION

In spite of an armed conflict between nations and the systematic extermination of an entire people of notable intellect, those who had been regarded as an endangerment to the Union of Soviet Socialist Republics, there came to be a curse appended to the land with a fury of the elements of atmospheric powers. This accretion caused the winter's temperature to exceed 45 degree centigrade, thus January 1940 became extremely cold to such an extent that our old folks claimed they had not experienced that kind of winter in their entire lifetimes. Many believed that this act of imprecating was caused by the atheistic Bolsheviks who through invasion opened their borderline and in this way let the Russian cold weather come into our country. Yet others said it was a freezing hell from Siberia that hit us with a blow by means of STALIN. Of course, his real name was Joseph Vissarionovich Dzhugashvili, born in the Caucassian village of Gori on December 21, 1879. Stalin entered the seminary at Tiflis, but because of his Marxist activities within the school of theology he was expelled from the seminary. His acts and deeds, which were inherently wrong in themselves, contributed to his downfall, and as a consequence many times he was held in jail; finally, it led him to an exile in Siberia at the age of 24. He had completely dropped his real name of Dzhugashvili in favor of Stalin, which means "man of steel," when he began to murder millions of people, including Lenin, Leon Trotsky, and his own wife, dearly beloved mother of his children. It is ironic then, when a man kills one or a number of persons, essentially then called a murderer, but when a man murders millions of people he is called the conqueror. Alike Stalin, by the blood of innocent people became a man of steel, one with machinations of the devil. Consequently, this world ruler of darkness turned his attention on Poland, with his crafty strength using men of steel to genocide the country's intelligentsia and patriotism, that which are called bourgeoisie and capitalist, who were considered to be the most implacable enemy of the Communistic regime.

Cramp and narrow our land appeared to the people educated and those unfortunate ones who toiled for the Free State of Poland, for their state of great distress had arrived and was at the threshold. With respect to this calamity, Szabunia had submitted his long prepared list of names and addresses of all foresters and chief foresters to the authority, NKVD, for their banishment to Siberia. I remember that it was in the early days of January during perilously freezing weather when over a thousand families from the territory of Nowogrodek were taken hold of suddenly and forcibly to thralldom. From the Wilderness of Naliboki alone were 350 families, or about 1,500 victims, including men, women and children. As it began to grow light in the morning, a large convoy traveled through Naliboki eastward under Soviet military escort to Siberia.. People subjected to suffering uttered prolonged, piercing cries of pain and terror. All their relatives and friends that were left behind became faint from fear and the expectation of the things coming upon the inhabited region of Naliboki. It came just as the old man of Terebejno once foretold, that on the ground of Naliboki there will be anguish of people, not knowing the way out because of agitation of evil men who will arrive here in their furnaces. But now this immense loss had struck, just like a plague of the Black Death, unexpected by anyone, and at such a tragedy there was not even a good-bye allowed to be said, or an affectionate clasp within the arms of another, or to touch with the lips as a sign of love and compassion to show pity for the suffering of another, with the desire to help or spare. To the contrary, this extremely fatal event of departure was cruel, enjoying the suffering of others and causing grief and strong emotions by shedding tears of many.

This Soviet military escort, however, was adequately equipped for the severe winter according to the Russian custom, but not so our people, being unfamiliar with their weather conditions. In this particular season their boots with large legs were made of pressed cloth of wool in thickness approximately half an inch, and the trousers, jackets, coats and hats that covered practically the whole head consisted of the same substance, but somewhat thinner, which as a whole provided guaranteed protection against Russia's dangerously cold weather. It has been reported that a demonstration confirmed the fact that an experienced Soviet soldier equipped in Russian winter clothes is able to sleep overnight outdoors without any harmful effects.

This horrifying, barbarous act of seizing so many people had enormously upset our family. My mother with kith and kin were crying all day, overwhelmed by grief, for among those unfortunate people was

A convoy of Polish families seized are taken down Wilno Street to Siberia, January 1940, under escort of the Red Army in single-norned hats, like an animal's horn attributed to demons.

her dear brother, Waclaw, with his wife and two sons, Czeslaw and Heniek. Czeslaw graduated with my sister Waclawa in 1939, and Heniek was just six years old, the same age as my brother Antoni. Lucky, Janka was a student at lyceum in Nowogrodek, and on this account she was left behind. However, her institution of learning as all others at this time was closed, but the young girl was apprehensive to return home because of great danger. The land was infested by evil activities, for it was a period of debauchery and violence because the badness of the Communist man was abundant everywhere, and every inclination of the thoughts of his heart was bad all the time.

The following day our grandparents came; they lived in Naliboki on the skirt of woods three miles from us with their son, Josef Lojko, the invincible legionnaire. Their special visit was to extend sympathy and to comfort mother since she was attached to Waclaw and particularly to his dear children, as daily she used to send them to school. My grandparents also were worried and greatly troubled about Boleslaw, who studied law in Wilno, because nobody knew anything about him, as well as Janka for that matter. Fortunately, all facilities of communication were nonfunctional everywhere, and therefore no news was considered good news, so expressed my father to my grandparents.

Due to the painful distress caused by the occupation of the Soviet Union, I noticed that my father had developed a new habit through nervousness. He began to squeeze a bit of bread in his fingers and kept continually rolling it into a pellet while he remained in a seated position of idleness. His habitual practice was so frequently repeated that it became almost automatic, which subsequently annoyed my mother. Many times she tried to restrain him from rolling bread pellets, but her efforts were of no avail.

In the first part of January, notwithstanding the fact that the temperature was 45 degrees Celsius, there was not much snow on the ground when the Soviet captors ordered the victims to use their own transportation. Therefore, they had to engage their four-wheeled horsedrawn vehicles instead of sledges, and because of it the whole convoy consisted of wagons. Subsequently, the victims' own transportation was confiscated by the captors for the USSR's public use as soon as they reached the railroad. But their livestock and poultry had been appropriated for public use before their departure; thus from this time on deprivation of property through confiscation began full scale, affecting all inhabitants.

Just as it was in Russia in 1928 when Stalin inaugurated the first Five-Year Plan, a vast program of industrialization and collectivization that by false assumption had as its purpose placing the Soviet Union on a firm economic basis. The concept of the Five-Year Plan was to burst national production to the highest point possible, and the concluding events of that period were celebrated nationwide and much publicized with respect to a norm. The average achievement for groups became competitive, which was supposed to lead Russia to a great abundance of everything. The Five Year Plan was carried on and on, despite the many hardships it brought on the population and opposition from the right side of the Communist Party. Then Stalin began to meet with serious resistance within the party. Moscow trials followed, and eventually many old comrades were sentenced to death. The stubborn population was deprived of properties through confiscation, and during this method of operations millions perished from lack of food because they repudiated an enormous program of collectivization. In like manner, cautiously and systematically the Soviets here made their demand from all inhabitants to surrender part of their livestock and poultry to the Bolshevik's Regime. For example, if any farmer had in his possession five head of cattle, hogs or chickens, etc., then one of five or two of ten and so on he had to submit to the authority. The principal idea was to strip the farmers gradually from all possessions so that finally they would be forced to work in a collective enterprise as a farm, called a kolkhoz.

In this Siberian freezing hell under compulsion to perform an act for mutual economic benefit, people commenced dragging their domestic farm animals out from the stables and pigsties and so on and so forth, and delivering them to Bolshevik's authority at the market ground next to gmina, the community building. Most of the men said nothing for fear of the Communists, but others, that is only a few, according to my father were mourning and groaning the loss of their livestock. As normally expected, one man was expressing himself in local Byelorussian language, saying that when the Soviets arrived in the square of Naliboki, "I remember they proclaimed that they came to set us free. Now it is obvious to me that they are indeed setting me free from that which I possessed." Another man grumbled and said, "I give my credit to the Polish prewar propaganda when it was written in a pamphlets, 'it is better to live in the Polish prison than to live in the Soviet's paradise,' the place of great beauty and delight." Father said so many animals were neighing and bellowing while the chairman, commissioner of NKVD and its officials were inspecting the livestock for any faults or defects. And only after their thorough inspection were the owners of the livestock able to be all dismissed, but none was accused of defraudation of the Soviet's regime. The livestock then was loaded onto the Russian heavy mobile military transport and without delay shipped to the USSR.

During the Soviet invasion many soldiers of the Red Army entered peoples' homes with curiosity, mainly to see how the Polish landowner lived under capitalism. One soldier came to our house and asked my parents if he could have something to eat, especially home-prepared foods because he was sick and tired of the army provisions. My parents then in a glad manner prepared a table for him in abundance of homemade food, including an alcoholic beverage. So, while he was experiencing pleasure in eating and drinking, he started explaining how he lived in his country, the Soviet Union, before he was drafted into the Red Army. He said that he worked in the Soviet's Kolkhoz from dawn to dusk and that all workers combined were fed from one large pot like hogs. One loaf of bread was separated into portions between five persons. The Kolkhoznicks, he said, were dissatisfied and complained when they were mobilized, saying, "Why on earth one rifle per one man when we used to be given one loaf per five men?" Of course, at that time my parents were skeptical; they thought the soldier was joking or was exaggerating his story, with a view to the military forces of a hundred divisions that had invaded our country. But now, however, my parents became doubtful and began to accept that what he said was true, and indeed their population was suffering from extreme hunger.

During the prewar time Szabunia's spying activities provided information about identities of certain individuals who lived in Naliboki and its surrounding area. Now, since such person was arrested by this apprehender, Szabunia, some of them who had been most distrustful and detestable were held at the NKVD headquarters for interrogation in Iwieniec. Among those was our former "Wójt Gminy," the community chairman about whom Szabunia had learned "Wójt" was a Polish officer in the rank of colonel and was engaged in combat action against the Bolsheviks, defeating them in World War I. Consequently "Wójt" himself was wounded and was left with a crooked left leg; that is why we noticed he walked with a limp every morning to the community building on Pilsudski Street while passing our residence. From the time when Szabunia had the people arrested, he frequently traveled back and forth to Iwieniec, where he was conducting the interrogations. However, the outcome was that Szabunia eventually tortured all his arrested victims to death. In the meantime, someone from Naliboki passed this unfortunate information secretly to our priest at the parsonage. In turn, the priest soon delivered this sad news to "Wójt's" wife. The bereaved parent of two sons, Zygtnunt and Ziutek, "Pani Wójtowa," chairman's lady, the priest admonished her, "Now you are in great danger, my child. We must find at once a safe place for you." Pani Wójtowa expounded her resume and referred to the fact that she used to work in a hospital as a qualified nurse. The priest was very glad to hear this and said, "Our Doctor Chwal is extremely busy at this very moment; it is advisable, therefore, for you to work as a nurse with Dr. Chwal." So Pani Wójtowa immediately began working with the doctor, and soon she had to abandon her residence by the lake on Pilsudski Street and move to Mr. Walon's dwelling, where the doctor's abode and clinic were located, right opposite our establishment on the same street.

Szabunia at this time was running around Naliboki like a rabid dog trying his best to capture Prelate Bajko, but unfortunately for him, Nalibokians hid the prelate in such a way even the devil himself would not be able to find him. Enraged, Szabunia began to exercise his power over Jews, compelling them against their will to search and find the prelate, Jan Radziwill and Alfons Toiko, that which Jews by now declined and did not want to have any part of it. Nevertheless, the search continued by NKVD and became a subject to contingency of apprehension.

As a subsequent result of being involved with Szabunia, the Jews realized that to remain faithful to the Bolshevik's regime was truly an effort without reward. "Till now," Mr. Machlis murmured, "we have gained nothing to show for and to be proud of."

"Gained nothing?" asked Mr. Szymanowicz. "Talk about what we have lost! Look at my business; it's empty. I cannot get any flour, yeast, salt or anything else for that matter to bake pastry, cakes, bagels or bread. See, what kind of baker I am? I ask you."

"True!" confirmed Mr. Jankiel. "We are all finished. All our businesses are wasted. We have absolutely no means of supporting or maintaining our existence anymore. No more can I gather shoddies and rags in exchange for soap. You see, under this regime you cannot possibly be even a rag-and-bone man. Besides, look at this Szabunia, what he is doing with Polish people; many he is sending to Siberia, and the others he is tormenting to death here."

"God forbid!" unanimously said the Jews. "We of all people must not immerse our hands in the blood of an innocent people."

It was lucky for Alfons that he was hiding in his own home and was together with his wife and his little girl. But Jan on the other hand, madly in love with Wierka, was hidden some half a mile from Wierka's residence where he used to live, now in his mother house on Poplawski Street. In this way he had no chance to be close with his greatly loved wife and his two children. Oh, how many times he wanted to wrest out and to cling close to Wierka, his most beautiful of God's creations. But his mother kneeled before him and implored with a lament, begging, "Please, my son, do not wrest out because this NKVD shall execute you and kill you on the spot. You shall make an orphan of your children. Oh, my God, think about the little ones." Supplicated mother, full of tears, did not know what to do and complained at our home, this tall and slim fine looking lady Radziwill. But Jan could not help it, he was tearing his hair off his head, and he was not afraid even to suffer death on account of his passion. His ardent affection for Wierka indeed was incapable of being expressed or put into words for anyone who knew his plight.

With respect to the detestable attitude, that of Hebraism, toward a corrupt Communism as it now had developed in our northeastern territory, "Wilenszczyzna," it was easily perceived as a start of gradual intense aversion among our invaders. Hence the Hebrew people were treated with hate by the Russians, just as much as Polish people throughout the centuries had been subjected to maltreatment and persecution on account of race. The endless wars between Russia and Poland is evidence sufficient to induce belief.

Through the centuries in this environment people developed unusual customs and traditions; no doubt these practices were borrowed from the previous invaders that swept this land some time ago, such as the Knights of the Tentonic Order of Prussia, Tatars, Turks and Swedes. For example, out of the Sweden nation there was a most influential character by the name Emanuel Swedenborg, 1688-1772, who developed a system of philosophy and mystic theology. He reported that he plunged deep into mysticism, heard mysterious conversations, saw visions, received revelations, saw heaven and hell, and conversed directly with angels and even with God Himself. He felt himself divinely commissioned to expound his revelations and perceptions, and even suggested that his theological writings were dictated to him by God. In spite of everything, our people were swallowed by perplexity of mind. They were confused, not knowing right from wrong; hence their acts, deeds and omissions were inherently wrong in themselves, morally wrong, "Mala In Se."

Old folks remembered the years long gone by and said that here in the wilderness were bandits, highwaymen, enchanters, sorcerers, witch doctors, astrologers and fortune tellers. Many were influenced by a belief founded on irrational feelings, especially of fear, marked by a trust in charms, omens, the supernatural, etc., also any rite or practice inspired by such belief. It is no wonder, therefore, that Satan, the devil himself, was predominating over the entire Wilderness of Naliboki.

People here were hunting animals for pleasure, just like Nimrod, a mighty hunter in opposition to God the Almighty. They were drinking and eating animals' blood. They were consuming strangled creatures from the forest, thus violating God's law, oath, agreement, etc. For did He not tell his people, you must abstain from things polluted by idols and from fornication and from what is strangled and from blood. Every moving animal that is alive may serve as food for you. As in the case of green vegetation. I do give it all to you, only flesh with its soul—its blood— you must not eat.

The nation was punished for transgressions of law that interdicted hunting animals for pleasure. That is why the extinction of animals was caused then, and later during World War I, followed by infliction of many people to death by starvation. Mother's baby sister and her continual struggle to obtain food led to her arrest and imprisonment at Krakow under suspicion of being a spy, then freed by her brother Jozef, the legionnaire. As any other people in this environment, my mother was superstitious. She keenly observed irrational feelings and was fearful. For instance, when I forgot something and then came back for it as I intended to go to play or perform some service, mother always warned me some kind danger may occur or misfortune if I was to follow my intent. Or again, if I was putting my socks on inside out, mother repeated a similar warning. She always cautioned me not to sing or whistle on Friday and so on and so forth. My father, on the other hand, had his own deep inherent ways that obviously had derived from our ancestors. I used to enjoy watching his skillful way of killing a hog. I remember it well, the way he habitually employed his skill. He used to grab hold of a hog's front right leg and then jerk it suddenly toward him, causing the fat animal to fall on its back, and swiftly pierce it in the heart with a pointed instrument called an awl or bodkin. (We called it "Szwajka.") At the same moment the end of the szwajka was vibrating and throbbing, causing the pig to squeak with a somewhat prolonged loud cry until it was dead. After a singe and thorough wash, Father cut open the belly and removed all internal parts of the body, then he used a cup to draw up the pig's blood, which he drank, and again he drew up another cup of blood and gave it to me and said aloud as with an order, "Drink it! It is good." Of course, following father's instinct in order to act in ways that are essential to survival, I drank the pig's blood, but I did not like it much, because it was warm and the fact that I saw this pig while it was still alive. So only a chill and shudder went through me as I drank this warm blood, as it was the first time in my life. I felt then that I was doing something wrong without anyone telling me, but what and why I did not know; neither my father, for he was accustomed to it, by which already he lost his conscience. So for many, many years I wondered, why at that first time drinking blood I had such a strange sensation and frightening guilt. But the answer was very simple, which I did not know nor anybody who lived in Naliboki. The proper answer to this forbidden act is that God in advance has implanted into every living soul His law, even before I was born. "Only flesh with its soul—its blood—you must not eat." Soul represents life as a creature. Both ne'phesh and psy'khe' are also used to mean life, not merely as an abstract force or principle, but life as a creature, human or animal. Once the blood is poured out from the body it makes the expression "deceased or dead soul," which also appears a number of times in the Bible, meaning simply "a dead person." That is why in regard to the human blood, when David's men risked their lives to bring him a drink of water, he poured it out on the ground, for in his eyes, to drink that water would be like drinking the human blood of his soldiers, which he knew would violate God's law.

Blood sausage, highly seasoned blood stuffed into the cleaned entrails of some animal, usually a pig, just like my father used to make, was most popular in our parts of the country. Yet, such a delicacy one could not get from a Jewish dealer in meats, and no one in Naliboki was curious enough to find out why? Is it not possible, therefore, that Naliboki and its region was the headquarters of Satan himself, precisely as it was in Babylon, an ancient empire of "Mesopotamia" on the river Euphrates, just like Naliboki on the river Niemen. The capital of Babylonia from about 2100 B.C. was celebrated as a seat of wealth, luxury and vice. Of course, vice denotes an immoral habit or trait, a slight personal fault, foible, habitual indulgence in degrading or harmful practices, something that mars, a blemish or imperfection. Undoubtedly, this Babylon's VICE fits Naliboki's description.

That is why in this haunt of vice in the early days and throughout many generations people here have been bewildered by the devil to grapple with death.

The ancient city of Babylon in the Hebrew scriptures is featured prominently as the long-time enemy of God and his people. It was outstandingly prominent during its entire history as a religious center. And from this center its religious influence radiated in many directions.

This haunt of vice originally began here in the manner similar to that of Nimrod, the grandson of Noah. The Dukes Radziwill in company with monarchs, the princes of Poland, Lithuania and Russia, hunted not just animals for pleasure but also warriors in order to improve their warfare skill to be invincible in future combats. Their hunting territory extended from the Wilderness of Naliboki throughout the land of Nowogrodek and Wilno. All this land combined is called "Wilenszczyzna," in comparison to that of Mesopotamia. The rivers and lakes of the land of Wilno belong to a confluence of Niemen and Dzwina, similar to Babylonia, that ancient land in the lower Mesopotamian valley through which the Tigris and Euphrates Rivers flow. In this land of Wilno there are well over 1,000 lakes in an area exceeding 1 ha., with the largest lake being Narocz (80.5 km square). In the southern and northeastern parts Wilenszczyzny is "HORN-BEAM OSZMIANSKI," created by the receding flood waters after the great world's deluge and exceeding heights of 200 meters above sea level. Today, however, the city Wilno is the capital of Lithuania and is called "Vilnius" or Vilnyus (Pol. Wilno; Rus. Vilna). A pagan settlement existed on the site until the thirteenth century, but the community's real importance dates from the building of a castle there in 1320 by the Lithuanian Grand Prince Gediminas, who made Wilno the capital of Lithuania in 1323. The following six centuries brought a series of struggles, sieges and bombardments to the flourishing commercial city and fortress. Here the "Ostra Brama Chapel" contains a highly revered image of the Virgin Mary. Regarding the Ostra Brama, which means sharp gate or arch, Adam Mickiewicz used it in his expressive masterpiece "Forefathers' Eve, Part III," and in his last poem, "Pan Tadeusz" (1834). In the first of these he develops his "messianistic" doctrine that Poland among the nations occupies the place of Christ among men. Poland has been crucified but will rise again and will inaugurate a new period in history. The background of "Pan Tadeusz" is rural Lithuania on the eve of Napoleon's expedition into Russia in 1812; its subject is a quarrel among the local Polish nobles, happily terminated by a wedding.

The university in Wilno was founded by King Stephan Bathory as an academy in 1578, raised to a university in 1802, suppressed 1830, and reopened in 1920. Vilnius in the western part of the Soviet Union, at 54 degrees 40' N. lat. and 25 degree 20' E. long. In this city was born well-known Godowski Leopold, 1870-1938, the Polish-American pianist, composer and teacher. Important among his works are "Studies on Chopin Etudes," "Symphonic Metamorphoses," and many transcriptions for piano. He died in New York.

According to some historians, in Naliboki Polish King Zygmunt August nearly lost his life during his mysterious hunt in 1540. He ordered a small Christian Chapel built upon the ruins of the ancient pagan temple of "Perkuna and Goddess of Animals." And again, upon this place Dukes Radziwill built the church of St. Bartholomew according to Gothic architecture in 1630 A.D. The votive offering of the king was moved from the small chapel and hanged by the main altar, which hung until our modern time when Nazis utterly destroyed the church by fire on the first day of August 1943.

In my childhood I remember how I gazed at the wonderful paintings inside the church. I always wondered how the artists created such beauty, since God, not in the manner of a niggard, favored me too with such talent. I looked steadily at the votive offering of the King and various holy pictures painted in splendid colors, as of St. Bartholomew, who was one of the twelve apostles, and is mentioned in the Acts of the Apostles and in the synoptic gospels of Matthew, Mark and Luke.

Oh, how I was enchanted and fascinated by the magnificent, inspiring to the imagination beautiful holy pictures of saints that we worshipped in our church. I could not understand why the Germans would burn to the ground such a splendid church, which I have missed so much when reflecting on the past. However, once I was gazing at the picture of the "Last Supper" because of a habit of mine. I noticed that there was absolutely nothing on the walls in the background of Jesus, so I wondered why. But when I read the book of Daniel about Sha'drach Me'shach and A'bed'ne'go I learned that because they refused to worship an image of gold as the king had ordered, they were thrown into the fiery furnace. They were ready to die but not violate God's Law because He commanded: You must not bow down to them nor be induced to serve them, because I Jehovah your God am a God exacting exclusive devotion, bringing punishment for the error of fathers upon sons, upon the third generation and upon the fourth generation, in the case of those who hate me. You must not have any other gods against my face.

Knowing that branch of knowledge concerned with past events, especially those involving human affairs, one would know what to expect from the future, and could also ignore the idea of destiny, the power that is thought to predetermine the course of events. But obviously it seems that nobody in Naliboki knew or did not wish to know its annals, thus the community that existed here for centuries was uninformed and therefore continued to live in a state of confusion just like the people in Babylon. While constructing the city, they suddenly came to a halt when confusion in communications occurred. Hence, the name is derived from the verb (ba'lal), meaning "to mingle, mix, confuse, confound." Babel's God-defying program centered around construction of a religious tower "with its top in the heavens. It was not built for the worship and praise of Jehovah, but with the motive of making a "celebrated name" for the builders. The approximate time of such building may be drawn from "Peleg," who lived from 2269 to 2030 B.C.E. His name meant "division, part," for in his days earth's population was divided—Jehovah scattered them over all the surface of the earth in the exact manner as the people from Naliboki and all its surrounding region, which includes Chotow, Kleciszcze, Kozliki, Jankowicze, Ogrodniki, Prudy and Terebejno.

Similarly, in Naliboki instead of the Tower of Babel people constructed a "blast furnace" in the days of those Dukes Radziwill. They produced steel, from which they manufactured on a large scale swords and hilts for the swords decorated with priceless stones. Their splendid product of swords was distributed throughout Europe and the Asia Minor peninsula of extreme west Asia, comprising most of Turkey. In return, people became rich and had many possessions, so that the whole abode became a haunt of vice, cursed by God. And from this time on people living here found themselves under machination of Satan, who was directing them constantly to grapple with death. That is why if one would travel now through this wildernesses one could see a multitude of graves, and far off mounds of dead bodies of the Polish people who were massacred by the swords of their own making in the hands of Turks, Mongols, Tatars, Swedes, knights of the Teutonic Order of Prussia, etc.

With regard to a curse, prophet Isaiah wrote: The land has gone to mourning, has faded away. The productive land has withered, has faded away. The high ones of the people of the land have withered. And the very land has been polluted under its inhabitants, for they have bypassed the laws, changed the regulation, broken the indefinitely lasting covenant. That is why the curse itself has eaten up the land and those inhabiting it are held guilty. That is why the inhabitants of the land have decreased in number, and very few mortal men have remained over.

The Hebrew and Greek words in the Bible that are translated by the word "curse" or similar expressions is basically the desiring, threatening or pronouncing of evil upon someone or something. There are different types of curses. The first curse employed was at the time of the Edenic rebellion and was directed by God against the instigator of the rebellion through the serpent. This curse was to end in his destruction. At the same time the ground was cursed on Adam's account, resulting in its producing thorns and thistles but not in its destruction. The curse that God placed on Cain condemned him to a fugitive life. A curse resulted in destruction of the people by a global flood. The first curse pronounced by a human was that which Noah directed against Cannan, son of Ham, condemning him to slave for Shem and Japheth. A curse of solemn pronouncement or prediction of evil, when made by God or by an authorized person, has a prophetic value and force. "Oath" as well as "curse" implies an oath that carries with it a curse as its penalty for violation of the oath, or because of the oath's proving to be false. Paul showed that all the Jews needed to be redeemed from the curse of the Law covenant by Christ's becoming a curse for them through his death on the torture stake. Jesus's action in cursing the "Goat" class and also in instructing his followers to "bless those cursing you." Accursed children, those who are covetous, "have eyes full adultery, and who entice unsteady souls." A curse that is "laid up" originally applied to votive offerings laid up or set apart as sacred in a temple.

Accursed, set apart as evil—Paul wrote to the Galatians that they should consider as "accursed" anyone (even angels) who declared to them as good news something contrary to that which they had received. Those who had "no affection for the Lord" were due to come under a similar designation. A curse was to end ancient Babylon in complete destruction, and finally, in contrast with earthly Jerusalem, the curse hit to the symbolic city "Babylon the great" as a result of God's judicial decree against her. The "anathema" pronounced against her, the world empire of false religion is evident from the command given at Revelation. It became evident, therefore, that the most accurate description contrast with Naliboki fits that ancient city of Mesopotamia on the Euphrates, capital of Babylonia from about 2100 B.C., celebrated as a seat of wealth, luxury and vice.

Babylon was a most religious place. The remains of no less than fifty-three temples have been discovered, without comparison to Naliboki because there was only one temple, but there were many more in the land of "Wilenszczyzna." The god of the imperial city was Marduk. Here in Naliboki was the goddess of animals in the temple of Perkuna. His temple was E-sagila, meaning "House of the Foundation of Heaven and Earth." Marduk is called Merodach in the Bible, and various authorities identify Nimrod with the god Marduk; it was ancient custom for a city to deify its founder. Triads of deities were also prominent in the Babylonian religion. One of these, made up of two gods and a goddess, was Sin (the moon god), Shamash (the sun god) and Ishtar; these were said to be the rulers of the Zodiac. And still another triad was composed of the devils Labartu, Labasu and Akhkhazu. Idolatry was everywhere in evidence. Babylon was indeed "a land OF GRAVEN IMAGES," filthy "dungy idols." The Babylonians believed in the immortality of the human soul. Nergal was their god of the underworld, "the land of no return," and his wife Eresh-kigal its sovereign lady.

The transposition of false religion from Babylon to Naliboki conforms to the law of logic and became actual after confusion of the people's language took place in the ancient city. Characteristics indicating the distinctive quality of Babylonian religion in the land of Wilno "Wilenszczyzna" was long before Babylon's fall to the Medes and Persians in 539 B.C.E. by Cyrus the Great.

Here, legends filled man's imagination. People professed that in the land of Wilno once existed large cities with the multitude of temples raised in honor and glory to the Trinitarian gods of the devil, where a human sacrifice was predominant, when victim's beating hearts were held up to them. Degradation of human quality was brought down by filth and dungy idols. Regarding these cities it was said that the earth had swallowed them suddenly, and that their places became lakes.

Stories of like characteristics continued in our neighborhood concerning a wicked city with its temple that supposedly existed on the site of Kroman. This ancient city, according to explanatory description, had its main entrance or gate on the southwestern location at the present hamlet by the highway that leads east-westward. By reason of its evil deeds, human sacrifice to the triad of devils, etc., the earth swallowed the city by sudden and violent motion, and it was plunged deep under the ground, causing its hole of expanse to be filled with water, which as a result became a lake in the area of 228 acres called Kroman.

I have heard many old folks say that the lake Kroman is extremely deep and that the water in its center is very cold, in all probability because of its depth. They further emphasized that all around in this particular location there is something that has perpetually terrified people. And of course, it was obvious to everyone that Kroman's hamlet was haunted for as long as anyone could remember.

The lake Kroman ceaselessly inspired me with dread, a terrifying anticipation, as of evil, when my herd of cattle headed toward the lake. This very fear always made me turn the cattle from the lake because I was very scared to even look at its expanse in the middle of the forest, especially when I was alone in that vicinity. Notwithstanding the fact that from the north bank I was able to see a little of hamlet, but it did not helped me in the least for I knew the place was haunted.

Haunted places are supposedly visited by ghosts, which allegedly are dead human bodies that demons are impersonating. The demons are attracted to the places where their artifacts have been laid, and thus they would reiteratively reappear impersonating some dead humans who themselves do not exist, for they are dead, unconscious of anything. For this reason Kroman seems to be their ideal location, since here undoubtedly existed an original demons' abode.

One may wonder where these demons come from. Well, before the flood of Noah's day, it appears that other angels of God left their proper habitation in the heavens and their assigned positions there and, materializing as human bodies, came to dwell on earth, marrying human women and producing offspring called Nephilim. These angels, having left God's service, came under the control of Satan. Hence Satan is called "the ruler of the demons." In one instance when Jesus expelled demons from a man, the Pharisees accused him of doing so by the power of "Beelzebub, the ruler of the demons." That

The North Bank of the Lake Kroman and Canal Lock.

Sacrifice to the triad of devils.

they had reference to Satan is shown by Jesus's answer, in which he said, "If Satan expels Satan, he has become divided against himself."

When the building of the Tower of Babel began in 2239 B.C.E., people said, "Come on! Let us build ourselves a city and also a tower with its top in the heavens, and let us make a celebrated name for ourselves, for fear we may be scattered over all the surface of the earth."

After that Jehovah said, "Look! They are one people and there is one language for them all, and this is what they start to do. Let us go down and there confuse their language that they may not listen to one another's language." Accordingly Jehovah scattered them from there over all the surface of the earth, and they gradually stopped building the city. That is why its name was Babel, because there Jehovah confused the language of all the earth, and Jehovah scattered them from there over all the surface of the earth.

So, from the time of the scattering of people over all the surface of the earth until Babylon's destruction in 539 B.C.E., these humans of false religion throughout the seventeen centuries flourished in the lands wherever they had reached their suitable place, such as the land of Wilno (Wilenszczyzna), and for example, a legendary island, Atlantis, and other legendary lands, such as Lyonnesse off the Cornish coast and the lost Breton city of Ys. Because of the wickedness of its inhabitants the island disappeared beneath the sea and the cities sank beneath the waters, about which the Bible does not mention. But nonetheless it is reasonable to take for granted that when Jehovah annihilated that ancient city Babylon, hence all other cities of the scattered people over all the surface of the earth were contemporaneously swept away forever, and thus they became to be beneath the waters as a legend. However, whether it is a legend or the historical fact that serves as a source for knowledge of the past, it is crystal clear that man till now has learned nothing from it to change his ways.

That is why only Jehovah can tell the finale from the beginning. The virgin daughter of Babylon is to sit in the dust, dethroned and naked, and the multitude of her counselors will be burned up like stubble. In one night Babylon had fallen, ending centuries of Semitic supremacy, control of Babylon became Aryan, and Jehovah's prophecy was fulfilled.

From that memorable date, 539 B.C.E., Babylon's glory began to fade as the city declined. Alexander the Great intended to make Babylon his capital but he suddenly died in 323 B.C.E. at thirty-three years of age. About the fourth century C.E. the city appears to have passed out of existence. It became nothing more than "piles of stones," just as it was foretold. Naturally, it is logical to conclude that if a city destroyed on the surface of the earth could not have been rebuilt, how more so those cities that sunk beneath the waters. Who can bring them into existence again?

Among John's visions recorded in the book of Revelation appear pronouncements of judgment against "Babylon the Great," as well as a description of her and her downfall. Thus, Babylon the Great must be viewed as a symbolic city, one of which the literal city of Babylon was the prototype. Because the ancient city gives the mystic city its name, it is helpful to consider briefly the outstanding features of Babylon on the Euphrates, features that provide clues to the identity of the symbolic Mesopotamia, "the land between the rivers," the name often applied to the Tigris-Euphrates Valley. Broadly speaking, Mesopotamia is the habitable area bound by the Persian Gulf on the southeast, the mountains of Iran and Turkey on the east and north, and by the deserts of Jordan and Arabia on the west and south. In ancient times it included the territory of Babylonia and Assyria; today, it is the kingdom of Iraq.

Similarly Wilenszczyzna, the land between two rivers, or in the fork of Niemen and Wilia, embraces the entire Wilderness of Naliboki and the black soil in the Nowogrodek region, where the descendants of Anak, who are from the Nephilim, the men of extraordinary size still dwell to this day.

Indubitably those giants and/or the people from ensuing generations wandered from the fork of the Tigres-Euphrates Valley through Asia Minor by the Black Sea and northward to the land of Wilenszczyzna, and here they settled down in the fork of Niemen and Wilia.

CITY OF JOHN'S VISION

A distinguishing characteristic of Babylon the Great is her drunkenness, she being pictured as drunk on the blood of God's people and the blood of Jesus's followers. She thus is the spiritual counterpart of the ancient city of Babylon, expressing the same enmity toward the true people of God. Significantly, it was to the charge of religious leaders that Jesus laid the responsibility for all the righteous blood spilled on earth, from the blood of righteous Abel to the blood of Zechariah. While those words were addressed to religious leaders from among Jesus's own race, the Jewish nation, and while persecution against Jesus's followers was particularly intense from that sector for a time, history shows that thereafter the opposition to genuine Christianity came from other sources (the Jews themselves suffering considerable persecution).

That is why John's vision admonishes God's people: Get out of her, my people, if you do not want to share with her in her sins, and if you do not want to receive part of her plagues. For her sins have massed together clear up to Heaven, and God has called her acts of injustice to mind. That is why in one day her plagues will come, death and mourning and famine, and she will be completely burned with fire, because Jehovah God, who judged her, is strong.

The Last Day of Naliboki

After the final judgment was executed upon the ancient city of Babylon and all contemporaneous wickedness had been wiped off the surface of the earth by Jehovah, following in time throughout the centuries new cities were built in Mesopotamia, alike Wilenszczyzna. Here came into view such cities as Wilno, Nowogrodek, Oszmian, Wolozyn, Lida, Stolpce, etc. The population of Mesopotamia remained largely Semitic, and the Persian overlords had to employ prevailing languages, Aramaic, to communicate with their subjects in this area. On the other hand, the population in Wilenszczyzna was Slavic, one of the most important families of Indo-European languages. In accordance with its geographic position, it shows some connections with Baltic, especially Lettish, on the one side, and with Iranian on the other. Here again, people built the temples in every city, and again worshipped false gods. In Nowogrodek at the side of the castle, a parish-church in the seventeenth century was raised on the ruins of a Perkuna temple, exactly as the chapel of King Zygmunt August was built on the ruins of the temple, Perkuna and Goddess of Animals. Subsequently, because of the blood that had been spilled of many, a church of St. Bartholomew was raised on the ruins of the pagan idol worshippers in honor to those who have been persecuted and suffered a violent and untimely death, in a like manner as the martyr Bartholomew.

St. Bartholomew's tradition represents preaching in India and being martyred by being flayed alive and crucified in Armenia (or in Cilicia). In works of art he has been represented as flayed and wearing his own skin as a cloak, as in the statue by Marko d'Agrate in the cathedral at Milan, or carrying his skin in his hand, as in Michelangelo's "Last Judgment" in the Sistine Chapel of the Vatican. His feast day is on August 24.

Because of an appeal for evil, people here have constantly ripped off strips of skin from their bodies; they were tortured, tormented, persecuted and killed. During World War I for their food they ate heather; from its seeds they baked the bread and ate it. Except for the time period between two world wars there was peace and prosperity.

The Hebrew word sha'lohm' is broader in its application than the English term "peace." Besides referring to the state of being free from war or disturbance, sha'lohm' can convey the idea of health, safety, soundness, welfare, friendship and entirety or completeness. Exactly this kind of shalohm in Naliboki I experienced from the day I was born July 15, 1929, until 1939, when the calamity of Naliboki took place, that which was foretold by an old man, Jozef Byczkiewicz. Just as Paul wrote to Thessalonians in Corinth 50 A.D., where it is that they saying "peace and security," sudden destruction is to be instantly upon them, just as the pang of distress upon a pregnant woman, and they will by no means escape.

After ancient Babylon was destroyed, some centuries later upon the hill in Naliboki overgrown with oaks a temple of PERKUNA was raised and dedicated to the goddess of animals. Later, at the end of tenth century A.D., that pagan temple began to deteriorate on account of a new Christian era in Poland, that which has prevailed, when most powerful Mieszko, as once was Attila in the eastern part of Europe, was lured to Catholicism by Otto III and the King of Czechoslovakia; thus he became the first Christian Prince of Poland, 960-992 A.D. However, Attila, 406-453, king of the Huns, raided the Eastern Roman Empire, gaining him the title of "Scourge of God," and threatened Rome, but was dissuaded by Pope Leo I. Naturally, Germany or Czechoslovakia had no desire for history to repeat itself, since these countries already had the doctrine and practice of a Catholic church. Following in time, when King Zygmunt August built the Catholic chapel in order to place his votive offering, the chapel was raised on the ruins of the Perkuna temple, at which time the ancient oaks had already faded away. Then, finally, on the same spot where the chapel was, Dukes Radziwill built the church of St. Bartholomew and the votive offering of the king was replaced to the new church and hung in front of the main altar. At that time the hill became surrounded by the growing alder trees and fir trees, which were growing till our time, as our folks remembered.

It seems that the prophetic words of Isiah had a significant effect on Naliboki and its surrounding in regard to a curse that befell our homeland. He wrote: the high ones of the people of the land have withered. And, the very land has been polluted under its inhabitants, for they have bypassed the laws, changed the regulation, broken the lasting covenant. That is why, the curse itself has eaten up the land and those inhabiting it are held guilty. That is why the inhabitants of the land have decreased in number, and very few mortal men have remained over.

How true it is that the high ones have withered, such as princes, kings, czars, dukes and generally the high ones of all the people of the land. These ones became dry, as a plant when cut down or deprived of moisture. The ordinary men were drafted for compulsory Soviet military service and never came back home. Many Jews fled to Palestine. During the Soviet invasion many politically inclined escaped to foreign lands. Many such were murdered by Byelorussian outlaws. Many again were arrested by People's Commissariat of Internal Affairs, and many of them were tortured to death. A great number of families were seized to Siberia. It shows indeed that the inhabitants of the Wilderness of Naliboki decreased in number, and very few mortal men have remained over.

In the beginning of Dynasty Jagellon, from the time when Poland was united with Lithuania until the final partition and extinction of Poland, the population in the land of Wilenszczyzna was rich and famous. People here lived in splendor, exceeding brilliance from emitted or reflected light, in conspicuous greatness of achievement and excellence. That is why about this golden age and the love for his country the poet Adam Mickiewicz expresses himself beautifully while being in an exile. His initiating words of "Pan Tadeusz" are as follows: Lithuania, my country, you are like health, how much you should be prized only he can learn who has lost you. Today your beauty in all its splendor I see and describe, for I yearn for you. Holy Virgin, who protects bright Czenstochowa and shines above the Pointed Gate in Wilno! You who does shelter the castle of Nowogrodek with its faithful folks! As by miracle you did restore me to health in my childhood, when, offered by my weeping mother to your protection, I raised my dead eyelids, and could straightaway walk to the threshold of your shrine to thank God for the life returned me, so by miracle you will return us to the bosom of our country. Meanwhile bear my griefstricken soul to those wooded hills, to those green meadows stretched far and wide along the blue Niemen, to those fields painted with various grain, gilded with wheat, silvered with rye, where grows the amber mustard the buckwheat white as snow, where the clover glows with a maiden's blush, where all is girdled as with a ribbon by a strip of green turf on which here and there rest quiet pear-trees.

Those were the days concerning which our native poet described in his renowned poem, the time when Naliboki had Europe-wide distribution of the most beautiful crystals, the best quality steel and fancy swords with hilts from the polished stone, that which excited mercantile traffic.

Now. as the days passed by under Soviet Union occupation, many individuals appeared to be missing just overnight; they were disappearing and nobody knew what was happening to them. My parents noticed that Katlarycha, called sister, a head nurse with her companion, Taciana, also mysteriously had vanished. My parents were aware of the fact that Katlarycha was a member of aristocracy under the czar's rule, about which Szabunia must have found out, taking into account that these two Russian ladies were number one on his list as enemies to the Bolshevik's regime. Except that the Communists did not bother to consider their innocence under the present circumstances, since during their regime in Naliboki Katlarycha and Taciana did nothing but care for the sick.

While the Communists were so preoccupied with the abduction of people, it seemed that they had forgotten to enforce the controlling power with respect to hunting and harvesting trees in the wilderness. Under such an irresponsible government for its subjects, where the store houses were empty of supplies, where the rubles had no value, where the Jews could no longer depend on their business but had to exchange their gold for a sack of potatoes or wheat from their next-door neighbor, the people secretly had to pursue game to have anything for food because of the critical time. Yet, on the other hand, others were cutting prime timber and hauling it home for the new necessary building structures of houses, stables and barns.

In regard to hunting wild boars, deer and hares in the wilderness, since the possession of any firearms was forbidden by the Soviets, folks for this purpose were obliged to use traps and snares. For the wild boars deep pits were excavated on their path to a field of potatoes. Trap devices for catching other animals were used, but out of all the most popular in the region were snares, loops of wire in which if anything was caught by the neck, the animal would strangle itself. Because of the political deprivation of necessary living provisions and intentional assimilation of all to Kolkhoz and Stalin's First Five Year Plan, folks under this condition took no heed of God's Law that prohibits Christians to consume things strangled on account of its blood. (Acts 15:29)

However, to catch a partridge or any small, plump game bird such as the ruffed grouse or the bobwhite, was quite simple. One would have to take a handful of grain and push it into the snow, at least up to the elbow, then release the grain and pull out one's hand straight upward, leaving a deep hole in the snow so that when a partridge reached its food, the feathers simply would not allow the bird to get out from such an awkward position. The game then is seized alive and ready to serve as food.

From observing other people I learned adequately how to set snares for deer and hares. In the outset of February during extremely cold weather and deep snow, I set out on skis to find a suitable location in order to place my snares. For the hares I arranged my snares in the skirt of woods, passing the sawmill, which was newly built and ceased to function under the Soviet's occupation, which also caused an interruption of electricity.

Since there was a lack of firewood at home, the following day I asked my father to harness our horse to a sledge so that I could ride into the forest and bring a load of timber for fuel. Father agreed, and he recommended I ride about five miles north to our meadow that was in the midst of forest where I would be able to find a lot of dead, dry trees, ideal for firewood. But he warned me not to cut any growing trees for it is contrary to law.

During my journey to our meadow, I remembered how my mother with Mania Baszuro, Mania klimowicz, Wierka Radziwill and Bronislawa, my sister Waclawa, brother Antoni, Baszuro Teresa, Jadwiga and Stanislaw and Radziwill all used to walk this way by the beautiful Jewish orchard northward into the woods for a whole day to pick whortleberries, a European variety of blueberry, also called bilberry. How most enjoyable those days were, as of a picnic and great fun gathering blueberries in the overgrown expanse farther than one's eye can see. Traveling somewhat farther through the forest I had a good sight of deer struggling in deep snow, far away from the road. The large trees growing in the low ground were suddenly bursting from the severe frost and causing most frightening explosions. Finally, when I reached my destination, the path to the right leading to our meadow was covered with snow some four feet thick. Therefore, I drove to and fro several times to trample the snow, making an appropriate way to pull out from there a load of timber. The meadow was surrounded by overgrown birch trees, and in between there was a thick brushwood full of footways made by deer as they walked to the stack of hay that was in the middle of meadow. Without hesitation I set my snares for the deer and hares and began to cut the trees and create a load, while my horse enjoyed eating his oats and hay. I covered the horse with a heavy blanket, and as for myself I knew I had to be on constant move in order to keep my body temperature warm. As soon as I completed my task, I was on my way home. Of course, on my arrival home I did not tell anybody, even my father, about my intentional attempt of hunt.

The following day I put my skis on and went behind the sawmill to examine the snares in the skirt of woods. When I arrived I was surprised to find four hares trapped in snares, strangled and frozen stiff. I put them into a sack so nobody could see what I was carrying, and this way I got home. Accurately, Pani Wojtowa and my parents were sitting at the table talking. So mother asked me, "What have you got inside that sack?" At once, I pulled the hares out from it. Surprised, mother said, "Oh, what I am going to do with them?

Pani Wojtowa interrupted and said, "Pani Klimowicz, if you permit me, I can make a pasty (pasztet) that will be enough to feed both our families." Mother agreed and I helped to carry the hares to Pani Wojtowa's house.

A few days later I set out to our meadow to inspect the snares. When I got there, I found in one of my snares a large ruminant animal having deciduous antlers, that of a male only. Farther on there was a white hare trapped also, the kind that exists but in the wilderness. Immediately, I shoved this deer on a sledge and placed the white hare beside it, cut some trees and shaped the load to conceal the dead animals. As soon as I was finished, I was riding on my way home. When I pulled into our yard, father came out and said, "What a fine load of firewood you have been able to bring home, son." But I thought I would console him more when I told him that under the wood there was a deer and hare. Instead, father became disturbed and worried. He told me that it was not lawful to trap animals like that; besides, the Golshevik's could arrest me if they found out about it. Then I understood why I was filled with fear while I was dragging these animals on the sledge.

After father had disposed of the animal meat by storing it, I then decided that I would never again set snares to trap animals for food or otherwise.

Often, as I walked to the spring to fetch a pail of water for mother's urgent usage, by the St. John column Szabunia and his NKVD members cut down with automatic guns, I recalled how some people when passing by the St. John took their hats off, others made a sign of the cross or bowed, and some even stopped by the column and said their prayers. But presently, I noticed, people passed through absolutely without paying obeisance, except those doing it just by force of habit, not realizing that the St. John column was no longer there.

The people in Naliboki were by inherent regulation very gentle and goodhearted. Instead of a salutation with the opening words of, "good morning," etc., they adapted a common form of greeting by a simple bow with the words, "Niech bedzie pochwalony Jezus Chrystus," or, "Praised be Jesus Christ," and the answer of the greeted person was, "Na wieki wiekow." "Amen. For the ages of ages. Amen."

The extremely severe freezing temperatures scared people walking by the lake when willows and alder trees were bursting in half from the bottom to the top, with a dreadful sound, as of a rifle. On this account the lake and all streams nearby were frozen solid, except that in the spring water flowed steadily and smoothly along. Its water just emitting a lot of moisture into the air, especially visible vapor floating as light mist. And many old folks were scratching their heads as they stood over the spring on the bridge, wondering why this abstruse water could not freeze. On Sunday as usual, people heavily clad, faces covered, only the eyes visible, and around the mouth white frozen vapor sent forth from the act of respiration as they all went to church. Everyone looked sullen and dejected, no longer amiable and joyous as we used to be six months ago. People now felt as if they were practicing deceit and felt guilty of something unrecognized; kneeling, they beat themselves in the chest, repeatedly saying, "Mea Culpa," while the priest Baradyn at the altar officiated the divine service. Miserable Prelate Bajko, a man of genius who was talented to exert a strong influence over others, had become a fugitive from pursuit of the NKVD.

In the past around the church and on the cemetery grounds during the night the place was consecrated even though it was repeatedly haunted. Folks used to talk about the ghosts and spirits that were supposed to recur persistently to the memory of some individuals who told their stories to others, and consequentially many were scared to walk at night by the sacred place. Except for my cousins who lived at the rear of cemetery. Their father, Michal Lojko, kept his children under strict discipline and thus he reassured them that there was no need for them to be filled with apprehension because there was no such thing as ghosts. When he sent Marysia or Lucjan to borough for an important mission, their father always emphasized to them to be courageous and bold. After completing the task, my cousins usually stopped at our house. Astonished, my parents were curious as to how Lucjan was able to walk by the cemetery at night, which their kids were incapable of for being so scared. But Lucjan, like his two sisters, said, "Our father taught us to obey him promptly no matter what, and above all not to fear some foolish narration of a fictional tale made up by old folks." Yet, my father, unlike his brother-in-law Michal, believed that there were apparitions that indeed were startling. That is why he used to tell a lot of scary stories to others about "Kamionka," a separate portion of Naliboki next to "Eascianki" on the same street, Nowogrodek. The street at the end of the borough through Kamionka climbed up the hill and thus was called Kamionka (stone jug). Nevertheless, directly from the very top of the stone jug undoubtedly was a haunting place, in all probability because this was the location of ancient worship and sacrifice inspired by demons up on the rock, just as Kroman, or the temple of Perkuna, the spot of archaios demonolatry upon which the present church of St. Bartholomew was built for permanent Christian worship.

However, from the time of invasion people ceased to talk about the ghosts and scary places. It seemed that under the period of the Soviet's occupation the visible representatives of incorporeal persons had a change of reality; they in fact became corporeal persons of the People's Commissariat of Internal Affairs. The plain truth about the change of reality is that determined Satan had summoned his angels to possess the mortal members of the NKVD in order to direct them to the systematic extermination of an entire people. This actually became an interim when there was left no one to trust; then one can only trust his own heart.

In March Chairman Szabunia anew made his nightly arrest of some number of human beings and NKVD imprison them in jail at Baranowicze. Among these victims arrested was my godfather, Jozef Lojko, my mother's brother. He and others with him underwent severe torture of a Russian method in Baranowicze. Jozef was found to not measure up to their standards because during World War I he was an invincible warrior in battle against Cossacks as Polish legionary in Jozef Pilsudzki's forces. Also, among that indefinite number of victims suspected of being some political threat to their regime was Mr. Guminski, my teacher, and father's first cousin Kazimierz Wolan, just a young student at a university.

In April Szabunia finalized his seizure of the remnant families to Siberia. Among such unfortunate ones was Grygorcewicz's family. Mr. Grygorcewicz was (Soltys) a bailiff and tax collector who lived with his wife, daughter and three sons in a hamlet between Naliboki and Terebejno. Apparently, his grown-up sons had decided not to stay at home for fear that at any time they may all be apprehended by Szabunia. At the time when Szabunia unexpectedly came with the NKVD to seize the whole family at night, he was disappointed that the two adult sons were absent. Enraged, Szabunia had their father, Mr. Grygorcewicz, flogged before the remainder of the family had been grabbed to Siberia. Consequently the two sons of Mr. Grygorcewicz henceforth became fugitives from arrest by NKVD. They swore that from that time on, no matter what, they would hunt Szabunia and impose upon him injury in return for injury received.

On a certain day in May, as usual, Szabunia was traveling on a bicycle to Iwieniec. However, he never reached his destination that particular day. NKVD in Naliboki and in Iwieniec became disturbed. Immediately from both ends they examined the road and found nothing, for there was no trace of Szabunia or his bicycle anywhere on that route. Szabunia was declared missing. On the third day a special squad of NKVD from Minsk arrived with some trained dogs and began their thorough search for the missing Szabunia, the Chairman of Naliboki. At last, during the midday, this special squad was able to find dead Szabunia about a mile from the main road in some chasm, a bottomless gulf; piled on top of his body was a mass of newly cut trees.

Szabunia's corpse was brought to Naliboki by NKVD and soon a solemn funeral was performed in accordance to the Communistic custom. He was buried in the consecrated cemetery at the church of St. Bartholomew, which he himself with other Communists had defiled, and upon his grave the Communists erected a monument, but instead of cross on its top they placed a Russian red star with hammer and sickle. When parishioners saw this monument on the consecrated cemetery they were all disgusted, because every parishioner was aware of the fact that even a Catholic who committed suicide or an unbaptized infant was not permitted to be buried on the consecrated cemetery, for such dead members of Catholic families were interred outside the cemetery behind the wall on the common grounds as to the doctrine of the Roman Catholic Church. Yet it was no surprise; rather it was expected from the Communists as being most capable of sacrilege at any possible time. So, in spite of their impiousness, somebody also during the night demolished Szabunia's monument and eased himself on his grave. When some people the following morning went to the cemetery they noticed that Szabunia's Communistic monument was destroyed utterly, and on his grave there was just a large heap of human excrement.

As my father happened to be in Maczylin in order to figure out a new way to plant a field, Mr. Kanawal came outside from his house to engage in chatter with him. Since Mr. Kanawal lived close to Terebejno, he knew a great deal about Szabunia, and also he heard a lot about an old man's predictions, a considerable part of which had already come to pass. With respect to the 108-year-old man, Mr. Kanawal allegedly affirmed to my father that his predictions had practically exposed Szabunia's Bolshevik activities to all the people within this vicinity, and that is why he undoubtedly had him killed and got rid of the body in an obscured way. Just for that reason the old man became missing. Szabunia probably had his body dismembered and boiled its pieces in a pot in which he boiled daily food for his pigs, thus the pigs ate this human flesh, but the bones he burned in his furnace and then scattered the ashes upon the stream near Terebejno so that the remains of the body disappeared without a trace forever. This was indeed a most horrifying story, and when my father came back home from Maczylin he told us all about the things Mr. Kanawal had described to him regarding the missing old man who was nicknamed Nostradamus by the people who heard his prediction concerning The Last Day of Naliboki.

My cousin at last somehow obtained a clandestine passage because it was politically dangerous for her to travel from the Nowogrodek to Naliboki, and thus she safely arrived home, but unfortunately in Trascianka there was no domicile for Janka since her family had been carried away with open force to Siberia. Our kith and kin therefore assembled together in order to determine the conclusion of a sturdy place for Janka, following upon the fact that all the students in Naliboki, as anywhere else, had been arrested and held somewhere in confinement in Russia and in Baranowicze. Obviously, it was dangerous for Janka to stay with us again or with Uncle Michal, and certainly not with Grandfather, where it was most threatening since from that residence Jozef was apprehended. However, decisively and unanimously they concluded that the safest place for Janka was with Eugenjusz Klimowicz, who by now had been known only by his secret name, "OKON." As planned, Janka stealthily was moved to stay on that day with Okon's mother, Mania, but in the night he came and took her away with him.

The Polish word okon means perch, a small, spiny-finned freshwater food fish; also having spines, thorny, difficult and perplexing. That is exactly how Lieutenant Eugenjusz Klimowicz was in disposition to the Bolsheviks. Later he was also called "ZBIK," wild cat, in his antagonistic inclination to the German enemy, notwithstanding that he fluently spoke both languages, Russian and German.

Under this tyrannical power the living conditions had become rapidly unbearable. The inhabitants began to dislike with intensity this National Communist System. Their Five-Year Plan and the idea of compulsory Kolkhoz grew to be most detrimental, if not outright pernicious, to anyone living under it. Even though without the burden of taxes the citizens had sacrificed for the system all they had, except their souls.

Of course, under the czar's regime it was different, Communists indicated for their own predisposition. For failure to pay taxes, they argued, the Cossacks used to impale a deadbeat by driving a sharp pole into his posterior, and then set the bottom part of the pole into the ground with its victim on top. Then they would fasten a notice on that said, if anyone from the family dare to get him down off that pole, he likewise will be impaled. Such a cruel way of collecting taxes in pre-Communism Russia originated from the Roman Empire. The Romans were noted for the cruelty and severity of their penal laws. Scourging, flogging, harsh prison terms and executions were frequently used in order to keep the people in line. That is why the Roman Empire fell from within, on account of taxes, and the same befell the czar's Russia, as through the intercession of "Judicium Dei," "The Judgment of God." Conforming to the laws of logic, that system too certainly was most repressive, if not outright oppressive, to anyone living under it.

Since the subjects were powerless and there were absolutely no preventive measures to change the system for betterment, where one can only expect retrogression, our folks started making up funny jokes about the Communist control. Many had enjoyed the sound of singing Russian songs, although these were Communistic pieces of poetry put to music, which the people have learned recently. But just for the fun of it, folks were converting these songs to suit their own ends, and purposely to scorch the system. For example, the most popular Communistic song, transformed to adopt new opinions, was as follows:

> If tomorrow is a war,
> We shall kill our boar.
> The meat and bacon we shall eat,
> The bones to the Russian store we must submit.

While the meeting was still in session on Janka's issue, another matter of importance was brought out to be resolved. Uncle Michal and Grandfather introduced an idea for my father's attention, urging him to take without lapse of time the possession and management of Trascianka because of our relatives' concern that somebody else would move there and the whole property be wasted. Obviously then there would be nothing left for Uncle Waclaw to come back to, as we all anticipated that he would one day return home from Siberia. Besides, Grandfather, using his best endeavours, said, "Wilhelm, you are the most suitable candidate since you have a Russian education and capability to manage the forestry, particularly Trascianka on account of your familiarity of it."

Meditative Father said, "Yes, it is a very good idea, I grant you, but let me think about it."

But Uncle Michal declared, "There is no time to think; one must act upon it immediately or else lose the chance."

It did not take long for Mother to persuade my father to act promptly to get the forestry job; it was just as quickly as he was convinced by Grandfather and Uncle Michal. The following day Father prepared himself ready for what and how to speak to the Soviet officials, the ones who were authorized to act for the government. Of course, these members of NKVD had their headquarters at the community building (gmina), where there also was an office of Chairman Szabunia. However, it was probably fortunate that Szabunia was deceased because he was possibly aware of the fact that the antecedent forester of the fascist state Poland, Waclaw Lojko, was his brother-in-law, whom he seized to Siberia just recently. Consequently, Father on his return home was happy and he told us that we could move to Trascianka immediately, and that on the first of June he and other men who applied for the foresters position had to present themselves at hamlet Budy for duty.

So, in order to establish ourselves in a new home, my parents decided the following day, Friday, the second week in May, Mother would ride with me to clean the house at Trascianka, and then as soon as we returned we would all move from Naliboki to reside there permanently. After a hard, long workday it became too late to travel to Naliboki, and naturally Mother was filled with dread to pass the night here; therefore she decided to lodge nearby at hamlet Kroman since some people still lived there who were of no importance to the NKVD. But here I grew to be the most terrified in my life because the house Mother chose to spend the night in was haunted, although a family lived there, with whom Mother made acquaintance. As I have set my foot into this house for the first time, I knew the locale where a particular event took place. I knew also from description the setting of rooms and the location of a corridor, and incredibly it all appeared exactly as it was pictured in my mind. What a dreadful place, I thought, indeed, it was for anyone to dwell.

After a long conversation the residents showed my mother rooms from which to pick. But the one she chose, I figured out, must have been the room in which the chief forester used to sleep, whom the ghost visited every night precisely at twelve o'clock. As I lay in bed I trembled with fear in expectation of the ghost that had haunted this place over the ages, and for a long time I could not sleep, but later at night eventually I became affected by drowsiness, and then soon obliviously fell into a deep sleep. In the morning when I woke up it was a daylight outside and I felt fine, realizing that nothing had happened during the night in reference to a visual appearance of a disembodied spirit.

It became more likely premature because it was my first displacement from the home I was born in, at the age of eleven now, concerning which for me all these had no fundamental ingredient of realism. The whole idea of moving to another place and forsaking the place of birth to me at this point was no longer shocking nor comforting, but it was most important above all that we were going to be entirely together as one family, for which I was grateful. As we left for Trascianka, I felt sorry for Aunt Bronislawa since she had to remain at the residence all by herself, for I saw her sad face when we were parting and saying good-bye, farewell.

Although I became affected by the interruption of school and regular church attendance, for this dilemma one must put the blame on the doom of war. From infancy mother taught me to pray, "Our father in the heavens, let your name be sanctified. Let your kingdom come. Let your will take place, as in heaven, also upon earth." And, as mother used to continue sending me, my brother and sister to the church, she knew it would result in the fear of the true God and the hating of bad, for in the fear of God one turns away from bad.

Trascianka, May 1940, Wilhelm Klimowicz is employed as a forester by the Soviets.

Nonetheless, our mother now plead, "Children, take heed, because we are going farther away from the people and the church; therefore, you must be bound to pray more regularly in the morning before breakfast and after supper before going to bed, that is each day as long as God permits us to live under the blessed condition in Trascianka."

Of course, it did not take us long to pack and load all necessary things on the wagon, and the first day of the third week of May we started our journey sixteen kilometers to the destined forestry. Father gathered together the cattle, but I drove our four-wheeled horsedrawn vehicle, with Mother, Waclawa and Antoni having the benefit sitting on it.

The road from Naliboki to Kroman westward extended uniformly in one direction without curve or bend. Starting from the borough, we traveled through Kamionka and Zasciarki, then entered the forest and began to ride on the wooden highway. This highway was constructed sometime before World War I, and then, during the war, it was most convenient for the armed forces. All along both sides of the highway there were a multitude of burial places for dead Russian soldiers who had lost their lives in that war. On their graves there were wooden crosses of the Russian Orthodox Church; some were still standing, other decomposed. In this forest land we passed by Smolarnia, the place where the production of grease, oil, gasoline, naphtha, benzene, etc., was in progress, but at this time remained inoperative.

Continuing our journey through this beautiful tract of land covered with trees and listening to the echoes of birds, we arrived close to Kroman, where at the junction we had to turn right onto a road that led to Lubcz across the river Niemen, or if one traveled straight ahead through Kroman one would get to Szczorce and Nowogrodek. Traveling about three kilometers, we came to a canal and crossed over the Glass Bridge, but from here there was another road leading northeastward to a hamlet, Budy, the headquarters of the chief foresters. However, from the bridge the road led straight to Trascianka, but halfway in between these two points curved northwestward to Lubcz.

At our arrival to the final destination, we all as one began to arrange things in proper order, making this new place into a splendid home. For the light at night mother found a box of candles, which of course Uncle Waclaw made some time ago from bees wax. The naphta lamps were here but there was no fuel, and there was a fireplace designed to illuminate the home by burning the resinous sap of pines shut in a piece of wood. This sticks, however, burned unusually long with a large mass of gas rising from the fire in darting tongues of light, thus serving to illuminate adequately the entire living space. As soon as all things were settled in the house, because it was the proper season to drop seed in soil my parents made immediate plans to cultivate the fields. Naturally our private land in Naliboki was caused to lie barren, so before the evening meal at the table we all prayed together, and shortly after we went to bed.

The next morning father ploughed the soil, and without delay I harrowed after he sowed the seeds. Gradually, day by day we cultivated the complete business of farming just before the end of May. On the first day of June, as it was appointed, father came before the Soviet officials at Budy, where he was authorized to carry out the forester's duty, working for their government agency. Without retardation we continued progressively setting in the ground young trees where the Pinus Sylvestris had been harvested some time ago. For this eight square kilometers of woodland called Trascianka, father now became answerable legally or morally for the discharge of his assignment, and hence he had to take good care of it and above all keep it clean. So, in accordance with good sense, father ploughed the forest lines that divided square kilometers approximately twenty feet wide, which should as a rule provide protection from fire hazard. The nursery Uncle Waclaw had left in dexterity and adroitness on the north side of the husbandry in the dense forest was protected by an enclosure of high fence from the wild animals. Father replaced the young trees that we had taken from this nursery with seeds so that they would germinate and begin to grow for future use.

Mother for the past two years had suffered from the infestation of tapeworm, a parasite on the intestines that unfortunately caused considerable loss of weight. In spite of everything, she had been given successful medical attention by Dr. Chwal, and since the solitary worm had totally been driven out, mother eventually regained her body weight and fully recovered. But adversity befell our father when he was ploughing the field during a very hot day. He had to take his boots off, which turned out to be for the worst because while he was working barefooted, the plough cut a snake in half, on which he put his foot down, as though on a barbed wire, but when he sat down and had a look father saw a snake rolling around his feet in the furrow. At this point immediately he moved quickly to the well, cut the wound open and sucked the venom from the contaminated area of a snake bite. After washing the laceration thoroughly, father came inside the house and drank one liter of eighty-five-proof vodka, and then he went to bed. There was nothing else he could have done, since Dr. Chwal was sixteen kilometers away from us. Incredibly, father slept all day and through the night, but the following day when he woke up he told mother that he was very hungry; other than that he was perfectly healthy. Except from this time on when he worked in agriculture he learned that the stings of bee venom could not produce an expected effect on him because of being made immune due to his plight.

Despite the war, here indeed was an abundance of everything existing that man's heart could desire. We had already sown the grain, cereals of wheat, oats, barley, rye that is widely cultivated about this place, which provides flour used for bread, and flax (Linum) for oil and linen, and buckwheat, ideal for bees to gather honey. We also planted potatoes and a variety of vegetables. In the small orchard there were a dozen of bee hives, similar to what we left in Naliboki. We possessed a sufficient number of cows of a breed adapted for milk production, such as Red Polled and Frisians, and we procreated a fine breed of Polish Lap-eared pigs. As for poultry, we kept only chickens, the best layers known as the Green-leg Polish breed, similar to Minorcas or Asian Andalusians, and of course we kept some Brahmas or Wyandottes for the table. Furthermore, I experienced pleasure in breeding my favorite Angora rabbits. From this Angora, Mother and Waclawa knitted magnificent hats for the winter season and other splendid fabrics. The entire forest was enriched in great varieties of mushrooms, rapidly growing umbrella-shaped fungi of which the most desirable is the Pine-lover, followed by Lepiota procera; Coprinus, the black-spored inky caps; Comatus, the shaggy mane; Micaceus, the glistening inky cap; Astramentarius, the common inky cap; Cantharellus cibarius, bright yellow chanterelle; Polyporus sulphureus, a large bracket fungus; Lycoperdon gemmatum, the gemmed puffball mushroom, etc. In spite of numerous tests devised to try to distinguish edible from poisonous fungi, there is no foolproof method to distinguish the edible ones from the toadstool. The only safe method is to learn how to identify the mushrooms. Unknown specimens should be avoided until the assistance of a professional mycologist has been obtained. The problem, however, is not as formidable as it seems—out of the hundreds of species, a large number are so characteristic that, once they are well learned, they cannot be confused with any of the harmful species. At least that is what I have found from my experience acquiring gradual understanding from my parents and in participation with others.

In the lea (chiefly poetic, an open area in the woods) that encompassed the canal where father used to do the hay-making with his friend, Antoni Szarzanowicz, there was indeed an abundance of gooseberries, currants and crab apples. The pine forest everywhere was covered with the blueberries (black Polish berry) and small strawberries, called here Pozioraki, but in a lower land of wood there was plenty of crabbed or sour berries called Zurawiny, of a dark red color, soft, abounding with juice and among other things ideal for jelly desserts.

The surrounding streams ponds and all small bodies of fresh water, including the canal and lake Kroman, were replete with a subdivision of fish species that afforded a superb fishing ground. In this body of unpolluted water the animated fish flourished in magnitude. Schools of perch and silver fish overcrowded the canal; the crawfish from the lake Kroman invaded all its outflows; every pond and puddle was filled with the eels, and large pikes concealed themselves under heavy roots of trees at the banks of rivers and canals. Eighteen-inch-long brown trout, common European trout, forced its way into the sinuosity of the river to spawn. This river, about ten kilometers long, once was converted into a mercantile canal from the outflow of lake Kroman to the river Niemen.

Uncle Waclaw had left behind a collection of different trapping or entangling nets, all in perfect condition, from which I had a choice to use for catching fish. My favorite was the isosceles triangle net with a widely open entrance designed to chase the shoal, mainly perch and silver fish, in the shallow places on the bottom of canal. This was the best net ever invented for this method of fishing. Another most serviceable device was the trap net with considerably long wings, enough to reach two banks of the old sinuous river. This particular net I set down in the river during the spawning season exclusively for the trout.

Uncle Waclaw owned an entangling net specially made for this deep lake Kroman. This device used to capture fish consisted of gill and trammel net. The net was fitted with floats along the upper edge and sinkers on the lower edge. By the proper use of floats and sinkers the net could be made to hang vertically at the surface or at the bottom of the lake. The net was placed where moving fish would swim into it and become entangled. The size of the mesh used was such that the head of the fish could pass through but not the body. Fish could not escape since their gills were caught on the netting; thus they were "gilled." Unfortunately, father never had time to use this valuable device and I on the other hand was scared of the lake because of its spooky open space having unspecified depth, that of an abyss. This haunted location by an apparition once was a wicked city that the earth had swallowed, and since it had rested beneath the waters as an unverifiable story handed down from the past. So the people, in particular those who believed the story was true, were terrified to be at that place for fear of being influenced, or even worse, possessed as by demons.

In this forestry father had a favorable position to hunt wild animals, especially wild boars. Besides them, there were plenty of deer and hares, a mammal allied to but larger than the rabbit. With respect to these animals father had no interest to hunt them for meat or otherwise. The Wilderness of Naliboki used to be abundant in elk, a large animal that resembles both a horse and cow, similar to an American moose, but the emaciated population during World War I hunted them down to the limit of extinction. The wild boars at Trascianka were going through the erected barriers into the potato fields and ruining most of the crop. Around the field in the skirt of the woods there were scaffolds, raised wooden platforms attached to the trees for the purpose of safety and delusion of the wild boars on account of human scent, which they easily detect. That is why, when someone happens to be near them in the forest, even though the person cannot be seen the wild boars will disappear from that area suddenly. And yet, when they are shot and wounded, then they viciously attack the shooter. Despite the safety measures that had been taken, such unfortunate incidents occurred repeatedly in the Wilderness of Naliboki, where many suffered injuries to the body and even death.

Furthermore, here for the forester was the most beneficial source of earnings directly from the people who resided on the west side of river Niemen. These folks as usual came to Trascianka to cut the trees for their use as building material or combustible matter as a source of heat energy, which naturally they appreciated more than their peat, also called turf, the natural resource created after the flood in the time of Noah, this substance consisting partially of vegetable material, found in their bogs. The peat was pressed and dried in blocks for fuel when the people behind Niemen ran out of the firewood, which obviously is not obtainable during the summer season, only in the winter when the river Niemen freezes solid. At such a time folks would take a shortcut into the forest on a sledge instead of a wagon, by means of which they were able to transport huge loads of firewood or building material. Usually, during their rush to have their timber or firewood stamped with a die or otherwise by the forester, only then were they permitted to commence their transportation. Under these circumstances, evidently, everyone wanted to be the first or at least have his task completed during that particular day, in which the forester's eight hours work was not enough, and thus he was compelled by them to work an unlimited period of time in order to serve everyone at hand. In such a situation, father was awarded with lots of presents, which consisted of sacks of flour and pealed grain, large legs of ham, slabs of bacon, etc., to the extent that the whole larder room was filled with articles of food.

The means of maintaining one's existence in this wilderness was indeed good and undoubtedly better than in any towns or cities. Our isolation from civilization was advantageous in many ways, apart from the lack of salt and soup, or a doctor in cases an emergency. Otherwise it was a utopia on earth. Obviously, the people from Naliboki and all surrounding areas were aware of the fact that life in the wilderness was superior in quality and it excelled their life in any closely settled urban district.

When the Soviet authority began to exchange the forest product for money to the citizens, then there became a high demand for employees in order to keep the forest clean and clear from fire after the trees have been harvested. Among many who came voluntarily to work for the Soviets in the forestries, the headquarters in Budy designated the family Ciechanowicz to Trascianka to work under the supervision of my father. This family from Zascianki, Naliboki, was in no way related to the noble Ciechanowicz, the last proprietor of the castle known presently as Majatek.

Later sometime a young married couple, Mr. and Mrs. Zielonka, came to Trascianka to work from Naliboki, and from then on the three families lived together in one dwelling with two apartments.

Actually the Communist system of almost everything being shared mutually was commonly acceptable and unobjectionable among the entire population in the Soviet Union. For instance, the Soviet radio and newspaper emphasized daily that if one comrade had no boots to wear, then he was obligated to go to his neighbor and take one pair from him, for he possessed two pairs of boots. Such was the established practice governed by the Communist law, which they only had the power to legislate and the people generally had to take or to give what was for them fixed in position for use or service, or else undesired objectors could find themselves somewhere in the salt mine or in Siberia.

Mr. Ciechanowicz was an ordinary, short fellow, but his wife was a tall, heavy woman with three adult children. Their son, Jan Ciechanowicz, was twenty-one years of age, over six feet tall, good looking but extremely delicate. Mrs. Ciechanowicz to him was more of a nurse than a mother and she kept him on his special regimen,. Both daughters were of the same height as their father, except that Zofia was a slim, young, hard-working individual, and Mary was solidly built, probably because of being a mother of two children, and yet she was very attractive.

The house at Trascianka had two apartments made sufficient to be occupied by two families. But when Mr. Zielonka came to live there, the Ciechanowicz family started sharing the apartment with us because our apartment was larger and by now we were well acquainted. When using the stove for cooking, mother with Mrs. Ciechanowicz prepared food individually in turn, respectfully.

However, during very nice days in the summer, mother would cook on the fire outside in the yard by the well. It was a most enjoyable experience outside at the fire in the course of the last meal of the day when all were gathered together gratified and singing old songs; some would tell stories and other funny jokes.

The wilderness in summer was infested with mosquitoes. The female of these winged insects having a long proboscis capable of puncturing the skin of man and animals for extracting blood. The proboscises of this mosquitoes after the extraction of blood usually caused some swelling on the skin for those who has recently arrived here, but as for us, we became not susceptible to this harmful influence. However, besides the loss of a certain amount of blood there was no danger of transmission by the European mosquitoes of yellow fever or malaria. Nevertheless, this noisy insect was most annoying mainly during the night, thus the windows and entrances to the house had to be secured with screens to exclude mosquitoes and admit air. Apart from that mentioned, another way of protecting was the smoky air by the fire or if alternatively one was smoking a cigarette or tobacco pipe; obviously then the volatilized products of the combustion of organic substances repelled the insects.

The Ciechanowiczes' main source of income was from their ten Frisian dairy cows that they had brought with them from Naliboki. And to that end, they hired a herdsman with whom I joined, having the pleasure to tend my herd of cattle. As soon as the dairy cows were milked at sunrise, we moved the cattle to pasture, and at twelve o'clock sharp we aimed always home with the herd for milking; then, finally, after two o'clock we tended the cattle at the pasture till sundown. Additionally, Mr. Ciechanowicz acquired a salary in USSR rubles for his services rendered in the forest. His daughter Zofia with her mother was involved in the production of dairy products, which they exchanged for other foodstuffs, and they were actively engaged in cooking food and managing the affairs of their home. But Jan most of the time was reading a book while on the sofa, for he did not care much about anything else in his life. Apart from that, they had no intent whatsoever to cultivate the land, which my father offered them to do so if they desired, but this year they came here too late for planting. As with regard to Mr. Zielonka's livelihood, his was based only on the salary obtained from his work in the forest.

From mid-May, before these two families came to Trascianka to live with us, my primary task was to tend the cattle in the forest. At eleven years of age I was fearful of the people traveling the highway, and for this reason I was compelled to become adapted to a new situation in the wilderness and its environment. Intrinsically I was vigilant, and because of it I was extremely cautious to cross the highway before I stealthily explored that particular territory. I could hear from far away when somebody was traveling by putting my ear to the ground, or by observing fresh tracks, knowing that someone just passed through. The presence of strange people in the wilderness terrified me; therefore, instinctively I learned how to hide and camouflage myself and at the same time to watch someone travel through. My innate tendency to act in ways essential to my preservation and survival had always been the first and foremost objective. That is why in every situation I inherently maintained cold blood, quick reflexes and twofold eyes and ears. In case of any danger, instead of advancing I knew how and when to retreat. After all, the battle avoided cannot be lost.

While hiding in a secret place of the forest, I acquired the ability to be patient and calm. My breathing was without a pause or break; it was deep and slow. My concentration was focused directly on one object only and my eyes gazed steadily to converge toward a center of danger or uncertainty to defeat an opposition by willpower. I knew that the Wilderness of Naliboki was exceedingly mysterious. Here bandits once gained dominion over this territory. The old tale about the threat and danger of wild animals and reptiles startled the mind of anyone who found himself alone in the midst of the wild kingdom. It also made one shudder to think that so many dead people were buried everywhere in the vicinity.

Throughout the ages generations had trampled their feet on ancient places of human sacrifices to the triad of devils, where the demons until the present time did not allow people to have peace. When the people supposedly were visited by ghosts, they had been brutally murdered and many were forcibly seized and had gone throughout eternity. Who had the courage or boldness now, to say, "I am fearless!"? Indeed, not even one able-bodied man. And where is protection left for the children? I wondered, was I in any way better than my cousins were, Czeslaw and Heniek, whom the forces of darkness abducted to Siberia. I did not think so, rather I too expected that soon I would be the next to face the same predetermined course of events. Again, I wondered, what is it that we as children became guilty of to deserve death?

I found out that the safest way to herd the cattle in the forest was to stay behind the herd, for they scare away all living creatures of the forest. Once I ignored this concept and moved up to the front of cattle, and I repeatedly then was confronting some sort of danger. One time after a sudden storm and very heavy rain in mid-June when the scorching sun came out of thick, dense, dark cloudlike mass, the ground saturated in rain water began to extend emitting steam above the horizon. Intending to cross the meadow through the straight footpath, I outran the herd and started walking ahead, but when I tried to step on the footpath it was covered with hundreds of deadly snakes, which evidently all slithered on this dry walkway to enjoy imparting warmth of the sun. Another time, I was eager to cross the pine woods to check the quality of grassland way ahead, and I came upon a gigantic wild boar that was about ten meters from me actively engaged in turning up the earth with its snout. As I glanced at its enormous size, my mind terrified, instantaneously I climbed a tree. At the same moment this dark, huge beast lifted its snout and looked at me climbing the tree, then turned around and took off at a full gallop with such speed and weight that, incredibly, the beast caused the ground to tremble.

Again, a most terrifying incident I encountered was being startled by a vicious wolf by the Glass Bridge. In the later days of June during beautiful sunny weather I decided to graze the cattle on the sides of the road in the direction toward the Glass Bridge because there was a glade, a nice clearing in the woods where the cows could be fed quickly on a good pasture. So, by the time my herd reached the highway, I began exhibiting a lack of patience and was determined to pass the herd in order to get on the bridge to see the fish before the cows scared them off. Unfortunately, just in front of the bridge a large wolf disconcerted my intention. This wolf unmistakably was running southward, following the course of the canal, but when he crossed the highway he stood still in the middle of it, turned his head and gazed fixedly at me. In this instantaneous tragic plight based on a distance between of only several meters, I had no choice but to face the fear and use willpower. So I stood still, without any movement and making no sound, just staring back at the wolf's glittering eyes. In this hostile encounter my mind began to grow clear and I started to concentrate, intensifying my visual focus of the wolf's image in my mind.

The Glass Bridge and the wolf.

As I continued to imagine a picture of a real creature in my mind, I acquired the ability to command the image and move it into the direction it originally intended. Remaining in the same capacity, continually concentrating, *You are moving ... Your head is moving straight forward ... You are walking forward ... I see ... You are moving ... You are going away from me ... Keep on going ... Go ... Go ... Go away ...* The wolf moved his head steadily forward, then slowly back toward me again, and again moved his head slowly forward and commenced to take a steady step forward, one after another, just as I willed. In actual fact it was happening exactly in harmony with my will, as I became more pure with conscious and subconscious thought that was not deluded with the irrelevant detail of apprehensive disposition. By the time the wolf in slow motion crossed the road and got to the forest, he suddenly disappeared. I rushed onto the bridge to see how fast the wolf was going, but strangely enough the vicious creature vanished without trace. However, from this time on I never again feared the wolves or any vicious dogs because I was able to use the same method of concentration virtually on any wild animal successfully. Afterward, when I elaborated on this event, I asked myself, what could have happened if I ran to climb the nearest tree? Then I realized that I would never have stood a chance at self-preservation; the wolf would have been on top of me and I, as a result, intelligibly could have been devoured. Besides, a boy of eleven years, physically as it is distinguished from the mind or spirit, would be afforded no ground for hope in such a despairing predicament.

Subsequently, I sat in a relaxed position on the Glass Bridge with my feet suspended from the structure and my face turned in a northern direction, while all the cows on the east side were grazing tasty, thick white clover and the waves of perch and silver fish swam in a schools, the pike with long snout roiled clear water at the bank of the canal. The fragrance from the various trees and vegetable kingdom of the forest ecstatically tended to induce drowsiness. In this susceptible state I began to be engaged in continuous and contemplative thought as I inculcated glittering water of reflected rays from the solstice sun. This twinkling water in my eyes was mesmerizing me; I was falling into a trance, a dreamlike state marked by bewilderment and an insensibility to ordinary surroundings. I was falling back in time. Falling ... falling ... falling ... falling, way back in time ... Then I saw the people, how they were filling the earth and subduing it, having in subjection the fish of the great body of salt and fresh water and the flying creatures of the heavens and every living creature moving upon the earth. Then I saw the dead bodies of the people and giants, how they were floating here on the powerful receding flood waters from the highest elevation on northward, then farther ahead by the sinuating "Horn Oszmianski" westward, carried swiftly into the Baltic Sea. Then I was able to see with my mind's eye how the scattered people came here to dwell and to indulge in debauchery, how they built great cities and temples and performed human sacrifices to the triad of devils, Labartu, Labasu and Akhkhazu, how they brought with them to this land their Iranian and Indo-European languages, which were converted into the Lettish and Slavic, and finally how these were disseminated into a multitude of languages and dialects in order that different groups of people sustained a hatred among themselves throughout the ages. These corrupt and wicked cities had been swallowed by the earth in the day when its center, the ancient Babylon, was annihilated, and since they remained beneath the waters as a nest of haunted lakes by the demons whom those people once idolized. Again, how heathenish temples of Perkuna were built in Nowogrodek and upon the renowned hillock of Naliboki in honor to a goddess of animals. How the noblemen worthy of all ranks, kings, czars, and kaisers were engaged in mortal tournaments. How King Zygmunt August erected his chapel on the ruins of the Perkuna temple in Naliboki, in which he laid up his votive offering, and henceforth the pronouncement of evil upon Naliboki and its entire territory was devised. How the Dukes Radziwill built the church upon the same cursed hillock and dedicated it to Saint Bartholomew. How the magnificent swords were manufactured here and how many Polish innocent people were killed by these swords on account of the increased curse. Who can remember their footprint or who else must follow their footsteps? How many loyal people puzzled why Russia, Prussia and Austria sliced off various parts of the Polish-Lithuanian state in 1772, 1793 and 1795, until the country was entirely partitioned for 143 years? Why throughout this period of time repeated national insurrections were defeated, and who can now recite the number of sepulchers of those faithful patriotic warriors? Then I saw with my mind's eye how the Polish people were stretching out their hands to Napoleon Bonaparte, imploring for emancipation. Alas! His strive for world domination was capitulated. His defeat at freezing Moscow was painted on canvas in oils, the picture that I could not take my eyes off that hung in our living room in Naliboki. How my godfather, Uncle Jozef Lojko, fought here like a tiger in company with the great warriors, Polish legionary, when at last Poland reemerged as an independent nation after World War I, in which I was born here to enjoy a briefly lasting peace and prosperity. With my mind's eye I saw the absence of war, in which time our house was full of people gathered together to hear the old man's prophecy as if it were made under divine influence concerning "The Last Day of Naliboki." How Satan the devil shall be unleashed with his sting of death, as a final scene in a play, to have his victory within the time of "man's number," indicating that it has to do with imperfect, fallen man, and seems to symbolize the imperfection of that which is represented by the "wild beast." How the people, just as they were told by the old man, shall behold the first sign which came about in school six months after his prophecy. How again, six months later in the early days of August 1938, the people witnessed fulfilment of another sign in Maczylin. How two most dreadful years had passed since the last sign occurred with supplemental year 1938 of the "Jewish Persecution;" thus I saw myself being present in its half of the last wild beast's number, 663, in August 1940, the number that presumed to be six hundred and sixty six.

As I maintained without interruption my relaxed mood of contemplation I proceeded to form a mental image of a Jewish merchant who once suffered the catastrophic loss of his wagon full of glassware on this bridge, and since it has been called the Glass Bridge. I visualized also an adult Jewish woman who from Lubcz along the west bank of the canal passed by, just as that wolf did, the Wilderness of Naliboki in the nude, even though exposed to predators. Seeing too a giant, Mr. Kostus, approaching this famous bridge from Smiejno-Budy to Trascianka, which was about at midnight, and suddenly took off into the direction of Kroman because he thought he saw a ghost just as tall as himself. But unfortunately, it was not a ghost, it was my uncle Waclaw Lojko who carried his son, Heniek, on his shoulders and covered him with a bed linen to protect him and himself from the mosquitoes. However, poor Mr. Kostus henceforth never ceased the act of running from danger.

In the meantime, my herd of cattle quit grazing and was ready to settle itself on the ground. But because it was time for milking, I disturbed the cows and drove them home. But when I got home a while later my Aunt Bronislawa flied breathless away from Naliboki here to us. Amazingly he had covered the distance in a much shorter time than usual. But now she appeared not only out of breath, but she was holding her breath from fear and making an earnest request for my father to run and hide from the Russian NKVD at once, because another commissioner of NKVD had arrived to Naliboki that very today from Smolensk and he was looking for Wilhelm Klimowicz. "So as soon as I heard this dire message I could not stop running here to warn you," she said. As I looked at my father's face becoming so pale, I realized that he was much more frightened than I facing the wolf. And that is why I was discouraged to tell my parents anything about it.

However, while this commotion troubled all of us inside the house, I looked outside through the window and saw a horse and carriage in our yard. I cried out, "Look! Someone is here in our yard."

At this point in time, scared Father walked out to meet his most distressing circumstance. As he approached the carriage, Father asked the man, who was clad most elegantly in a Russian uniform, "Can I help you, sir?"

The man stepped from his carriage to the ground and replied, saying, "My name is Ivan Klimowicz. I am looking for Wilhelm Klimowicz, my uncle."

Father answered and said, "I am Wilhelm Klimowicz."

Then Ivan said, "Oh, what a relief, at last, I found you."

At that, they both embraced and slowly entered the house to make acquaintance with all of us inside. Here, father introduced unknown Ivan Klimowicz to his aunt, Bronislawa Klimowicz, and my mother, then to Waclawa, me and Antoni.

It was most fortunate for my mother since she had relief on account of our aunt's presence and her skill and extraordinary ability to entertain the guest. Thus, all of a sudden the room set apart and equipped for cooking food became extremely busy. Father stretched out the table and placed the liquor upon it, then went outside to unharness the most beautiful Siberian horse and led him inside the stable. He covered this fine animal with a blanket and filled his trough with hay and oats. When father came back inside the house, shortly thereafter our extended hospitality to Ivan, our kin, began.

In the course of behaving in a kind and generous manner toward this most unusual guest, we all were astonished looking at Ivan, our flesh and blood whom we never knew or had a chance to meet. My father and Aunt Bronislawa were lost in deep thoughts, having a feeling of doubt and also strong curiosity in regard to their two brothers lost from long ago, Edward and Edmund. They both were impatiently desirous to put forth a question about Ivan's father to find out if he was alive and which brother was actually his father. But there was not enough courage as yet to force this momentous information out of him. Father then took for granted with a feeling of confident expectation that Ivan himself voluntarily in due time would reveal all that was needed about his father. Unfortunately, the outcome of it became most peculiar and rare for the son not to mention or to say anything about his own father over a couple of days. Finally, my father effectively asked him and said, "Ivan, my dear nephew, tell me, how is your father?"

Ivan reluctantly replied and hastily said, "My father is dead." Because since World War I Father had not communicated with his brothers, he insisted on getting some kind of facts concerning them, but his nephew absolutely declined to discuss it. Rather, he proudly expressed his point of view of how the Soviet Union became the mightiest empire in the whole world. How he as commissioner of the People's Commissariat of Internal Affairs from 1937 helped to decontaminate his motherland from the parasites and poisonous country's element, which at all costs and inevitably must be neutralized and exterminated.

As I secretly listened to my cousin, the kind of life-and-death language he used in his expressions, it scared me enormously. Immediately, I envisioned him not as my cousin but a brutal monster, a cold-blooded murderer. Then I realized also that he must have been an actual executioner of the fifteen thousand Polish officers of divers ranks late in 1939 in Katin near Smolensk, not to mention how many millions of people in Russia were massacred from 1937 until the present day by the People's Commissariat of Internal Affairs. It is probable, therefore, that Ivan's name was decreed beforehand by the devil himself in order to exert an invigorating influence upon him of exactly the same characteristic as that of Ivan the Terrible, the first Russian ruler to use the formal title of tsar (1530-1584). With such a disposition, indicating the distinctive quality of the czar, Ivan (cousin) was selected by a supremacy of wicked spirit to be its cruel person, as in ancient times who held up the beating hearts of their victims to the triad of devils. Now, however, in modern days on a much larger scale Ivan had been granted the power and authority to hold up the beating hearts of his victims to the triad of up-to-date devils; namely Stalin, Molotov and Voroshilov.

Strange luck that our posterity would have someone coming from an ancestral line who perhaps then and indeed now was involved in paranormal activities governed by the forces of darkness. To this end, our grandfather constantly used to read from the Bible some passages for my mother, and I participated in hearing: Go on acquiring power in the Lord and in the mightiness of his strength. Put on the complete suit of armor from God that you may be able to stand firm against the machinations of the devil.

Subsequently my father had an unimaginable conversation with Ivan concerning the periodic oscillation and frequency on which a harmonic system of the Marxian doctrines and policies of the Bolsheviks are based. Cousin Ivan was interested because of the strange sphere of the forest Father had responsibility for, so he began to inquire what it would do, if anything, for the state's economy. Naturally, Father gave some reasons to him as to how essential the science of planting and managing forests is for the Soviet Union.

During an extensive period of time in which both were engaged in conversation and appreciating the resourceful value of the forestry they decided the following morning to saddle the horses and have a ride in order to get a full inspection of the eight square kilometers of forest over which my father assumed an obligation of duty. While they were riding on horseback, father showed his nephew magnificent Pinus sylvestris, oak, birch trees, ash trees, and fir trees. Ivan was immensely impressed with a feeling of wonder and approbation, as at the sight of anything rare, excellent or sublime. Just as father had expected, knowing that Ivan had been brought up to believe that all things originated from nature, hence God does not exist.

Meanwhile, this interrogative cousin of mine, having the ability of a spy, approached me and started asking a lot of questions, particularly about the erudition of Russia. And then, of course, he wanted to know how much I was advanced in the German language, since it became most popular in the Soviet Union. At that very moment he began to speak to me in German:

Ivan: "Do you speak German?"
Mieczyslaw: "Not so much. I am not very good at that."
Ivan: "How are you?"
Mieczyslaw: "Very well, thank you. And you?"
Ivan: "Fine. Do you mind if I smoke?"
Mieczyslaw: "No. May I get you a drink? And, what would you like to drink?"
Ivan: "I'd like a vodka."
Mieczyslaw: "I can quite believe it."

After a considerably long talk with me, Ivan went to my father and told him that I was wasting my time there in the capacity of a herdsman. "This young boy is very bright and talented," Ivan implored. "Please, let me take Mieczyslaw with me to Smolensk. There, I shall send him to the best educational institution in Russia, and when he completes his study he will be an erudite young man. You'll see; we shall all be proud of him."

Father was stunned and did not know what to say to Ivan. After a few deep breaths, he said, "I do not know, Ivan. However, it appears to be a very good idea. But first, I think, we must ask Mieczyslaw himself if he wants to go into the world through this open window from the actual place of his birth."

"All right," said Ivan. "Tomorrow, I shall take a ride with Mieczyslaw in my carriage and we shall talk about it, then I shall learn what will be his decision on this matter."

Later my father stealthily told me, "Ivan eagerly wants to take you with him to Smolensk for an acquisition of knowledge. Also, he will alter your Christian convictions by means of intensive, coercive indoctrination. Moreover, you will be brainwashed without subtlety or affection, and in this way Ivan will make a Communist out of you, in an exact manner as he became himself."

In response to Ivan's most generous proposition and father's admonition, I honestly said to my father, "Please do not worry, because to go with my cousin to Russia it would be as if I sold my soul to the devil ... God forbid. His offer is extremely frightening."

Strangely enough, at this particular time the people in general within the confines of our vicinity did not know exactly the significance of NKVD or its potential capacity of accomplishment, capable of being realized aside from the Russian people themselves. However, later we learned that it was actually equivalent to the German SS or Gestapo, the German state secret police under the Nazi regime that was noted for its brutality, just as NKVD in the Soviet Union subsequently became apparent. But who on earth could imagine the bounds of power and authority of father's nephew, who was a commissar, an official in charge of a commissariat of the Soviet government, or so-called People's Commissariat of

Internal Affairs, that which existed in its cruel capacity from 1935 to 1946?

In the warmest season of the year, the following day as it was planned. Father helped Ivan to harness the horse in his carriage and then we went for a ride through the odoriferous forest in the direction of Lake Kroman. A stillness had mastery over the environment. The steady trot of a horse alleviates one to drowsiness. Good-looking Ivan with his smiling face glanced at me, and I cast a glance at him. Then he said, "Well, shall we sing before we fall asleep?"

"Sure," I replied. Then I said, "Look, Ivan, how broad it is, the Wilderness of Naliboki. Let us sing the song:

> The wide country of my birth.
> In her there is plenty of forests, fields and rivers.
> I do not know any other such a country,
> Where a man can breath so freely.
>
> From the Moscow to Ukraine,
> Up to the Northern Seas.
> A man is passing through like a master,
> In his own endless native land.

Following this melodious song, we gratified our desire and sang a few more songs. Lo and behold, here was Lake Kroman. Astonished, Ivan stopped the horse and suddenly jumped with joy, getting out from the carriage walking toward the lake, glancing in every direction, stating positively, "I am sure I have been in this place before. What a well-acquainted and sociable place it is. Somehow this champaign, overgrown with trees around the lake, recollects the ancient days prior to my present existence."

Indeed, I could hardly believe my ears what I was hearing from Ivan, as if it were an unconscious utterance of his, since all Communists are Godless and nonreligious persons. Yet here and now he was implying a rebirth of the soul in successive bodies, the becoming of an avatar again, or the incarnation of a god. "A god?" I wondered in my mind. Most likely, a demon that has wrest out from beneath the waters of the lake and possessed Ivan beyond self control. It seemed to me at that time that the demons from this depth without any doubt effortlessly possessed a great number of atheists in Russia not long ago who were coming back to its originally occupied cursed location purposely to stain their skirts with innocent blood.

After a long while, Ivan reluctantly said, "Mieczyslaw, let's ride back home."

Soon, as we got into the carriage, Ivan opened one of his compartment to get something, in which I noticed there was a lot of armament such as pistols, rifles, grenades and finka, a small Russian machine gun with a cylindrical metal container that holds seventy-one bullets, and ample ammunition. So, as he turned the horse around and we started riding home, Ivan made his attempt to persuade me to go with him to Russia in order to become an educated man. Without being rude, but rather in dignified manner, I wanted him to see this idea from my point of view, and at the same time endeavor to show him a gratitude for his kind generosity. In this decisive nature situation I proposed to my cousin by asking him to consider my own personal desire and allow me to stay with my parents just for this one year at Trascianka because it is a new place for us to enjoy. "But next year I will be ready to go with you to Smolensk."

Ivan of course agreed, and he said, "Okay, but remember, Mieczyslaw, next year I will be here, especially for you. Do not forget." So as the horse was trotting, we began to sing again before we arrived home for the food and drink.

Father told Ivan, "Tomorrow I have to go to Smiejno-Budy regarding official business with my state employees."

Ivan said, "That is good. I shall go with you to see those state employees and find out what they are doing there for the Soviet Union."

The following day they both got into the carriage and drove to Budy, Ivan as usual tastefully ornate in uniform with a pistol at his right side and a round hat on his head, fashioned similar to that of the late Szabunia. As soon as Ivan entered the building full of Russian state employees, all present became faint out of fear and expectation of the things he might do to them, for the power he had bestowed upon him was to kill a man just as to eject saliva from his mouth. But, in spite of everything, Ivan ordered them all to be calm and declared that, "Henceforth you are dealing here with my uncle, Wilhelm Klimowicz, your forester from Trascianka. My name is Ivan Klimowicz and I demand that you all here will take very good care of Wilhelm Klimowicz, not just because he is my kin, but on account of the fact that he is most importantly a proficient forester, and as such he is essential for the Soviet Union. Therefore remember, let him serve you as a model whom you must imitate to be productive of results with a minimum of wasted effort for the motherland."

Unanimously all present declared, "Yes, we obey Commissar Klimowicz, and we shall remain faithful to father Stalin and our native land."

Somehow as the days went by Ivan familiarized himself and became more agreeable, delightful and gentle toward the members of the family. Eventually he opened up and disclosed to us all things about his family and Uncle Edmund. He told my father that his father was Edward, that is my father's firstborn brother, and he said, "In October 1918 Bolsheviks came to our house and arrested Father when I was just eight years old. Since that day, mother and I, we never saw him again. Probably the same thing has happened to my uncle Edmund, because from that time he had vanished too.

"During the revolution," Ivan continued, "death embraced a mass of people in Russia, which was inevitable for the Communists to prevail. A brute czar's regime for a failure to pay taxes, Cossacks used to impale such deadbeats simply by driving a sharp end of a pole into one's posterior and setting the bottom part into the ground with its victim on top of the pole, with a notice attached to it which read: 'If anyone from the family dare to get him off the pole, he likewise shall be impaled.' Today, however, taxes of all sorts in Russia have been absolutely abolished, and in this way the whole population became free from the czar's tyranny as no other nation in the world has yet experienced."

Nevertheless, my father thought in his mind that every side has its own unique story which will never justify the other. Besides, concerning the taxes, Jesus recommended to pay back Caesar's things to Caesar, but God's things to God. Naturally, one under no circumstances could dare argue or contest an opinion about God's things with Ivan prior to his exorcism, for one could bring calamity upon himself if in regard to this matter he did not stay mute.

It is true that the Romans were noted for the cruelty and severity of their penal laws. Scourging, flogging, harsh prison terms and executions were frequently used in order to keep the people in line. No doubt that such a system was certainly most repressive, if not outright oppressive, to anyone living under it. The taxes that the Russians had to pay in money and kind were exceedingly heavy, and they were all the heavier in that two forms of taxation ran side by side for them—civil taxes and religious taxes—and neither was light. Those cruel ways of collecting taxes in Russia were adopted from the Roman Empire, which had fallen from within on account of taxes, and it seems that unfortunately the same befell Russia, as through the intercession of "Judicium Dei."

In spite of everything, father took a Russian accordion and started to perform delightful music. He played some old folk songs and then shifted his performance to modern songs, at which accompaniment Ivan melodiously sung, in particular a song most popular in the Soviet Union which reads: With us is Stalin the kinsman, with his iron arm, to the victory leads us Voroshilov. On the earth, in the heavens, and on the sea, our tune is mighty rigorous.

Following a division of those extended melodious poems, all gathered at the table to enjoy the meal.

Ivan pronounced, "Well, my dearest relatives, the time is getting near to my departure. On the twelfth day of August I must leave for Smolensk. I will have to submit the horse and carriage in Iwieniec, and there where I first landed I shall get to my airplane and fly home."

Father said, "We shall get ready for August eleventh, and early in the morning we shall ride to Naliboki, and there before your departure I will introduce you to the rest of Klimowicz family."

So, my parents began to pack some foodstuff for Aunt Bronislawa, such as homemade cheese, butter, sour cream, eggs, bacon, ham, ray flour for bread, which is common in Europe, wheat flour for cakes, buckwheat grits, peeled barley, honey, vegetables from the garden, and so on. The following morning father joined our horse and wagon to Ivan's carriage. This chestnut colored horse with a white blaze on his face, black mane and a long black tail was called Mashka. This obedient mare once underwent ill luck, when debauchee Leon limed her white and cut her tail off, the incident that took place near the carrousel site on the common pasture. However, after an emotional parting, hugs and kisses, Aunt Bronislawa got into the carriage, then followed Father and Ivan to Naliboki, while we four souls waved our hands, standing in the yard saying good-bye with tears in our eyes ... "Good-bye, prosperous voyage!"

As soon as they arrived in Naliboki, Aunt Bronislawa started performing in her kitchen, preparing a go-away party for her nephew. In the meantime, father and Ivan went to gather all the relatives, especially those who were not suspicious in the Soviets' eyes. Among those were Benedikt Klimowicz, Alzusia, Arszula and Regina Klimowicz, Gabryjela and Jozef Kosciukiewicz, Edward Wolan and his mother, Genefa Klimowicz, with her sons, Boniutek, Gienek and Michal. The total gathered was about fifteen people, and together they went to the cemetery to show Ivan the burial place of loved ones; his grandfather Kazimierz Klimowicz, grandmother Elzbieta Klimowicz, great uncle Dr. Peter Klimowicz, grandmother's brother Kazimierz Wolan, our baby sister Zofja Klimowicz, and Wladyslaw Klimowicz, Genefa's husband and Gabryjela's brother.

This going-away party took place in our residence on Pilsudski Street, 5A and 5B, where Ivan's father, Edward Klimowicz, his brother Edmund Klimowicz, Bronislawa Orszula, Wilhelm my father, sister Waclawa, myself, our late baby sister Zofja and my brother Antoni were born. Father told Ivan that his aunt Orszula Klimowicz soon after World War I took off to Wilno and there she promptly married Von Metro Majer, a native of Berlin, Germany. Subsequently they settled down in Lithuania as a family with a son and daughter, and then he became the prime minister of Lithuania, but unfortunately just a few years in the past Von Metro Majer was assassinated, and we did not know what really happened to the rest of the family because from that time we became disconnected. Obviously, Father could say absolutely nothing about Lieutenant Eugenjusz Klimowicz, the son of late Dr. Peter Klimowicz, who actually jumped the train near Stolpce headed to Katin, Smolensk, where all Polish officers, 15,000 of them, were murdered. Now lucky Eugenjusz was a combatant band leader, operating behind the enemy in opposition to commissar Ivan Klimowicz. And similarly, no one could dare mention to him anything about unfortunate Waclaw Lojko, seized to Siberia, or Jozef Lojko, imprisoned in Baranowicze, alike the university student Kazimerz F. Wolan, nor Jan Radziwill and Alfons, my father's cousin, both pursued by NKVD. What a world, one that is squeezed tight in the hand of the devil. I deliberated, who was it that once prophesied by saying, "Brother will deliver brother over to death, and a father a child, and children will rise up against parents and have them put to death"?

Our Benedikt as usual came in with a violin under his arm in order to diversify this sudden and unexpected reception. Certainly, he was glad to perform some classic music created by the Russian renowned composers according to the conventions of Western Europe, such as Balakirev, Rimsky Korsakov, Tchaikovsky, Anton Rubinstein and many others. Just a moment before assembling, Benedikt at his home played a favorite classic of Ivan's on the grand piano. When his fingers struck the keys of this huge musical instrument and his artistic execution caused to form a piece of melodic music, the previously unknown to all Klimowiczes, Ivan, became enchanted and captivated to the extent that he felt hurt and was sorry to be leaving the next day. In addition, Benedikt asked his sister Arszula, an ex-school teacher, my father's aunt, and Father to sing an opera entitled "The Prince and Peasant Girl." In this opera the Russian prince is madly in love with the most beautiful Polish peasant girl. But no matter how much he loves her, she declines to believe him because he is a prince and she is just a simple peasant girl. As this introductory event of a short play appears, the peasant girl sings in her alto voice:

The peasant girl: You are telling me, and I believe,
You will go with another, and forget about me.

The prince: Let God strike me dead into Hades,
If I am thinking about another.

If I am thinking about another,
then my soul yearns for you.

After such a magnificent performance, Ivan affectionately hugged Arszula, Benedikt and my father, and said, "What a singing voice, what music, indeed. This is incredible; it can only be compared with performances of the Bolshoy Theater in Moscow."

Benedikt added, "Your grandfather was indeed some musician, for he had an extraordinary, unique talent."

Then, meditative Ivan said, "I know, because I have read his letters written to my father long before I was born. Of course, among his letters there were yours, Benedikt, Peter's, grandmothers, Orszula's, Bronislawa's and Wilhelm's. That is why grandfather's funeral was the largest ever held in Naliboki, on account of him being gifted with musical and medical abilities, and also the fact that he died so young."

I remember this, as my father told me many, many times.

Later during the day at the gathering, Ivan was absorbed looking at the portraits hanging on the wall in Aunt's Bronislawa living room—there was a portrait of his grandfather, grandmother, his father Edward and uncle Edmund.

The following morning on August twelfth Father told us that all the relatives came out to wish Ivan a prosperous voyage. As he was departing, he gave the impression of being in aberration of mind, perhaps, because he never knew that he really had many relatives by blood, whom he had just encountered. This phenomenon, however, indicated that Ivan was at any rate part human after all. I wondered why. Then my grandfather, Franciszek Lojko, my mother's father, told me that God made man in his own image, and therefore man reflects God's four axiomatic qualities, namely Love, Justice, Wisdom and Power. So, grandfather said, "No matter what force of evil motivates Ivan, he cannot escape the fact that he was created in God's image. No one can, because of God's will and his supreme power of the law."

Could someone say that the apes in Russia built such powerful tanks to invade Poland? Of course not, because they do not possess man's qualities. Or, if someone enjoys eating a beef steak, would he honestly say that he was eating a chicken? Certainly not, because God created all creatures according to its own kind.

During an inspection of the forest, Ivan noticed strangely a great number of trees devoid of moisture. He asked my father, "Why in this endemic land of yours are there so many trees dead everywhere?"

Father explained to him, "From December 1939 to March this year we had here the coldest winter ever known to any living man in this present generation, and curiously enough no one seems to know why. Through severe frost the trees were split in half from the stem to the crown of the entire self-supporting trunk that grew at some distance above the ground, and as a result they became dead due to the arctic condition that just encircled our entire region."

"Well," Ivan commented, "this cannot be anything else than the force of mother nature, which of course, is quite normal and unavoidable."

But here old folks professed to know differently. They had intuition that it was a sign that signified something worse yet to come upon the entire Wilderness of Naliboki than just a great number of dead trees in it. These old folks, undoubtedly, attempted to behave in the same way as distinguished "Nostradamus of Terebejno" in their anticipation of "The Last Day of Naliboki."

There were frequent reports of fires occurring in one place after another, terrifying fellow citizens in the Wilderness of Naliboki. Despite the established law and order by the Soviets, there were dreadful rumors about violent crime being diffused everywhere, out of control. Apparently the Byelorussians, after robbing Polish families, burned them alive in their own homes. Unverified reports circulating from person to person gave the impression that the victims deserved blame for some offenses to Byelorussian residents under Polish rule, or perhaps they fell victim, some were saying, because of their selfishness and grasping desire for possessions. Either way, this certainly was an extremely scary plight of a dangerous nature to anyone living under it.

Father was called to appear for a meeting in Smiejno-Budy. There was a discussion conducted between foresters about the serious problem concerning a physical force unlawfully exercised under the Soviet's wing. Then my father was issued a firearm for self-protection and to be able to keep his assigned territory under control. On his arrival home from that meeting, he brought with him two rifles, one pistol and lots of ammunition. In his happy mood, he said to our mother, "Jozefa, I have noticed that these Russian officials in Budy have some respect for me. You know, it seems that Ivan's position of NKVD has a mighty influence on the Russian people in general. No wonder they all were scared of him when he approached them in their office when I was with him. They told me not to worry, that if I notice anything unusual not to hesitate but report it to them in Smiejno-Budy immediately. They said that they will send an army to any region that will put an end to this kind of atrocious deeds."

By the end of October our process of gathering a crop in Trascianka was completed. Also, most of the thrashing was done. Some wheat was ground in the mill to flour and groats from barley, oats and buckwheat. The last crop was the potatoes that we picked in the fields; however, a certain part was ruined by the wild boars during some summer nights. Nonetheless, the potatoes yielded well and we had more than enough to last us till the next crop. After all the potatoes were sorted—ones for the table, seeds and small ones for the hog feed—we stored them in a buttery over the winter. This buttery, a pantry-like room to store food, was built specially in a similar way as the house in order to keep the freezing temperature out. This facility was constructed by my uncle Waclaw on the southern side of the property near the house, and it was very convenient for one to obtain anything needed for the kitchen. I remember once in this place Uncle Waclaw was extracting honey and at the same time I gluttonised myself with lots of honey. My parents here this particular year also extracted lots of honey from the honeycombs by means of centrifugation, a rotary machine for separating substances having different densities. My parents filled jars with the pure honey and the honeycombs were preserved in frames, ready for the beehives. Father had several new swarms gathered from the trees and housed them in the spare beehives. There was indeed a lot of honey this year; the bees gathered not only from all sorts of blossoms in the forest and clover in the fields but also the fact that we grew a great deal of buckwheat. The harvest was good ... my parents were satisfied and most thankful to God, our heavenly father.

All of a sudden Mr. Ciechanowicz began to tease Mr. Zielonka for some reason in a facetious manner. At first our parents thought it was of little worth and insignificant, but soon it became a serious matter. While Mr. Ciechanowicz was working together with Mr. Zielonka in the forest he was telling him that his wife was seen to have been flirtatious with men coming here from the other side of river Niemen who obviously were in a business transaction with my father. This, of course, was not true; it never happened, but nevertheless Mr. Ciechanowicz continued to annoy Mr. Zielonka at any occasion possible. Inevitably, soon we heard through the wall a loud noise. There in Mr. Zielonka's apartment a situation had developed to violence. However, this violent agitation did not last long because Mr. and Mrs. Zielonka packed their bags and left for Naliboki, and in this way their apartment became vacant. Then, without any lapse of time, Mr. Ciechanowicz and his family moved in to occupy that apartment. Eventually it came to light why Mr. Ciechanowicz was teasing Mr. Zielonka ... simply because he desired his apartment.

At the same time Mr. Ciechanowicz was teasing my father in order to divert his attention from Mr. Zielonka, to have his guarantee of getting rid of Mr. Zielonka from Trascianka permanently. To this end, he told my father to keep his close eye on my mother and also on his son, Jan Ciechanowicz. On some occasions Jan was rejecting his food prepared by his mother as usual, Mrs. Ciechanowicz. My mother felt sorry for the young lad for not having eaten any food for a while, so, as she was well trained by Aunt Bronislawa, she could cook much better than Jan's mother. She took pity on him and prepared a delicious dish, which Jan enjoyed eating and for which he was most grateful. Since this occurred repeatedly, my father became jealous. Of course, his improper jealousy led to a quarrelsome disposition. When I drove my cows for milking, I found my mother extremely upset and crying. I wondered why mother was so upset and crying. "Mamusia, what is the matter ... why you are crying?"

"It is your father, son."

"If he is so hard on you, why did you marry him?"

"Well, every man has his own qualities, some good, some bad. I married your father for his good quality."

"What was his good quality, Mamusia?"

"Because of his incredible singing voice and the way he played accordion I fell in love and married him," said mother.

But, in spite of everything, as soon as Mr. Ciechanowicz moved away from us to the next door apartment my father had no reason to be jealous and we incessantly lived in harmony, love and peace.

In November the Soviet government came up with a new idea in order to have people occupied with some useful work in the Wilderness of Naliboki. They proposed to pay twenty-five Russian cents for each broom made in the forest. This brooms here were normally made from twigs of young sprouts of birch and tied together by the bark of a linden tree, and finally a stick from which bark was taken was driven into the center and served as a handle. In bulk the brooms were delivered by people to Smiejno-Budy, and from there the lot was shipped to the Soviet Union to use in factories, yards, streets, etc.

Mr. Ciechanowicz actively began to make these brooms as specified by the government. He was working in the yard by the porch some eight hours daily and was able to make forty brooms each day. After the first week of my eager observation and learning a knack that of Mr. Ciechanowicz, I asked my father if he would let me to make the same brooms as Mr. Ciechanowicz. Undoubtedly he was very skillful with his hands. I knew ... I watched him weave a fishing net by interlacing strings, and also the way he interwove strands to weave a basket. I enjoyed watching him too, how swiftly he twisted (lapcie) bast shoes from the fibrous inner bark of the linden tree. Lucky for me, Father with pleasure told me to go ahead. "Start making your brooms. I shall deliver them for you to Smiejno-Budy."

Out of all excitement I harnessed the horse into a wagon and drove to the birch tree forest to get a lot of twigs and sticks of the linden tree. At home I immediately began to follow Mr. Ciechanowicz, but unfortunately I could never catch up with his speed of work. The best I could do was twenty brooms per day, which surprised my father because he said I'd be lucky if I manage to make ten brooms in one day at my age.

Because of the Soviet's attack on Finland there was a considerable gap in the hundred divisions of Red Army occupying Poland. Stalin ordered the immediate mobilization of all men in Poland from twenty-one to twenty-five years of age in order to fill the gap and to have enough man power in reserve. Many thought that he was getting ready to invade another country but some were saying that Stalin could not trust Hitler. Anyway, a great number of men from our native land were drafted to the Red Army and we never saw them again. Some five hundred young men from Naliboki alone, including Jan Ciechanowicz from Trascianka, produced just a particle of the diminished population in the Wilderness of Naliboki. Once again in a different way Mr. and Mrs. Ciechanowicz were mentally and physically disturbed. For days we noticed they did not eat any food. For a while I felt strange and empty, as if someone died ... one person less, probably never to be seen again. After all, Jan was a nice fellow who never bothered anybody; he was just lying down and reading books.

As the Christmas holiday drew near my parents loaded a horse-driven vehicle with foodstuffs and sent me on a journey to Naliboki to deliver the provisions to my Aunt Bronislawa. Once our Maszka had been placed on the right road to Naliboki, she knew the way home. She did not mind at all if I altogether fell asleep, for her instinct expected that I would awaken as soon as she walked into the old yard. Traveling through the wilderness a considerable distance alone, at first I grew sad from lack of companionship, then it became spooky and frightening. As I watched Maszka pulling the wagon reliably and at the same time looked into a density of the forest and heard the sounds of wildlife and glanced at the endless blue sky, I buried myself and sank inside the wagon in order not to see, hear or think about anything. In such a state of mind I was involuntarily getting drowsier and drowsier yet as the wooden highway was rocking me to deep sleep, until my dear aunt roused me from sleep in our yard. I was very happy to see her but she was surprised when she saw so many things on the wagon, thinking that she was not forgotten in the family circle.

After passing the night I went to the church for nine o'clock mass on Sunday. At the end of the celebration of this liturgy I had to see our priest, Baradyn, and ask him to provide our family with wafers of unleavened bread for the Christmas holiday. I received them and placed a donation according to the will of my parents. On my return from the church I left on the table my aunt's share of these consecrated wafers in manifold colors, and promptly harnessed the gear of a draft animal and attached it to a wheeled vehicle; then I was ready to go. Before my departure I hugged and kissed my dear aunt and said goodbye. As the wagon moved and I looked back, my aunt was standing with tears in her eyes, waving a handkerchief and saying, "Prosperous voyage, Mieczyslaw!" Then, I drove out from the yard onto the main road for a long journey again in the dry, cold December weather.

The season of fourteen days prior to Christmas was observed strictly according to the custom of Catholicism, whereby all members of the Roman Catholic Church were obligated to keep a fast. In our family mother took the lead in the fasting agenda during advent, and also every Friday of the week, including the (Wielki Post) Lenten Fast. She abstained from prescribed kinds of food as in observance of religious duty. Therefore, we were not allowed to consume meat, animal fat and all dairy products; however, it was permitted to eat fish and to use vegetable oil for cooking. Notwithstanding the fact that one might feel undernourished during such fasting period, it proved to be time and time again most salubrious and conducive to health providing one endeavors to persevere in this manner to abstain from the restricted foods. Besides, what a feeling it is to look forward to Christmas Eve, the evening meal that was constituted of twelve courses and served at one time as a matter of fact only at this special occasion once a year. And each such delicious dish was made up of fasting foods. This most joyous celebration at our home, like in any other family, began with prayer and then the parents breaking and sharing the wafers with their children and next of kin if they are present. Then was the moment to enjoy the twelve courses of food that were prepared over the period of two weeks. The cold night of December twenty-fourth was peaceful at Trascianka. Our domestic animals were fed and watered, housed in the warm stables as usual. The candles on the Christmas tree from the windows illuminated the whole dark yard situated in the midst of forest, which is under pretence of friendship in the open air. Following the carols during such a happy evening, a somnolence became dominant and carried us through December twenty-fifth, held as the anniversary of the birth of Jesus Christ.

After the Christmas holiday the weather got colder and colder, the ground harder and harder. Consequently, when canals, rivers and lakes became frozen solid, and in particular the marshy land with its river Niemen, then the thick snow covered the surface of the earth so that man could travel on his sledge as the crow flies in any direction he had the will. This was the time when people from the western side of river Niemen were able to travel eastward through Trascianka into the forest to obtain their firewood or green wood as building material useful to the attainment of some end. Normally, at first they purchase an indeterminate quantity of trees, then they cut these trees down and stack them. The forester then comes along and stamps their wood or timber according to its volume in cubic meters. The customers only then were permitted to transport their felled timber home across the frozen river Niemen.

But of course, once the weather conditions became favorable to cross the river Niemen, then the people rushed impetuously, and thus our forest land was filled with drivers on sledge vehicles pulled by the most magnificent horses that have been fed and raised on that extremely fertile black soil. Our yard was daily packed with vehicles and the house was overcrowded by men who spent some time in waiting for my father to return from the forest and in turn to get their felled timber stamped. Some of these men were tremendously huge; they were giantlike men of supernatural size and strength. Inside the house they settled down on the floor on their buttocks, and for a snack they held one loaf of bread in one hand and a leg of ham in the other and washed it down with vodka that was contained in a large pitcher. Every time Father came home from the forest they treated him with vodka and snack before he went out again to stamp felled timber for the next customers. By the time the day was over, Father had

Giants from the other side of the river Niemen.

drunk vodka to excess, but because of very cold weather and as he was on constant move in the forest it was certainly conducive to his health. However, he did not complain; rather he was feeling great and was happy in spite of long hours of work.

Eventually, while waiting for their felled timber to be stamped, the ordinary men tried to persuade these giants to demonstrate their strength in order to have a pleasant diversion, and of course some fun to bet, making an agreement to risk something of one's own in return for the chance of winning something belonging to others, such as tools, sheepskin coat, foodstuffs, etc. But these huge men were in no way embarrassed, shy or timid; on the contrary, they were daring and fearless. That is why one said to the other in the Byelorussian language they all were fond of speaking, "Wasil, let us go outside and show them how we can lift some horses!"

"OK," said Siergiej, "let us all go outside."

As they all appeared outside in the yard, they noticed large logs laid by the fence. So Wasil said, "Hey, instead of a horse, let's try to lift those logs." And, as it happened, this incredible power lifting of the logs then began, which would take average men to use a lifting device in order to load or unload the logs to convey them from one place to another.

Ultimately, after several weeks, my father's hectic life and this officiously active job finally slowed down and he continued to work officially at a regular pace. The customers persistently continued to transport their felled timber home to its completion before the melting of the snow. They were most generous, rewarding father for his effort regarding their assistance. The outcome was that our buttery (spizarnia) was filled with foodstuffs abundantly so that it caused Mr. Ciechanowicz to be extremely jealous. Undoubtedly, he observed the people with whom father had business, how they were carrying bags of gifts through the door into our buttery. Out of this felled timber rush was only one consolation—the fact that his daughter Zofja fell in love with one man by the name of Karol Marawiej, who was one of these people from the other side of river Niemen, the very ones that Mr. Ciechanowicz regarded with wonder, pleasure and approbation, because most of our people on the eastern side of the river Niemen believed that it would result in good fortune if one was betrothed with one well off of the other side.

Mr. Karol Marawiej at the beginning during the first several weeks traveled back and forth beyond the river Niemen until his transportation of felled timber was completed, then he stayed with Zofja at all times in Trascianka, and of course she became pregnant. So, as it turned out, Karol took the place of Jan in the Ciechanowicz's family.

At this particular time it was apparent that my mother also was carrying a growing fetus in the uterus. We all were glad about it because life here was very good. The employees such as my father who worked for the Soviet's regime were excused from an obligation to which other people were subjected by submitting their domestic animals to the state. That is why our livestock began rapidly to increase, also due to the fact of unlimited pasturage at this beautiful forestry.

Mr. Ciechanowicz was riddled with jealousy in the presence of my father and it became more evident from the time when his son, Jan, was drafted to the Red Army. Indubitably, he felt that the position my father was holding indeed belonged to him, that my father did not deserve it because Mr. Ciechanowicz had learned that most of our relatives were enemies of the Soviet Union. So, on a certain day Mr. Ciechanowicz appeared before the Soviet officials who resided at Smiejno-Budy and told them that his neighbor, Wilhelm Klimowicz, was a sole enemy of Russia. When they asked comrade Ciechanowicz to elaborate on this subject, he told them that Wilhelm's brother, Eugenjusz Klimowicz, was one of the Polish officers wanted by NKVD, that his brother in law, Jozef Lojko, was a Polish legionary presently being held in confinement at Baranowicze. Also his brother in law, Waclaw Lojko, a Polish forester, had been removed from Trascianka to Siberia. Then they asked Mr. Ciechanowicz, "Can you tell us, comrade Ciechanowicz, where was comrade Wilhelm Klimowicz educated, and in whose army he served?"

Mr. Ciechanowicz responded, "I do not know, comrades."

"Well," one of the officials answered, "we have here on file comrade Wilhelm Klimowicz's resume, which states that he was educated in Russia and that he also served in the Russian army. Is it false or true, comrade Ciechanowicz?"

"Yes, it must be true," replied a stuttering, surprised comrade Ciechanowicz.

"Well, besides this fact, what else do you have to say about comrade Wilhelm Klimowicz? Is he an enemy of Russia?" asked one official.

"No," said the accuser. "I have nothing to say about comrade Wilhelm Klimowicz. I was wrong. I am sorry."

Mr. Ciechanowicz never knew that my father's nephew, Ivan Klimowicz, was as a matter of fact the commissar of NKVD, residing in Smolensk, which of course the Soviet officials at Smiejno-Budy were not at liberty to disclose to Mr. Ciechanowicz, who was to them nothing more or less that just a kolkhoznik.

In the beginning of March Father drove to Smiejno-Budy to make his report concerning a metrical volume of felled timber sold and the square area of land that was occupied by trees but was now being harvested, that which must be estimated for the replacement of young trees in the early spring. While he was talking to these well-acquainted individuals, they told him, "Comrade Ciechanowicz was here the other day in our office making his formal accusation against you, but of course we did not take any notice of his complaint, which after all did not make any sense to us. If you wish, comrade Klimowicz, we shall dismiss him from Trascianka and instead we shall send you another worker."

But father intervened by explaining to them, saying that his dismissal would cause greater problems for it would create a deeper-seated unfriendliness permanently between them. "Therefore it would be beneficial for all parties concerned if comrade Ciechanowicz remained at Trascianka; perhaps then his unfriendly disposition would become wearisome. Besides, he is an exceptionally good worker."

Consequently, the Soviet officials went along with father's proposition concerning Mr. Ciechanowicz, and we like good neighbors continued to associate and work together as usual.

Later, I overheard my parents talking to each other and realizing how lucky our family happened to be on account of Ivan's Klimowicz's visit. How strange that some unforeseen force brought forth an effect on the mind of Ivan to come to us here with such an enormous influence, that which embraced us with full protection. Mother said it must be a miracle, apparently caused by the direct intervention of a supernatural power. Otherwise, after the things Mr. Ciechanowicz told the Russians about us, we would definitely have perished somewhere deep in Siberia. In the process of being saved by a miracle, and because of its eccentricity, we began to pray now more than ever. From this time on when our principle meal of the day was ready at the table we prayed all together daily, thanking God for keeping us safe from danger and all evil.

During eighteen long months Alfons Lojko had already endured hiding from the NKVD underneath the structure of the furnace, in which commonly wood is consumed for heating and cooking. He had no idea how long yet he would have to continue to persevere under these inhumane conditions. In spite of the daily danger surrounding him and the uncertainty of the outcome, he was mentally and physically amazingly strong. Many times he had been seen by neighbors inside the house who eagerly observed Alfons from outside. Some collaborationists parallel in character to Mr. Ciechanowicz had been revealing selfishly information to the NKVD. Naturally, the NKVD repeatedly raided the house, terrorizing wife and child, but unfortunately always failed to find Alfons, the ex-member of the Polish Youth anti-Communist and Jewish organization. Finally, in the middle of March one day two Russians of NKVD clad in army uniforms and fully armed came inside Alfons's house and ordered his wife to pack her things because, they said, "You and your child, as of now, you are under arrest. We are going to take you to Russia."

So, while she started packing as they ordered, she was crying, but they were sitting at the table, talking and laughing. On the other hand, Alfons, hidden under the furnace, was hearing everything to

Alfons Lojko reluctantly surrendered to NKVD.

the point that he could not bear it any longer. So, in his rage he jumped out from underneath the furnace and all of a sudden he appeared in the room with two guns pointed directly at them. Both Russians were benumbed from fear, but Alfons only for the sake of his wife and child said to the Russians, "Since you are taking my wife and my child, take me also." At that moment he surrendered himself to the occupants and submitted his weapons to them. They in turn were banished, as some convicts, without a trial, his wife and child to an unknown place in Russia and Alfons in the prison at Baranowicze that already was full of Nalibokians from the start of the Soviet Union's occupation.

In the last year I had learned that in early spring the brown trout, S. trutta, of Europe migrate upstream. This trout is of great beauty and splendid game qualities, as well as this excellent fish is praised by all. From the upstream canal into the old twisted river the brown trout moves seasonally to such an extent that all sinuosities are filled with the fish. Catching the fish was the least of my problems because my uncle Waclaw Lojko left his trap nets, which were designed for this purpose. So, I carried them quickly to the canal and set them in the sinuosities of the river at the location near the Glass Bridge and gave some number of days to pass over before pulling the nets out of the water. When finally the time had elapsed, as a matter of curiosity I came there to drag out the trap nets and to see actually what was there inside. The net, of course, was floating easy when I was pulling it, but dragging it out onto the bank was indeed extremely hard, for the net was full with large fish about twenty inches long. After considerable effort and struggle dragging all nets out onto the bank of the river, I came back and told my father to help me to get the brown trout home. He then in a hurry harnessed our Maszka into a wagon and we drove to the canal, whereby we loaded all fish on the wagon, and on our return home we emptied the fish into a water trough by the well outside in the yard. Consequently this large trough was filled with trout, and when mother came out from the house she could not believe her eyes. Father passed a remark saying, "You see, Jozefa, now our fasting period will not be so hard ... being thankful for such a wonderful gift as if it came from heaven."

Mother replied, Yes, fast we must, but Mieczyslaw is the one who caught the fish."

In response I truly said, "I only put the nets into the water, but I never knew that fish would be there; this must be a miracle. That is why we must enjoy and eat the fish, although it is a fasting time before Easter."

By the way, Father himself at this time was engaged in distilling vodka from rye flour and getting it ready for the Easter holiday. To distil alcohol under the Communistic regime was a common practice everywhere, and it seemed that it was not in any way restricted by law, since it was forbidden to operate for private profit under capitalism. Therefore, now vodka was in abundance here on account of the fact that it was simply and easily produced. Thus, Father was not acting stealthily but was making his distillation of vodka openly in the yard by the well where he had close access to water for the cooling system. Obviously, this process depended on separating the more volatile parts of a substance from those less volatile by heating in a retort and then condensing the vapor, thus produced by cooling. When the faucet actually started dripping from the cooling system then it was a full-proof alcohol, but gradually it become weaker and weaker. For this reason, father and Mr. Ciechanowicz were tasting it, and eventually both got drunk right there by the apparatus. However, I remember at that particular time out of one sack of rye flour (zytnia maka) Father was able to rout forty liters of ninety-proof vodka.

My parents decided to share some comestibles we had obtained by our own endeavor with relatives living in Naliboki, so Father had to deliver these foodstuffs to them before the Easter holiday. As soon as he completed his distillation, he took with him some vodka, brown trout, ham, bacon, beef, wheat and rye flour, butter, cheese, eggs, and many other things homemade, and he drove to Naliboki and distributed between Benedikt's family, Mania Klimowicz and Alesia, and of course Aunt Bronislawa. On Father's arrival home he told mother that Alesia's daughter, Wierka Radziwill, was not feeling well and there must be something wrong with her.

"Well," mother said, "Wierka is very young nice lady. She is in her prime; I am sure she will be alright."

Then father added, "As for the rest of kith and kin, seems they all are feeling great, just as we do, except for Jan Sadziwil and Prelate Jozef Bajko; they both are concealed from the NKVD."

Mother said, "God knows how long they will have to endure this affliction, unfortunate poor souls."

"Also, in town I came across some old Jewish friends," father said. "Then I stopped by our neighbor, Mr. Michal Machlis, and we were talking for quite a while. Mr. Machlis was saying that the living conditions for the Jews have deteriorated badly because they cannot obtain any merchandise from the Soviet Union for the stores. The Polish remnants that they yet possess they are exchanging for food, and that whatever some of them harvest from the land they share with others who have nothing. It is evident in these days under Communistic rule critical times hard to deal with are here. Mr. Machlis was saying, 'A man is not allowed to obtain possession of one's property; he is even not sure if he is the owner of himself. You see, my dear Wilhelm, how many innocent people here have been snatched over night and they disappear for ever, We are not sure anymore when and who next will pass from sight. This is Bolshevik's madness, and their madness is very plain to all. Nothing good will come from it ... they will make no further progress,' Mr. Machlis concluded.

"I sympathized with the neighbor, went outside to the wagon and brought a sack of wheat flour to his house," continued Father. "Of course, he did not want to receive with favor but I told him that for his gratuity during our past association I owed him much more and to please if he needed any help or anything at all not to hesitate but call on me."

Mother was very pleased with what our father did with respect to Mr. Machlis. She said, "Next time when we go to Naliboki, we take some butter, eggs and a live chicken to his family."

As a consequence of so much distress and not knowing what the next day held for anyone under Bolshevik's tyrannical exercise of power, my parents decided to set up a self-inflicted penitence to abstain from eating and drinking on the last day of Lent, which is the period of forty days, excluding Sundays, from Ash Wednesday to Easter, observed annually as a season of fasting. We as children were not allowed to pass any food or drink through our mouths the whole day until the following day of Easter, regularly set aside for a religious purpose in honor of the resurrected Jesus Christ. The feast day ought to commence with consecrated bread and hard-boiled eggs that people bring to the church on Sunday morning for the priest to dedicate to sacred uses by sprinkling holy water on it. Because of such a special necessity, my parents sent me in a hackney-coach with the bread and eggs to Naliboki and told me to ride directly to Uncle Michal Lojko. There, they told me, I shall pass the night, and in the morning I shall go to the church to have my bread and eggs consecrated. Alas, I can never forget that day!

I left Trascianka for Naliboki around three o'clock in the afternoon on an empty stomach, and by the time I arrived to Uncle Michal's it was already dark. Uncle Michal kindly attended to our horse Maszka and told me to go into the house and take it easy, as if he were waiting for my arrival, I thought, and so I felt relieved. But of course when I got inside the house I found that my uncle's family was in the same predicament as ours, under a strict Lent, because here Uncle Michal was the one who administered discipline, just the same as our mother did. Then I appreciated fully why my parents did not want me to go and stay with Aunt Bronislawa, for they thought that she would definitely feed me and thus I would break our family's vow. Soon, however, my cousins and I went to bed. But in the morning Uncle Michal woke us up and sent us to the church with the victuals for consecration. The mass started at nine o'clock and I began to feel physically weak; the church was extremely overcrowded. I was with my cousins Lucjan, Marysia and Helena, situated up in the front close to the altar where a votive offering of King Zygmunt August was hanging and the large picture of Patron Saint Bartholomew painted in colors on the internal structure. Subsequently the crowd was squeezing me tighter and tighter, so that in the end I could hardly breathe. I kept looking intently in the direction to Priest Baradyn officiating, and I was wondering how soon he would start to sprinkle the holy water on people's victual, but the more I thought about it, it seemed to be dragging longer unbearably, as I was completely exhausted from strength on account of the state of being starved. The army priest and Priest Dadis were engaged with confessions; therefore many after confession pushed themselves from the altar in a long line throughout the church to take communion. But when Priest Baradyn began to give communion it really became harder for me to bear my weakness. At this very point in time I was afraid that I was going to faint. Finally, throughout the same line on the left and right people started opening their baskets, and soon Priest Baradyn walked sprinkling holy water on the both sides. Shortly afterward I tried to push myself in the direction of an exit, but it was hard. I had to move with the crowed. As soon as I got outside with my basket I headed straight to Uncle Michal, not even waiting for my cousins.

In a hurry, as I reached the gate of beloved uncle's husbandry I saw him standing in the yard with my transport prepared for me to ride home. At the same time, he lowered his head forward briefly and told me, "Climb up the wagon and ride home quickly because your parents are impatiently waiting for you." Aunt Orszula was standing on the porch saying good-bye as my uncle was opening the main gate, and there my returning cousins from the church were waving farewell. Maszka, of course, after being well fed and having a long rest, was full of temperament to trot back home without pausing. I arrived home sooner than I expected but unfortunately extremely weak. My parents walked outside to meet me.

Father grabbed the horse to unharness, but mother took the basket with consecrated food and I followed her into the house, where I sat by the table and weeped. When father walked in and saw me crying, he embraced me with strong emotion and sensibility, then took me by my hand, opened the door to our dining room and showed me a large table prepared with marvelous food and drink, and said, "Now all this is for us to enjoy, for we were just waiting for you."

At this very moment I forgot I was hungry, and we all were gladdened by this great occasion. Immediately after Mother had seen to the filial preparation and told us to take our seats at the table, Father opened the holy scriptures and read Matthew 6: 16-18, as follows: When you are fasting, stop becoming sad-faced like the hypocrites, for they disfigure their faces that they may appear to men to be fasting. Truly I say to you, they are having their reward in full. But you, when fasting, grease your head and wash your face, that you may appear to be fasting, not to men, but to your Father who is in secrecy, then your Father who is looking on in secrecy will repay you.

Now, father continued, "Let us pray, our Father in the heavens."

And so, we all together prayed aloud.

Uncle Michal's magnificent husbandry was enclosed with a fine fence, just as the contiguous parsonage was, and thus presented itself incomparable to all other proprietors of the land situated on the same elevation of the perimeter of St. Bartholomew's church and cemetery. On this elevation, the highest point in Naliboki, there have been no other dwellings except those people's cultivated fields. But farther beyond in to the west from the cemetery there was a village called "Zarecze."

An unauthenticated story from earlier times preserved throughout generations and popularly thought to be most a perplexing phenomenon was often observed as an appearance of tall "gleamy" figures in our old consecrated cemetery, yet nobody knew for sure what it was exactly. Appearing in the night, these large gleamy figures people used to call "gleamy pillars" (jasne slupy). Because of an agitated feeling aroused by awareness of threatening dread and terror, some endeavored to take courage and be able to explain this phenomenon scientifically. They claimed that when for the most part some fat corpses are buried, they are inclined to discharge a chemical element, for instance, such as phosphorous, which evaporates from under the ground and subsequently comes into view above the surface in the shape of a gleamy pillar. But the gleamy pillars frequently used to follow those who encountered them, always behind at a certain distance. If a person became frightened and started running away from this apparition, then regardless it maintained exactly the same distance behind him, and indeed this phenomenon was the scariest of all to anyone who had experienced it. Nonetheless, the scientific explanation continued that when a person walks or runs, he dashes through the air and therefore creates a vacuum behind his body, a chasm, into which this phosphorous pillar is absorbed to occupy an empty space, and thus no matter how fast a person would move the pillar would follow the vacuum instantaneously. Of course, such an interpretation in theory or in practice made a lot of sense, and for this reason it caused many to be less fearful.

Again, some folks superstitiously inclined believed that this phenomenon was nothing else than the representation of dead, tormented souls to whom the gate of heaven had been denied, and that in the meantime they had lost their way to purgatory and apparently could not find the way to hell. So, such unfortunate disembodied spirits were just wondering around on their burial ground until such a time when they reached their proper destination in one way or the other. When someone asked these folks why the ghost when encountered followed people, the strong believers always answered, "They mean no harm; they just seek an indispensable direction and desire assistance from a person they meet." That is why on a day of commemoration, November 2, intercession is made for the souls of all the faithful departed, but on November 1 a festival commemorative of all saints and martyrs is celebrated, to whom we pray for their clemency and guardianship on behalf of faithful departed souls.

Well, one may ask, does this conception make any sense? Surely it does, because it is an absolutely logical explanation. But again, one may ask, is this conception in any way scriptural? Certainly not, for anything that is unscriptual does not originate with God the almighty.

Yet, in spite of everything some old folks who were familiar with the holy scripture categorically declared that this phenomenon was really an impute of demons, having a superhuman power and ability to invade and possess any human being. On this account throughout the ages we have had people possessed by demons who manifest unexplainable power of healing the sick, ethers, to foretell the future, and many have been stricken by psychosis. The term is more or less synonymous with mental illness or insanity. Those who had severe mental disorders, often involving disorganization of the total personality, without organic disease, have been taken into custody at the police station in Naliboki and immediately afterward sent to the asylum in Stolpce. Such unfortunate victims were called here "Opetaniec," a madman, a man or woman possessed with the devil. However, the enlightened old folks made absolutely clear that this phenomenon was to be considered unmistakably as the only cause and source of demons and nothing else.

Early in 1939 a certain number of individuals had seen a legion of tall gleamy pillars that rose from under the ground on the cemetery and moved directly toward the east, inconsequential of vacuum or even in which direction the wind was blowing. On account of this, most people were scared to be near the cemetery at night, knowing that it was haunted exceedingly. But as soon as the Soviets invaded Poland, a new terror and consternation embraced the people to such a degree that they lost the memory of the haunting place, and for a long while nobody talked anymore about these tall ghostlike pillars. Until now, when again people observed a host of tall gleamy pillars, how they were rising from the cemetery ground and started on their journey toward the west. Certain individuals tried to match this phenomenon with the prophecy of an old man from Terebejno, and they concluded that definitely these were evil spirits that had existed here from remote antiquity, and that in the present age they had been organized as a military unit for its assigned function. It shows that two years ago when they had gone east, they brought here ungodly men who defiled our church, destroyed the Pillar of St. John and seized a great number of local people who were subjected to most cruel death. Struck with amazement, some listeners added, "God

Generally spoken of as "gleamy pillars" that were observed to rise up from under the ground and set themselves in motion toward the west; however, less accepted as superhuman creatures in Tartarus on the consecrated ground in Naliboki, from where they exercised the rule of darkness as wicked spirit forces.

knows what else these demons will bring here from the west." Some older men understood the purpose of this course of action and said, "Soon it will come, the last day of Naliboki, just as the Nostradamus of Terebejno predicted."

However, anything that is impossible or improbable remains the truth, which conforms to rule, standard, pattern or ideal, and therefore corresponds to the reality. For example, when the sons of the true God took for themselves wives from among the attractive daughters of men in the days of Noah before the Flood, the Bible then mentions the presence of "Nephilim." It is believed to mean fellers, or those who cause others to fall down, and the word is plural. In those days, as well as afterward, there were giants (Heb. nephilim) on the earth, who were born to the sons of the gods whenever they had intercourse with the daughters of men; these were the heroes (Heb. gibborim) who were men of note in days of old.

So, the fathers of the Nephilim have been angels, spirit "Sons of God" who did not keep their original position but forsook their proper dwelling place. Angels had the power to materialize in human form, but to dwell on earth and to forsake their assigned service to have fleshly relations was rebellion against God's laws, and perversion. The disobedient angels are now "spirits in prison," having been thrown into "Tartarus" (the lowest places) and reserved with eternal bonds under dense darkness for the judgment of the great day. This seems to indicate that they are greatly restricted, unable again to materialize as they did prior to the Flood, but yet they have power to invade and possess a mortal man.

Naturally, before the Flood the Nephilim and their families traveled the world, and of course had no difficulty reaching the most fertile land of Nowogrodek and Wilno, which chiefly is called Wilenszczyzna. Here they took up their abode, the place that for some antecedent generations has been called Naliboki. These fallen angels that materialized married women, fathered a hybrid generation known as Nephilim and then dematerialized when the Flood came, and the outcome was that they became "demons," invisible wicked spirit creatures. During the Flood every man was trying to reach the highest elevation, upon which they all finally were inundated. The highest elevation in Naliboki happened to be the church location, but then probably must have been much higher since the receding Flood waters diminished the hill. Inevitably then, henceforth this site considered in regard to its surroundings became the fixed place of Tartarus, an underground prison for superhuman creatures from where they exercise a rule of darkness as wicked spirit forces.

It is no wonder, therefore, that only here, on the other side of river Niemen as nowhere else in Poland, Lithuania, or Byelorussia are found animated giants, such as forester Talun, Mr. Kostus and many others. However, this phenomenon can be enlightened and fully convinced by Mendel, Gregor Johann (1822-1884), the Austrian botanist and biologist. He kept a careful record of his observations and made counts of the dominant and recessive characters in each generation of hybrid crosses. From the results of his experiments he formulated three basic laws known as the Mendalian Laws of Heredity.

After destruction of the world, about 130 years later, when the building of the Tower of Babel was, in one of the first cities to be built after the Flood, here God confused one set of language people had and scattered them from there over all the surface of the earth. Babel's God-defying program centered around construction of a religious tower with its top in the heavens, and it was dedicated to false man-made religion. When the scattered people reached the land of Wilenszczyzna, here they built cities and temples, and they worshiped the triad of devils over the period of seventeen centuries until these wicked cities sunk beneath the waters and became a legend, antonym ... history.

From the rule of Cyrus the Great during two centuries people came here from Mesopotamia, when the Tigris-Euphrates Valley was divided into two satrapies known as Chaldean and Assyria. Conveniently, they came to a similar geographical site between two rivers, Niemen and Wilia, into two palatines, Nowogrodek and Wilno, carrying with them fiendish religion, also Arabic and Iranian languages, which in due time evolved into Slavic and Lettish languages. Thus, an evil existed here through the ages, intentionally favorable for the demons dwelling in Tartarus. In Nowogrodek and Naliboki, temples of

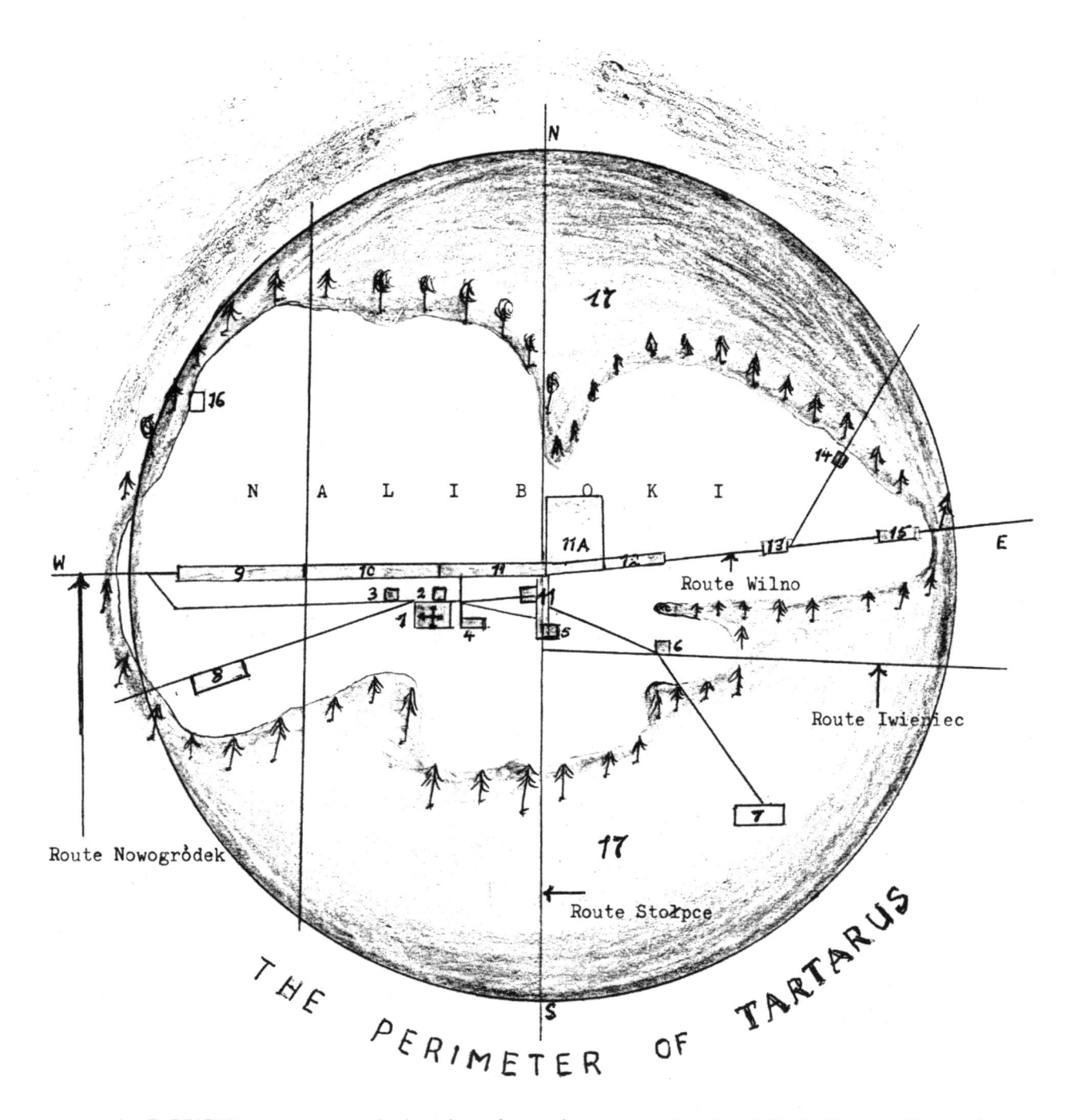

1. TARTARUS, consecrated church and cemetery ground. 2. PARSONAGE. 3. Husbandry of Michał Łojko. 4. MAJĄTEK (Castle of Radziwiłs) 5. SCHOOL. 6. DEATH VALLEY, Bokales.
7. CEGIELNIA, Brick-kiln. 8. PAZARECZE, Hamlet. 9. ZAŚCIANKI. 10. KAMIONKI.
11. MIASTECZKO, Borough. 11A JEWISH ORCHARD and their residence. 12. PLACE.
13. NAWASIOŁKI. 14. MACZYLIN. 15. TEREBEJNO. 16. Husbandry of Józef Łojko.
17. FOREST, appurtenant to the Wilderness of Naliboki.

Perkuna were raised in honor to the goddess of animals, where since mighty hunters used for game not only animals but also famous warriors.

Ultimately, after fifteen centuries had past, the first Christian prince of Poland, Miecislas I, ruled his kingdom, then the temple of Perkuna began to deteriorate. King Sigismund II Augustus (1520-1572), last of the dynasty of Jagellon, on the ruins of the temple built a chapel and laid up votive offerings there, which are accursed and set apart as evil or execrated. Then eighty years later the chapel was reconstructed into the church of St. Bartholomew by the Dukes Radziwill, and the king's votive offerings were transferred and hung in front of the main altar. Then, ever since, generation after generation as far as one can remember, the natives experienced a dread of haunt by demons.

Alike some other old folks in Naliboki—my grandfather, Franciszek Lojko—had a keen interest in the holy scriptures. He knew inwardly regarding the presence of demons in the midst of mankind which originally used to be an angels, but having left God's service came under the control of Satan. Grandfather was conscious of the fact that Satan continued to wage a bitter fight against Christ's followers, and for this reason he endeavored to live by the word of God. When the grandfather out of all his children tried to convince his son Michal concerning the actual wicked spirit forces, for some reason unknown he rejected such an idea with disdain and refused to belief in the existence of demons or Satan. In a like manner, he disciplined his children not to fear ghosts or wicked spirits because simply they did not exist, so Uncle Michal claimed.

Family, relatives and friends were deeply sadden by Wierka's perplexed illness. Dr. Chwal incessantly attended her sickness, yet with no hope of saving Wierka's life. The doctor's diagnosis and prognosis lastly disclosed acute leukemia, a generally fatal disease of the blood and blood-making tissues for which in her case there was no remedy. It pains me to recollect that on the twenty-eighth day of April this most beautiful blond person, twenty-five years of age, a wife and mother of two, passed away, and in the absence of her beloved husband, on account of superhuman creatures that at such a time exercised a rule of darkness over mortal man. For Jan Radziwill this particular moment was as if heaven and earth split in half and were no more. His own life became meaningless. Debilitated, Jan struck his head into the wall and lamented extremely. Incontinently and uncontrollably he wanted to wrest out to Wierka, but his mother desperately endeavored to restrain her son, saying realistically, "What good it will do? Wierka is dead and her house is surrounded by NKVD. They are there ... just waiting for you. If you go to Wierka now, my son, they will never let you see her; they will seize you, and you will cease to exist. What about your children? Think, and get a hold of yourself. Because God only knows how hard it is to endure this timeless loss, our beloved Wierka is no more."

As his mother was expressing herself and wept, Jan embraced her, and then they both manifested grief by shedding a lot of tears.

Jan, in the agony of unbearable pain and lamentation caused by the departed Wierka, just for the sake of two little ones concurred with his mother and said, "I shall be watching the funeral procession from my hiding place through the vent hole in an attic."

Jan's reluctant determination to not be captured by the NKVD suddenly relieved his mother from the mental strain and fear for her son's life. The vent opening in an attic was a low story beneath the roof where Jan was so far successful in hiding from the Soviets. Here he had a full view of Pilsudski Street at a distance of approximately 400 meters, which was a straight way to the church and cemetery. Of course, the other possible way to the cemetery was through Nowogrodek Street and then turning left into Poplawski Street, passing by the residence of Radziwill, which could create suspicion for NKVD if the funeral was to go this way, for they would presume that Jan was hiding in his mother's house. Therefore, it was unanimously decided from the assent of all concerned that the funeral would be conducted through Pilsudski Street on the fourth day after Wierka's departure.

On this mournful occasion all relatives who were under no suspicion or were in any way a threatening element against the Soviet regime were placidly gathered for the funeral procession held for the final disposal of the body of our beloved Wierka at the late Dr. Peter Klimowicz's residence, where actually Wierka, his daughter, was born and ended her life. During this unfortunate event our parents from Trascianka spent several days in Naliboki. Four pallbearers clad in black carried the coffin on their shoulders, walking with a slow pace. In front of the coffin was Priest Baradyn walking with two service boys. Following their mother's coffin were two little ones, Danusia and Jurek with grandmother Alesia and Mrs. Radziwill, followed by my parents with Natasza Makarewicz and her son Arkadjusz, Wierka's half brother, then Benedikt Klimowicz with his two sisters, Arszula and Alzusia, with her daughter Regina, Following them were Gabryjela Kosciukiewicz with her husband and two daughters, and her sister-in-law Genefa Klimowicz with her three sons Boniutek, Eugenjusz and Michal. Among them was Bronislawa Klimowicz, who at our residence throughout many holidays tutored her cousin Wierka and Gabryjela to bake the most delicious cakes. Following the relatives was a considerable crowd of friends and neighbors.

Without regard for moral turpitude or for family grief, this gathering of an individuals at the funeral was under the surveillance of NKVD in an attempt to seize the fugitive, Jan Radziwill, but their effort was beyond the realm of possibility.

From not far away, there was secretly concealed Jan, who was gazing through the vent in an attic at the living picture of his most beloved Wierka being carried away in a coffin. His mind was flashing through many thoughts. For everything there is an appointed time. Now, a time to weep, a time to keep away from embracing, and a time to give up as lost. *Oh, Wierka! Wierka, my love, my life, let me be devoured by this evil destiny too, to be able to squeeze and lay by your side forever. Not fair or just. Who can deny my dream I was dreaming constantly about you? My dream of eternal love for you, my dar-*

The funeral of Wierka Radziwil (1916-1941).

ling, is flourishing ceaselessly, even death cannot hinder. My dearest, where you are? My heart is with you always. Seated shrunken and contracted, Jan contemplated those sweet days when he was holding Wierka in his arms and kissing her while standing on the porch surrounded by a garden full of raspberry ... hearing her mother's repeated call, "Time to bed, Wierka!" *Now, my beloved Wierka, since you cannot breathe nothing else matters. How dear you are, I only know, because I have lost you.*

As Jan looked fixedly at the funeral procession from this vent in an attic, an image of Wierka's face appeared before him for a spell. In that he heard her voice softly saying, "Good-bye for now, my love, till we meet again."

In such a plight, distracted to despair and to dejection of spirit from the loss of hope, this phenomenon of Wierka's declaration lingered in Jan's mind henceforth. He believed that his fate was to die in Naliboki sometime in the near future, eventually to be combined again after separation. That is why from this inspiration Jan became extremely courageous and began to risk his life at any occasion possible from this time on.

From the attic in the Radziwills' dwelling one could clearly see a vast region of land including some buildings that was an appurtenance of Naliboki's borough (Miasteczko Nalibockie). On the northern side corner of Stolpce-Pilsudski Street there was the house of Mr. Machlis, and next to his property a residence of Mr. Baszaro. Then it was our place of residence, and formerly there was a clinic of my grandfather Dr. Kazimierz Klimowicz, who likewise was an organist of the church of St. Bartholomew and untimely died of leukemia just as his niece Wierka. I have noticed that my parents were alarmed by it and talked about this strange peculiarity of leukemia striking twice in our family. So they wondered who would be the next victim of this fatal disease. However, on the southern side of the same street was the house of Mr. Srol and next to it the residence of Mr. Walon, where also was the clinic of Dr. Chwal, and farther down toward the lake there was the residence of Wojt, the late Chairman of Naliboki. From the view of the Radziwills' house, Popiawski Street leads directly to Majatek of Ciechanowicz, which originally was the manor house of Dukes Radziwill. Stolpce Street and the highway to Iwieniec went through the land of Majatek. On Stolpce Street there was an elementary school of Naliboki giving a course of education of seven years, with pupils usually entering at about seven years of age. On the western side was the residence of Mr. Farbotko with an orchard; here used to reside Sister Katlerycha with her friend Taciana. On the eastern side of Stolpce Street there was the residence of teacher Mr. Guminski and a house of sinister Natasza Makarewicz, Arkadjusz's mother. The right side of Poplawski Street bordered a parsonage and the left bordered Mr. Jesc's orchard; all these remained subject to exclusive ownership of the late Mr. Poplawski.

From this point of view it was obvious that we had to be eyewitnesses throughout the years of a great number of funerals passing by our house or being conducted through Poplawski Street, which we always watched. On All Saints Day and All Souls Day, November first and second, I remember the whole hilltop of the cemetery was glowing, lit brightly by innumerable candles each year. Those were the days of commemoration on which intercession was made for the souls of all the faithful departed.

The worship of the dead points to this origin. The mythologies of all the ancient nations are interwoven with the events of the Deluge. The force of this argument is illustrated by the fact of the observance of a great festival of the dead in commemoration of the event, not only by nations more or less in communication with each other, but by others widely separated, both by the ocean and by centuries of time. Moreover, this festival is held by all on or about the very day on which, according to the Mosaic account, the Deluge took place, the seventeenth day of the second month—the month nearly corresponding with our November. Thus these celebrations actually began with an honoring of people whom God had destroyed because of their badness in Noah's day.

Such holidays honoring "spirits of the dead" as if they were alive in another realm are contrary to the Bible's description of death as a state of complete unconsciousness.

From my childhood during a catechism I learned that the human soul is immortal, is not subject to death. Yet in spite of the Roman Catholic edict a priest himself at the pulpit in the church of St. Bartholomew was announcing people's names who had purchased a mass consisting of various prayers for the dead souls. By the way, these expressions sound exactly the same in Polish. So I wondered how it is possible for the dead soul to be immortal, having an eternal life, not even subject to the authority of resurrection; it did not make any sense, at least in my mind. And yet, looking at the hilltop I was extremely apprehensive of something far more powerful than a human soul dead or alive. To mistake one for the other, I was terrified looking at the cemetery through the window of my bedroom in the night, and especially on the All Souls Day, just as I had an overwhelming impulse of fear when I was near the Kroman lake, the legendary drowned city. Searching, concerning the dead, later in my life I was convinced that they are conscious of nothing at all; neither do they any more have wages, because the remembrance of them has been forgotten. Also, their love and their hate and their jealousy have already perished, and they have no portion any more to time indefinite in anything that has to be done under the sun.

Nonetheless, the fear and terror that was in me was inheritably genuine, induced by sinister spirit, as it is in every human being, which impels a man to worship something more powerful than himself. Certainly, those disobedient materialized angels whose bodies were destroyed by the Deluge, but their immortal malevolent spirits throughout the ages stayed powerful enough to force a mortal man for their adoration in the manner most pleasing to them. Therefore, it is no wonder that the cemetery hill of Naliboki, just like many other similar locations in the world, continued from the time of the Deluge to be in observance of a great festival of the dead in commemoration of the event when God delivered the angels that sinned to pits of dense darkness to be reserved for judgment. Apparently the disobedient angels were cast into Tartarus in Noah's day, which is not a place but a condition, and was not presented as a place for humans but for superhuman creatures. So in that regard there is a similarity, since the scriptural Tartarus is clearly not for the detention of human souls but only for wicked superhuman spirits who are rebels against God.

In the beginning of May, father started to cultivate the ground for early planting. Now he allowed me to help him plowing, and while he was sowing the seeds of a different kind I was harrowing the plowed ground behind him. After we spread manure from the stables, we planted potatoes, and by doing this we completed our cultivation. At that point at least father did gain some extra time, which he used to work our land in Naliboki for the benefit of Mania Klimowicz and Aliesia, also his sister Bronislawa, our aunt. But our exclusive land in Maczylin was left barren this year for the second time. On his return from Naliboki, he was engaged plowing the lines of the forest which were necessary for the protection of spreading hazardous fire. At that time I already joined the herdsman hired by Mr. Ciechanowicz, who authorized me to help my father, for which, of course, my parents were kind also to share our crop with the Ciechanowicz family. On account of pregnancy, father forbid mother from helping in any kind of work outside the house, and in this respect Ciechanowiczes were mindful too, because their daughter Zofja was pregnant also; both as a matter of fact were in advanced stage.

At this time, being still in my puerile state, I experienced pleasure in constructing articles by a joiner. I was already skillful making brooms from the white birch twigs, which were tied with bark of a linden tree, and also I had acquired proficiency of making baskets, those common ones in our homeland that normally are made out of roots from the pine tree and its frame shaped from the hazelnut cane, or furze. These canes are easily bent and once they are devoid of moisture such baskets are capable of holding heavy weight when used for harvesting potatoes. Now in June the bark of the linden tree peels off effortlessly and smoothly. Just as the old saying was formulated in following words: "In June one can climb the linden tree barefooted, but when descend, this being is booted." As deceitful as it may seem, yet it was quite a simple task for any man who knew how to twist his bast shoes. Bast, of course, is the fibrous inner bark of trees, originally of the linden, also used in making cordage.

During the time when I was tending my herd of cattle with the Ciechanowiczes' herdsman I learned from him how to twist my bast shoes. From that time I was able to twist them all in various sizes for my mother, sister and brother. But father, as most men in this environment, twist his own bast shoes, furnished with a sole so that they would last longer in the summer or winter. In the Wilderness of Naliboki it was appropriate to wear these bast shoes on account of the fact that it was most convenient and safe for one's feet to walk through a boggy land overrun with vipers and other poisonous snakes once the feet were soaked in water till saturated; but in the meantime walking on a dry surface it repels the moisture rapidly, thus the feet become desiccated soon, which does not occur when one is wearing leather boots or caoutchoucs. During the summer we wrapped our feet with linen rags when in use of bast shoes, but in winter we used the woolen socks and then wrapped our feet with woolen rag remnants also, so that the feet had no chance whatsoever of frostbite, which often resulted in gangrene.

Now I was eager to learn how to use a scythe, but all the scythes we had were too big for me. So father had to make a special order and the blacksmith made it somewhat small, but just right to suit my growth. Then in the middle of June I began to cut the grass in a glade by the canal, where some years ago my father with his friend Antoni Szarzanowicz had been hay-making and saw a naked, unprotected, possessed middle-aged woman in this wilderness. Here, after turning swathes till my cut grass became dry, I built a hay-rick, just as my father use to do. When I came home, father was very curious to know where I had been over the last five days. I told him that I was hay-making in a glade behind the canal and as a result I had there a considerable size of hay stack. He could not believe me. In that case, he got on the horse and went to see it. When he came back, he told mother what he saw about this incredible occurrence and they both laughed themselves sick. When I asked them what was so funny, they looked at me and laughed more, saying, "You are so small. How did you manage to load the hay so high, since there was nobody to help you?"

I said, "Quite easy, I handled this job in the exact manner as father does constantly. At first, I prepared a bed of logs, and in its center I buried a long post with rope tight to the top of it. Then I started to pack the hay on beds around the post. When it got too high, I used the rope to climb up. I trampled the hay, climbed down and packed some more hay. And, I kept on repeating the same process until I had finished my hay-rick; and when it was done, I came home."

While hay-making I was alone in the forest, and naturally I became preoccupied with various thoughts, in particular about my cousin Ivan. It bothered me a lot thinking about the fact that one day soon he would come for me because I agreed that he could take me to Russia. On the other hand, I was pondering ideas of his promise, when he said that I would be provided with the best education there was and subsequently acquire power and authority precisely as he did by becoming a commissioner of NKVD. Here, I was given reason for expectation, concerning which I was forming a mental picture of Ivan's sincere gratuity. Fancy, free sustenance, free education; after that, possession of enormous power and supremacy. But, for all these, the first step I had to take was an oath of becoming a Communist and to have exclusive devotion to our father Stalin. Of course, after that it is expected that all things will follow smoothly, absolutely without anxiety. What an offer! How can one refuse? But in the back of my mind I knew there was a catch and a very good one at that, which meant that once I accepted such an offer I would be automatically obligated to renounce my faith in the true God. It goes then without saying that I would find myself on the side of the devil, befit manipulation of his atrocities. I would be playing into his hands, becoming a killer of men, since the devil walks about like a roaring lion, seeking to devour someone. It is unthinkable. How on earth could one man could kill another whom God created in his own image, according to his likeness? Following upon the fact that God's Son stated that his Father is "a Spirit," this rules out any physical likeness between God and man. Rather man had qualities reflecting or mirroring those of his heavenly Maker, qualities that positively distinguished man from the animal creation. Though in the image of his Creator, man was not made to be an object of worship or veneration, as it is wont in the case of Stalin.

As I was engaged in continuous and contemplative thought such as this, I began to shiver from fear. At once I laid my scythe on the ground and sat on the swathe cross-legged, bowed my head and began to pray our Lord's prayer. Then I concluded with my usual entreaty, which I was saying from the day of Ivan's departure: "Oh God, our heavenly Father, please protect me from this temptation and prevent Ivan of coming here for me."

Later, when I came home, I asked my father, "How shall I extricate myself from going to Russia when Ivan comes for me?"

Father answered, "I do not know, Mietek. But do not worry; if he comes, then I am sure we shall find some kind of explanation that will exculpate you from the promise you have made."

Nevertheless, my worry did not stop by a long shot, for I continued praying each and every day, asking God to impede Ivan and have him not come here at all.

Only two days had passed since I finished my hay-making. I remember so well that it was a most beautiful morning at sunrise as we got up to milk the cows, and soon after I was ready to put them in the pasture to graze. The sun was huge, deep red, as if stained with blood, and had just begun to peep in the line of the apparent meeting of the sky with the top of the trees of the wilderness. The overmastered stillness under the blue sky initiated to dictate an admonition. But of course, nobody was paying any attention. Besides, who would be observant once under subjugation in this inanimate Polish world? Yet, in this extraordinary beauty and calmness in the early part of the cloudless twenty-second day of June, my mother began to have the pangs of childbirth. In her travails the tranquility of the environment was roused, for she was screeching and screaming aloud. Her mom, that is our grandmother, with excellent childbirth experience, stayed with us intentionally to help the bringing forth of offspring. Father was milking our cows with my sister Waclawa, and I was standing by him listening to mother's cry. At the same time the Ciechanowiczes, as always, were milking their cows too. Mrs. Ciechanowicz suggested to my father to have me retained in case help was needed. "Anyway, our herdsman will take care of Mietek's herd," she said. So I was left behind, cutting the wood for fire and carrying water into the house from the well outside.

Though possible to have the baby born at any moment, at 10 a.m. the blue sky began to roar with melodious sounds of enthusiasm, that which may or may not create a preternatural miracle. In this amazement and rarity our neighbors dashed out from the house and father queried them. "Hey, what is happening? What kind of sound is this that in its own novelty invests golden views?" Soon, the sky became overclouded with a massive and ponderous German Luftwaffe, the air arm of the German aggressive forces no man had ever seen. Rejoicing inwardly, one may ask, what's the matter? Echo from the sky ... Das ist ein Blitzangriff! This is a lightning attack. Yet for Poland it meant simply, deliverance from the Bolsheviks' paradise and plunging into the Nazis' hell, the habitat of evil spirits, where literally is only death and condition of great mental or physical suffering.

In this actual process of time, father said, "To live or not to live, that is the question; whether it is not a struggle over death or life, who knows?"

At this precise moment the baby girl was born, and we named her Krystyna. Mother's delivery terminated in success and she remained in good health.

At noon father received a draft from the Soviet Union. Immediately, he was ordered to report in Lubcz, which was west of Trascianka about sixteen kilometers on the other side of river Niemen. So he took his identity with him and left for Lubcz. The Soviet Union's concept was to grab the remaining part of the Polish manpower and use it in an anti-German attack, but unfortunately it did not turn out that way. Because the following day, Germans bombarded heavily large concentrations of the Red Army troops, including Lubcz. Under such a predicament the Soviet officials ordered the Polish men to scatter and head for home. The next day, father safely came home.

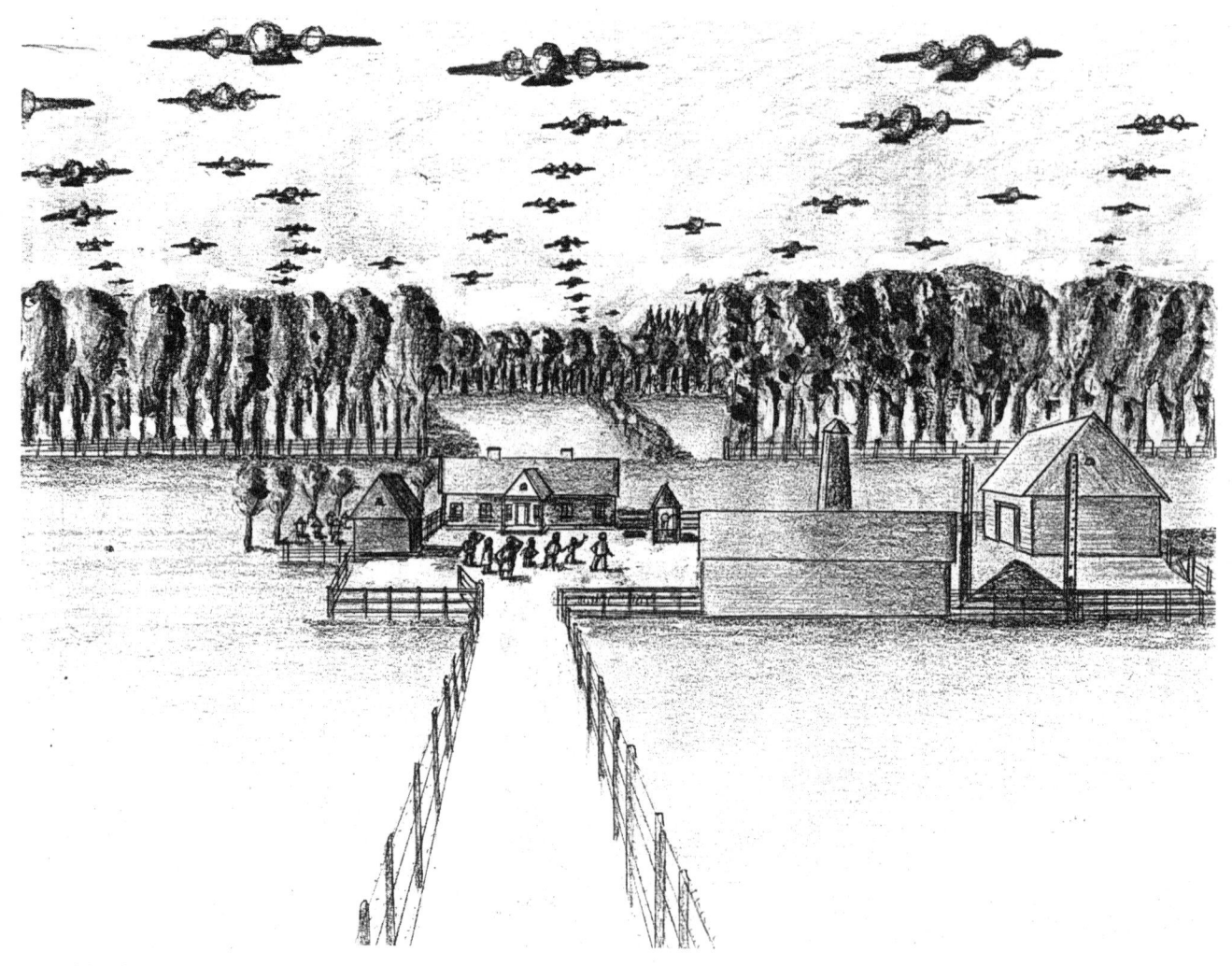

June 22, 1941, German "Luftwafffe" airforce attacked the U.S.S.R.

At 2 p.m. the German air power reverted from the distant part of civilized Russia to Germany. This time, of course, the airplanes did not create much of a disturbance because they were empty and light flying back home. One airplane we noticed was flying very low with a heavy discharge of smoke behind. Finally this flying contraption burst in flames and crashed in the forest just a few miles south of Kroman. Men who operated this aircraft descended by parachute and thereafter were hidden from the Red Army by the local people.

Russians searched for the German pilots in vain; they found wreckage of an airplane but no pilots, dead or alive. Later, of course, those folks that lived on the forester's husbandry were handsomely rewarded, perhaps to show the Polish people that whosoever treats Germans right, they in turn shall be taken care of by the German National Socialism, which presently was being dominant under the dictatorship of Adolf Hitler.

In this most significant, momentous day, an enormously massive air raid launched on the USSR was indeed "Blitzkrieg und der Kampt gegen die Armut," lightning war and the war against poverty. The outcome was that one hundred Stalin divisions in Poland came to be paralyzed. The minority members of the Communist party lost total control over the majority of non-Communists. But both the Communistic patriots and nonpartisans endeavored to scamper away from Poland in a panic. But for them there was no place to run, hastily or otherwise. One may ask, why? Simply because at the outset the Germans heavily bombarded the line across Russia, and on the following day a complete front was created by the German paratroopers. Once this objective was done, henceforth a massive delivery of military units continued daily. Thus the Nazis' military objectives were the destruction of the Soviet armies in the field, the seizure of Kiyev, Moscow and Leningrad, and the occupation of the oil fields of the Caucasus and the Caspian Sea, as well as the industrial centers of the Urals. By mid-November 1941, the armies had laid siege to Leningrad and Moscow and had taken Kiyev, Kharkov, Zhdanov and Kerch in the eastern Crimea.

On that very second day Nazis propaganda was discharged in a shower from the airplanes, which nonpartisan peasants apprehended meant what actually was written concerning their long-awaiting expectation of being free from subjugated Communism. These plain pamphlets declared as follows:

#1. STALIN IS DEAD AND THIS IS THE END OF COMMUNISM.
#2. ABANDON YOUR WEAPONS AND GO HOME TO YOUR PARENTS.
#3. NO NEED FOR YOU TO FIGHT FOR THE POVERTY.

The most effective Nazis propaganda caused the majority of the Soviet soldiers to lay down their arms and move east, some in military transportation and the rest on foot. The forests by the highways were filled with abandoned weapons and military equipment, including heavy transportation and Stalin Tanks. Most of these vehicles could not travel any longer for a lack of fuel because of panic and disorganization.

On the third day, however, at 10 a.m. a multitude of German airplanes flying east had a full view below of the Red Army heading home. But in order to disorganize and to scare away a military unit, a German airplane dropped two bombs by the side of the highway in Smolarnia. The holes in the ground were so enormous that either would fit an ordinary house. The explosive effect shook the entire region and the house we were in at Trascianka, but no Russian soldier in Smolarnia was killed. Unfortunately, the blast was exceedingly thunderous and frightening to such an extent that I was left with horrible dreams for a while.

The Communists in Baranowicze were lining up the Polish political prisoners for execution, but the German bombardment interrupted execution and all Polish victims dispersed and came home. Over the period of almost two years these Polish prisoners endured inhumane torture. Fortunately enough, all the victims from Naliboki returned home safely, and among them were our relatives, Jozef Lojko, Kaziraerz Wolan, and Alfons Lojko.

Since the first day of the Soviet Union's occupation, Jan Radziwill came outside from his hiding place, but the sunshine and fresh air prevailed over him, and at once he fell face down to the ground. Neighbors carried him inside the house. Dr. Chwai came to do medical scrutiny and testing on Jan but found nothing wrong with him, apart from the fact that in his plight he was made feeble or languid without sun and fresh air.

My godfather, Jozef Lojko came to Trascianka to narrate to our parents his ordeal in Baranowicze prison, where he suffered agony inflicted by the Communists. For example, one of their effective methods under interrogation was for the victim to sit on the corner of the chair for a long period of time with his feet stretched in front on the floor while water fell in drops directly onto the center of his head, and so on, and so forth. Then, I could not believe what I heard, yet gradually I learned what the Communists actually were in their disposition toward the Poles and why in our plight Russian roulette was applied.

As soon as the NKVD officials deserted their post in Naliboki, Radziwill came to his children and lived with his mother-in-law, Alesia, as he used to reside there with Wierka in this large Klimowicz house. My uncle Zenka, Eugenjusz Klimowicz and my cousin Janka Lojko came from undercover here also, and they lived with Zenka's mother, Mania Klimowicz. Prelate Jozef Bajko returned from his concealment to the sacred service and married this young couple, Janka and Eugenjusz. Now, all from undercover Eugenjusz's men were reunited with their families, those that once were members of the Polish Youth like Radziwill, students of universities, and Polish legionaries, veterans from World War I, just like our Jozef Lojko.

The German propaganda proved to be persuasive and susceptible to the Russian people.

At the celebration of this modest marriage all kith and kin were gathered, at which occasion the bridegroom, leader of the Polish guerrilla movement in the Naliboki region, delivered a harangue. On the outset, he spoke about the Communists and their long-lasting systematic extermination of the Russian people, which followed the extermination of Polish intelligence, and at the present time a mass execution of their own soldiers who hungered and longed to be free just for a moment without fear of death. As Zenka continued, he urged caution to all present to be aware of the Nazis' trap. He also reminded them of the fact with respect to Jozef Filsudski's forgotten and unfinished plan, the way he was going to eliminate Adolf Hitler and disengage Communism in Russia. Then he enthusiastically concluded with a question, saying, "My dearest patriots, who can be now the assistant or supporter of Jozef Stalin? I tell you, only Satan the devil."

Nonetheless, since inside the Soviet Union and its occupied territories communication from outside the western world was subject to a blockade or obstruction, we had no way of knowing about the fact that on the day Hitler invaded the USSR, Prime Minister Winston Churchill had promised Britain's full support to Stalin and the Communist people.

In Smolarnia, where the German bombs were dropped on Russians several days ago and did not kill any, Communists traveling in limousines stopped there and massacred the Red Army soldiers who were walking home unarmed. In Naliboki five unarmed soldiers came to Mr. Skniut's tavern and asked him if he could provide something for them to eat since they suffered from extreme hunger and had not eaten for days. Obviously, Mr. Skniut was well acquainted with the commissioner of NKVD, who was of Jewish descent and an official in the municipal building of Naliboki. So Mr. Skniut called him and told him that some five Soviet soldiers came to his establishment and were demanding food without pay. The NKVD commissioner arrived in his limousine at once, parked by the tavern, walked inside and got the soldiers outside. He took their identities from them and as they were standing in the line, shot them in their heads and left them dead on the pavement. As soon as he took their identities, he said, "Now I execute you because you are unarmed." Immediately then the commissioner got into his limousine and drove east, and disappeared from sight forever.

During this day a great number of soldiers, most of them unarmed, were passing through Naliboki. When they saw these poor young men laying dead by the tavern, they were very concerned and made an inquiry to find out what had happened to the soldiers, why they had been executed? Naturally, certain locals explained to the Russians what had happened. So, as these soldiers were on their journey east, they took with them Mr. Skniut, and later somewhere near Iwieniec he was found dead. Mr. Skniut was buried in that city at the Jewish cemetery by his family and friends from Naliboki.

Mr. Skniut was in his fifties but he looked much older because he was wore a long beard. My friend Arkadjusz and I used to bring Mr. Skniut forest mushrooms, sorrel, and fresh water fish. He was a strict businessman. We were paid cash by him for our stuff, and in his bar we used to buy and enjoy his Polish smoked dry sausage. Of course, then we had some change left from the amount, derived from the disposal of goods. His tavern was always packed on Sunday afternoons after mass. It was indeed fun for us to watch men coming out drunk in the evening at closing time. Mr. Skniut was a family man with a wife, two beautiful daughters and a son. All his children were adults. His tavern business in Naliboki was highly appreciated by all natives.

A taste of freedom proposed death.

In accordance with the universal rule of militarism, when one or more soldiers forsakes arms, in such a case they may face the firing squad for desertion. But when millions of soldiers abandon their weapons, then it is the will of the majority of the people to say that they are dissatisfied with their oppressive regime; hence they are not under regulations of the militaristic policy or statute. Therefore, since such is the case, a change of government remains undeniable. So, in order to obviate such a future predicament, Stalin compelled each and every soldier to take an oath that the last bullet will be left to shoot himself before he became a prisoner of war to his enemy. Further it was forewarned that if this dictated command was not carried out, then Stalin personally would kill violators once he got hold of them. Inevitably millions of Stalin's troops had fallen into Hitler's hands. But at the end of World War II Stalin made his demand of Great Britain and the USA to return the Soviet prisoners of war from the German occupied zones. When the British soldiers in Germany came to collect Russians in order to put them on the train to their homeland, many escaped, but of those who had no chance to flee, a multitude committed suicide, concerning which their captors had no idea why.

Tatars is the name originally applied to the Mongols. After the Russian Revolution of 1917 the Kazan and Krim Tatars were organized respectively into the Tatar and Crimean Autonomous Soviet Socialist Republics. The Volga (Kazan) Tatars, who numbered about three million, from 1926 were gradually assimilated into the Russian population. However, this Asiatic tribe of people were known to be forcible, characterized by malice, corrupt in conduct or habits, and above all most dangerous. My father had an opportunity to be with them in World War I near the Black Sea, and he learned there that for the Tatar to kill any man is as easy as to spit on the ground. Now, since they had a right of self-governing power in the Communistic regime and were in the Red Army, Tatars exercised that power by putting to death by legal authority those who gave up; thus a large number of Russians died at the hands of Tatars.

Two armed Tatars were heading on foot eastward over the Glass Bridge. Obviously, they saw our lane, walked in and came to our house. In the house, the Tatars asked my mother to provide them with food, and at that they sat down behind the table. Naturally, she started to prepare a meal for them. When father walked into the house, they both stood up and asked him sternly, "Why are you not in the army like us to fight the enemy?"

Father answered, "I was drafted, but when I presented myself I was relieved of duty. The superior gave me my discharge papers. Please, let me show you these papers."

One nodded. But actually there were none. Father then walked into another room, climbed through the window and escaped in the forest. The Tatars waited for a while, then opened the door and saw the window wide open. As they came back to the table to eat, they were cursing in their own native language. As soon as they had enough to eat, they put their rifles on their shoulders and hurried in the direction intended because on the highway there was a heavy and noisy movement of troops and German airplanes were in the sky.

Several hours later the esoteric tumult calmed down. Mother told me to go call father home because the Tatars had gone and it seemed they would not be back. I went to look for my father everywhere and kept calling him but there was no sign of him anywhere.

Not till the following day did father appear home and tell us that he watched the Tatars crossing the bridge and all the Russian troops heading eastward throughout the day and night. He said, "I knew when it was safe for me to come home."

The retreat of the Red Army continued till mid-July, the exact time when the German front in the Soviet Union had been firmly and densely established with the great soldier, fifty-one-year-old Friedrich Paulus. He commanded a panzer army and was promoted to colonel general and field marshal on the Russian line of contact of two opposing forces. Paulus was chief of staff for General Walther von Reichenau's army throughout the Polish and French campaigns of World War II, in 1939 and 1940.

Again in the Wilderness of Naliboki, probably as anywhere else in the country, the German pamphlets were discharged in a shower. But this time not as propaganda, rather a command given to the Red Army instructing them that there was no place to run. "You all are in our captivity, in thralldom. Now, you must take a temporary employment with the Polish farmers and work for your food and lodge until the German authorities demand your presence to be a prisoners of war." This was indeed an unconditional ultimatum of the German Socialist Republic's power and superiority with respect to over one hundred divisions of Stalin's armed forces that were incredibly taken by surprise. At this point in time, the boisterous movement of the disorganized Red Army in the German pot came to a halt.

Now, as they are the prisoners of war, they quit to sing:

> With us is Stalin our own dear,
> with his iron arm, to the victory leads us Voroshilov.

Chapter IX

THE GERMAN OCCUPATION

September 17, 1939, was the day the USSR advanced with one hundred divisions to take half of Poland, according to a previous agreement with Germany, and in spite of the Soviet-Polish nonaggression pact. Twelve days later a line of demarcation in Poland was agreed upon, and in October Soviet Byelorussia and Soviet Ukraine annexed the territory east of the line. Thus, for the second time in history, Poland ceased to exist. But now, since June 22, 1941, the Soviet Union was being attacked by the Nazis, and the partition of Poland planned between the two powers was terminated—Poland became completely under German occupation. And yet, unfortunately, from this time on the people of the Wilderness of Naliboki were persecuted by both sides, the Nazis and the Russian Communists alike, to suffer death by war crimes, torture, executions and systematic extermination.

Again in the Wilderness of Naliboki, probably as anywhere else in Poland, German pamphlets from airplanes were discharged in a shower. But this time, rather than an order given to the Red Army, the propaganda instructed them, there is no place to run; you have been captured; you are in thralldom; you all must take temporary employment with the Polish farmers and work for your food and lodging until German authorities demand your presence as prisoners of war (in Kriegsgefangenschaft sein). This was indeed an unconditional ultimatum of the German Socialist Republic's power and superiority with respect to over one hundred divisions of Stalin's army, how they were taken by surprise in a single day. So at this point in time, the boisterous movement of the disorganized Red Army in the German pot came to a halt.

A Russian sergeant arrived on a black horse to Uncle Jozef Lojko's farm and offered his service in exchange for food and lodging. Further, he said, "If I stay on your farm and work, I would like to leave this Siberian horse with you."

Of course, my uncle was very pleased to have most needed help on the farm and a beautiful horse, an animal that he always admired. And there was a lot of work in his place since he was held in prison over a year and half. Now, as he became free, he needed help desperately, and it was just luck that this sergeant, Wladimier Mikalajewicz, came in a most convenient time. However, it was not a surprise at this particular time, since every farmer had a Russian soldier working for him just for food and bed. Yet, no soldier came to our place at Trascianka. But Wladimier was a very hard worker, and after a while Uncle Jozef brought him to Trascianka and he worked for us over a period of two months.

Wladimier was quite a decent human being, for he did not approve of the Communists' way of life in Russia. He did not wish to be as other millions of Russian citizens subjugated by Stalin's Five Year Plan. This idea he strongly compared to exploitation or enslavement of mankind in an antiquated way. He specifically said, "We the people in the Soviet Union are classed as working hard peasants who toil just for a little food because all the earnings are being used up to support other countries with a notion that when the whole world becomes converted to Communism, then Russia will be prosperous and its people will live in luxury, which shall compensate for all the impoverished duration. Obviously in the beginning we were deceived by this plan, but later we felt that every other Five Year Plan was getting worse, not better. Then we realized convincingly that the thing we hoped for would never come to pass. Now, at this present time we are better off as prisoners of war than being free in the Soviet Union."

Nevertheless, Stalin's propaganda pamphlets on the subject of the current situation were discouraging Russian soldiers to surrender to the Germans on account of the fact that once the Nazis got hold of them, in Germany they would be tortured, starved, flayed alive, burned alive, and so on and so forth.

During the first week of August a baby girl was born to Zofia Ciechanowicz, whose father was Karol Marawiej. At the same time the Ciechanowiczes had a message from some men of Naliboki who were together in the Red Army in Russia with their son Jan Ciechanowicz. They encountered a bitter fight against the Germans there and eventually were seized. In reprisal the Germans made them walk day in and day out without any food or water. Consequently many died, among them Jan Ciechanowicz—the only ones who survived ate grass or leaves off trees and chewed the same to obtain moisture, and Mr. and Mrs. Ciechanowicz were aware of the fact that their son, Jan, would not eat grass or leaves off trees and live.

Our parents the following Sunday after a meal while sitting at the table began to deliberate about this strange and unusual occurrence. They marveled and said, "What a coincidence, when one is born in the family, one also dies."

Mother added, "How true it is ... when our beloved Wierka died, Krystina was born."

Father said, "But if Jan was not so fastidious about the food he would definitely have survived his ordeal, just like the others from Naliboki. What a pity, because he was nice and quiet guy, the best in their family; he was always engaged reading books."

When the Russians ran away they left behind their equipment. The forests everywhere contained an abundance of weaponry, ammunition and motor-propelled vehicles. While I herded the cattle, I came across many such things near the highways. Then I decided to bring home a rifle with a lot of bullets, binoculars and a large tire, which later we stripped off the layers of rubber and used as a sole for our bast shoes.

In Maczylin, where the woman was possessed by the power of healing, her two nephews, the sons of Mr. Kanowal, while tending a herd of cattle in the forest found a pile of grenades. They took some of these round, egg-shaped, explosive bombs designed to be thrown by hand with them and sat by the fire with other boys to show them what they had found. While they looked at and handled these Russian grenades, one boy drew out the pin, causing a grenade to blow up. The sudden explosion killed almost all boys by the fire who were about my age. This unfortunate tragedy brought to the attention of every youngster in the entire region to be cautious with the Russian stuff left behind.

In the meantime when my father was away on business, I pulled out the rifle fully loaded and came outside to Mr. Karol Marawiej, who at the time was just standing in the yard doing nothing. I asked him to have a good look at this rifle that I found in the forest. Then I proposed, "Let's go, Mr. Marawiej, and try to shoot something in the woods."

As we walked trough the field, a hare came out in front of us from the skirt of woods and sat about ten yards away. Mr. Marawiej aimed and fired at the hare. In a twinkle of an eye, I saw only a cloud of dust where the hare was, but when the dust vanished slowly, the hare was not there. Yet, a moment later the same hare came out again from the woods and sat on the same spot repeatedly. Mr. Marawiej aimed and fired again, but the same thing happened. And in the same way Mr. Marawiej had a chance for a third time, but when he fired the rifle at this hare he missed again. The hare in its confusion wobbled straight in one direction without a curve or bend, not knowing what had really befallen him. I was very surprised at Mr. Marawiej's shooting. I was disappointed at how a grown-up man could miss a hare at such a short distance. Then again, I was not sure whether it was the rifle's problem or not. In order to try it out, I placed some cans and bottles on the fence; I regulated the distance on the rifle and commenced shooting, which happened to be quite simple and easy, for I knocked each target from the fence. But suddenly I realized that my bullets were flying into the forest facing our lane, and at that instant I saw my father riding on a horse back home. This unfortunate incident scared me so much that I was really sorry to bring this rifle home. Eventually in good time I gave the rifle to my father and played only with the bullets I had found.

In mid-August Uncle Jozef and Alfons arrived with the Russian soldier, Wladimier Mikalajowicz. Alfons decided to stay with us for a long while because he could not live in his house alone without his loved ones, that is his wife and baby daughter. And naturally he was not sure with the German occupation what to expect. Here in the wilderness he had a better chance to disappear in case Nazis came looking for him. Because of what he went through under the Soviet occupation, Alfons had no trust in Germans neither.

Uncle Jozef was kind to my father and allowed Wladimier to work for us in the harvest, since he himself had nothing to harvest due to his imprisonment in Baranowicze. Nonetheless, there was ample work at his place, he said, but it surely could wait because it was not as urgent as harvest. So, as I remember, father was very grateful for his brother-in-law's kindness, and at the same time while drinking vodka together he threw a couple of good jokes and they all laughed.

During the time the klansmen were at the table drinking vodka with a snack of fried sausage and sauerkraut, they asked Wladimier about his annals. "Of course, there is nothing much to tell about myself," said Wladimier, "except that when I was eight years of age I was taken away from home, because my parents were starved to death by Stalin, for they did not want to let go of the farm. At fifteen, I was put to work in kolkhoz, then after some period of time they moved the best workers to toil in the factory on piece work in order to produce a norm for the Five Year Plan, which Stalin was expecting to be higher than the previous five years. Among others, for broken working records I was publicized throughout all the advertising medium in Russia, but for me it did not put more food on the table. We all nonCommunists suffered starvation, excluding those who had been tyrannizing us, namely the national political group of Communists."

"You know, Wladimier, this same group of so-called People's Commissariat of Internal Affairs imprisoned me and Alfons," declared Jozef. "Alfons was seized just at the end of its occupation and so he is free, but his wife and child were instantly displaced; nobody knows where in Russia."

"Well, it is nothing unusual where I come from," said Wladimier, "because in our country under the Communist regime a lot of people have vanished just in the twinkle of an eye and never shown up again. This happened to be a common phenomenon, and in the course of time we got used to it. Besides, some imagined that they were moved to a much better place to which all others hoped to get. Unfortunately, not long ago we found out how ghoulish it was, because Stalin did genocide them all. Now I tell you that as long as this devil rules there, I'd rather be a prisoner of war in Germany in spite of his oath," so categorically expressed Wladimier.

At the end of October father sent me with Wladimier on a journey to Uncle Jozef because, he said, "Jozef needs him more than we do." Also he allowed me to stay there for a few days. We all were sorry that Wladimier was departing from us, especially since I became attached to him through working together. He was a very happy person, an optimist with a disposition to look on the bright side of things. So, as we traveled, we were singing contemporary Russian songs throughout the journey until we arrived to Uncle Jozef. Here, at my uncle's husbandry, I smelled an aroma of grandmother's cookies, small, thin, dry cakes, usually sweetened with honey, which I enjoyed so much.

Grandfather as always had me help him cut the wood for fire, and the following day we went into the forest to look for champignon mushrooms, here called "rydze or pieczarki," which are ideal to preserve or flavor in pickle. These crispy champignons are found growing normally at the end of summer and in autumn. In the course of being able to find a lot of champignons with lovely greenish tops, grandfather called to me, "Ty molodiez," which means, "You are a fine fellow, brick, an admirable fellow, well done!"

Of course, for a youngster to be called molodiez by his father or better still his grandfather was indeed a great honor. I was thrilled by it and thought that grandfather was glad because I helped him find a great deal of mushrooms. In that case, I said, "Today is a very lucky day for rydze, Grandfather."

"Not rydze," Grandfather answered. "It's your prayers, Mietek."

"What do you mean, Grandfather?"

"You see, Mietek, your prayers have been answered. Your cousin, Ivan from Smolensk, will not be coming for you. That is what you feared most and prayed for," said Grandfather.

"Yes, it is true, Grandfather."

"You see, Mietek, God is the hearer of prayer, and has power to act on behalf of the petitioners. That is why in everything by prayer and supplication along with thanksgiving let your petition be made known to God, for he that is trusting in Jehovah will be protected. The determining factor, then, is the heart of the individual and what his heart is moving him to do. Those who observe God's commandments and do the things that are pleasing in his eyes have the assurance that his ears are also open to them. The individual must have faith in God and in his being the rewarder of those earnestly seeking him, approaching in the full assurance of faith. Recognition of one's own sinful state is essential, and where serious sins have been committed the individual must soften the face of Jehovah by first softening his own heart in sincere repentance, humility and contrition. Then God may let himself be entreated, grant forgiveness and a favorable hearing; no longer will one feel that God has blocked approach to himself with a cloud mass, that prayer may not pass through. Though one may not be cut off completely from receiving audience with God, his prayers can be hindered if he fails to follow God's counsel. Those seeking forgiveness must be forgiving toward others," and so concluded Grandfather with respect to prayers.

From Blitzangriff, the military lightning attack up to this point in time, Naliboki continued to be without the German local authority, which in fact was abnormal and devious for some peculiar reason. It appeared to be reality that the devil himself, the prince and ruler of the kingdom of evil was in control over the Wilderness of Naliboki, having to his disposition the Soviet partisans, Byelorussian and Ukrainian bandits, AK, the Polish army of the country, Nalibokians guerrilla, and of course the German army, Nazis, SS and Gestapo. In such a predicament and atrocious plight of a dangerous nature, who could be expected to survive or persevere? Certainly not until the intervention of Judicium Dei, for it being supposed that the interposition of Heaven was directly manifest in these cases on behalf of the innocent.

However, a certain Deutche Stabschef, the military colonel chief of staff, Herr Carl Sawinola presiding in Iwieniec, had been appointed to watch, inspect, guard and protect Naliboki. He was a rufous, short man in his forties. His unit of soldiers was constituted of volunteers who were Ukrainian and Byelorussian men clad in dark-blue uniforms similar to that of the Polish Youth (Mloda Polska) of 1938.

After spending a marvelous time with my grandfather, the following week Uncle Jozef sent me home. From my uncle's husbandry it seemed that Mashka knew its way home instinctively as I drove through Zascianki and Smolarnia, bypassed the Kroman, and then soon arrived home to Trascianka. My parents wanted to know what was new in Naliboki. I told them that there was nothing new at this moment, except that people felt an emptiness because there was no authority and no Germans. All those who were hiding from the Bolsheviks hesitantly stayed now at their own homes—but for how long, Uncle Jozef said, no one knows.

As the winter was approaching, my parents began their preparation, as was accustomed annually in this environment for the season of Christmas, extending from Christmas Eve to Epiphany, January 6. The celebration of the Christmas holiday excited everybody to the point that everyone was involved to get something done by expenditure of physical and mental energy. Our house interior was entirely painted and decorated. Plenty of wood for fire was gathered. Food for the livestock was made ready at hand to feed them in the easiest way possible. A lot of special food for Christmas was made ready beforehand. Then finally, the Christmas tree and its decorations, the presents of Saint Nicholas, and consecrated wafers, when after Advent and two weeks of fasting, Christmas begins with a divine service in the church of Saint Bartholomew, called "Pasterka," or Shepherdess, the magnificent and most glorious to see atmosphere between people of good will on earth and in heaven, true God be praised! What a glorious, splendid celebrated seriousness it was indeed for a youngster to be brought up in such a fascinating pervasive influence. I thought and believed that it was heaven on earth. Yet despite the glamorous attraction and charm of the Christmas celebration, to my mind and understanding it was essentiality for our family to remain together as one body, which truly embraces the Christmas spirit, if there is one. However, I had no way of knowing that this particular Christmas was indeed the last one in my life I celebrated undividedly with the whole family. How sad, because later I wondered why we really became separated, why for me the Christmas celebration all of a sudden stopped. Who was to be blamed? God? Then I was puzzled ... Pantokrator? The Almighty God? I thought it was preposterous! There must be some other explanation that yet I did not understand.

Throughout the years searching for the true and correct answers to these questions I have learned that the observance of Christmas is not of divine appointment, nor is it of New Testament origin. The day of Christ's birth cannot be ascertained from the holy scriptures or, indeed, from any other source.

Luke 2:8-11 shows that shepherds were in the fields at night at the time of Jesus's birth. From this alone it may be seen that the traditional date for Christmas, in the winter, is unlikely to be right, since the Gospel says that the shepherds were in the fields.

Wise men, or magi, led by a star were actually astrologers from the east. Although astrology is popular among many people today, the practice is strongly disapproved in the Bible. Would God have led to the newborn Jesus to persons whose practices He condemned?

Matthew 2:1-16 shows that the star led the astrologers first to King Herod and then to Jesus, and that Herod then sought to have Jesus killed. No mention is made that anyone other than the astrologers saw the star. After they left, Jehovah's angel warned Joseph to flee to Egypt to safeguard the child. Was that star a sign from God or was it from someone who was seeking to have God's Son destroyed?

Note that the Bible account does not say that they found the babe Jesus in a manger, as is customarily depicted in Christmas art. When the astrologers arrived, Jesus and his parents were living in a house. As to Jesus's age at that time, remember that based on what Herod had learned from the astrologers, he decreed that all boys in the district of Bethlehem two years of age and under were to be destroyed.

Demonstration: Suppose a crowd came to a gentleman's home saying they were there to celebrate his birthday. He does not favor the celebration of birthdays. He does not like to see people overeat or get drunk or engage in loose conduct. But some of them did all those things, and they brought presents for everyone there except him! On top of all that, they picked the birthday of one of the man's enemies as the date for the celebration. How would the man feel? Would you want to be a party to it? This is exactly what is done by the Christmas celebration. And by the way, the birthday of one of the man's enemies was Nimrod, born approximately on December 25 and celebrated prior to Christ and concurrently with Christmas.

Soon after the Christmas holidays passed, mother started to make necessary preparations for the christening feast. Our baby, Krystina, was already six months of age and mother was afraid that in the case of an accident or death the infant would not be permitted to be buried inside the walls on consecrated cemetery, because as a rule unchristened infants were buried outside the wall on unconsecrated ground. Of course, at the time nobody realized or distinguished which site was more appreciative—the consecrated one, where demons, the superhuman creatures, were being detained in Tartarus, or rather the unconsecrated one, which was free from the evil spirits. Besides, is it by sprinkling or by complete immersion in Christian water that baptism ought to be administered? Or, again, was infant baptism practiced by first-century Christians?

Mark 1:9,10: "Jesus ... was baptized, 'immersed,' in the Jordan River. And immediately on coming up out of the water he saw the heavens being parted."

Origen (185-254 C.E.) wrote, "it is the custom of the church that baptism be administered even to infants."

Religious historian Augustus Neander wrote, "Faith and baptism were always connected with one another; and thus it is in the highest degree probable ... that the practice of infant baptism was unknown at this period (in the first century) ... That it first became recognized as an apostolic tradition in the course of the third century, is evidence rather against than for the admission of its apostolic origin."

My parents selected for Krystina's godparents Eugenjusz and Janka Klimowicz, which in my opinion was a most appropriate choice, because for one reason, the christening feast would take place at Janka's recent home, and for the other, they both were connected to us by blood and were united in marriage. I was thrilled that my cousin Janka would be my baby sister's godmother and also delighted that Uncle Zenka would be her godfather.

Under the circumstances, in order to protect and maintain the forests in the Wilderness of Naliboki, there was no affecting influence from the authority following the German occupation. Thus, my father as a forester was destitute of power to control things. Either way, the people from beyond the river Niemen came here as usual when the river froze solid to obtain an adequate supply of firewood at their own discretion, and of course, free of charge. At such a contingency, others were cutting and hauling timber suitable for building or structural purposes. This winter the forest became overcrowded more than ever. The people hauled heavy loads of timber day in, day out. But some thoughtful individuals were asking father for advice as to where it would be proper for them to harvest the wood for fire in order not to cause any damage to the forest. Naturally, at the same time when father was showing them a suitable place he was rewarded with comestibles in the same manner as occurred the last winter. This was the time that everywhere people began to build new homes, barns, stables, storehouses and butteries. It was amazing watching them working so arduously, and again perhaps presumptuously in vain. Besides, who wanted to accept as fact that it was nothing else but vanity—especially when one is excessively eager for acquisition or personal gain. Most people obviously had forgotten the augury of the old man from Terebejno, namely the last day of Naliboki, which definitely was approaching and lingered with imminent axiom.

Our neighbor Mr. Carol Marawiej, as soon as he furnished himself with wood for fuel, took his wife and baby and went to live at his own place of birth on the west side of river Niemen. And as a consequence Mr. and Mrs. Ciechanowicz were left on their own to support themselves by means of resourcefulness at Trascianka. Of course, they occupied the south end of the building and we lived at the north side, which originally was inhabited by our uncle Waclaw Lojko.

On March 22, 1942, our baby Krystina reached already the age of nine months and was christened at the church of St. Bartholomew by Prelate Jozef Bajko in the presence of Janka and Eugenjusz Klimowicz as godparents. After this formal ritual was performed in the prescribed manner, all participants arrived to Trascianka and commenced to celebrate this happy occasion with rejoicing. Here with godparents was a group of some fifty people who came to observe this Christian water baptism over several days, but after parting all relatives remained and continued having a party over two weeks. Among kinsfolk besides Janka and Zenka was Jozef Lojko, Alfons Lojko, Benedikt Klimowicz, Jan Radziwill, Michal Lojko, my grandparents, Aunt Bronistawa, Mania Klimowicz, and Arszula and Regina Klimowicz. Naturally by this time there was a great deal of food and beverage consumed, but our parents were sufficiently prepared for this exciting occasion and most importantly the family reunion.

This delightful reunion in the face of an armed conflict between nations was indeed something to remember. At this gathering there was no shortage of entertainment either, for everyone present was extremely talented on account of the fact that God was not parsimonious to bestow on them those dexterities. During these days, there was the sound of splendid music and a canto with marvelous voices. Unending laughter was stimulated by funny stories and various comedy acts, having always happy endings. Also an incredible demonstration, a show of military force or readiness to be valiant in combat, was made by my godfather, Jozef Lojko. So, as we all stood and watched Jozef perform on horseback exactly as he did in an actual battle against the invincible Cossacks during World War I, it was indeed something to behold, for Polish legionnaires were not only excellent and renowned combatants but also great acrobats, ones skilled in feats requiring muscular coordination in order to be positioned in diversified or changeable ways at a full gallop. It was generally described that the legionnaire could ride a horse on top, behind, on each side, under and over again at full tilt. In the eventual attack of enemies, an adversary could only see some herd of horses galloping into their direction, but no riders, and therefore no threat, until the moment when the antagonists were taken by surprise.

In the fields during spring we always had an effigy set up to scare the crows or other birds away from the growing crops. Naturally, it was something frightening but in any way not dangerous. So this was what Uncle Jozef opted for his target and told us to observe. Instantaneously he took off from the stables in full gallop toward the skirt of wood, but we only saw the fastest gait of a horse without its rider as it appeared. From there, while the horse was turning around, Jozef was shifting his position from the left side on the horse to the right, and when this sensitive, easily excited black Siberian horse was heading our way it appeared again that it was without a rider at all. In this lightening moment, as the horse was taking his curve by the scarecrow, Uncle Jozef fired a shot ... and bull's eye! Wow, what speed, strategy and muscular coordination. It was absolutely unbelievable. This was the reason why the Polish legionnaires had been unassailable warriors whom not only the Cossacks used to hate, but even the radical Bolsheviks. Yet, Jozef Lojko did not despise anybody, but certainly, in the case of an assault, he was ready to stand in his own defense if some opportunity presented itself wisely to be in just cause.

A tilt of artful stroke by the Polish legionnaire, Jozef Lojko.

On the first day of April Uncle Jozef got up early in the morning and went for a ride on his horse. Mr. Ciechanowicz next door was expecting his flour to be delivered by his daughter early on this day, and my father anticipated at any day to have two cows to calve. When Uncle Jozef arrived home, he went straight to Mr. Ciechanowicz and told him that his daughter had some accident on the Glass Bridge, nothing much to worry, and needed his help indispensably. So immediately Mr. Ciechanowicz in his desperation dashed out from the house and went off to aid his daughter. Then my uncle came to our house and woke my father, that is, his brother-in-law, and told him that he needed hot water at once because the cows were about to calve. In a hurry, father set the water up to boil and ran to the stable to see the sows. In a short while father came out from the stable and was walking slow, at which time he saw Jozef laughing in the window. After a short while Mr. Ciechanowicz was came back from the Glass Bridge with a mean and nasty look on his face, but he did not want to speak to my Uncle Jozef anymore. So, much as always, it was for Jozef's April Fools Day.

When I drove the cattle home for milking, Uncle Jozef came to me and said, "Mietek, we have not much food left, let's go and catch some fish in your canal."

At once I started getting my fishing net out, but he stopped me and said that this time we were going to catch fish without a net. In response I said, "Uncle, are you trying to fool me too, because it is April Fools Day?"

"No," he said, "come and see. I will show you an entirely new fishing method."

As we walked through the woods toward the canal, he said, "Mietek, lead me to the deepest water you know in this canal."

In that case, I was going toward the lock of the canal, which was about half a kilometer north of the Glass Bridge, for there was indeed a deep hole created by the waterfall from the lock. When we got there we could not see any fish because the water was so deep. My uncle, as he was looking into the depth of water, told me, "Take cover, Mietek. Stand behind the tree," and as I did that, he threw a grenade into the midst of deep water. Suddenly, about a forty-foot-high jet of water was forced up by the explosion. The entire area was covered with foam, and shortly after there happened to be a lot of fish floating on top of the water surface, which I went inside to collect, and we brought it all home for our food.

A few days later my mother said to me, "Mietek, we need more fish." Then I approached Uncle Jozef and asked to him if he would like to see my way of fishing. With some curiosity, he agreed to come to the old sinuosity of a river near the canal where I set my trap nets for the fish that were spawning at this particular time.

Once we arrived, I went down into the water up to my chest and started to get the wings of the net out in order to pool the trap net onto the bank. Of course, when we were pooling it my uncle saw some large trout inside the net. At that moment he had a pleased expression of his face and said, "I am very glad I came here with you. What a fine fish." In the end, we filled our sacks with trout, set the trap net in the same sinuosity of the river and came home with the great deal of fish.

April 5 in Naliboki it was the German callout for the Russian prisoners of war, "Das ist aufrufen fur Russische kriegsgefangener." The German military trucks came to town to gather all Russian soldiers and transport them to Germany, and this process was being executed immediately, like lightning, "wie der Blitz." Wladimier Mikolajowicz from Uncle Jozef's went to surrender in Naliboki to the Germans, and so did many Russians who were piled up on trucks and taken to Germany. But a great number of the members of the Communist party declined to surrender and instead went to the Wilderness of Naliboki, whereby they organized themselves into Soviet partisans on Polish soil. These men no doubt were Communist fanatics and Stalin's faithful ones who found themselves clashed with AK, the Polish country's army, and Naliboki's guerrilla under the leadership of Eugenjusz Klimowicz. In order to become powerful they invited local Byelorussian and Ukrainian robbers and bandits to join them; thus the Soviet partisans in the wilderness were propagated to a multitude.

Promptly, after all the Russian prisoners of war had been removed from Poland, the genocide of the Jews began in the territory of Wilenszczyzna and Nowogrodzszyzna. In the middle of April the Nazis were rounding up Jews to the specially selected locations in this domain. Before doing so, first the Nazis destroyed the Jewish public records in archives in order to cover up their crimes of war, and in the future the national allegiance would unanimously say, "Here, Jews never existed."

The German systematic extermination of Jews in this country was expeditiously executed in accordance to the Nazis' tactical background. Our Hebrew neighbors in Naliboki were forced into the middle of the street from their homes in the matter of minutes and violently were made to walk under a harsh and oppressive escort of German SS directly to the selected location in Nowogrodek. Here, in this hour, the victims weeping and gnashing their teeth, they saw the last day of their lives. Unfortunately no power on earth could deter or prevent their destiny. About five hundred Hebrews walked out from the borough of Naliboki and abandoned their birthplace and beautiful homes with majestic orchards—innocent, fatal families with babies, children, adolescents, adults, and old folks together. Henceforth, who will remember them, who will recall their family names? Who could say, "Once I knew Mr. Skniut, a good businessman with a long, distinguished white beard; he was killed by Russians, but his beautiful wife with three adult children were exterminated by the German SS in Nowogrodek"? Who could say, "Hey, I conducted a very good Geschaft in the borough of Naliboki with Mr. Sanagoga, Mr. Matus, Mr. Malka, Mr. Ick, Mr. Szlomka, or Mr. Leiman"? Who will remember Mr. Jankiel and his soap in exchange for rags? Who can taste again palatable cracknel (obwarzanek), or halvah from Mr. Chaim's bakery? Who could say,

The seizure of Jews in Naliboki, April 5, 1942, for annihilation in Nowogrodek committed by Nazi atrocities.

"Once I went to school with Mr. Srul's two sons; they were my best friends, and I had great pleasure playing with them"? Again, who can remember the Turkish bath of Mr. Brocha, which was near gmina, the municipal building, and next to the carrousel and livestock market, or who can really remember them all, such as Mr. Chaim, who resided behind the school, Mr. Szymanowski, who used to sell clothes, Mr. Machlis, Mr. Kwartacz, Mr. Rozowski, Mr. Wajner, Mr. Ela Kagan, Mr. Nachama Graf, Mr. Szmuit, Mr. Czorny Isho, Mr. Herc, who resided next to gmina, and many, many other families whose names have been completely forgotten?

Besides the family names that cannot be remembered, there were also Jews residing with the locals who escaped from the Polish zone occupied by the Germans in September 1939. Of course, then their names were unfamiliar to us, the people living here. In the Wilderness of Naliboki Nazis seized all Jews in Wolozyn, Bakszty, Lubcz, Delaticze, Szczorce, Korelicze, Rubiezewicze, Rakow, Klieciszcze, and many other cities and towns in this palatinate, from which they were escorted on foot to Nowogrodek by the Protective Squadron, the "SchutzStaffel," the SS. Naturally, this Nazis' operation continued for many weeks, and at the same time the Communist partisans were growing rapidly in numbers; thus they were getting invulnerable, but had no interest whatsoever in rescuing Jewish men, women and children from the Nazis' holocaust. Yet in 1939 the Communists professed to be on friendly terms with the Jews when they were in pursuit of a patriotic organization, namely the Union of Polish Youth, which stood against the Communists and Jews. Now, however, the Polish Youth guerrillas and AK were gathering Jews under their protective wing and were vigorously fighting shoulder to shoulder against the Germans.

Consequently, from proclamation of independence on May 14, 1948 to 1954, 107,400 Jews entered the country from Poland, but the origin of the immigrants entering the country between 1919 and 1947 was approximately 41.1 percent from Poland, which was higher than from any other country in Europe.

It was the first week in May when we planted potatoes in the field behind the stable. A few days later in the evening a huge wild boar came and rooted out a great deal of potatoes, causing extensive damage to the potato field. The following evening, afflicted, father came out with a rifle to guard what was left of the potatoes. But as soon as he set his foot in the field, he saw a mountain of a boar turning up the earth with his snout. So he bent down, took his aim at the wild boar, fired a shot, and the boar fell down on his side; then all of a sudden got up and ran warped and writhed to the skirt of wood, the place where Uncle Jozef took his turn on horseback when he demonstrated his wit. At this point in time father was scared to follow a wounded wild animal in the dark. Father came home and told us that he hit the boar, which we knew because there was some blood where this native hog of continental Europe had fallen.

Nonetheless, early in the morning father went to track the wounded beast and noticed that it fell several times before it got to the skirt of the woods. Here the boar was laying down and facing his own tracks, looking at my father, ready to attack. Frightened, Father was about to shoot the wild boar again, but then it appeared to him that indeed the animal was without vivacity or instinctive fear; that is, an innate tendency given this category of animals to act in ways that are essential to its existence. Finally, Father picked up a stone and threw at his body, and it became apparent that the wild boar was dead. Soon, he used the horse to drag this huge wild boar into our yard and left it by the well to be dressed for food.

After a whole day's hard work, father converted this huge wild boar into sausage and hung it up on top inside the smokehouse in order to be smoked. Then in the pit, a bottom part of the smokehouse, he lit the fire and instructed me to maintain constant smoke by using a lot of furze bushes (Ulex europaeus), which we called janowiec. This furze, freshly cut, when burned obviously creates plenty of smoke and gives a nice flavor to sausage made even from the wild boar. Eventually, Father had this smoking process for a great amount of sausages set up, and I carried on an action to keep the fire going.

Meanwhile, Mr. Ciechanowicz was noted to have been for some reason spending much time in the forest each day. My parents wondered what he was doing there on his own, but it seemed that nobody knew anything about Mr. Ciechanowicz's intentions.

On May 10 it was already getting dark outside when the dog started barking with alarm and fright, so we looked through the window and saw some strange men armed with rifles and automatic weapons walking down the lane toward the house. When they entered the yard, two men, as if they were well informed, came directly to our house, and one emphatically said to my father in Russian, "We came to shoot you ... step outside!"

As Father walked outside with them, I was fainting out of fear and expectation of the murder of my father. I had no idea how my mother, sister or brother felt, but I was never so scared in my whole life, knowing that these Russians would kill my father right now, any second at the sound of a rifle shot. What a dreadful feeling during this very moment; in words it simply cannot be expressed. To me it was precisely the end of the world when I awaited a bullet to be discharged from a firearm. But then after a while I heard a conversation and hoped that they would not shoot my father after all.

Subsequently, after about twenty minutes of chat, the partisans let my father go back in the house. They had our horse and wagon, drove to the smokehouse, loaded our sausages on the wagon and were ready to go to the wilderness. Some men came into the house to search for weapons, concerning which Father told them he had none because they were hidden outside. But unfortunately they found some bullets under the mattress in my bed. They told Father he had lied, but Father said, "There is a lot of ammunition laying around in the forest; the boy picks them up and he plays with them."

They muttered some and then left to join the rest outside. We looked through the window and saw them going away.

Father said, "When they had me outside, first they introduced themselves to me. One said, 'My name is Petro Bywalowski and I am the major of the Red Army. This is lieutenant Hryshka Porazit. Presently we are engaged in a struggle with the German enemies. We came to shoot you because your brother is one of the Polish officers in the rank of captain. His name is Eugenjusz Klimowicz and your name is Wilhelm Klimowicz.'"

Father then asked, "You want to shoot me because he is my brother?"

"Yes," said the major, "your brother is the leader of the Polish guerrilla; therefore, he is our enemy."

"Well," said father to the major, "my nephew, Ivan Klimowicz, is the commissar of NKVD in Smolensk. When you shoot me, will you shoot the commissar also?"

Momentarily all partisans got stunned and instantly assumed a different attitude. Then the major said, "OK, it seems that we were badly informed about you concerning this matter, comrade Klimowicz. But I need food for my men right away; we have to borrow your horse and wagon in order to take your kielbasa from the smokehouse."

"So then I harnessed the horse for them and they let me go," said Father.

At that mother stepped in saying, "How would they know all about Zenka since they are strangers in the land on whom we never set our eyes? And besides, how would they know all about our sausage in the smokehouse?"

Soon, father began to murmur and said, "Wait a minute, Jozefa. That must be Mr. Ciechanowicz."

Then mother said, "No wonder he spent days on end in the forest. He surely met these partisans there and educated them in his own cunning old way. What an evil man he is."

With respect to our Jews and their ordeal, some visitors came from Naliboki to see the way we lived at Trascianka. But their main topic of conversation was to let us know how the Germans seized our Jews and made them walk all the way, about fifty kilometers, to Nowogrodek. In the beginning, the Germans, clad in army uniforms with helmets and rifles, chased the innocent Jews, not tainted with sin, evil or moral wrong, beating them with rubber cables from their homes outside in the middle of the street in town. On this most horrifying morning, some even had no time to make a sudden grasp of things, if they could, to come out with a case or bundle, and were lined up ready to march in an inhu-

Mr. Machlis, Michal took his final rest in Smolarnia under unfeeling, pitiless German SS.

mane and barbaric manner. Women were full of tears, but men were as pale as linen sheets. There was no crying, yelling or screaming—the entire crowd, free from blame or guilt, especially legally, went calmly like lambs to the slaughter house, whether they knew it or not. Yet, some could not be fooled by the Nazis' enigma; for instance Mr. Machlis, because at his age it did not matter where the demon-possessed monsters were going to kill him. By the time the column of approximately five hundred people reached Smolarnia, where two large German bombs were dropped on Russians, Mr. Machlis sat on the grass at the gutter of a highway. Meanwhile, some travelers were passing by in front and back of the column. One of the German monsters who inspired hate or horror because of cruelty and wickedness came to Mr. Machlis and started yelling, "Aufstehen! Los gehen! Schnell! Schnell!" But Mr. Machlis did not move a muscle. The unfeeling, pitiless killer aimed his rifle phlegmatically at the head and fired. Mr. Machlis fell dead sideways from his sitting position and the German fiend continued to follow the column of people.

When the Hebrew people came to cross the river Niemen, an elderly Mr. Szlomka happened to lean on a rail of the bridge to cease from effort of walking for a time. Another German SS came close to Mr. Szlomka and shot him, and as he fell the killer kicked the dead body off the bridge into the river. After they crossed Niemen they came to Szczorce and stayed there overnight. The following morning they advanced on foot through Karelicze, and in the evening they came to Nowogrodek, where the German SS piled them up with others, worse than any animals, in a ghetto, a temporary enclosure of high barbed wire fence, and there, indeed, was weeping and the gnashing of teeth.

It was estimated afterward among the locals that in Nowogrodek alone there were over 60,000 Jews, but combined with the Wilno territory the total population of Jews exceeded 150,000, annihilated by the German SS's systematic extermination between the beginning of May and the end of July, 1942.

This large national group of Hebrew innocuous people ceased to exist without a trace just in a matter of three months. Innocuous apart from the fabled accusations that broadcast Jews use human blood for ritual purposes. A charge of ritual murder is referred to as early as the first century of the Christian era in a polemic of Josephus against the anti-Semite, Apion, but such charges did not become prevalent until the twelfth century. There has never been any basis for them, particularly since Jews, according to Biblical injunction, are forbidden to consume blood and Jewish dietary laws enjoin the scrupulous removal of blood from meat. The accusation has varied in details and assertions, but usually it has been made in conjunction with Passover, the Jews being charged with murdering a Christian child by means of a barrel full of nails sticking out, inside of which the child was rolled, and its blood used in the preparation of Matzoth, the prescribed unleavened bread. Yet, no Jew accused of ritual murder has ever been found guilty. But the charge has persisted and been made in almost every country in which Jews have lived up to the nineteenth and the twentieth centuries.

However, despite the falsehood of blood accusation, the accusers themselves committed ritual mass murder, and thus spilled some million pints of Jewish blood on the soil of two palatinates where the innocent Jews once had settled, but during the present days the authority denied the fact they ever existed. Undoubtedly convenient—no trace could be found by Byelorussian or Polish justification because in advance Nazis had destroyed the Jewish records of existence.

At this monstrous act of murder, who could have been more pleased? None other than Satan and his demons. These superhuman creatures had the first kind of cotillion in Tartarus after a stretch of three milleniums, when in those ancient days human beating hearts were offered in sacrifice to the triad of devils namely, Labartu, Labasu and Akhkhazu, in this very same land of Wilenszczyzna and Nowogrod czyzna.

Several days had passed since our Jews from Naliboki passed through the wilderness to Nowogrodek, and Father sent me to Naliboki to deliver some groceries to Aunt Bronislawa on a hackney coach. When I neared Smolarnia, I slowed the horse down and looked for the place where Mr. Machlis was killed. I thought that his body would still be there, but when I found just a pool of blood it was obvious that somebody buried him already, most likely inside the hole where Germany's two bombs exploded since it was the easiest way to bury in the forest. Whenever I passed through Smolarnia I always looked at that spot of blood of our dear neighbor and best friend of my father, the spot where the grass was burned and did not grow over that summer.

During the time of the German's systematic extermination of the Hebrew race the rumor was spread among the local people that those families of multitudes who were social workers and/or persons of aristocracy seized to Siberia in January 1940, the survivors had been miraculously released. Apparently Premier Stanislaw Sikorski ventured his life on behalf of his people and went to Moscow to confront Stalin in order to demand his citizens be set free. The significance of the premier's encounter was that by December 4, 1941, all Polish people had been removed from Siberia and placed in Uganda, an independent member of the Commonwealth of Nations, in Africa. After their convalescence in Uganda young men were drafted for service in the Polish armed forces and vigorously fought against Germans on the foreign soil until the end of World War II.

During this tumult between different parties in the same state we had no idea whether the family of Uncle Waciaw from Trascianka was alive or dead. But after the war we learned that Waciaw, Mania and Czesiaw survived the Siberian ordeal—except Heniek, with whom once his father scared Mr. Kostus on the Glass Bridge; he died from old and starvation in Siberia.

In August and September 1940, Britain stood alone against the full force of the German air and sea attack. But the Battle of Britain was won, although destruction of buildings and civilian casualties continued throughout the war. During Premier Sikorski's stay in London the German sea attack was ready to invade Britain. Disturbed, Prime Minister "Winnie" had no idea how to stop the German invasion. Sikorski instead suggested to Churchill in determined protection of his country to pour the gasoline and all flammable liquid hydrocarbon into the sea and to light it when the German fleet got near. Of course, the gasoline, oil and anything else of the sort, soluble in alcohol and ether but not in water, floated on top of the sea. When the enemies got close, the chemical element was lit, and the outcome was that some seagoing vessels had been burned up and sunk, but the remaining German fleet escaped for safety, and thus all enemy warships of great size scattered away.

Owing to such a brilliant idea, Winnie became a close friend to Sikorski, naturally for the love of his country Great Britain. Under this kind of amicable disposition, eventually Sikorski revealed to him his own plan for the love of Poland, which was namely to liberate the country from both Hitler's and Stalin's oppression. Sikorski's Plan signified an insurrection in Warsaw when the line of contact of two opposing forces got close to the capital city; at such a precise moment the country's organized resistance would rise up against the enemies and his armed forces from abroad would join the insurrection in Poland and strike both oppressors together as one.

Whether Premier Sikorski betrayed his country or merely showed his self sacrificed spirit, the following questions first must be asked. Was it lawful for one leader to disclose to another who was his friend and ally his country's secret plan? Or was it permissible for one leader to seek a necessary support from another, that which already was promised before September 1939, and as yet was not honored? Had Sikorski's Plan been, executed would it not be most beneficial not only for Poland but also for all the nations? Certainly then there would have not have been a long-lasting cold war and the race of atomic power that only caused the global increase of famine and pollution.

Unexpectedly, during the night on May 15, Eugenjusz Klimowicz with 250 men surrounded Trascianka so as to cut off retreat or to catch in a trap partisans who had recently threatened the life of my father. He detected the true nature of this incident instantly and became very angry toward Mr. Ciechanowicz. After all night waiting in an attempt to catch those partisans who unfortunately did not show up, in the morning Uncle Eugenjusz went straight to the apartment of Mr. Ciechanowicz and menaced him, saying, "If any harm should come to my brother caused by the Russian Partisans with whom you have had contact, then rest assured the same you shall get from me together with all your family." Hence a frightened Mr. Ciechanowicz made a solemn affirmation with appeal to God that this would never happen again and acknowledged with regret of any given offense.

A few days later, Major Pietro Bywalowski came from the field of operations assigned to his unit at the railway track in Stolpce. He successfully sabotaged the railroad and obstructed German delivery of war materiel to the frontline, but at the same time unexpectedly met in battle with the Germans and thus lost some of his men.

While these Russian partisans were resting in our yard, I was seated on a log nearby pretending to splice my bast shoes in order to hear what the Russians were talking about. Between them there was one eulogist, Lieutenant Hryshka Porazit, who was boasting about some men he killed a while ago. He was saying that two young men were passing through the wilderness and when he stopped them he began to interrogate them. And it came about that they did not have any identification on them. "So I decisively told them, 'you are a spies!' Of course, they denied ... hah hah hah. Again I repeated, 'you are nothing else but the spies.' 'No, we are not,' the fellows answered unanimously. Then, I said to them, 'if you will tell me that you are spies, I let you go, do you understand?' 'Yes,' they answered. 'So, what, are you spies!' 'Yes.' 'I cannot hear you.' 'Yes, we are spies.' At that point I ordered them to go, but as they moved, I shot them in the back of their heads. Hah hah hah. I had my comrades remove the bodies off the highway and dump them in a ditch. Some dumb Poles," he said, "I killed," and the lieutenant continued laughing together with all the partisans.

As I looked at his face, I saw it was full of holes. He must have had a small pox, an acute, highly contagious virus that usually leaves permanent scars such as this monster had. He was a horrible looking guy and obviously possessed by demons, since such a creature is capable of performing deeds of a devil, but not that of a human. He was the one who insisted being in a hurry to kill my father, and for this reason he was impending him to speak, because simply he did not want him to be justified.

A few days later after these partisans had gone away, one hundred more came, and an officer in charge demanded my father feed his men. During the time that they were laying down in the yard, Father butchered a cow and mother prepared a large pot outside, in which we used to boil liquid food for our animals. I carried some firewood and lit the fire under this huge pot. Without delay, this pot was filled with water and beef, and it was boiling. Mother and Mrs. Ciechanowicz brought all the bread they had to the partisans, and after a short while a hundred men consumed a cow, for which they expressed gratitude to us, got up and left.

Consequently, at this point in time it was quite obvious that the Soviet partisans had greatly multiplied in the Wilderness of Naliboki. And, because of such a swarm, people living here in some remote places began to suffer a loss of properties and death, for they had been robbed and many murdered or burned alive in their own homes by the Byelorussian and Ukrainian bandits who professed to be partisans of the Soviet Union. But their main purpose was to gain possessions and to take vengeance on the Polish nation in this opportune time mixed with Russians, and really they had no interest in participating with them against the Germans.

The signal calling troops to form ranks occurred in Naliboki on May 29. Russian partisans were gathered here to a secret position for a surprise attack on German SS who had already committed genocide on the Jews in the eastern part of the territory surrounding Minsk. Therefore, now they would travel from Iwieniec through Naliboki in order to continue their systematic extermination of the Jews in Nowogrodek. The Soviet partisans learned that German SS would arrive to Naliboki precisely at 2 p.m. On the little hillock behind the school they fortified themselves with trenches, placed in them machine guns, CKM, RKM, and heavy machine guns, called maxims, and the ambush was all set.

In the meantime they were celebrating on the streets in town, drinking vodka and laughing with women. Benedikt Klimowicz happened to walk through the crowd of Russians, as usual with a violin under his arm. When the Russians saw him, they asked to play for them. Naturally, Benedikt performed pieces of their Russian music, to which they listened and danced.

Just before the Russians were about to take their secret position for the surprise attack, one of the officers in charge, being himself partially intoxicated, said, "Let's go, lads, to kill at least two birds with one stone."

The locals who heard him say that at first did not comprehend fully its meaning, but later it became clear exactly what the officer of Communist partisans meant, because what he had in his mind was the purpose for them to ambush and kill the German SS unit, but Naliboki would be held responsible, and thus befit being blameworthy in the eyes of the Germans.

Undoubtedly there were much better and more suitable locations for the ambush between the cities of Iwieniec and Nowogrodek, a stretch of highway where partisans could have destroyed these superhuman creatures, but then it would not fit the prophesy of the old man from Terebejno, since the last day became focused on Naliboki exclusively.

Precisely at 2 p.m. on May 29, 1942, there was a sign that the German SS unit was approaching; the partisans were ready waiting. A certain man tending a herd of cattle in the forest ran to meet the Germans and tried to warn them that ahead there was an ambush, but they did not believe such a thing to be possible. Inebriated SS, overwhelmed by their own powerful emotion of superiority despite the warning, continued to move forward. As soon as they passed through the forest, they appeared in an open field of Naliboki. Everybody in town was able to see them coming. Just as the international race we used to watch, when the cars popped out from the forest and sped toward the school. The first car in the German convoy passed through the valley unharmed, turned left and got away on the highway to Stolpce. All the rest of the SS vehicles were trapped in the valley. When partisans opened fire, nineteen German SS were killed, and three were captured alive. These German SS were of distinguished superiority, because they had scars on their faces, as in duels cut by swords according to the German national custom of nobility. The Russian partisans' operation was swift and speedy—in the matter of twenty minutes the battle was over. One wounded German SS crawled to the skirt of the woods and died.

The most beautiful, sunny, bright day turned to darkness; suddenly the sky became covered with clouds and it was windy, stormy and dark as three noble Germans stood with their hands above their heads while others were laying dead or suffering the pain of death, but all with the mark of distinction.

The townspeople came to see the battlefield. They saw Russians taking into custody three Germans alive, and in that darkness they saw gleamy pillars rising above the surface from among the dying men and shifting as with the wind toward the cemetery. Folks were standing and looking at the dead and dying Germans; among them was Benedikt Klimowicz watching the evil act of a possessed young lad whom some called crazy—he was smashing a dying man's head with a stone and pulling off his wrist watch. Benedikt was shocked, so he called attention to this crazy lad and said, "Do you not fear God? What is it that you are doing?"

Vanquished SS by the Soviet partisans in Naliboki on May 29, 1942.

At this precise moment the possessed young lad from his kneeled position looked straight into Benedikt's eyes, got up, dropped the stone and walked away without saying a word.

Some older folks marveled at the scene of this phenomenal occurrence and said from experience based on their observations that the demons in the shape of gleamy pillars last year seen heading west influenced some Germans to be frantic and caused them to come to this cursed land to murder the people in cold blood, in which process they appeared to die here for demons to get free and return to pits of dense darkness, an abased condition into which God cast such disobedient angels. But several old men used their best endeavors and said, "This is not the end yet, make no mistake about it, for we shall see more similar occurrences."

These Communist atheists and diffidents, without taking any notice whatsoever of the sudden change in atmospheric condition, darkness or gleamy pillars, since to them such a phenomenon attributes to nothing else but only the laws of nature, grabbed hold of these three Germans and came with them to the school ground. Among other locals here was school teacher Mr. Guminski, who some time ago came to Naliboki from the city of Poznan. He was familiar with the German language, and while he was standing close to the German SS they asked him to ask the Russians what they intended to do with them. When Mr. Guminski expressed in their language what the captives had said, the Russians burst our laughing and murmured, "No need for you to worry."

At this point the partisans locked up the Germans who wore a human skulls on their hats in the third grade classroom. These were no doubt nobles of high rank, officers, SS, who had completed systematic extermination of thousands of Jews in the territory of Minsk and presently were on their assignment to the palatine of Nowogrodek to genocide a mass of Jewish people prepared for them in a barbed wire compound.

"Uh-oh," said Mr. Farbotko, who resided next to school.

"What is the matter?" asked Mr. Arciuszewski.

"Well, did you notice what really happened just now?"

"What?" asked Mr. Arciuszewski.

"You see, they put these three devils, just like an ancient triad of devils whose names were Labartu, Labasu, and Akhkhazu, straight into the third class. And this is the class where our children encountered a vision of the Virgin Mary in March 1938. Do you not remember?"

"Oh, yes, you are right, Mr. Farbotko, I remember now. That is what the Nostradamus of Terebejno had predicted, namely about two visions and that very cruel men shall come to occupy those two locations where the signs occurred, and that they are men so wicked, as if possessed by demons, and will cause the destruction of many people who will become dead just like them. Furthermore, only on account of them the last day of Naliboki will be determined."

"What a terrible thing; it seems that every word the old man said will come to pass. What kind of a man was he, to know exactly what is going to happen in the future?" said Mr. Farbotko. "Some people thought that he was a holy man or a living saint, but others said that he must have been an angel, a heavenly messenger who materialized into an old man, lived among us for a while, prophesied and disappeared."

After an hour or so having last the meal of the day, the partisans took the Germans along with them and went in the company of evil destiny directly to Maczylin. Here by the skirt of woods at the exact spot where a visual appearance of a disembodied spirit that looked just like the Virgin Mary was encountered by so many in August 1938, Russian partisans lit a fire, and then they stretched those three German devils on the bent young white birch trees, tied by their hands and feet. They whipped them with birch rods and began to torture them by means of a cross-cut saw throughout the whole night and the following day till the Germans had expired. The partisans buried their dead bodies there and vanished into the wilderness.

Three high-ranking SS officers were killed by means of torture at the sight of the apparition in Maczylin, as predicted by an old man from Terebejno in 1937

During the day of torture a certain shepherd girl in that neighborhood heard unusual human screams, about which she told her parents. When all things had quieted down the people went there and saw some bent trees, whip rods, and a cross-cut saw covered in blood, including, of course, a mark of interment.

Comparable with this interment was the grave of a notorious hindermost bandit, apprehended in the Wilderness of Naliboki, found guilty after a trial for mass murder, and sentenced to death by hanging. His execution was carried out on the crab tree behind the school at the junction in 1922. Coincidently, a similar occurrence took place, but in a plural sense, at the same location in 1922, whereas the intermediate lapse of time until 1939 was a time of peace and prosperity experienced by the society as a whole. This intermediate span in time was indeed divine, because all people were actuated by reverence for a supreme being. They were extremely religious. But now, since the war, they had been enclosed by sacrilegiousness and evil, violence and murder. Yet strangely enough, nobody knew why we all were suffering excruciating mental and bodily pain in this atrocious spell, apart from some old men who emphatically exclaimed, "for the sins of our forefathers who transgressed the divine laws in the third and fourth generations!"

Such an exclamation or vociferation no doubt caused a lot of talking between folks. Many disturbed by this outcry and the recent experiences of evil in world war had heightened the objections of a belief in the omnipotent God. They had found no satisfactory answer to their question, why does God permit suffering? Some had lost faith in God. They felt that he was not interested in mankind. Others who accepted suffering as a fact of life, by the loss of loved one's became embittered and blamed God for all the evil in human society. At the same time, others observed that these experiences increased the need of humans for divine truth on this matter and a closer relationship with true God in order to understand clearly that the suffering was not from God. The Bible assures us that the suffering we see around us is not caused by Jehovah God. For instance, the Christian disciple James wrote, "When under trail, let no one say: I am being tried by God. For with evil things God cannot be tried nor does he himself try any one."

In addition, even though many terrible things have been done in the name of God or of Christ, there is nothing in the Bible to suggest that either of them has ever approved of such actions. God and Christ have nothing to do with those who claim to serve them but who cheat and swindle, kill and plunder, and do many other things that cause human suffering. In fact, the way of the wicked one is something detestable to Jehovah. God is far away from the wicked ones. (Proverbs 15:9, 29)

Again, others wanted to know exactly what had been happening in the past fourth generation. Of course, the ones who were historically minded were able to enlighten these concerned ones to the past events in reference to that particular generation. They said that the people back then built the church in the year 1630 on the ruins of a pagan temple and dedicated it to the martyr Bartholomew, and at the same time they transferred the king's votive offering and hung in front the main alter. Then they began to produce enchanting weapons and sold them to our invaders for profit. Subsequently, there was much blood of the innocent spilled, and because of gain there was gross indulgence of one's sensual appetites. That is why God was bringing punishment, for the error of our fathers upon sons, upon the third generation and upon the fourth generation, in the case of those who hated him and did not keep his commandments. They did not approve of holding God in accurate knowledge; God gave them up to a disapproved mental state to do the things not fitting.

A few days after the shocking consternation that gripped Naliboki, our Benedikt came on foot to Trascianka to narrate to my parents about the Russian partisans' ambush and neutralization of the German SS unit. He stayed with us over a period of two weeks. We all experienced great pleasure listening to his performance of music, of such infrequent talent and virtuosity, a technical mastery of an art intended to be heard with reference to a story, idea, situation, event, etc. He was bachelor, an unmarried man, never smoked tobacco or drank any alcoholic beverages in excess; he was a splendid organist, pianist, violinist, and an old organ restorer. The violin was virtually his girlfriend, for wherever he went he had it under his arm and played always at his convenient time.

Uncle Benedikt promised me that soon he would make me a new violin and would instruct me how to play on this particular instrument. But I knew that at his home he had about five of those violins, so I insisted that he give me one and teach me to play straight way, not later, because I was extremely eager. Then he responded in my favor, saying that those violins were too big for me. He said, "I intend to make one especially for your size, and then I'll really show you how you can play a violin."

At that instant Father said to Benedikt, "You know, Mietek is pretty good with his accordion. I only had a brief session with him, showed him to play just a few pieces of music, but now he is playing all different pieces on his own."

During Uncle Benedikt's first week with us the weather was out of the ordinary, bright with a serene sky and a fragrance in the air from the various growing flowers and pine trees ascending high as if to heaven. A cuckoo somewhere in the forest cried without cessation and a skylark sang in the air as it climbed to praise the beauty of the day. And here I was in the yard getting ready to go fishing, but Uncle Benedikt came out from the house asking me what I was going to do today.

I said, "Uncle, I am going fishing because it is a very nice day today."

So he said, "Can I come with you, Mietek?"

"Sure, Uncle, I am very glad that you have asked me since I at all times have done all my fishing by myself, and it feels lonely once in a while being without companions."

After I stretched my triangle net tight I went to the storehouse and got a sack that used to hold grain, and then I started walking with Uncle Benedikt through the forest to the Glass Bridge. Uncle took particular notice of the forest and commented how beautiful it was there and what a pleasant odor there was from the trees. He said, "I would like to go here one day and find me a fir tree (Picea excelsa), which is most suitable for making a violin of best quality."

Farther ahead he noticed pine-lovers, champignons and leaf mushrooms growing. Then he vociferated, "Look! There is a squirrel ... see ... climbing up the tree, and over there a white hare."

As we walked on, we saw a roe buck with majestic horns and a doe with two young ones. Uncle was so enormously impressed by this magnificent environment that he said, "Mietek, all this surrounding beauty in its complexity and unity inspires awe to our creator, the omnipotent God. Who can really appreciate all this creation under heaven but one who is meek, humble and lowly in heart?"

Of course, knowing the fact that my uncle spent almost his lifetime as an organist in the churches of large cities, he was versed and thus was cognizant of God's bringing of the universe into existence and all these living things.

Once we got to the bridge, we commenced fishing in the canal toward Lake Kroman. Halfway up there was a dam to control the flow of water built by a beaver on account of a sluice being down by the lake, and therefore the water in the canal was shallow for the beaver. However, since these clever creatures had constructed the dam for themselves, the water on our side in the canal was not deep, just right to fish. What I had to do was to set the net in an appropriate place in this canal and run ahead on the bank, spot a large number of fish and then chase the whole school of fish into the net. Consequently, as I was repeating this same process over and over again, emptying my net on the bank, it made my uncle very busy filling the sack with a perch, silver-fish and pike. Shortly he called me saying the sack was full and there was no room for any more fish. Because of exceptionally fine weather I was in my shorts only. I suggested for my uncle to take off his trousers and use them as a sack. Naturally he did not mind when he saw such a great catching of fishes, and besides, by disposition Uncle Benedikt was not bashful or shy; to the contrary, he was adventurous and audacious at all times. But soon his trousers were full with fish, and then he took off his shirt, and the shirt was filled too. Then I hid my net and we began to struggle to get this bulk of fishes home as my uncle walked only in underpants worn over his loins. Subsequently upon discharge of garments and sack into a trough by the well, Mother could not believe her eyes when she saw so many fish caught at one occasion.

After a fortnight father told Uncle Benedikt, "I wish you would stay with us longer. Do not try to go home yet because of the Russian partisans, for they are everywhere in the forest at this moment. In a while things may change and then it will be safer to travel in this perilous wilderness."

But uncle said that he moved into his friend's house, Mr. Szlomka (the third house from Mr. Skniut's tavern), with the hope that his house may be safe from the people who plundered Jewish properties, so that when he returned with his family they shall have their home to come back to. "That is why I must go back home, besides, I have a job to rearrange in some new way all the furniture, including my own, in order to make room for my grand piano."

Inevitably, Uncle Benedikt had to bid farewell to us all and left for Naliboki as we stood in the yard with tears watching him go, his violin under his arm as usual.

After Benedikt left Major Pietro Bywalowski and Lieutenant Hryshka Porazit became habitual visitors at Trascianka. They facilitated themselves to eat and drink in our house as if we were their servants.

In the intervening time Arkadjusz Makarewicz came from Naliboki and stayed with us over a few days. I was surprised to see my friend after nearly four years, because now he was seventeen years of age and fully grown. Father was afraid for his safety and therefore told him that he took a high risk coming here, since the whole area was infested by partisans. Father said, "You know, Arkadjusz, at your age they could easy mistake you for a spy and kill you just like the others they murdered."

But Arkadjusz said, "Uncle Wilhelm, I am a spy. Eugenjusz Klimowicz sent me here to find out how large the concentration of the Soviet partisans is in this region and their location, and he told me that you would be able to help with this information.

On the morning of June 19, a young man in his early twenties came to us exhausted critically and also wounded. Mother dressed his wound and then put a lot of food on the table for him to eat and drink. This young man while eating began to feel better and started telling my parents his most horrifying story. He said, "My name is Abraham Jachin. I am a Jew from Szczorce. My whole family of seven were seized by the Nazis with many other families and we all were driven and goaded by them to Nowogrodek. There, they had already dug a massive pit by use of bulldozers and then they were engaged in the systematical killing of all the people. Subsequently they ran my group to line up alongside a pit, and we were standing ready to be shot and killed. I remember I was hit and fell down with others into a pit, but I felt I was still alive. During this terrible murder more people fell on top of me but I tried to persevere till the night came, then I crawled out from the pit and have walked since through the night until I got here. Now I want to keep on going with the hope that soon I might meet someone like me who escaped his death from the Nazis, then perhaps together we could hide better from the Germans."

Under the circumstances my parents suggested to Abraham that he lay down on the couch and have a good rest, and in the meantime, mother said, "I shall prepare you a bag of food for your journey."

After about five hours in our house, Abraham Jachin thanked my parents for their kind service and was walking out through the door when Lieutenant Hryshka Porazit and his men arrived. They stood in the yard and watched this young man come out of the house. Porazit sat on one log in the pile in our yard and called to the man, "come here." Then, after talking with him for about a half hour, Porazit got on his horse and ordered the Jew to run in front of him. As they passed from sight in the woods, some fifteen minutes later we heard an echo from the discharge of a rifle. Shortly afterward Porazit returned and was laughing, saying, "I have executed that Jew."

Some Nalibokian folks with whom, of course, our parents were well acquainted were traveling from Nowogrodek and stopped in Trascianka for refreshment. Father had their horse released from the harness and gave him food and water. The people came in the house and laid their food on the table, upon which mother put a bottle of vodka, and she boiled some water for coffee. Naturally, my parents were extremely eager to hear from them the news about the city of Nowogrodek. So they narrated the fact that many, many, not hundreds but thousands of Jews had been murdered there by the Germans in the last couple of weeks and that they were buried in huge, massive, deep graves. A great number of Jewish children in this repulsive and most horrifying plight had been hidden by the local people in the city. But somebody squealed, obviously a German collaborator, that a lot of Jewish children had been concealed in the Nazarethans' convent. The German SS consequently seized the children and executed eleven Polish nuns together with those innocent Jewish children.

Subsequently in a favorable circumstance the bodies of eleven nuns murdered by the German SS had been removed from a massive grave and buried alongside the parish church. This church was raised close to the castle of the Dukes Radziwill in the seventeenth century on the ruins of a pagan temple, Perkuna. Outside the parish church there was a monumental tablet that narrated the wedding of king Ladislas Jagello and Sonka Holszanska in the temple Perkuna, which previously existed on this place in the year 1422, and also there was a marmur monument that endured the unforgettable nine knights fallen in the battle of Chocim in 1621, and now the grave of eleven Nazarethan nuns murdered in 1942.

At this particular time in the Wilderness of Naliboki was spread an onslaught on the Polish people by the Soviet partisans. Many families had been plundered, murdered, and burned alive. The German ascendancy over this territory had been reluctant to keep law and order or deal with the Soviet partisans in their midst. This sudden rise of partisans caused confusion among the country's army, AK, and Polish guerrilla, since the main objective was to resist the German enemy by all parties for the common interest. However, in that way, the Soviet partisans' malicious assault on the civilian people induced the Polish underground forces to hostile acts against them henceforth.

These evil-minded Communists, obsessed with vicious and depraved thoughts, came to my uncle Jozef Lojko's house and told him that they were there to shoot him because he was a Polish legionnaire during World War I. At that, they shoved and jostled him outside in the presence of his four young children, his wife and parents. Grandfather fell down on his knees and prayed, but it was unimaginable how the rest of the members of the family felt or how they were drowning emotionally. They took him to the barn on his farm, where my uncle stored hay and grain. Then over a half hour there was absolute stillness, and all of a sudden a shot. Grandfather fell face-down to the floor. Grandmother thought that he was unconscious, yet he still prayed but in a low voice; all the rest of the family cried. About ten minutes later, partisans opened the barn door and they came out—with them miraculously was Uncle Jozef. The partisans then terminated their connection with the victimized Jozef, and as an outcome of this frightful experience Grandfather's son came into the house unhurt, aside from some powder burn on his face from the explosion of a gun when they fired it by his ear.

Evidently, as a professional warrior having cool blood and a remarkable technique for achieving some end, Uncle Jozef said, "I extricated myself from this perilous entanglement for the time being merely by telling them that if they shot me, they would not gain much because in this region there is a great number of Polish legionnaires."

Uncle knew out of hand that these ungodly Communists would easily go for his idea for the reason that they were murderers on the large scale. He told them that if they gave him at least two days he would be able to produce for them the names and addresses of these Polish legionnaires. In order to make sure that Uncle Jozef would not betray them by failing to act as promised, they fired a rifle right by his ear and warned him that the next firing of their rifle would be directly through his head. In this way they gave him two days time in which he must furnish them with information regarding the Polish legionnaires. At that moment they dissipated in their dissolute pleasures elsewhere.

In such a trying situation Uncle Jozef got on his horse and immediately went to the Polish army, AK, concerning which he knew their secret location in the Wilderness of Naliboki. His actual intention was to bring the Polish underground force to Naliboki and stop the plunder and barbarous murder simply by defeating the Soviet partisans who had greatly infested this area. Once he reached one considerably large unit of the Polish fighting men, they informed Uncle Jozef that there was no need for them to go to struggle against Russian partisans in Naliboki because right at this moment the Germans were coming to Naliboki to wipe out all Russian partisans. They would bombard by means of German air force everyone in the location; that is to say, the places occupied by local people in the forest with the expectation of eradicating all Russian partisans.

On July 1, 1942, 120 German soldiers arrived to Naliboki with most sophisticated weapons and at once placed themselves in the fortress, that of old Dukes Radziwill, now known as the Majontek (Estate) of Ciechanowicz. However, their arrival to Naliboki was late on that particular day, and therefore they were tired and went to sleep. Yet this unit was not an ordinary group of soldiers, but rather they had been specially trained to be exterminators, the German SS that consisted of an inhabitant of Latvia who innately spoke the Russian language.

Early in the morning before dawn on July 2, some ten thousand Russian henchmen launched their surprise attack against this sleeping German unit. The Soviet Communists for the occasion had exercised their superior authority over a collective mass of bandits who professed to be partisans, namely Ukrainians and Byelorussians, armed them with rusty rifles of World War I and shoved them up in front to clash with the Germans. This great crowd commenced to move from the west side of Naliboki through Zascianki toward the east and directly to the center of Tartarus, where apparently the disobedient angels (spirits) were cast into pits of dense darkness in Noah's days. Such a prisonlike abased condition into which God cast the wicked superhuman spirits to be reserved for judgment could easily be differentiated between the Devil's Triangle, also known as Bermuda Triangle, of course, if there were such a place where supposedly people and things had perished and no trace of them was ever found, and for this reason it remains a mystery.

A certain Polish resident in Zascianki obviously had a clear understanding of Christian submission to the superior authorities, and in this way he risked his life to warn the occupants. When he saw a cloudlike mass of partisans in motion, he ran in front of them through the backyard gardens, portending he was picking out cabbages, but when he could not be seen by them he ran fast till he actually got to Majatek to alarm the Germans that they were under heavy attack.

Half the men in the unit got ready just when the shooting started, but the other half was still getting dressed. Once the whole unit was intact, their approach to the battle was swift. From the fortress Germans cut down and curtailed most of the partisans, then they came out to pursue them westward through the cemetery. The struggle here was rancorous naturally because of a great number of monuments, where actually two Germans were killed. But when the Germans got through the cemetery, the Russian partisans were out in an open top field and this was where most of the Russians died. The casualty total was several thousands partisans and three Germans. Unfortunately, some partisans died from an explosion of their own guns since the weapons they had were never used.

In the square of the borough one German masqueraded between large stones in an enclosed area; he was there to shoot and kill anything that moved. A young man, Mr. Baszuro, who was married with two children, happened to be curious and wanted to see what was going on outside, so he thrust his head through the forge window and got shot right through the head. Mr. Baszuro was the only local from Naliboki who died in the morning of July 2.

On the open top field by the cemetery on the western side one German burst into the house of my uncle, Michal Lojko, and he put his gun in my uncle's chest with the intent to kill, looking straight into his eyes, saying, "You have been shooting at us." But Uncle Michal froze and could not say a word.

Instantly Aunt Orszula and my cousin Lucjan unanimously replied, "Nobody was shooting from this house. We do not have weapons."

Shortly this German-speaking Russian realized the truth and left the house. But unfortunately Uncle Michal became pallid, as if he had seen a ghost. Yet to all appearances no one could say for sure what in real life he had encountered at that particular moment, for he himself henceforth was silent. However, some old wise men said what he saw in that German was a devil himself in person, but he refused to believe in such things as devils or demons. That is why once he saw the real image of the spirit, the shock of a sudden and severe agitation of the mind was killing him.

Since then, Uncle Michal did not eat any food and could not speak, for he became affected with disease. Dr. Chwal tried everything in his power to help my uncle, but there was nothing he could do except recommend some specialists in the hospital in Stolpce. Immediately the family took him there and he was admitted, but unfortunately their efforts were of no avail. After a month my uncle was discharged from the hospital, and he was at home for several weeks until he faded completely and passed away.

I remember that day so well at thirteen years of age when all my relatives came to the funeral. I was with my mother and father at my uncle's home, looking at him laying in the coffin clad in a black suit and black socks. He was very thin. I was thinking how good he was to me the last time at Easter. Then I wondered why he had to die just because of sudden, violent fear. Then again, I visualized how the Russian partisans in exactly the same way put a gun in my father's chest and it did not have such an effect on him. And also I thought about Uncle Jozef, his brother, who underwent the same experience in his barn, and yet he was not scared to death. I also wondered about what those old men were saying in regard to the spiritual phenomenon, since like no one else Uncle Michal supposedly resided practically on the top of Tartarus and had entirely ignored the existence of superhuman creatures. These demons no doubt must have been greatly offended by my uncle's confutation, and therefore appeared before him in that possessed exterminator of humans, the German SS, which indeed frightened Uncle Michal to death.

At 9 a.m. the Germans ordered all inhabitants of Naliboki to go out with shovels and bury the dead, the Russian partisans who were laying around the fortress, by the church grounds, on the cemetery and, of course, in the vast field behind the cemetery on the western side of the hill. So everyone was engaged in digging a burial place for the dead bodies wherever they were killed. Because there were so many corpses they were buried in unmarked, shallow graves, because instead of one day it would probably take weeks to bury the dead properly.

At noon more Germans arrived, and immediately they all spread out in town questioning everybody in an attempt to connect someone to the waylay of May 29. Obviously they had planned in advance to execute two persons from Naliboki for the one German who died that day. Naturally, by use of pressure and violence they succeeded in finding some people who had been involved, under compulsion of course, to provide the Russians with the food, drink, tobacco and entertainment. Forty-four persons they sought to arrest, and eventually they confined them in a smokehouse in the yard of the Estate of Ciechanowicz.

The Germans were determined to discover the three dead superior officers of the SS. Finally a shepherd girl led them to the locality where the three Germans had been murdered. The local people from Maczylin were compelled to dig out their bodies and thoroughly wash them before the Germans shipped their corpses by air to Germany.

Among the most unfortunate arrested people of Naliboki were some entire families with children, and also my great uncle Benedikt Klimowicz because he played his violin for the Russian partisans. Mr. Sienkiewicz, who resided in the Estate of Ciechanowicz, became downhearted and dejected knowing that Benedikt Klimowicz was detained, for he loved his music very, very much. Without hesitation he went to the German higher-ranking officers in that fortress he lived in and told them that the man with the violin was absolutely harmless and innocent because he carries his violin no matter where he goes and plays it all the time so that everybody can listen because his music is sweet. The German officer ordered to release the man with the violin. So Benedikt got free, but as he was walking home from Majatek and passing by the lake the Germans had with them that possessed young man and they were flogging him with a rubber rods until he fell down to the ground. When this disordered young man was getting up, he saw Benedikt and said, "He was there with me also." The Germans in that case thought Benedikt helped him finish off the dying German, so they grabbed him and confined both in the smokehouse, reserved for the execution.

When Uncle Jozef found out from the Polish underground army that the Germans were coming to Naliboki and were going to destroy all dwelling places in the forest, the most indispensable responsibility for him was to inform us immediately in order to abandon Trascianka. In his determination to rescue us from danger or death, he sent a messenger who as a matter of fact arrived to our place at seven o'clock the morning of July 3. Our parents then without delay packed the wagon, and we were on our way to Naliboki. Mr. and Mrs. Ciechanowicz saw us leaving, and they too vacated and went to Zascianki.

My father and I were driving the herd of cattle, and the rest of the family was riding in the wagon. At one o'clock in the afternoon we reached Naliboki, and we were traveling through Zascianki when all of a sudden a drunk German SS obstructed our right of way and walked toward us, pointing his handgun directly at us as he swayed from side to side. I got scared to death and in an unnoticed fashion hid myself behind the wagon, and then in a like manner passed through somebody's gate, pretending I was walking into the house. As soon as I by passed that house, I ran through the gardens like the man that warned the Germans, and got to the back road that led to Uncle Michal's. I bypassed his house and then the church and finally came breathless home telling Aunt Bronislawa that the German probably killed all our family, for I had just escaped.

Some twenty minutes went by after I appeared on our premises, and the family, all in tact with the livestock, were pulling up in the yard. I was so glad that nothing bad had happened to them, because I did panic and run, thinking too that my behavior had upset them, yet nobody said a word about it, so I left it at that and kept quiet.

In a hurry we unloaded the wagon, arranged all things accordingly and began to hear about what was happening in this old miserable town of Naliboki. Suddenly, we learned that our beloved Benedikt, together with many other people, was locked in the smokehouse at the Ciechanowicz's Estate and that the Germans were going to kill him and nobody could do anything about it. We also realized that Eugenjusz Klimowicz, Jan Radziwill, Alfons K. Lojko, Kazimierz Wolan, Jozef Kosciukiewicz, Prelate Jozef Bajko, Priest Baradyn, Priest Cadis, and many others who were persecuted under the Soviets' regime now were staying at their own homes. But the Germans were walking around like rabid dogs and all folks were emotionally disturbed, not knowing the way out because of their madness.

Still, on this day in addition to the turmoil, Herr, Chief Carl Sawinola and his men clad in dark blue uniform from Iwieniec arrived to Naliboki. The whole place now was being swarmed with the German power and authority, but nobody was sure as to what they were going to do next.

A demented Orszula from Terebejno happened to be going to the church, and yet she never before was near the church. She was passing by a sentry who occupied the exact spot in the crossroads where the Pillar of Saint John used to be. Evidently, this German guard made some sexual remarks to her, and in turn she reached for a stone from her bag and threw at him. The sentry started loading his rifle to fire, but Orszula jumped the fence on the right side of the road opposite the lake and ran away through Poplawski's field. He aimed and fired his rifle and Orszula dropped dead. Some folks used to call her "Opetana Orszula," meaning Orszula possessed with the devil, and because of that they said that she was in the end set free from confinement at his abode; that is, three miles away from her home, in Terebejno. Naturally at her death an evil spirit did creep forth at the most convenient space, and her body was buried in the resting place by her kinsmen.

Father was standing under a covered structure at the entrance to our house and exercising his mental capacities, endeavoring to grasp some kind of idea in order to resolve an urgent complex matter that was contrary to nature, reason or even common sense. Interruptively I approached him querying about the same thing that was uneasy in his mind. I said, "Father, the Germans are going to kill Benedikt."

He answered, "Yes, but there is nothing we can do about it."

Then I urged him, "Why does Uncle Eugenjusz not go to the Germans and speak on Benedikt's behalf since he is fluent in the German language? They will listen and will respect him for it because he speaks their language."

But unfortunately my father told me that if Zenka went to the Germans concerning Benedikt, they would also kill him because at this point in time they were raving mad. From that time on in my life I realized that the mastering of a foreign language is absolutely of no importance, at least in such a situation as this; nevertheless, I was very disappointed.

On the fourth of July in the morning my mother sent me to bring two buckets of water from a spring by the lake on the lane to Majatek. When I looked there I saw a German guard with a rifle standing in the middle of this lane, and by the fortress itself two Germans were flogging a naked man to death with rubber rods as he screamed. Another German turned around and started walking toward the flogging execution because the other two needed help. As soon as he got there, then three of them together began thrashing systematically that victim in a manner of grain. For a while the victim's body was bouncing suddenly and violently until his consciousness was entirely lost, but they continued flogging him even after he was dead. Such an event to behold at thirteen years of age, this horrifying death, made my hair stand on end. As never before I was terrified, and yet inwardly I was glad it was not I suffering such a cruel and inhuman death.

Apparently, the victim was a partisan, a USSR colonel disguised in civilian clothes, who was in his thirties with a wife and a one-year-old child. They killed his wife also, but the baby girl Mr. Sienkiewicz

The USSR colonel being flogged to death in Majatek.

was feeding, and he asked the Germans if he could keep her for himself. The Germans reluctantly allowed him to keep the child. Consequently, the parents of this child were buried on the premises of the Estate where they actually encountered their own tragic end.

However, Mr. and Mrs. Sienkiewicz, two of their own sons and this little adopted girl survived the war, and in 1946 I met them personally in the German DP camp that was called Camp Kosciuszko, in Menden, Westfalen, where I remained temporarily as a resident being a displaced person.

The enraged German movement in the wilderness was without mercy; only the vengeance of death was upon those who were found there. On this day, July fourth, Nazis formed extremely long lines of men and swept the forests like in a hunt for wild animals. Any confronted partisans were killed on the spot without being taken captive. The German Luftwaffe air force was searching for Soviet partisans and bombarded anything they saw move in the forests. They flew over Kroman, Trascianka and Smiejno-Budy. While flying over Smiejno-Budy they saw am unusually big man running across the field, but it was Mr. Kostus and his baby girl trying to reach the woods and hide. Unfortunately, the German flew over him and dropped his bomb, which fell directly on top of Mr. Kostus, and from that time on no trace was found of the giant or his baby girl. At the same time the German lines cut through the thick forest at Trascianka and killed a Russian partisan woman. A great number of partisans were killed on this day and their carcasses were left behind to be devoured by the wild beasts.

Chief Sawinola and his men were conducting a thorough investigation of the German SS massacre on May 29, 1942. While he was walking on the school grounds he met Mr. Guminski and they recognized each other from the old days, when they used to be friends in school at the city of Poznan. Naturally, they had a lot to talk about. Mr. Guminski invited Chief Sawinola to his house for the principal meal of the day. The chief of course had never expected to meet his old friend here, for it was a remarkable concurrence of events. So in his excitement he expanded and began to relate to Mr. Guminski the real fact of the situation that presently faced Naliboki. He emphasized this criminal deed of savagery against the three loyal men to the Fuhrer who had been murdered in Naliboki. The superior officers in the fortress had not decided yet whether to annihilate the town by killing every living soul in it. "But in case they make up their mind for the worst, do not worry, my friend ... I shall rescue your whole family and take you with me to Iwieniec," assured Chief Sawinolam.

However, Mr. Guminski in defense of Naliboki began to explain to the chief how much the people of the town had already suffered from the Bolsheviks and now from the Soviet partisans under the German occupation, with the hope that the influential chief would persuade the officers otherwise. He brought to the chief's attention a great number of individuals who actually underwent severe persecution inflicted by the Soviets. Then Mr. Guminski said, "You know, Carl, I have lived here since I graduated as teacher, and in 1939 Mr. Eugenjusz Klimowicz was here employed as teacher by the commissar of NKVD. He taught arithmetic, Russian and German language. He was an excellent instructor and a law-abiding citizen, but it was not long before the Communists began to hunt him like an animal. They tried to seize him because Mr. Eugenjusz Klimowicz came home as an officer of the Polish army."

Father came to me and he said, "You know, Mietek, today the Germans are going to kill our dearly beloved Benedikt. The execution will commence at 5 p.m. of all the people who are being held in the smokehouse at the little valley between the two skirts of wood, the actual place where the Russian partisans killed the German SS. There, they have already excavated a large hole in the ground to bury all the victims of our borough. Obviously, we all are scared of the German actions; not any person dares to go there and watch the execution. But you can go there, Mietek, to herd the cattle on our land that borders with the Ciechanowicze's, and if you lay down low there you will be able to see among the others our Benedikt being killed."

Imagine me of all people, a stripling, going there on my own to watch a mass murder performed by the Nazi monsters. When my father said this to me, I began to shiver and felt goose pimples all over my body. Nevertheless, in obedience to my father and in the company of my cattle I ventured to go there. I said to my father, "Soon after milking I shall drive the herd to our meadow, and if the Germans see me there, let them think that I am nothing else but a herdsman minding my own business."

As the heavy traffic of the Germans continued around the school, the neighbor Mr. Farbotko observantly formed an opinion of some paranoia. He soon went to Mr. Guminski after the Germans had left to find out what it was all about. In response to Mr. Farbotko's query, Mr. Guminski said that the man in charge of his task force was conducting an investigation concerning the Germans who had been killed, "and he told me that the Nazis feel very bad about it. In fact, they are thinking about destroying the entire Naliboki, which means that this is the last day of Naliboki."

So Mr. Farbotko began to ponder the German's idea, and he said to Mr. Guminski, "You know, if they really destroy Naliboki now, it would not make any sense because it would be contrary to the prophecy of the Nostradamus of Terebejno, for everything that he has predicted has been fulfilled, except the last day of Naliboki. On this account his very words were, 'All these things which must come to pass, shall be executed in the range of the devil's number.' And we all know what that number is—it is 666. On the day of his prediction at the residence of Mr. Wilhelm Klimowicz in August 1937, six months later a vision occurred in the school, then six months later another vision appeared in Maczylin, and from the time of his prophecy up till now, that is from 1937 to 1942. That is exactly five years, which the principle number is unlikely to be 665, but if this year was by any chance 1943, then I would believe that in fact it is the last day of Naliboki."

Although scared, yet in accordance to my promise, father watched me drive the cows from the stable to our meadow between two skirts of wood. I drove them straight through on the "wygon," a common pasture ground, behind the sawmill eastward and south to the corner of both the Ciechanowiczes' and Klimowiczes' land. Here I made an opening in our fence and let the cattle graze in this tract of grassland which was reserved for hay. I looked around in this vast region but saw nobody, not even one living soul, except for some horses tight with front hoofs and other varieties of livestock grazing on the pasture. I got as close as possible to the crossroads in this little valley and lay down in a ditch. Here I waited and waited, having all sorts of pleasant memories of past events. I was thinking how just a fortnight ago Uncle Benedikt and I were fishing in the canal between Kroman and Trascianka. I was thinking too about the violin my uncle promised to make me and to instruct me how to play. Then again, I contemplated, why we as human beings were being wasted by the senseless killing. Is there any limit to it, or is there no limit at all, and in this way we all are going to suffer such a violent and untimely death? Being drowned in such emotion I wondered why I was ever born.

Precisely at 5 p.m. all of a sudden I heard a great noise and a roar of automobiles in the Ciechanowiczes' yard. Then some German army trucks began to show up, loaded with people and heading to the pit with the German SS.

The first truck stopped on the road by the excavation and everybody got off, but there were two more trucks with people and the last one was carrying quicklime to cover up the corpses. The Germans were lining up the victims in a hurry along the side of the excavation ready for the killing. One could only

It was my last piece of music I was permitted to play.

hear, "Los! Los! ... schnell! ... mach schon schneller!" The Nazis' bestowal of death upon their victims was constantly speedy by nature, for they called it "Blitzaktion," a lightning operation.

Uncle Benedikt somehow was the first in a row standing by his executioner, and he was talking to him. Apparently he was making his last request in the Russian language to this Latvian killer to be allowed to play his violin. Consequently, the killer made Uncle Benedikt stand on the northern corner of the excavation and ordered him to play his violin until he exclaimed vehemently, "I shall kill all these people, then you will be last!"

Uncle Benedikt, as he was standing with his two feet on the ground—that is, between the earth and heaven and on the sides between two skirts of wood—placed the violin under his chin and began to draw the fiddle bow, forming a melodic sound of "Bokalis." In his musical parlance undoubtedly he was exchanging thoughts with the heavenly messengers, letting them know about his and all these innocent victims' geographical position, which will remain their resting place until the omnipotent God actually swallows up death forever, and He will certainly wipe the tears from all faces.

In his last performance under the sun of this classic musical parlance, he was gaining momentum, like he was inspired by special divine influence to be able to play "Bokalis." And so, Benedikt played it not as a man condemned to death and being consumed by dread or horror; but with boldness and confidence he played as a virtuoso at the concert of a great audience of heavenly angels.

BOKALIS, this Russian word in the plural sense means "the skirts of woods." Obviously, Uncle Benedikt was standing before his death in the little valley between two skirts of wood; thus he communicated with the supreme authority above and was without interference of actual surroundings, by which he was not in any way impeded to function on the musical instrument. Because no man by his own power is able to perform as Uncle Benedikt did in the moment of his untimely death.

"Bokalis" is a piece of music composed by the Russian composer Rachmaninoff, Sergei Vasilyevich (1873- 1943). This renowned composer left Russia just before the Bolsheviks revolution in 1917, and from that time on he lived, composed, and played chiefly in the United States. He died at Beverly Hills, California, on March 28, 1943, the year after Uncle Benedikt Klimowicz was murdered on July 4, 1942.

During the extolled deep mourning piece of music, the skirts of woods resound some prolonged echoes from a gun of the dying souls that Satan was so eagerly counting. In a short while forty-three persons had been killed without disposition or power to show mercy or compassion. Uncle Benedikt moved to the brink of a precipice as he continued to play the violin. The killer aimed his gun for the forty-fourth time against Benedikt's head and fired. At that moment the sound of music stopped and was only followed by an echo. The last truck reversed to the pit and tipped its quicklime. The Germans then leveled it and covered it with earth. Finally, all drove back to the fortress, and after that this surrounding became quiet again, as if nothing had ever happened, but inevitably the mark of this mass grave remains there till this very day, and up to the end of this system of things.

Since the cattle grazed on good grass or herbage and were well fed, I drove them out from the meadow, closed the gap in the fence and arrived home. Father came out to meet me in the yard and said, "Benedikt has gone, Mietek?"

"Yes, Father, and very courageously and fearlessly, for he did play sad music till the end. I wondered how his fingers could move so free from dissipation and distraction of the mind with steady nerves on the violin during his execution."

"Well," Father said, "one thing to his advantage was the fact that he played organs in the church for funerals so many times in his lifetime. As a matter of fact, he played organs in church at the funeral of your grandfather, Kazimierz Klimowicz, his brother and my father; that was a long time ago. So, you see, Mietek, the music itself was making him brave because when he played, he performed it as to God."

July fifth in the early part of the day I came to my grandaunt, Orszula Klimowicz, to tell her about the death of her brother, Benedikt. Her pain and sense of deep loss made her feel that she was drowning emotionally. At such a moment, driven into despair, she was pulling her hair from her head and contemporaneously uttering sobbing sounds of grief accompanied by tears. In this ravaged lamentation I became moved emotionally too and cried. My aunt embraced me and we both continued to cry. Then she said, "Look at his violins and his grand piano. Who can play these instruments now as Benedikt did?" At that she sat at the grand piano and began to play Benedikt's the favorite piece of music, "the First Piano Concerto," composed by Pyotr Ilyich Tchaikovsky.

Now since Benedikt Klimowicz was gone only one organist was left in the parish of Naliboki and that was Mr. Pietraszkiewicz, who resided on the church ground with his wife, but two their sons, college students, never did return home during the war time. With Benedikt, unfortunately Mr. Hasiuk's entire family was wiped out by the German SS.

The organ of the Saint Bartholomew church was very old, yet it was the best playing musical instrument in the country because it was cherished, repaired, and tuned regularly by Benedikt for the reason that his own brother and my grandfather, Kazimierz Klimowicz, played this organ long before him. However, presently Mr. Pietraszkiewicz was worried and was saying, "Who will see to this beautiful organ now since the man who maintained it is no more?"

The German officers, including Chief Sawinola, came out from the fortress and were marching directly to the parsonage. In the parsonage they made sure that the priests and Prelate Bajko all were present. At that point, Eugenjusz Klimowicz was summoned to appear before them in order to answer to the criminal homicide of the twenty-two German SS on May 29, 1942, in Naliboki. By inherent nature Eugenjusz knew exactly what one could expect from the furious Germans, for one wrong word could result in a bullet in his head. So he used diplomacy and laid the entire blame on the Soviet partisans by implying that for the last three years not only he personally had suffered anguish and torment, but the highest percentage of people in Naliboki. "The Wilderness of Naliboki presently has become infested by these Russian partisans, and therefore Naliboki desperately needs the German power in order to eliminate these kinds of bandits and outlaws and permanently to control and to police this entire region," Eugenjusz concluded his argument in defense of all the people, including himself.

For a moment the officers and Chief Sawinola began to lay heads together. And at the same time Uncle Eugenjusz related to Prelate Bajko what he had told the Germans in their language. Instead, Prelate Bajko put his hand on my uncle's shoulder with a slightly pleased expression of his face.

Abruptly one of the superior officers promulgated the fact that the German armed forces were unaccustomed to staying behind the front line in the time of war. He concluded by saying, "Our specific obligatory service as a priority is to use all power in battle against the enemy at the front line; therefore, we cannot afford to provide you with protection."

Immediately another officer, a Latvian lieutenant, began to speak. "We in Latvia have had a similar problem as you have here, Herr Klimowicz. Yet without anybody's help, we ourselves managed to clean up the mess and to control the affairs of our society. Therefore, likewise, I suggest to you, Herr Klimowicz, to organize your people as one unit and defend yourself from the attacks of Russian partisans." At that instant, the lieutenant raised his voice and said, "Do I hear a second?"

All the rest of the officers, including Chief Sawinola, seconded the motion and formally acted as supporters of the present resolution and incited it to be an active fortitude.

Consequently, Eugenjusz Klimowicz stated, "Now I must assemble the people and put to them this proposition. If they can be persuaded, then we all would need a lot of weapons and ammunition necessary for attack or defense."

The Germans concurred and said that regarding an armament there was no problem. "We shall make sure before we leave that you be left with ample weapons and ammunition, and additionally Chief Carl Sawinola will do his best to assist you in any way he possibly can from his headquarters in Iwieniec."

So, finally this verbal meeting had a peaceful ending and my uncle came home free from danger. Of course, the Germans had no way of knowing the fact that they had been dealing with "okon," the leader of the Polish guerrilla, and his being in a rank of captain, fully armed and secured, ready to strike the enemy. However, okon means a perch, which in its secrecy referred to Captain Eugenjusz Klimowicz, about whom at that time nobody knew was the guerrilla's leader, or if such a combatant band that often operated behind the enemy ever existed.

While at home, Eugenjusz sent his password for the immediate assembly of all members, and at once some five hundred men stood at the square ready to hear what their leader had to say. The leader came out from his home and arose on that large stone at the square for everyone to see him and proclaimed, "Friends, today the war is not at an end yet, but rather we are in the middle of it. The Germans, instead of destroying Naliboki, gave us an option to patrol the town from being trampled by the Soviet partisans. If you decide that we must protect Naliboki from the Soviet atrocities, then at least we will have to contend with one enemy, but on the other hand, if you decide not to go along with the German proposition, then we must disappear into the wilderness, abandoning our people for the German discretion, and you all know of what they are capable doing. So, those in favor of protecting Naliboki, please show your hands. ... Those who are against, please raise your hands."

However, the outcome of this vote was unanimous in favor for the safety of Naliboki. In that case, Eugenjusz went to Chief Sawinola and told him, "The people of Naliboki are free from uncertainty. They have decided to stand against the Soviet partisans."

Forthwith, Chief Sawinola on May 5 commissioned Eugenjusz Klimowicz "Kommandant von stadt Naliboki," and henceforth he was called commandant. In this way every resident from the age of twenty to forty-five was implicated as a sentinel of Naliboki—whom we called "Samochowiec," meaning a self-preserver or self-defender.

On July 6 my parents decided to go back to Trascianka to get some potatoes because we did not have any here at home. But father would not dare to go, knowing that if partisans got hold of him they would kill him. Mother, too, was afraid to go by herself. So she asked our neighbor, Mrs. Mania Baszuro, if she would go with her to Trascianka. Of course, she said, "I do not mind. I would really like to go with you."

At that, father prepared the wagon and instructed me how to engage the plow on my own and how to unearth the rows of potatoes. When we arrived there I followed father's directions and turned over some rows of potatoes just as he told me. Successfully, I put the horse at rest and hung a sack of some oats on his head to eat. The three of us began picking potatoes and putting them into the baskets, but then all of a sudden we saw a partisan with a rifle on his shoulder walking toward us as he came out from the forest. Mother was benumbed from fear. I had no idea how Mrs. Baszuro felt, but as for myself I thought nothing of it, except I did not like the fact that he was armed. Nonetheless, when he got closer to us, it appeared in all probability that he was more terrified than we were. He tried to speak, stuttering with spasmatic repetition, asking us, "Have you seen the Germans anywhere nearby?"

Mother said, "No! We traveled sixteen kilometers from Naliboki and we did not see any Germans on our way here. But Naliboki is full of them."

At that point he calmed down and began to narrate his ordeal to us. He said that a large number of partisans suddenly moved out from this area, except he said, "Myself and one lady, we were left behind. So, we hid ourselves in a thick brushwood. Two days ago I left the lady because I had to urinate and defecate, but at that precise moment I discharged my machine gun. At once, I buried myself in wet and spongy ground and covered my body with sod. The Germans must have walked over me, but somehow I remained there unseen. For a long while I stayed put, until I realized that it was safe to come out. When I got to my lady, she was laying dead, shot right across her chest with machine gun."

Then he asked us if we would like to come along with him to see the dead lady.

Naturally, my mother and Mrs. Baszuro replied, "We do not mind. Please, show us."

So the man in his forties began to lead us to the dead body, which was laying in thick brushwood near the nursery between the meadow and arable land on the eastern side of where we came to pick potatoes. Once we entered the forest, after a while we started crawling in the thick, compactly overgrown young fir trees. Finally, we crept to the actual place where the dead lady was laying stretched out prostrate in her beautiful brown fur coat. As the man had said, she was shot across her chest, which was covered with blood. After seeing this corpse and exchanging thoughts with the unfortunate partisan, we separated and came to finish our job. Finally, we traveled back home.

On the following day our grandfather came to us on a visit and talked to my mother about his dread when partisans tried to kill Uncle Jozef. Grandfather said, "After that I could not sleep for several nights. And then, because of great fear for Jozef, I copied from the holy scriptures Psalm 23; 'Jehovah is my Shepherd,' in the form of a letter and gave it to Jozef to read and to carry these holy words with him wherever he goes."

Then, of course, mother started telling her father about the incident we encountered in Trascianka the previous day. She has told him that in addition to all those Russian soldiers that were killed and buried around Trascianka during World War I, now there was a Russian woman in her thirties from the city of Minsk whom Germans had killed three days ago. "She is laying dead by the nursery in a fur coat that used to be beautiful, but now it is full of holes and soaked in her blood."

When grandfather got home, he told Uncle Jozef about the Russian woman the Germans killed at Trascianka. Of course, Uncle Jozef for his curiosity ventured there fully armed on his black horse. When he examined the dead woman's coat he found Russian golden coins the size of a US dime that were sewn up in the bottom hem of the fur coat. He came to our house and gave mother a souvenir, a gold coin that actually was current currency in the time of the czar's reign.

At home, as usual, there was nothing much to do. Father was in an easy chair sitting down, looking through the window; at the same time habitually he was rolling a bread crumb in his fingers and thinking as if he were soothing his nerves. Then mother looked through the window too and saw people dragging some old Jewish stuff for themselves. Now, in the materialistic aspect of life, she said to my father, "You are sitting here and watching the people carrying all different things from the Jewish homes. Why don't you get up, go there and bring something for yourself just like those people?"

At that, Father turned around and said, "Jozefa, Jozefa, who knows how soon the things we possess in this evil plight somebody in a like manner will be dragged out also, for we don't know really, whether we shall be fortunate enough to avail ourselves of the things we own. It is most likely that we may land in exactly the same predicament as our poor Jews did."

Naturally, mother heard what father was saying, but in turn she had no answer.

Since the German power was heavily engaged on all fronts in the war action, they had been deficient to dominate completely their internal affairs in the occupied countries. Thus, here we had no administrative management over the forestry as we used to have under the Soviet Union occupation. The people felt that they were free from any and all restrictions or control in the Wilderness of Naliboki. They began to cut down the prime trees of the forest and use this timber for building or structural purposes. They started to construct systematically new houses and barns. In order to acquire knowledge by imitating them, at the age of thirteen I was keenly observant of the way construction was performed, since I was anxious to follow in their footsteps because we had a complete absence of a buttery, a storage for potatoes that must be preserved over the winter season. Of course, this type of storage in the country was built in the exact style as a dwelling place. So my first objective was to stick to the way the house was built, and for that reason I watched them building houses.

After a period of two weeks the German armed forces commenced to leave Naliboki. Nevertheless, as promised on their day of departure they delivered two wagonloads of weaponry and ammunition, which they left by the residence of Eugenjusz Klimowicz. However, these weapons were mainly Russian, appropriated by them from the Soviet partisans whom they killed in combat. Finally, when these implements for fighting were arranged into kinds, there appeared to be three Russian maxims, powerful machine guns; six Russian CKMs, heavy machine guns; about ten (Finka's), the light Russian machine guns with a metal cylinder that contained seventy bullets; and the rest of the firearms consisted of German and Russian rifles.

As soon as the German armed forces had left, immediately the boundaries of town were established and the sentries were permanently placed all around Naliboki. The first and essential post was placed high on the scaffold of the unfinished new church with two maxims, and the other maxim was placed by the school. The heavy machine guns were set out in various places encompassing Naliboki. In the case of sudden attack, the siren that existed from the prewar fire department was ready to discharge a sound alarm three short times, but for revocation used to be just one prolonged sound for everyone to hear. In any event of danger it was well organized according to plan that every self-defender was obligated and compelled to be in action on the sound of the siren three times. When the Soviet partisans got to know this fact, they began to avoid Naliboki, and in this manner they placed themselves at some distance, and stood aloof, unsympathetically toward the Polish people now more than ever.

In the beginning of August I was standing by the window looking at the people passing by on Pilsudski Street. Suddenly I could not believe my eyes, for there walking was Abraham Jachin, a Jew whom Lieutenant Hryshka Porazit shot and killed June 19 at Trascianks, who also claimed that he previously was attacked in Nowogrodek by the German SS but miraculously escaped death. Now, there he was walking again directly into the clinic of Dr. Chwal, which was opposite our house. When I told the parents whom I just encountered, they sat by the window and waited until he came out to see really if it was Abraham Jachin. And the outcome was once he come out from the clinic, my parents were convinced that in fact it was the same Jew, Abraham Jachin.

In the evening father went to Dr. Chwal and told him the story about this Jew. But the doctor already knew all about it. He said, "This young man was laying by the highway near Trascianka and a certain farmer from the hamlet of Pazarecze was passing through and saw he was still alive. He put him on his wagon and brought Abraham to his home. Since then, I was making home visits at this hamlet and treating his wounds. However, the last wound from June nineteenth, the bullet went right through his body but luckily did not penetrate any vital organs. Now after six weeks he is able to move around. So I instructed him to come to the clinic, but cautiously and secretly, not to talk to anyone or to enter anybody's house in Naliboki and go straight to Pazarecze. The farmer told me that he is happy to have him because now he is helping him on his farm."

Subsequently, since this incident we saw Abraham Jachin entering the clinic regularly once each month, and concerning his safety Dr. Chwal did not tell Abraham about us or that we moved from Trascianka and now were residing next to his clinic. So, as Abraham was instructed by Dr. Chwal, every time he was going in, the same way he was going out from the clinic, always in a silent manner, that is to say, completely taciturn and without vexation. At the end of father's conversation with Dr. Chwal, he commented, "It seems that Abraham unfortunately was haunted by the demon of death, and yet he was miraculously rescued by the angel of heaven, and thanks to you, Dr. Chwal."

By the end of August we had managed to salvage all we could from Trascianka, and in this way we gathered sufficient stock on hand to last us over the winter. However, the main bulk of our crop was abandoned in the fields there, except the already made hay, which was left in stacks to be transported in the winter.

On August 30 our neighbor Mr. Jesc lost his youngest son, Franek. Mr. Jesc's residence was situated on Nowogridek Street next to the Wolan family, our relatives, but his orchard was extended to Pilsudski Street, behind our house on the west side. Franek, at nineteen years of age, took a ride on his bicycle to Iwieniec to visit some of his relatives there. Unfortunately, on his way to Ivieniec he met his tragic death, for Russian partisans got hold of him and murdered him in cold blood. Mother and I came to our neighbor's house during the viewing hour, open to the public, and there I saw Frank laying dead in the middle of the room in his coffin, clad in a black suit and in boots with large legs. At that moment I tried to remember him when he was a kid and I was just a child, how Frank ran around in his big orchard and threw apples all over the place. Yet, when I asked him to throw some apples across our fence, he used to express amusement and laughingly run away home. All along, from my childhood onward, I knew this neighbor of ours as selfish and stingy because for some reason or other they never offered us any fruit from their immense orchard as long as we were adjoined. But despite their unsociableness and not being congenially inclined, we all were gravely sad because of such a tragedy taking place, which we knew undoubtedly was facing us all sooner or later.

In September the members of our guerrilla band, under the guidance of Jozef Lojko, began to make dreadful inroads directly on the Soviet partisans in the perimeter of Naliboki. This was my Uncle Jozef's idea, and he emphasized to the commandant, Eugenjusz Klimowicz, that the partisans had to learn to fear Naliboki, and thus they would stay far away from our town. It was no doubt that he was concerned about himself, including his family and other Polish legionnaires who lived in remote places as himself on the skirts of wood. Living in such an isolated location certainly was most dangerous at the time of being overrun by the Soviet partisans. This kind of infestation was occurring in large numbers so as to annoy and threaten without exception anyone.

On several occasions by this time Naliboki's patrol had encountered the partisans near Maczylin and Terebejno. However, not with intent to kill, but instead the combat group fired their machine guns above the intruders' heads and caused them to run away from Naliboki. So the outcome was that the more the patrol was intensified, and indeed they all performed strenuously, the less there were such unexpected meetings with the Soviet partisans.

Chief Carl Sawinola with his military police arrived from Iwieniec to Naliboki. He visited my teacher, Mr. Guminski, with his loyal body guard, a native of the Ukraine. While everybody was at the table dinning, the chief professed that if he failed at killing someone early in a morning, then, he said to Mr. Guminski, his old friend, "I cannot enjoy eating my breakfast. You see, my friend, this Ivan Tomaszenko saved my life by an unusual and unexplained event. That is why I trust Ivan to be my personal guard. And so he is, since the day when I led a man to his death by execution. But he was a manlike being of supernatural size and strength of Byelorussian nationality. Once I shot him, he grabbed me and was crushing me to death. If not for Ivan, he would definitely have killed me and gotten away. Lucky for me, Ivan appeared as if from nowhere and suddenly emptied his gun into this giant, and thus I was rescued."

In October Jozef Lojko selected three men for himself, and soon afterward they engaged one dweller with a hackney coach to drive them around the perimeter of Naliboki. One of these three men was Jozef's friend, Stefan Arciuszewski, clad in civilian clothes, as naturally Jozef was himself, but the other two, Leon Szarzanowicz and Zygmunt Dubicki, they were clad in regular Polish army uniforms. Of course, the enlisted driver, Mr. Kunicki, was just a plain civilian fellow.

However, Leon Szarzanowicz used to be a notoriously debauched lad, but not since he beheld the vision five years ago in Maczylin, just like Mr. Kostus, Benedikt Klimowicz, Edward and his brother Kazimierz Wolan, the priests and Prelate Bajko, the old organist, Pietraszkiewicz, and many, many others. Leon as a matter of fact has radically changed and became a perfectly normal human being. Now Leon was very proud to be "Samochowiec," defending his community and his place of birth.

This time, however, Jozef Lojko decided to scare off some demon-possessed partisans in the southern part of Naliboki, which was north of his husbandry. On this southern side resided his brother Michal at the very center of Tartarus, and certainly from this center on the same elevation toward the forest was the actual location of hamlet Pazarecze. And in this hamlet lived Jozef's ex-concomitant from World War I, who used to be also a Polish legionnaire. He lived there with his wife and teenage daughter.

But once they arrived to Pazarecze and because being adequately armed with automatic weapons and hand grenades they choose to move on somewhat farther beyond the perimeter of Naliboki into one village and then even to another village where the most Byelorussian people lived. At that second village they stopped and stayed for a while and immediately afterward Jozef suggested and intelligibly said, let us go back to Pazarecze and there we stop at my friend's house and have something to drink, besides it was a long ago since I saw him last.

So Mr. Kunicki was driving his hackney coach steadily back northward to Pazarecze, but when they reached this hamlet it was already growing dusky. As they arrived, they stopped by Jozef's friend's house. Mr. Kunicki took care of his horse as Jozef knocked at the door, which of course without delay was opened, and at such an unexpected occasion there was some truly affectionate embracing with salutation. Everyone passionately was welcomed to the dwelling place as honorable guests. At that point in time in all excitement a preparation of the table began, as was the habitual practice of the Polish community. But being in action of such incitement the dwellers forgot to draw the curtains in the house. The young men, of course, Leon and Zygmunt, were sitting at the table, and the teenage girl was seated on Leon's lap.

In the meantime 150 Soviet partisans came to that second village, in which Byelorussian residents told them that a while ago some Polish soldiers had been there but had just left. When the partisans asked the people how many of them and which way they went, the partisans were told only five of them and they went northward, presumedly to the next village. Evidently the Soviet partisans followed the trail of the Polish soldiers to the next village, but when they arrived there, again they were told they had just missed those Pols. Despite everything, the Russians were determined to get the Poles, and therefore they followed them all the way to Pazareczo. Here, finally they spotted them through the window inside the house. Instantaneously, they aimed directly at the two soldiers sitting at the table, fired and killed them without contrition or qualm, and also at the same time Stefan got hit in his shoulder. The dwellers of the house somehow dived into the basement beneath the main floor. Mr. Kunicki in a panic dashed impetuously throughout the door with his hands up and a loud appeal, "Please do not shoot. I am just a driver! I am innocent!"

After World War II, a passport photograph of Jozef Lojko, one of the most renowned, invincible warriors in the history of Naliboki.

Nevertheless, Jozef exhibited adroit maneuvering and stood alone against the 150 Russians, just like Samson went striking a thousand Philistines. Evidently, Samson's strategy was to stand with his back against the rock in Lehi so that no spear would pierce him from behind. Likewise, Jozef's sudden plan was to stand away from the flying bullets; therefore he climbed up to the attic.

Immediately after partisans killed Zygmunt Dubicki and Leon Szarzanowicz, and at the same time that Mr. Kunicki surrendered to them, they came to the house and argued as to who would be the first to open the door. At that precise moment Jozef reflexively sprayed the whole crowd with his machine gun through the window in the vestibule, and instantly he got to the attic. While above the ceiling, Stefan Arciuszewski was dejected in spirit, and in his despair he said, "Jozef, I am going to shoot myself rather than to surrender, for I just have been hit."

"No!" said Jozef, "climb up to the attic to me. I need you up here."

During the time that the partisans were retreating and dragging their dead with them, Jozef came down and took the weapons and all hand grenades from the dead, burst the lamp and climbed back to attic under in complete darkness.

In this lightning operation the Soviet partisans lined up at some considerable distance from the house and commenced firing at the house level between the floor and window sill until the entire wall became as a sieve. Now, as they were free from doubt that anyone was possibly left alive in this house, they decided to come again to the house to make sure that all Poles were dead.

At the door repeatedly the partisans began to argue, saying to one another, "You, Vanka, open this door! Yes! You, Alosha, open this door!" At that particular moment, Jozef commenced his action, first by dropping hand grenades into the middle of the large crowd gathered at the door, and then in a lightning manner he came down and emptied all machine guns at the Russians, by means of which he killed most of the men who had attempted to destroy them. However, only a few escaped alive, and they took the driver with them and fled.

At that instant, Jozef said to Stefan, "Now is the time for our decampment."

So then they both came straightaway to the borough to the commandant's residence, where Jozef reported this occurrence that took place at the hamlet Pazarecze.

I remember that evening I was out in the street opposite our house and I heard continual disorderly firing. I thought the Germans were coming again and that they were wiping out the Russian partisans somewhere far behind the church. I came quickly into the house and told Mother to come outside and listen to some kind of a fighting going on there on the western side of Naliboki. So we all were attentive in order to hear, but none of us knew that it was Mother's own brother, Jozef, in a dangerous combat with Russian partisans at Pazarecze, until next morning when he told us all about his ordeal.

Naturally, that morning commandant Eugenjusz Klimowicz had 250 men ready whom Jozef was leading to the battlefield at Pazarecze. On arrival they examined the actual casualty and destruction. Apparently, in this place the house in question was in fact just like a sieve, a utensil for straining or sifting, all the way from the window sill to the foundation. The bodies, however, of Zygmunt and Leon were penetrated with bullets a great number of times. Jozef's friend with his wife and daughter survived because they knew where their basement was; otherwise they would have been killed. Outside, however, the Russian casualties were great. Many partisans were torn apart beyond recognition. Parts of their bodies were hanging on the trees and fences all over the place. The fact was that more than one hundred Russians died in their act of pursuing five Polish soldiers.

The folks in town were passing remarks and saying it was obvious that the dead Soviet partisans were demon-possessed men, even including our Leon Szarzanowicz. And that no doubt, these superhuman creatures allured them and or attracted them to come closer to Tartarus for the purpose that they could be finally released from the bodies of these men once they died. Then by inherent nature these spirits went back to their dwelling place in the appearance of "gleamy pillars."

On the other hand, these folks were mumbling that there was nothing on this earth that could possibly harm Jozef Lojko. Many marveled, why? But the others answered, "Because he is protected by the saints."

"What saints?" asked old men scratching their heads.

"Well, Jozef is carrying some letters with him written by the saints, and that is what protects him from exposure to evil. Therefore, it seems that not only the Communist partisans, but even the devil himself cannot harm Jozef."

Yet, in our family, we knew that the saints people were talking about was really King David, who began his rule over all of Israel in 1070 B.C.E., and of course the letter was his Psalm 23 with its caption, "Lord is my Shepherd." Anyway, Psalm 23 is not so much applicable for the dead as generally assumed but rather for the living to take heed and trust in Jehovah that surely goodness and loving kindness themselves will pursue the one all the days of his life.

The psalm as a matter of fact was copied from the Bible by our grandfather, Jozef's father, for his son's protection and God's blessings. For this reason Grandfather's constant prayers and inculcation of God's word the Bible in the son's mind was richly rewarded and blessed. Certainly, even though Jozef walked in the valley of deep shadow, he feared nothing bad. God's rod was the thing that comforted him, and he dwelled in the house of Jehovah to the length of his days.

The sentinels during the night on top of a scaffold at a brick structure of the new church beheld an assemblage of gleamy pillars in the cemetery. These young men after a long time hearing repeatedly a legendary tale of such ghosts now had a chance for the first time in their lives to observe these phenomenal apparitions. But what they had really seen, they could not believe. In astonishment they looked at the ghosts, and at the same time they stared at each other. During this particular night they heard from the graves abnormal groans and they saw flames ascending above the burial places of the families Popiawski, Lukaszewicz and Adamcewicz. Under these circumstances, who could explain to these sentinels the actual meaning of this illusion? Besides, it was just a war zone, in which one had to keep his senses and reflexes in the proper order for self-defense.

At daybreak when there was a change of guards, these disturbed young men climbed down from the scaffold and went to the graves of those families, but they saw nothing unusual there; the entire cemetery was calm and not in a state of any commotion, as it was indeed during the night.

In November one of the self-defenders by the name of Kozuszko was involved for some period in courting a local girl in order to marry her. Kozuszko, of course, lived in the borough on Nowogrodek Street, on the north side, but his fiancee lived alone in a small log house opposite, on the southern side of the street. Finally for some reason she quit courting Kozuszko and fell in love with another fellow. So this Antoni Kozuszko became extremely troubled. He calculated by measuring tiers of logs and arrived at the exact level with the bed inside the house. Then one night when Janina Makowska was asleep with Jozef Hodyl, Antoni Kozuszko fired his rifle from outside through the wall and killed both Janina and Jozef with a single bullet while they were in bed fast asleep. A few days later, however, an investigation concerning this homicide disclosed that Antoni Kozuszko was the number one suspect. He was arrested for murder and confined at the prewar police station in Naliboki, and there he awaited for the final judgment to be determined by superior authority of Chief Carl Sawinola.

In the meantime while Antoni Kozuszko was held in confinement, a certain Russian young man clad in civilian clothes, without any identification whatsoever, came to Naliboki. The self-defenders apprehended this young man and locked him up at the same police station for further questioning. After a thorough interrogation made by Commandant Klimowicz and others, the local authorities considered this Russian undoubtedly to be a spy. So as it happened, he and Kozuszko both awaited Chief Carl Sawinola's verdict on his arrival from Iwieniec.

Several weeks later the chief with some twenty men arrived at Naliboki for his desired aspiration, as always eager to put someone to death. It was at the end of November when he showed up, and the weather was bitter cold. I remember him walking in the borough, clad in a sheepskin overcoat down to his ankles, and his men following him like a bunch of hounds. On the next day, he came to see the prisoners. He listened for a short while to the report given on behalf of the accused by some individual in charge of the criminal sector, then the chief looked at Commandant Klimowicz with a smile and said, "These two men are guilty as charged. I pronounce death by hanging!"

A message was delivered to the parsonage in regard to the death penalty pronounced upon the two persons convicted of murder and espionage. Priest Baradyn, a tall and very good-looking middle-aged man, came to the police station in order to shrive the victims, that is to receive confession and give absolution to these men condemned to death. Naturally, Antoni Kozuszko, being a Catholic, was submissive and docile; he confessed his sins to the priest, but obviously nobody in town knew whether Kozuszko really was the killer of the young couple, Janina Makowska and Jozef Hodyl, because the priest's vow prohibits revealing a man's sin. However, once the priest approached the Russian young man, he was on the other hand rather rebellious and or intractable, for he was neither a Roman Catholic nor Greek Orthodox—he was a stone Communist and had no faith in God. In this way the Russian spurned the confession and Priest Baradyn departed and went on his way to the parsonage.

The first week of December was pretty cold, but the ground was devoid of moisture and there was no snow. Chief Sawinola decided to carry out his execution of these two men on Monday at noon. A lot of people gathered at the square, and everyone was frightened, having a pale face with anticipation to actually see someone being put to death by hanging, one a local person and the other a total stranger. I remember as if it were yesterday. I was there with my father and mother standing in the crowd. I looked around and saw the priests, Baradyn and Dadis, both standing in the crowd. There was Dr. Chwal, Jan Radziwill, Alfons L. Klimowicz, Jozef Kosciukiewicz, Kazimierz and Edward Wolan, Witold Baszuro, teacher Guminski, Eugenjusz Klimowicz, all the relatives of Antoni Kozuszko, and many, many other local people. After all, it was a public execution, and Chief Sawinola made his demand for all the people to be present at this killing as an example designed to warn or deter others.

Before the commencement of the actual execution there was no final request made by the victims. Nonetheless, the Chief Sawinola permitted them to have their last say. The first, Antoni Kozuszko, was given a minute to speak, but as time passed he said nothing. Then one minute was allowed to the Russian young man. He cried out with a loud voice, "For Russia, mother of birth!"

Because of determent from the malicious and intentional killing of one human being by another, and the practice of spying, Chief Sawinola compelled by order that these two convicts condemned to death were to remain hanging on the telegraph poles for a period of three days. And so they hanged there for three days and their bodies were plainly seen from our back windows on Pilsudski Street. Every time I looked there, it gave me shivers and I remembered Dr. Chwal's timing. When Chief Sawinola fired his gun, which was unexpected, automatically I had my eyes closed, as did anyone else affected by it in the

Antoni Kozuszko on the left and the Russian spy on the right, hanged December 1942.

crowd. But as I opened my eyes, I saw the two men already hanging, because the stools they were standing on the Germans had kicked from under the victims' feet on the signal given by their chief. From that moment Dr. Chwai looked at his watch, and I heard him say, "They are still alive ... still alive."

As he was saying that, I saw their faces changing color, going dark blue. Then Dr, Chwal said, "The life is ended."

Soon after the frightening death scene the crowd separated from this execution and all the people went back home.

The following day, however, extremely low temperatures embraced the Wilderness of Naliboki; it was about 35 degrees centigrade bellow zero. The dead bodies of the victims hanging on the telegraph poles became frozen stiff, and of course there was nothing anybody could do about it, since we all through them had been castigated and thus had to endure looking at the corpses for three days. On the third day there was a heavy fall of snow on the ground and it turned out to be just like in the winter season. As usual the people engaged their sledges as vehicles for riding or moving heavy loads over the snow and ice. After noon the family of Antoni Kozuszko came out in to the street, took him down from the pole and prepared his body for a proper interment. Likewise, some compassionate folks took down the Russian

Antoni Kozuszko was a happily married man with one child and he finished his service in the regular Polish army together with Alfons Lojko and Jan Radziwill. After military service, they were habitually associated in Nalboki, and both Alfons and Jan knew he could not have perpetrated such a murder. Besides, Antoni was going out with Janina before he was drafted a long time ago, and had no reason to jeopardize the life of his family.

man from the telegraph pole and buried him properly. Naturally, under such severe weather when the ground was frozen solid, it was not an easy task for one to excavate a pit to bury these dead bodies.

Father's protracted contemplation concerning the present situation of Naliboki became crystal clear, for he knew that based upon the existing outlook and the prophecy of the old man from Terebejno Naliboki was doomed and soon would face destruction. He was aware of the fact that sooner or later all men would be killed by the Soviet partisans since everyone was involved in the protection of the town, known to the enemies as self-protectors. He also knew that those Russians who tried to kill him previously, this time certainly he would have no explanation or any excuse in order to escape his death. Taking into account that his brother-in-law, Jozef Lojko, killed over one hundred partisans and his brother, Eugenjusz Klimowicz, was the commandant of Naliboki. Because of these principal factors Father began to formulate a plan for himself in order to survive by avoiding an inopportune death. So he told mother that Naliboki did not stand a chance against the great multitude of Soviet partisans, and once they got there they would kill him. He said, "I must get away from here and go to Nowogrodek to my Uncle Jakub Klimowicz," who was the brother of Benedikt and resided there almost all his life. Of course we believed him, but we had no idea that Father intended to join the Polish underground forces, A.K. That is why he told us in case we were asked by any stranger where he was, "You must answer that I am dead."

Wilhelm Klimowicz joined A.K. December 1942.

To make sure that the family would be left with adequate supplies over the winter season Father made necessary predispositions, and in addition it was essential to deliver our hay from Trascianka. But he was fearful to ride to Trascianka; instead, he sent me to bring the hay and instructed me how to load a stack of hay on the sledge. Of course, this stack of hay was situated in the meadow close behind the dead body of the Russian lady who was killed some months ago by the Germans and it was not interred. And by the meadow her comrade who survived had buried himself in the wet and spongy ground. After seeing this dead lady, I could not get it out of my mind and it had haunted me. In such a plight, being alone in the wilderness, I even lost the perception of horror and trepidation that was facing me from the incensed and furious partisans that were at large in this vast region. As Father was scared to go there himself, he also feared for my safety, which I did esteem lightly since my mind was filled with a dread of the dead woman.

By the time I arrived at the Glass Bridge I was traveling easily because the snow was trampled down by the movement of sledge vehicles, but I did not see or meet anyone on the highway throughout my journey. When I finally reached our lane that led to Trascianka, it was covered with heavy snow and was free of tracks. Actually, there was not a single footprint of a man or even animal. So as I drove, I left my sole track on our lane. I entered the yard and passed through it behind the dwelling, getting to the meadow in thick snow, and at last there in the glade was our stack of hay. At once I placed the sledge next to the stack, released the horse and hanged a sack of oats on his head. Then I laid logs across the sledge, climbed on top of the stack and began to pack the hay in a rectangular shape on to the sledge until the whole stack of hay was transferred in a hurry. The more I thought I was surrounded by demons and ghosts in this legendary haunted place, the harder and faster I worked on the hay, but I could not blot out of my mind the face of the Russian lady that was laying dead in the thick woods close to me. I was so terrified that I wished to move out from there as soon as possible.

I quickly pulled down a pole at the rear end, which in front the top end was jammed between the rope, and I tied it after pressing the hay tight. Then, of course, I gird about the load twice with the rope, and I was ready to pull out from this forsaken place. As I followed my own mark in the snow, just then in the yard I encountered four partisans on horseback who unmistakably traced my fresh track. At my first glance I got scared, but soon I recognized Major Pietro Bywalowski, who I knew was a reasonable man. He approached and asked me, "Klimowicz, where did you come here from?"

I answered, "From Naliboki."

Then the major said, "Are there any Germans in Naliboki?"

"Yes!"

"How many?"

Then I exaggerated and said, "Oh, must be a couple hundred."

At that, the major said, "Have you seen anybody on your way here?"

I truly answered, "Not a soul, except you just now, major."

"OK, then, carry on."

So in a like manner I returned home with a large load of hay, and Father was very glad to know I was safely home. I told him that I met Major Bywalowski in Trascianka. Father remarked, "It was lucky for you that it was not somebody else."

As everything was made to be in order to last us over the winter season, a few days later Father bid farewell to all of us and set out for Nowogrodek; that was, as far as we knew. From this day on, one week before Christmas 1942, my mother, sister Kristina, brother Antoni and I never saw our father again in our whole lives. Of course, for the record Kristina was seventeen months of age, Antoni eight years, and I was thirteen years old.

This unfortunately was the loneliest, most deserted, desolate and depressed Christmas holiday I ever had because of being bereft of all hope not having my Father, whom I loved so much. At that point in time I hated the Christmas holiday, its Christmas tree, Santa Claus and his presents, and all its tradition because of evil so invoked that I was deprived from my father in my childhood. I truly knew Father left us because of Satan's atrocious acts and his machination of bringing woes upon earthly men, but I was not sure then whether the Christmas celebration was his idea also. Surely, the omnipotent loving God would not bring misery and distress upon the children on the Christmas day if such a holiday was indeed of His origin. That is why throughout many future Christmas holidays I shed tears while others were eating and drinking and were full of mirth and laughter. So I cried because of the state being afflicted by an armed conflict between nations, which denied me my father. Since then only the tinkling sound in my mind was left when Father said, "In case you are asked by any stranger where I am, you must say that I am dead." And so it appeared to be.

After the Christmas holidays some folks came to load firewood on their sledge near Smolarnia, where they accidentally stumbled upon the body of Mr. Kunicki, the driver who surrendered to the Soviet partisans several months ago at Pozarecze. It became apparent that Mr. Kunicki suffered death by inhumane torture since he was missing various parts of his body. This body was found frozen stiff in the forest and was brought to his family to Naliboki, where finally Mr. Kunicki was properly buried.

Subsequently in December after the execution of Antoni Kozuszko and the Russian man, Chief Carl Sawinola and his squad pulled out from Naliboki back to Iwieniec. Since then, the people here had sustained their own protection from partisans' atrocities. However, at the end of January some large concentration of partisans moved from the south toward Naliboki. Four delegates representing the Soviet partisans marched in through Stolpce Street with a white flag directly to the commandant's residence. The commandant, Eugenjusz Klimowicz, came out and invited these Soviet officers into the house, using the Russian language in communication. In the house was a crowd of his, Okon, or Perch, and loyal guerrilla members who were known by their code. Among those were Jan Radziwill, Jozef Lojko, Alfons L. Klimowicz, Kazimierz Wolan and many others.

These partisan delegates without lapse of time expressed their need by demanding immune and unobstructed passage through Naliboki from any direction they chose since it was a point of ramification of roads in the Wilderness of Naliboki. Because, they said, "As it is now, according to the present statute, we are compelled to go round about Naliboki many miles through the forest on our missions assigned against the Germans, which is most inconvenient." At the same time they emphasized by saying, "It is imperative you must grant us free and open passageway in order to perform our tasks."

In response to the Soviets' demand, which meant to stamp Naliboki again, Eugenjusz Klimowicz said, "If we allow you, the Soviet partisans, to pass through Naliboki continually, then it would certainly result in atrocious deeds and acts caused by the Byelorussian and Ukrainian bandits who claim also to be your partisans. Of course, there is no guarantee on your part that such barbaric conduct will not reoccur. Therefore, we the townspeople categorically deny you open passageway through Naliboki, and furthermore you must avoid us at all costs."

Without hesitation the officers of the Soviet partisans unanimously declared, "In that case, we have no alternative but to launch an attack on Naliboki in the near future."

At that point in time, they got up from their seats and thanked all present for the kind reception, and they walked away the same way they came.

The following day, the people of Naliboki were assembled at the square in town and Eugeniusz Klimowicz, as commanding officer of the self-defenders, delivered a powerful speech with respect to resistance and the inevitable confrontation of the Russian partisans. He urgently expressed exhortation concerning everyone involved to have quick reflexes and extrasensory sight and hearing, "for there is no room for those who are sound asleep, since every self-defender here relies one upon another. We must double our sentries around Naliboki and entrench ourselves. If it is impossible to dig on account of frozen ground, we must fortify ourselves with trenches formed out of snow and ice. You must exercise physically and mentally regularly in order to be ready in combat against your enemy. Because it is only by your determination, a decisive tendency toward this end, that we can accomplish what is intended by your volition. Above all, remember the sound of the siren; once blown, be fit to stand for your duty as the controlling force to protect your families."

Immediately, at the conclusion of commandant's speech and his instructive counsel, all present self-defenders declared in unison repeatedly, "We shall defend and safeguard ... we shall defend and safeguard ... we shall defend and safeguard Naliboki."

In view of such a terrible situation, all "Samochowcy" self-defenders without exception started working hard to strengthen Naliboki against attack. The circumference of three kilometers in diameter that surrounded almost the entire environment without procrastination was barricaded. About a thousand sentries stood guard day and night to avoid danger, and they were changed regularly every four hours. Obviously, the weather was very cold. Bare hands were sticking to the metal of firearms and the skin was peeling off if one tried to free his hand. Then many wondered who on earth would be stupid enough to attack Naliboki under such extremely freezing conditions. To die or to inflict a wound for anyone was certainly a horrifying thought. So, many weeks went by and there was no sign of any attack on the part of the Russian partisans. The people's state of mind with reference to confidence, courage, hope, zeal and so on was very great. Naliboki as a whole became self-assured; thus a suspicion of stern inspiring fear gradually faded away in the hearts of all people.

At the very end of February, the same officers of the Soviet partisans came with a white flag through a number of sentries and saw to what extent Naliboki had been strengthened against their attack. Nonetheless, after an hour of talking with Commandant Klimowicz they stated that based on the denial of free passage through Naliboki, "We are going to attack you on Easter, and then you will have to contend and repel."

However, the position of Naliboki at the time was incapable of being taken by force easily. Every self-defender was well prepared and ready to fight and protect Naliboki. The morale of folks in town was high. All had the confidence of being on the right and justifiable side, and that is why they had to stand firm against the Russian fallacious demand. The church was full of people every day and everyone was praying for deliverance from evil and ungodly Communist men. Prelate Bajko and Priest Baradyn, Priest Dadis and the priest of the army all were extremely busy every day at the confession booths. On each Sunday the church was overcrowded, many as a matter of fact were standing outside because there was no room for all of them in church. For that reason the pulpit was placed outside when Prelate Bajko delivered his sermon as a formal exhortation for the people to pray continually for the state of being relieved from restraint, evil and danger.

On account of the fact that at this period of time there was no restriction in the forest made by the authoritative administration of the affairs of a nation, the people helped themselves to cut down prime timber suitable for structural purposes. In early March many started to actively engage in building new houses, stables, barns, etc., not taking into consideration any approaching calamity. In spite of all uncertainty, the people were leading normal lives, as if nothing would ever happen. They began to build and work in the fields, preparing their land for cultivation.

At almost fourteen years of age I was very eager to follow people's indispensable course of life, for it served as drug, intended for treatment like preventing the spread of disease, but in actual fact it was the fear of death. So after a day's hard work, a meal and prayer before going to bed, being not in the state of anxiety because of tediousness, I slept sound and felt good the following morning.

However, early in February the same officers of Soviet partisans came with a white flag to Eugenjusz Klimowicz to make an ultimate request for secured passage through Naliboki. Of course, by the formal expression of will and opinion of all people in Naliboki concerning this question having been already submitted for decision, the commandant categorically denied their passageway. The Russians in turn unanimously said they were going to launch their attack on our town precisely on Easter, and at that point they terminated their meeting.

For several months everyone with an intuitive prevision looked forward to a certain partisan assault on Easter Holiday, but when such time arrived nothing happened, for there was not even a sign of Russian partisans in entire vicinity. Logically, all people in Naliboki gained confidence and became self-assured. They imagined that the Russians would not venture their effort against Naliboki during their critical conflict with the Germans. Conclusively, they did esteem lightly the Russian sense and consciousness of inimical disposition toward the Polish people, embedded deeply from the ages in their personality. Of course, to perceive their innate obscured hostility one can only learn from experience by direct contact with Russian people. Other than that, the Poles themselves, unfamiliar with Russians oftentimes refused to believe that they would have some kind of a concealed hatred against the Polish nation. Nevertheless, not all Russians were prejudiced or narrow minded; on the contrary, many were tolerant and progressive, just like Katlarycha and Taciana were.

Ironically enough, despite possible indications of impending danger from the Russian partisans and a potent prophecy of Nostradamus from Terebejno, the people in Naliboki became more busy than ever planting and cultivating the fields and constructing new buildings.

As a rule most people placed reliance on their hope, taking for granted all things optimistically—understandably everything was being ordered for the best. By such comprehension of others I was inclined to be, and hoped that someday soon my father would return and would be proud to see what I had built and planted. Because of my love for him I eagerly followed mother's instructions and help, by which I cultivated all our fields, even those that father used to leave barren. Additionally, I planted potatoes for Dr. Chwal on his landlord Lawon's land since father was cultivating this land for the doctor as a favor. Then, of course, at any spare time I was engaged in building a log structure for the winter storage of potatoes and other vegetables and fruit, since such commodious facilities we did not have like Uncle Waclaw did in Trascianka. My parents here at our husbandry used to store potatoes for the winter in large underground pits covered with planks, straw and a heap of sand, as it was a practical way applied by many people in our community.

The means by which I was constructing my building was from my keen observation of old men who were building houses and similar buildings in a regional fashion. The closest pine trees were growing next to the mass grave where my great uncle Benedikt was murdered. Here I drove into the forest and cut down some fine straight trees to the size I required, loaded them on the wain wagon and delivered them home. In the yard I shaped these logs in tiers, first by peeling bark, gouging a groove, notching the ends for a tight fit, arranging convexity in a proper place, then putting the first tier on the foundation of stones, placing a layer of moss on top of the tier, and carefully fitting the second tier, and finally driving the notched ends with a sledge hammer into the permanent position. By the time I was fixing the last tier some expert builders came to examine my work, and they indeed marveled, because I was just a kid and the craftsmanship was flawless. They passed remarks by saying, "He even laid the convex logs upwards so that the weight of the structure will press down the hump evenly in a middle."

Certainly, I was delighted hearing them praising my work because I hoped that their opinion would spread as a rumor and eventually reach my father. And, indeed, somehow it did reach him, but of no avail because five years later I was told about it.

To tread in other farmers' footsteps, by mid-May I managed to complete our cultivation, the planting and sowing of seeds in the ground. At the same time I had also accomplished my log storage, which required only a roof and completion of the interior. Now at last I had some extra time on hand for my leisure and pleasure.

During May as usual the weather was favorable for the larks and swallows to perform in the sky sensational acrobatic feats while the self-defenders on Sunday of the third week declared the anniversary of an independent year at Naliboki; thus all men decided to celebrate this significant occasion. As for alcoholic beverages, they used mainly a great deal of vodka, which was presently licit of being distilled commonly from rye. In commemoration of this event, in spite of war, there was an abundance of food and the people were having a pleasant diversion. There was music and dance. Naliboki held a banquet, in a manner of speaking, as the ancient Babylon on the night of October 5/6, 539 B.C.E., except of course there was no ominous writing on the plaster wall: "MENE, MENE, TEKEL, and PARSIN." Nevertheless, during the summer in 1937 something similar was uttered by the middle-aged Jewish woman entangled and possessed with the devil, which was, "ERE, MENE, NA, ROBILO." From Lubcz to Mir, across the Wilderness of Naliboki she carried this forewarning message, but of course nobody took notice because plainly she was considered to be a madwoman from the asylum in Lubcz, and besides, no one knew its interpretation.

On Saturday Arkadjusz Makarewicz came to me with an idea to go fishing somewhere. Therefore I told him about my last fishing with Benedikt in the canal at Trascianka. Naturally, he was thrilled and suggested to take a trip there the next day. So early in the morning on Sunday before sunrise we harnessed the horse to the wagon and left for Trascianka without realizing a potential danger of Russian partisans. Arkadjusz was seventeen years of age, prime prey for predators in this wilderness—undoubtedly we could be killed just as easily as our neighbor Franek Jesc was killed by partisans on his way to Iwieniec. As we journeyed through a bumpy wooden highway in the forest, presenting an extraordinarily imposing appearance, where the birds and all wildlife enjoyed freedom, we likewise felt unrestraint and very happy without thinking of any danger. On our arrival at the Glass Bridge, I unharnessed the horse for grazing fine clover in the glade by the canal and I went to get my hidden net. Here from the Glass Bridge in the direction of Lake Kroman we commenced fishing like never before. Indeed, Arkadjusz was enthusiastic on account of such a great catch which he never knew existed. After a few hours of effortless fishing we filled two large sacks with pikes, perches, bleaks and silverfish, and then we loaded them on top of the hay in the wagon. Immediately we engaged our horse to this vehicle and were on our way home.

As we traveled through this majestic woodland ornamented in its splendor, Arkagwsz said, "I would like to gather some flowers for my Pani Wala Achramowicz (Pani Wojtowa, residing with Dr. Chwal)." At that he jumped off the wagon and began to pick these fragrant flowers until he had enough to decorate the entire living room.

Subsequently, traveling on such a bumpy road, we were drowsy and fell asleep. At the same time our sacks full of fishes vibrated off the wagon and we lost them. As we emerged from sleep, Maszka was getting into the yard, and then, when we tried to unload the fish, the sacks were not there. Disappointed, Arkadjusz had only an enormous bouquet of flowers to present to Mrs. Wala Achramowicz. After we separated, I felt stupid because I neglected to tie the sacks to the wagon since I was aware of the bumpy ride on this wooden highway; besides, because of the fish the sacks were slippery and disposed to get away. But again, I had no idea at this moment that it possibly could be a sign of some kind of immediate exposure to evil. Furthermore, I wished I could talk with somebody about it, but I could not because my friend Arkadjusz left and it was impossible to reason with my mother since I lost my fish. So in distress and worry, I ate my supper and went to bed.

In the meantime, after offering flowers to Mrs. Achramowicz, Arkadjusz was invited to the last meal of the day at Dr. Chwal's residence. Here, following supper, they all played cards until late in the night while self-defenders continued celebrating the anniversary all night. However, at the table playing cards were Dr. Chwal, Wala, the doctor's nineteen-year-old nephew who just came on a visit from beyond the river Niemen, and of course Arkadjusz. Soon after the game of cards Arkadjusz went to Jan Radziwill to pass the night there.

Exactly at daybreak, all of a sudden our house began to be shattered and penetrated with numerous bullets without any sound of alarm intended to apprise of danger. The Soviet partisans' attack on Naliboki began before dawn at maximum intensity, with an extreme effort of concentration that comprised fifteen thousand men according to discernment of local folks and an admission of partisans themselves.

To gain one's purpose Arkadjusz had to go to Jan Radziwill, for it was his turn to be on guard with him and Alfons at the Pillar of St. John by the lake. Apart from that, he was a steady visitor at Jans' residence since Wierka's mother, Aleksandrja, was the sister of Natasza Makarewicz, mother of Arkadjusz; thus Danusia and Jurek, Wierka's children, were his niece and nephew.

In view of the fact that all Klimowiczes had been admirable musicians, cantatrices and songsters, undoubtedly such an inborn talent was bestowed upon Arkadjusz, since his father happened to be Dr. Piotr Klimowicz. However, prior to the formation of the self-defenders in Naliboki, when the Russian partisans had been roving and rambling about, among them was also a tall woman of Jewish descent from the Soviet Union. During that time Arkadjusz became acquainted with her publicly in Naliboki, and recognizing that she was Jewish he sang for her some excellent Jewish songs, which indeed she admired and lauded his wonderful voice.

This obstinate Communist, a tall Jewish woman, was a high-ranking officer in the Red Army. She presumedly had killed a great number of Russian soldiers during the German invasion on the USSR when the privates underwent perturbation due to German propaganda and in confusion abandoned their weapons. Now she was fanatically engaged as a Soviet partisan mounted on horse.

Just like any other human being, Arkadjusz had some good qualities and, of course, bad. From his bad side, unfortunately, he was accident prone and oftentimes his nonessential attributes were almost capable of causing death. For example, once he was running with a knife in his hand, and suddenly he tripped and fell on the bridge near our residence, stubbing himself in his throat. Again, on the common pasture patting some strange horse he was kicked almost fatally in his head. But recently, Jan Radziwill asked him to clean his machine gun, a Russian C.K.M., which Arkadjusz undertook, and in its process this powerful weapon jammed. As he tried his best to release it, the gun went off out of control, nearly killing Jan's children, Danusia and Jurek. Then, when Jan entered his house, he saw his entire wall had been shattered with bullets, and Arkadjusz was white as a sheet.

On Monday at 4 A.M., as usual, it was time to change guards. During this function, Alfons K. Lojko came to wake up Jan Radziwill and Arkadjusz for duty. They occupied their position at the crossroads of St. John by the lake. But at this particular time the Soviet partisans ambushed our fresh guards, and instead they climbed up the watchtower and thus silently eliminated Naliboki's most essential strategic point, which existed on top of the structure of the unfinished church. Following that, the partisans invaded our parsonage, two of them clad in cassocks. These two partisans impersonating priests in the dark appeared walking directly to Jan Radziwill's position. He, of course, without any hesitation was about to discharge his machine gun, but Arkadjusz declared, "Wait a minute, Jan. I think I can see ... they are our priests. Don't shoot!"

"Yes, they are priests!" confirmed Alfons.

Accordingly the partisans continued walking disguised as priests and successfully bypassed the sentries, advancing directly to Majatek (the fortress). Immediately as they reached Majatek, they began to hammer at the door with a sudden loud outcry in Russian, "Open the door!"

Instantaneously Jan opened fire and thus silenced those spurious priests.

At that precise moment the siege began. A swarm of partisans like ogres from the top of the cemetery hill commenced descending and overcrowding the footpath bridge in the valley parallel to the horizon of this ancient mythical lake. Jan Radziwill turned his C.K.M. gun from the line of Majatek and aimed at those demons, with lightning speed mowing them down off the bridge. The spring that began to flow in the time of Noah from the mouth of the lowest place (Tartarus) now had been obstructed by a dam of godless dead bodies. Once again the devil lured Jan Radziwill into his snare, simply to be killed without sense or discretion, for when the Soviets failed to seize Jan in order to kill him, not because he was a member of the Polish organization but rather because his name was Radziwill. The devil then bereaved him from precious Wierka in order to make him come to light, but by the intervention of the ruler of life and the universe Radziwill was saved.

In such a dreamlike state Jan Radziwill, responsive to the devil's suggestion, was fighting here to the finish. When Alfons, Arkadjusz and many other self-defenders requested to retreat from this position of danger, Radziwill refused. So, in such a hopeless predicament, a massive advance of the enemy grabbed Jan and dragged him out from his trench, and here again Radziwill's life was saved.

Indubitably, the partisans' objective was to possess immediate occupancy of Majatek. That is why in great numbers they swiftly moved like gleamy pillars from the cemetery onto the other side, where once the Germans, they experienced, were impregnable. Certainly, here was again the Soviet partisans' greatest loss, as Radziwill mowed them down, casting evil spirits back to their original condition from these possessed Russian dying men. Nonetheless, despite Radziwill's heroic achievement, the incursion continued to be enormous. Being in the state of consternation the self-defenders knew that it was time to withdraw.

As they all began to fall back, Jan, Alfons and Arkadjusz took a shortcut across Poplawski's and Jesc's orchard, and this way passed through Wolan's property urging Edward and Kazimierz Wolan to flee from the borough to the north side of Naliboki, but only Kazimierz, being an ex-student, followed them. Edward, his brother, declined, thinking that he was of no importance to the Soviets and therefore no harm possibly could come to him.

Alfons Klimowicz Lojko, a member of the Polish Youth organization (1938-1939), hidden under the stove over a year and a half, improsoned by the Soviets, a guerilla and subsequent soldier of A.K.

At dawn the Soviet partisans from the south besieged Naliboki completely and opened the heaviest fire one can imagine. Innumerable bullets contemporaneously discharged by thousands of men sounded just like wheat poured into an empty tank. Soon after Zascianki and Kamionka were aflame.

Radziwill, Alfons, Arkadjusz and Kazimierz, in the company of hundreds of other self-defenders, kept moving northward by the Jewish orchard, then over the sandy hills overgrown with brush and pine trees, straight to the forest. From Place, however, the self-defenders were falling back through the Jewish orchard. Here, Jozef Kosciukiewicz bravely held the Soviets for other colleagues to retreat, and as a result some partisans were killed in the Jewish orchard; however, Jozef escaped.

At this particular moment Naliboki was overridden by partisans, aside from Kamionka, as the legendary haunted hill became preposterous for the Soviets to subdue. Here, over many years as far as one could remember, people were terrified. At midnight they saw rolling barrels from the top of the hill and white horses in motion that used to disappear from sight. They heard the sounds of horses and swords engaged in battle, with the sounds of crying voices of fallen men, so that nobody at night had the courage to pass by on that street. However, it appeared as if a legion of demons once again for the last time had complete command of situation. The town's professional masons, Mr. Hodyl and his two sons, who actually had been building the church at the same time they constructed a brick mansion with a flat roof and a barrier on top of it, became invincible like a handful of Germans at Benedictine Abbey on Monte Cassino, where 15,000 Polish soldiers died subduing it. Similarly here, no Soviet partisans were able to get near Kamionka hill unless they fell down dead. So, as a final resort, the partisans had to fall back, brought in a large cannon, and from the distance commenced continually shooting until the mansion was annihilated together with Mr. Hodyl's family.

On the church grounds the partisans broke into organist Mr. Pietraszkiewicz house, drove him outside, shot and killed him. They broke into Dr. Chwal's residence, got his nephew outside and killed him at the door, the very spot where I once as a child amused the newly arrived doctor while I was playing in the heap of sand.

As the Soviet partisans were already invading Naliboki, the siren then sounded a warning signal. Obviously, it was too late for resistance to hinder enemy motion; if anything, there was not even much time left to flee. Such a sad circumstance of a sudden, unforeseen defeat is certainly worthy of comparison with the fall of the ancient Babylon Empire; hence history repeated itself on account of the fact that there is nothing new under the sun.

When the bullets penetrated our home I dived from the bed under the stove compartment where the wood was usually kept dry to light the fire. My mother slid all the featherbedding and pillows onto the floor, barricading my sister Kristina, brother Antoni, Waclawa and herself. In the course of this most horrifying shooting we all continued to stay put, enduring an unendurable time that we never experienced before or after in our lives. It is no wondered that Waclawa all of a sudden lost her mind. She became subjected to hysteria and therefore could not keep still. Subsequently, she got up and was looking through the window, where at the same time she was producing characteristic physical manifestations expressive of merriment, elation and amusement. Bursting with laughter she kept saying, "These men are ours, they all are wearing white bands on their heads."

In fear for her life I visualized Mr. Baszuro, who peeped through the forge window and was hit with a bullet between his eyes. Of course I did not want this to happen to my sister, so in order to prevent her from being killed, I shouted out, "Get your head down!" Waclawa of course, did not pay any attention. Nevertheless, in anger I threw a billet at her, and at that moment she fell down. Under such indefinite continual disorderly firing, I wished I could change into a mole and find myself instantly underground because upon the earth surface it was inconceivable to survive from such a rapid and heavy showering of bullets. The partisans' inroad and sudden rushing in persisted over a period of two hours, but those men with white bands on their heads were unfortunately the partisans of the Soviet Union.

The Last Day of Naliboki

By 8 a.m. the partisans had already gained dominion over Naliboki, and inside this inhabited place, the city of fallen angels, they began a savage and indiscriminate killing of unarmed, innocent human beings, as in acts of persecution and revenge. Arkadjusz's acquaintance, a tall Jewish woman armed with an automatic weapon, Russian finka, on a Siberian thoroughbred horse from Cossak's cavalry emerged as a devil in the street of the borough. While she was tying her horse to the fence, the partisans were actively engaged driving men and boys out from their homes into the street. Others were in a quick manner lining them up in a long row along the pavement beginning from the telegraph pole (on which Antoni Kozuszko was hanged) and all the way down to a curving of Nowogrodek Street. When the killing started some victims standing in the long line became affected with panic and were jumping the fence trying to escape through the backyards and orchards, but the partisans were there and were shooting them with Russian lacerating rifles. No one was able or lucky enough to get away from death. Mr. Arciuszewski, who lived next to Mr. Jesc and was in his late twenties, was lying dead partly on our and on Wolan's strip of land, having been hit in the face, but the back of his head was torn and his cranium was empty. In the street the Jewish woman at a short range with her finka was mowing down the row of defenseless men and boys so that their blood was flowing in the gutter simply like water used to after a heavy rain. Among many killed in this row was my uncle Edward Wolan. This fanatical Communist homicidal woman mounted her horse, turned around and waved for partisans to move on, at which time quickly they all advanced toward the south in exactly the same way they made the raid.

When the persistent disorderly firing had ended, Mother got up from the floor and I crawled out from underneath the brick structure (stove). A Russian partisan dug into the house, leapt to my mother and uttered with a shriek, "Where is your husband?!"

Mother said, "He is dead."

"I need your transport," demanded the partisan.

Mother politely replied, "Sir, please let my son harness the horse for you because he knows where all the gears of a draft animal are."

The partisan said OK, and at that Mother turned around and said to me, "Mietek, go harness the horse."

Now I wished I was hidden somewhere so that even my mother did not know how to find me because of the tragic incident I was about to encounter, but the outcome was a miracle for me to remain in existence. As I stepped out onto the porch, I saw in the street a short Russian partisan aiming his rifle directly at me as I walked through our yard to the stable. At that, he fired the rifle and it surprised me, for he missed me. Being numbed by not having any fear, I thought that if I dashed down to the stable he certainly would shoot again and kill me. So instead I decided to keep a cool position, as I once experienced with a wolf at the Glass Bridge. Therefore, I continued walking with a steady pace and just curiously rotating my eyes. When I moved my eyes to the right I saw him again aiming at me, and he fired. The bullet just whistled by my ears but I did not even oscillate. So I turned my eyes to the left and there I saw a boy Waclawa's age who was hit on Mr. Jesc' fence and was falling on the other side of Poplawski' ground. As I was pulling our horse from the stable, I observed this short partisan exercising his demonic power, getting to the wounded boy and shooting him point-blank without circumlocution while he was laying on the ground. At the discharge of the rifle his body instantaneously sprang once and the boy landed dead. Of course, looking at the figure of this particular partisan, I shivered again, as I did when our Benedikt was killed.

Anyway, I got our Maszka and wagon ready for the partisan and then I walked into the house all in one piece, telling mother, "I did my job."

After the partisan left Mother said to me, "On account of conflagration, clothe yourself with your Sunday suit first and then cover it with clothing of the day."

As I did that, I resembled a much bigger boy than I truly was. So I walked outside to see how extensive fire was in town. But at this particular time probably the last partisan was pulling a cow on a leash toward the church, and he called me and told me to walk in front of him. As I placed myself walking directly ahead of him, my mother and Aunt Bronislawa saw that he was getting ready to shoot me. They both dashed down to his feet and began to beg him, "Oh please, sir, he is just a little boy ... please, spare him ... please ... please ... please, sir," and at the same time they were kissing his feet.

At that, the partisan shook off my mother and aunt, since they were holding on firmly to his feet, and proceeded pulling that cow, of course, leaving us as we were behind.

However, after Naliboki was invaded and the heavy shooting ceased, I was for some strange reason devoid of fear, not realizing being killed now was easier than when under the stove—until the partisans left town and I saw so many laying dead on the street in our borough. Then I was filled with dread as never before. At this point it became quite clear to my mother that if father were at home, he would most certainly be killed, unless he had stayed with all those who fought and fled. As it happened, mother changed her mind, that father had left us because he did not love her. Of course, it was obvious too that he would not wait like the others did simply for the partisans to come to the house and kill him. No, rather he would be with Eugenjusz, Radziwill, Alfons, Jozef Lojko and many others who on their own endeavored to persevere in such an hour of trial. Besides, he foresaw the shattering of Naliboki in the very near future based generally on various facts that inevitably manifested such an evil destiny. And this was his essential reason for departing suddenly and secretly from Naliboki, for the acts of war work in ways that are difficult to understand because of their complexity or profundity.

For fear of running into massive German forces or Polish A.K., the Soviet partisans like desperados at 10 a.m. sharp suddenly pulled out from Naliboki southward, the direction from which their assault had been initiated. Moreover, being exhausted they did not have the courage to go northward because they would have to face "Okon," who with his loyal warriors was prepared for them at the sandy hills.

At 11 a.m. Chief Sawinola, like a man possessed with the devil, and two hundred of his addicted mounted cavalry emerged from the eastern part of the forest on Iwieniec highway. He drove as far as the square of the borough, glanced at the dead, more than he could rapidly count, then took an irascible look at the burning town, revolved his horse once or twice, and suddenly took off at the fastest gait of his horse with all his men directly to Iwieniec. Some local old folks were standing by and said, "What a shame. Look at him. It is unbelievable, a butcher of human beings, scared out of his wits when his own life is concerned."

At noon, the day was filled with the light and warmth of the sun, except that the whole atmosphere was thickened by the black smoke of burning houses and strong smell of gunpowder that propelled an enormous quantity of bullets. The surroundings became calm apart from the constant resound of the dreadful cries of many women who had lost their loved ones. In this atmosphere, Mother decided to take a walk, and I followed her as far as the late Dr. Piotr Klimowicz's residence on Stolpce Street. Here Mother wanted to know what happened, if anything, to our relatives. But when we came around the bend, they were all intact, thank God, standing outside in the street. As soon as they saw us approaching they came to meet us and we all stopped opposite the late Mr. Machlis's residence. Here with us was Janka, her mother-in-law Mania, and Aleksandrja with her two grandchildren, Danusia and Jurek. While mother was talking with them, I saw Eugenjusz at the square walking toward us, a bandage on his head. As he reached us he embraced all and spoke calmly. Then he looked at me and said, "Mietek, go into that pond and pull out some rifles." By the time I got several rifles from the bottom of that muddy pond, Eugenjusz bade farewell and with Janka his wife departed from us to the Wilderness of Naliboki, and that was the moment of our last meeting in this old bitterly wicked world. Ironically, I recalled that the previous day I had blamed myself for losing the fish I caught with Arkadjusz, but it was really not my fault, for it was merely a sign, a symbol of the people we had lost.

On our return home from Stolpce Street I wanted to show Mother the body of the young boy who was shot over my head, but when we got there his body was already carried away by kin, as well as the body of Mr. Arciuszewski. Yet, at the farther end of Poplawski's orchard there was laying Antoni Szarzanowicz's son, Michal, agonizing at the point of death. The partisans got him outside and shot him through his mouth. His mother and sister Wala were standing by him and weeping. My mother embraced affectionately her long devoted friend, manifesting grief by shedding tears together. The young lad Waclawa's age expired at sunset. His mother kept saying, "They just rout him outside and shot him. Why? Why? What has he done to deserve this?"

Such questions, of course, puzzled many Nalibokians, particularly those who had lost their loved ones, but it seemed at the time that nobody had a truly satisfying answer. However, shortly after they put the blame on Eugenjusz Klimowicz, and thus their false incrimination spread, and in time developed to its extremity within the Communistic regime behind the iron curtain; that is to say, an impenetrable barrier of censorship and secrecy imposed by the Soviet Union between its sphere of influence and the rest of the world.

After a year of self-protection it came about that on May 23, 1943, Naliboki suffered defeat from the Soviet partisans under German occupation, with minimal casualties to the self-defenders, who tactically participated in the actual combat. However, after the Soviets prevailed against Naliboki they took inhumane measures and thus massacred over five hundred unresisting and defenseless human beings in acts of persecution and revenge. Moreover, despite the Soviet's record and the admission of perpetrating this criminal act of murder, one hundred and several ten men omitting persons in the period of adolescence, the preponderance of evidence conspicuously presents over five hundred identical graves of the victims who were buried contemporaneously at the only cemetery in Naliboki. Therefore, this conformity to fact or reality of outcome on May 23, 1943, is the truth and cannot be confuted.

Weighing all the suffering and misery of the people in Naliboki from 1939 until this time, and considering the victims murdered and those who vanished without trace, there was not a single family left that was not touched by the loss of a loved one, and many families had been wiped out entirely. Unfortunately, it is also impossible to recall from one's memory all the names of inhabitants from the Parish of Naliboki, since the records of identity were destroyed by Nazis before displacement; nevertheless, here are just a few sonorous names in the subconscious mind to recall: Adamcewicz, Achramowicz, Adamczuk, Adamowicz, Arciuszewski, Andrzejczuk, Barancewicz, Baszuro, Bogdanowicz, Byczkiewicz, Ciechanowicz, Chilicki, Ghmar, Farbotko, Filicki, Guminski, Grzybowski, Grygorcewicz, Hale, Hleszczewicz, Hubar, Horoszkie, Hosiuk, Hodyl, Jankowski, Juncewicz, Karniewicz, Karp, Klimowicz, Kokiel, Kunicki, Koziomko, Kosciukiewicz, Kozuszko, Kanawal, Lawon, Lojko, Lukaszewicz, Miszuk, Makowski, Nowak, Nowicki, Okulicz, Ostapiej, Ogiejko, Pietraszkiewicz, Poplawski, Puzowski, Szarzanowicz, Szucko, Wolan, Zielonko.

Eugenjusz Klimowicz, as a rancorous officer of the Polish army and patriot of the Free State of Poland, persisted to lead his guerrilla warfare till 1944 within the perimeter of the Wilderness of Naliboki. On June 19, 1944, Eugenjusz, as commander of his company, captured Iwieniec after some twenty hours of battle, destroyed the German radio station and held the town over several days. After the annihilation of Naliboki by the Germans in mid-August 1943, Eugenjusz Klimowicz successfully defeated the German army at Kroman. Subsequently, with his company Eugenjusz Klimowicz, known at all times as Okon, was attached to the battalion of Major Ponury, and thereafter was a permanent commander in the Polish underground army, A.K. (Armia Krajowa). In June 1944 under Chief Commander Ponury in Jachnowicze they conquered the German watchtower of a border, and by the end of June 1944 this battalion conquered six more German watchtowers at Karzety, Rudnia, Sumy, Sobakince, Puchacze and Jewiasze.

At Rudnia, however, Okon was taken prisoner by the Germans. One of the superior officers ordered the Polish captive to be shot, and so he said to the subordinate German: "Take along this Polish swine dog and shoot him. Obey my command at once." But fortunately enough Eugenjusz understood the German officer perfectly, about which the Germans had no idea, knowing that Poles do not speak German.

So, as ordered, the German was leading "Okon" to the skirt of woods in order to kill him. On his way to the place of death, Eugenjusz overpowered the German and escaped.

After Naliboki was flattened by the fifteen thousand Soviet partisans in a uncivilized manner on May 27, a massive accumulation of Polish army was passing through Naliboki all that day. They were dragging along with them by horse power heavy military equipment and cannons. The people came outside to admire this colossal army. Many were saying, "Why are they passing through now? Why not three days ago when we needed them? Naliboki would be spared and our men would not be butchered by the Russians."

A tall man in charge of the A.K., General "Wilk" (General A. Krzyzanowski, secretly known as "Wilk," which means wolf) stood on an elevated place at the square and delivered an openhearted speech to our tormented and persecuted people. With regard to the Bolshevik's massacre in Naliboki, the general expressed his deepest sympathy and sorrow concerning such a great loss of lives by this extensive and bloody slaughter. He added, "The Soviets' malevolence and carnage practiced on our people throughout this century will never be forgotten. Citizens of Poland, I am saying now, soon we shall be liberated from the Soviet and German oppression and it will be no more, for their despotic power will be crushed."

Of course, with respect to Naliboki's fate General Wilk had no idea about the prophecy told by the Nostradamus of Terebejno, which was on the verge of fulfillment. But as for the liberation, we had no idea about Sikorski's Plan, concerning which General Wilk was not at liberty to disclose to the public because of being a top military secret upon which at this time all the Polish leaders had placed their confidence, namely that once the plan suppurated then the country would become a free state of Poland. The leaders waited for the Germans to reach Warsaw, at which point they would be ineffectual and weak, and the whole assemblage of Polish forces within and those abroad would strike together, and thus the Polish country would be liberated. However, in spite of the military secrecy, the general's speech was uplifting and improved to some extent the condition of the underprivileged and dejected people of Naliboki.

Subsequently, in 1944 General Wilk liberated a part of Wilno from German occupation, but unfortunately soon after he was apprehended, confined, and tortured to death by the Soviets.

On June 2, the Soviet partisans crowded into Naliboki, this time with the intention of apologizing to the people gathered at the square. They offered an absurd excuse for their error, saying, "It was our mistake to kill so many defenseless men, and it shows that some of our people undoubtedly had gone crazy; they were disordered in their minds. Now, however, we are promising you that this will never happen again. In order to demonstrate to you our sincerity, we are asking you to tell all your men who are intentionally hiding from us to come home and we are not going to bother them no matter what they think they have done. In this partial fulfillment of our obligation, we only want you to submit to us all your weapons and ammunition that you possess."

Obviously, our folks had no use anymore for such devices, so they all started carrying their weapons and piled them up in the borough, which came to three wagons full. At their departure, the partisans pulled the wagons loaded with the weapons along with them and they drove away to the wilderness.

Now that the Soviet partisans had left, the people began to argue among themselves as to whom from the men in the forest would be brave enough or stupid enough to come home. But they all were astounded when they saw Jan Radziwill walking into his house, of all men widely known and generally disapproved of by the Soviets. Immediately the following day officials of these Soviet irregular troops marched into Radziwill's house and looked at him as he was laying down on a sofa free from physical and mental distress, encircled by many guns which he had to his disposition.

The Russians said to Radziwill, "You are the one who killed a lot of our men on the bridge with this C.K.M."

The Last Day of Naliboki

1. Jan Radziwill; 2. Arkadjusz Makarewicz

Radziwill answered them, "Yes, I am the one; it is true."

They in turn said, "Well, it is something in the past, but now we must take with us all your weapons." And they left and did not haunt Jan Radziwill again anymore.

What a phenomenon, an inscrutable occurrence that nobody understood. One local woman said, "My husband was impartial and they got him outside and killed him. Whereas Radziwill is concerned, they were hunting him like rabid dogs trying to execute him, but now he killed hundreds of them and yet they did not lay a finger on him."

Of course, when Radziwill decided to go home it did not matter to him that the Soviets would kill him because this is what he anticipated. Otherwise he would never give himself up to his enemy, such a noble man as he was with innate dignity and honor.

Then some old folks said, "This matter is beyond a mortal man's comprehension because it is God's hand intervening, for he is the One who has dominion over the Soviets and Satan. Therefore, Radziwill is just like Daniel in lions' pit, where God's angel shut the mouths of the lions and thus they were unable to devour him."

As the men in hiding from the Soviets came to know about this peculiar unexpected incident, more self-defenders ventured home to their families. Even those who had been subjected to suffering, for instance Kazimierz Wolan or Jozef Kosciukiewicz, they too appeared at their homes. Nonetheless, many individuals like Alfons K. Lojko and Jozef Lojko had more reason to be skeptical. To them this knowledge was unattainable and such judgements had to be continually questioned and doubted so far as the Russians were concerned. Based on skepticism and the fact of being their ex-thralls, those men chose to remain free and henceforth stuck by Eugenjusz Klimowicz, not having a chance ever to return home since the last day of Naliboki was foretold.

When Jan Radziwill suddenly left the forest, many thought that he had become deranged and totally crazy, or otherwise the bravest man they ever knew. But those who knew him better accepted the fact that he desired to die on account of Wierka, for without her his life had been absolutely worthless. Yet to see how this situation developed, they cut the hair of Arkadjusz Makarewicz and sent him home. Without the hair on his head, he resembled much less than sixteen years of age; thus they thought the partisans would not kill a mere lad as they did during the raid.

Although existing under German occupation in submission to their authoritative power, this contemporary space of time once again began to be under the loathsome atrocities of the irregular troops of the Soviet Union. Fining oneself in such a plight of a most dangerous and complicated nature, when one's life came to be cheap and meaningless, where one was forced to adopt a similar attitude to that of Jan Radziwill, people in general lost track of living. They appeared to be as if under a supernatural power by which only a dead body is believed to be reanimated, or perhaps just like a corpse reactivated by sorcery but still dead. The subjects of such bewilderment were aware of their own existence and of external conditions; they were suitably most susceptible to an inspiration of demons, and they walked like zombies without anyone to take notice of them in order to scoff or perhaps jest as once they used to during peace and prosperity. This was our dungeon, in which everybody was trapped without a chance to escape or hope to become free.

When one is not cognizant that he is under a curse, one has no idea why the evil is upon him. So I pondered and wondered why God had abandoned us. Why we are surrounded by the demons and evil force, not knowing the way out? Why was I left ignominious and without God? Certainly here we were going to die, not knowing why. Since I was in no way better than those that had already fallen in death, it was quite obvious to me that soon I would be killed too. But I said to myself, *If by any chance I survive, I will search for the true God, and definitely then I will learn a sacred secret of God.*

Now that the Soviet partisans had established their permanent residence in our town, they were freely eating our bread, slaughtering our domestic animals for their covetousness, drinking our liquor, using our horse-driven transport, and ravishing our women. They were killing any man they wanted just because they did not like his countenance. Here in this city of fallen angels we were puffing and wheezing with a sound of hopelessness in anarchic confusion and general disorder of the supposed unformed original state of the universe. Here, where once the people lauded Christ Jesus daily, now they wondered, "Does God really care about us? If he does, why has God permitted wickedness throughout the ages?"

Of course, even well-known philosophers and clergymen have dealt with this matter but failed to arrive to satisfying answers. And so it seemed that nobody in Naliboki knew why God had permitted wickedness. However, much, much later I solved this conundrum, simply because I desired to know what God himself says about wickedness. Based upon our experience of painful and inhumane misery in Naliboki, we all can appreciate the Hebrew prophet Habakkuk's reaction to violence and injustice.

He lived at a time when the Jews had fallen into many bad practices, which sorely troubled Habakkuk and moved him to ask God, "Why do you make me look at injustice? Why do you tolerate wrong? Destruction and violence are before me; there is strife and conflict abounds. Therefore the law is paralyzed, and justice never prevails. The wicked hem in the righteous, so that justice is perverted."

Though convinced of God's righteousness, Habakkuk was distressed by the violence and injustice among his people. Also, at that time the Babylonians were on the rampage, terrorizing and despoiling other nations. It seemed that wickedness prevailed everywhere. The prophet Habakkuk wondered why God, who could see it, seemed to do nothing.

In a vision God assured Habakkuk that the seeming prosperity of the wicked was only temporary. God not only saw what was occurring, but also cared. He had an appointed time for meting out divine justice. Even if humans thought that this was delaying, Habakkuk was assured that it without fail would come true. It would not be late.

History tells us what happened. When the time arrived, God acted to end violence and injustice on the part of the Jews. The land was conquered and many of the people were taken captive. Later, God had an accounting with Babylon. As God Jehovah foretold through his prophets, the Medes and the Persians under Cyrus defeated the seemingly all-powerful Babylonian Empire.

This small-scale illustration shows that our creator does not close his eyes to wickedness. He is aware of it and he does care. Because high above the blue sky promulgates the glory of its guilder and the solstice sun gazing throughout the ages disdainfully on the erroneous erudite men. The stars at night that shine so bright that no man is capable to render account of, but one who has created these things is bringing forth the army of them even by number, all of whom he calls even by name, and he moves them by the abundance of dynamic energy, so that not one of them is missing, for the reason that he does care.

Since the whole world was laying in the power of the wicked, no one was safe unless he put on a complete suit of armor from God that he may be able to stand firm against the machinations of the devil in order to resist in the wicked day. Otherwise, without the complete suit of armor of God, it may be impossible to turn away from the snares of death. The scriptures say: None that rests his faith on him will be disappointed, For everyone who calls on the name of Jehovah will be saved. However, how will they call on him in whom they have not put faith? How in turn will they put faith in him of whom they have not heard? How in turn will they hear without someone to preach? How in turn will they preach unless they have been sent forth?

As I looked out through the window, I saw Abraham Jachin walking to Dr. Chwal for the dressing of his wounds. Unfortunate Abraham missed his death in Nowogrodek that was inflicted on him by the German SS, and again he supposedly was killed by the Russian partisan lieutenant Hryshka Porazit at Trascianka. I called my mother and she had a look at him walking, and said, "What a poor young man, left on his own like a single ear in the field after the harvest."

How on God's earth would he stand all alone exposed to the windy conditions of this wicked day. For this reason kind Dr. Chwal warned him not to stop here, or enter anyone's house, nor talk to anyone, just to keep going straight to Pozarecze, which is where he has found his refuge. Now that the Russian partisans were at large, it was more dangerous for Abraham because, after all, he was a Jew, but of course none of them knew him. Yet in spite of everything, an unforeseen occurrence was possible. But here was something more unbelievable than that, for Abraham Jachin was about to be caught in the snare of the wicked one just like a fly in the spider web.

On July 14 my mother was removing weeds in our garden and I was out in the street playing around with a hoop as I always did from childhood. Coincidentally, two partisans on a horseback were riding toward me from the St. John's crossing. When they got close to me, Lieutenant Porazit immediately recognized me and of course when I looked at him I knew what he was and what it meant having him around. He asked me, "Klimowicz, where do you live?"

As I was taken by surprise, I had to point out with my hand the direction to our house, but at the same time my mother saw me doing it. As they both marched in the house, Mother behind me made a bad facial expression at me, taking for granted it was my fault they found us. But, too bad for us indeed, for it was determined beforehand where we lived since they had made their inquiry at the parsonage in regard to our abode.

Inside the house Lieutenant Porazit first made himself quite comfortable. Then, he asked my mother, "Where is your husband?"

In reply, Mother said, "He is dead!"

The lieutenant jeeringly replied, "He is not dead; we know where he is."

Then Mother said, "If you know where he is, why are you asking me, because I do not know and as you can see, my husband is not here with me."

At that point in time Lieutenant Porazit commenced to relate his business in accordance with Communism. He said to my mother, "Your husband, Wilhelm Klimowicz, is in the Polish underground army, A.K., near Nowogrodek, and we are aware of his exact location. I want him to come home to you, and I guarantee we shall not kill him. You must therefore send your daughter, according to my instructions, and she will tell him what to do before he comes home. I am going to issue a pass for her safety throughout the wilderness, which will provide full protection in the face of our comrades. However, it is imperative

Lieutenant Hryshka Porazit and his comrade.

that he sabotage a military installation of A.K. to determine the genuineness that your husband is on our side. The round trip on foot is expected to be completed in three days."

Fearlessly, mother declined to comply with the lieutenant's demand, for she knew that if Father came back, no matter what he would still kill him. Undoubtedly, since the time when he tried to kill my Father, new developments took place of a detrimental nature to the Soviets on the part of Jozef Lojko, Eugenjusz Klimowicz, Jan Radziwill and Alfons K. Lojko. Father would not stand a chance. Therefore, it was obvious Porazit would blow his head off sooner than just killing anyone, as it was in his inspired demonic traits.

While Lieutenant Porazit was engaged talking with my mother, undetectably I was paying attention to his speaking, and for that reason I was standing away from them and looking through the window. At that particular moment, I noticed someone was walking out from Dr. Chwal's clinic. Looking at that person intensely, I recognized that it was Abraham Jachin. He then all of a sudden turned straight into our gate and was approaching our house. I froze stiff, unable to move or speak, as if some supernatural force descended from Lieutenant Porazit was possessing me to be in the state of catalepsy. No matter how much I wanted to dash out to turn Jachin away from entering our house, I could not move or do anything to stop him. Being in this state of a trance, I could only view this dramatic event, how Abraham Jachin walked in our dwelling just like a lamb into a slaughter house, allured by some mysterious evil force, how he entered our house as if by appointment or engagement to be there at a specified time for his third and final extirpation. He stood at the threshold and gazed in the predator's eye, then unpretentiously accepted his doom, for the face of this man appeared to be exceptionally white.

This merciless annihilator lured Abraham Jachin like a serpent. He scoffingly said, "Perhaps a glassful of vodka, a snack of kielbasa or a piece of bacon. The enchanted Jew was just shaking his head, implying, no, no, please. After a few jokes and laughter that caused degradation to his victim, where no one was laughing except the devil himself with his partner, Porazit called Abraham Jachin outside. In the yard he mounted his horse and coerced the young man to hurry in front of him. Riding his horse, Porazit drove him rapidly through the borough and alongside the Jewish orchard to the sandy hills, the place where the locals used to bury dead horses throughout the centuries, the spot that can only be familiar to the fallen angels from Tartarus, but certainly not to a stranger such as Porazit from Russia. Shortly after, Lieutenant Porazit appeared back in the yard; he tied his horse to the fence and came inside the house. Now he began to take by storm my mother. Obviously, we knew that he murdered Abraham Jachin in cold blood without any reason or cause. Now, the question in our minds was, what is in store for us?

Such a populously spread tension, a terrifying anticipation of evil overwhelmed the people in the entire region. We as a single family unit posed as a mere symbol, representing preceding families who likewise had suffered to the extent that as a consequence they remain among the dead. As the saying goes, now only the living know they will die, but as for the dead they know nothing. This infestation of godless men, known as Communists, involuntarily overpowered the Wilderness of Naliboki like the mighty ones who of old, the men of fame, when God saw that the badness of men was abundant in the earth and every inclination of the thoughts of his heart was only bad all the time. And God felt regret that he had made men in the earth, so he said, I am going to wipe men whom I have created off the surface of the ground. And indeed, so He did. Likewise, Naliboki must await its doom until God's appointed time. And after that it will only exist as a myth in the memory of descendants, who will indubitably say, "Look! There once lived and diminished our ancestry, in the land of legendary inundated ancient wicked cities that became haunted lakes, a place that is worthy of comparison nowadays to the mysterious Bermuda Triangle."

Lieutenant Porazit intimidated mother to such a point that she had to agree with his demand and act in conformity by sending Waclawa the following day to bring her father home. He at the same time insisted that above all, the sabotage to the military installation of A.K. must be carried out without fail and that the complete mission had to be accomplished in the duration of three days. "Beyond what has been said, we shall be back here on the fourth day to be sure this imposed task has been attained."

On the morning of July 15, Waclawa left on her digressive journey to locate our father that was made possible by the inculcation of Lieutenant Hryshka Porazit. An enormous dread compressed us as soon as the two partisans departed from our house and Waclawa had gone to find and bring our father.

From the USSR invasion 1939, we had no idea that it would be possible to survive under such dangerous circumstances. So we prayed incessantly to God to save us from a sudden and unexpected death. However, it seemed that the time had come for us to face our sudden and unexpected death because it was imminent, since the evil force bloomed like red poppies in the field, where there was no escape from it or chance to cheat this kismet, for we were in the devil's snare just like Abraham Jachin was trapped. In such a plight of great physical suffering, as in hell, some were saying, "If there is really a God the Almighty, then he will rescue us, but if not, then we shall be killed without fail, and die not knowing that God ever existed." This kind of contemplation was haunting us too, but ultimately it came to light that no power on earth could snatch us from the devil's snare, only the loving God himself. Yet if I died with my mother, sister and brother, then at least we would be thankful the fact that we lived much longer than our little sister Zofja, since we had an opportunity to frequent the church and pray to God that he may keep us in the memorial tomb to a resurrection of life.

Incessantly mother was mumbling to herself, "He is not going to come home because he knows Porazit will kill him. But if he is not going to be here, Porazit will kill us. Anyway, we are as good as dead."

At the same time, I remembered how scared I was at Trascianka when Porazit was eager to shoot my father. Only Major Bywalowski had forestalled the killing; otherwise he would be dead. Besides, Father used to serve in the czar's forces and he fought at the Black Sea against the Bolsheviks, and presently he was in the Polish army, which had nothing in common with the Communistic regime; therefore, to Lieutenant Porazit Father appeared to be a prime enemy to his fanatical system. Of course, not to mention Eugenjusz Klimowicz and all the other relatives whom the Soviet partisans despised and detested. So, based on this criterion, it was crystal clear to us that we would not see our father and that Porazit would certainly kill us, but at least with the relief of knowing that Father and Waclawa would remain alive.

On July 17 Waclawa came home alone, without father, for she had to comply with his decision. He instructed her to go back home and say to partisans the following: "I have failed to find my father because he was not where you sent me to reach him. Additionally, I have also failed to find out why he was not there."

On July 18 Lieutenant Porazit and his comrade arrived promptly. They tied their horses in the yard and came into the house. Seeing that our father was not present, they became enraged and extremely incensed. Porazit impertinently shouted to my mother, "Now you have pushed me to the limit!"

Mother started begging him to let Waclawa go again. "Perhaps this time she will find him and I am sure she will bring him home."

After a long altercation I noticed, in the midst of their ungovernable rage, that both Mother and Waclawa were in tears. Porazit concurred to let her go again on the condition that failing to exert influence on Father, "You all will have to die."

At noon I brought our cows from the pasture for milking and walked into the house. Mother with tears in her eyes was frying bacon for the partisans. They both were sitting at the table giggling while drinking vodka. In the face of peril, Waclawa absentmindedly walked out with a bucket to milk the cows. Our baby Krystina and brother Antoni were in bed for their afternoon naps. Having my ears set and eyes open imperceptibly, I distinctly heard a comrade saying to Porazit in a low voice, "This young daughter is beautiful with fine calfs, and yet the mother is something too."

As soon as Waclawa came back with a full bucket of milk, Porazit said to me, "Well now, boy, go give drink to the horses."

The Last Day of Naliboki

Who can measure their strength in our bad circumstances? I thought as I was walking outside to lead the horses to water. Inconsiderately, I untied one of partisans' horses, jumped on its back and drove as usual to the spring at St. John's Crossing. Here, as the horse was drinking this cool, crystal-clear, fresh water from the day's of Noah spring in the presently deserted place, my mind began to wonder. I was thinking and imagining that once Waclawa got to our father, she would never return, nor our father. But at least our plight indicates that they both would remain alive. And of course now it appeared to me that I had a good chance to escape and to survive, except there was nothing I could do to save my mother, sister and brother. I thought, *If only Antoni were somewhere outside playing, I would flee with him*, but he was in bed. I also pondered about the fact that taking such a chance to escape and leaving three members of the family behind would make me a self-centered person. Thinking this way, I had a guilty feeling inside me. But then again, I thought, *What about my father and sister Waclawa? They will be left alive. In that case, why should I submit myself willfully to death, which is equivalent to the intentionally taking of one's life, which is a violation of divine law.* So based on this line of thinking, I made up my mind and was determined to escape from the killer Porazit.

In the process of attending to another horse, I provided them both with fine hay, and then I pulled my own horse from the stable and rode it to the spring. As soon as Maszka had enough to drink, instead of home I made a turn in the direction of the school and was heading to Maczylin. Here from our long strip of land I followed deep into the forest to a glade, where our meadow was abound in rich pasture reserved for hay. At this glade I was alone, and by the lowest possible estimate I felt save from Porazit, an ogre-like man, as one of those Nephilim, designed to strike terror and cause panic among the people in Naliboki. However, being still in a sudden and severe agitation of the mind, also in great sorrow, I endeavored to calm myself down by thinking about the past, when we enjoyed ourselves at this glade during the days of peace and prosperity. I remembered when Father was haymaking here and I was playing with my sister and brother, and we were gathering all sorts of eatable berries and mushrooms. Later in August each year in Maczylin my parents had harvested our crop, and so did the multitude in this splendid neighborhood. The environmental external circumstances were seemingly blessed, since everyone was happy. The land resounded with a voice of magnificent songs, sang in native Byelorussian by young women as mermaids until the vision of the Virgin Mary, when the people poured in here to behold their own day of doom. In consequence, whosoever claimed they saw the Virgin Mary had already died.

In proportion to our regional custom, I entwined the two front feet of my horse with a short piece of rope in order to stop him from wondering away from the meadow, and then I was looked to find a suitable place for myself to pass the night. It was immediately evident that I dare not light a fire or sleep on the ground, for fear that something or someone may sneak upon me at night. To settle this determination, I found a large ramified tree and when it was time to retire I climbed upon it and fastened myself with the reins of the bridle to make sure that I would not fall off wile asleep. Thus, in my considerable trouble, I remained concealed to some extent, being able to see all things around me with confidence that nobody would notice me.

Now that I came to be free from the entanglement of extirpation, I found myself worried stiff about my mother, baby Kristina and brother Antoni, completely understanding the reality that they would be killed and I would never see them again. Being so embraced by such a horrible situation, I could not help but sob. Although at the same time I was thinking, *If only my uncle Jozef Lojko knew about mother's paleness of death, he would be instantly upon Porazit and kill him, and thus his sister would be rescued from the cold-blooded killer.* Undoubtedly, such a task would be imperceptible in comparison to that of the Pozarecze conflict, an encounter that surprised over one hundred Soviet partisans in a shameful defeat by just one man. I was thinking again about my uncle Eugenjusz Klimowicz. *If he knew about it, he would be on top of these two criminals like a ton of bricks.* Knowing his astuteness, how once he encircled Trascianka in an attempt to capture Major Bywalowski's band with Lieutenant Porazit, where only by a slight chance he missed them for ensuing adversity. Deliberating in such a way, my wishful thinking, obviously, was a hopeless idea that only tormented my mind unduly, since really it happened to be beyond the power of any man, for only supernatural intervention could rescue my innocent mother, sister and brother from the current sting of death. As I was upon this large three, I began to pray the way my mother taught me: "Our Father in the heavens, let your name be sanctified." Then I asked him, "Please, God, save them from death," and as I was asking God to bless all the members of our families in the name of our Lord Jesus Christ, I was tired, getting drowsy and sleepy, and at its conclusion I fell sound asleep.

Maczylin's nightmare and the tree of my family uprooted to time indefinite on "The Last Day of Naliboki."

In this cursed, God-forsaken land entrapped by a godless race, as in the ancient days of Nephilim to the legendary drowned wicked cities and subsequently from worship of a goddess of animals to the hunt of the noble warriors until the present time of such an evil propagation, I was dreaming an extraordinary dream in which I saw myriad dead on the surface of the ground before me. Among those dead, I saw rising up and coming to life three men whom I recognized: Szabunia, Nostradamus, and Ivan Klimowicz, my cousin, the son of my father's brother. They were moving toward me in a straight line, side by side. Behind them rising up were also three aristocratic Germans who were murdered here in Maczylin a year before. They too were moving toward me with the intention to hurl me down from the tree. At this point in time in my horrifying nightmare, the tree started to rise and float away from all those dead bodies. At that I felt safe and secure. When I woke up, I thought I was still floating in midair but it was daylight, and as soon as I came to my senses I realized my tree was intact. Then I looked around and steadily climbed down from the tree.

On this morning the second day after Waclawa left, the partisans at our home were waiting for her return. Here in Maczylin, since the surroundings were quiet and Maszka was grazing, I decided to come out from the forest to see what kind of commotion was going on at the highway, if any. Before I reached the skirt of woods on our strip of land, through which the highway ran across slantingly northeastward, I heard people and horses moving into the wilderness. Of course, in the past this road was extremely busy. This way where my grandfather, Franciszek Lojko, and so many other people from the Parish of Naliboki made their pilgrimage on foot to a sacred place in Wilno. They walked many miles as self-sacrifice through Klieciszcze, Rudnia Nalibocka, passing by the hammock "Garb Oszmianski," through Oszmian and directly to Wilno. Here at the skirt of woods I laid low and saw a heavy and rapid movement of Russian partisans, and it seemed that they all were fleeing deep into the wilderness, as in a panic. I laid and waited until this flight on the road stopped, then I came to our neighbor Mr. Kanawal's residence to ask anyone there what had happened, why the Russians were running to the forest from Naliboki. At that, Mr. Kanawal and everybody in his house shouted with laughter, the Germans are in Naliboki! Exultantly I jumped for joy and thanked Mr. Kanawal for his glorious news; so in a hurry I drank some water at their well and I ran as fast as I could to my Maszka. Soon I arrived home, but on my way to Naliboki I saw a lot of German soldiers everywhere.

My mother was very glad to see me all in one piece, and indeed I was thrilled to see them safe, thank God. Of course, as for Waclawa, she was separated from us for good. Later we learned that when she reached father, he told her that the scheme of Lieutenant Porazit and his accomplice had failed on account of the German hindrance, and furthermore that we in Naliboki were safe for the time being, and thus she remained with father permanently.

What a miracle, apparently caused by the direct intervention of a supernatural power. When I prayed to God on that tree, he not only saved us, but also in advance showed me that we would float away from death. Thinking this way, I came to realize that my dream was timely and instantly fulfilled—had it been a day or two later my mother, sister and brother would have been killed.

However, I had no idea at the time that this dream of mine had another implication of greater importance concerning not only the people in Naliboki but the entire population in the Wilderness of Naliboki. Yet, logically speaking, who would ever imagine that in the matter of a fortnight every single family would be uprooted and subsequently planted again somewhere on foreign soil, bringing forth posterity to time indefinite, and that this old settlement would be annihilated and not even one person would be permitted to return to his homeland. Without any doubt, such an eradication of the family tree from the permanent place of birth for our family was salvation, but the Germans considered it as pacification of the wilderness.

In any case, Maczylin's nightmare was an actuality impressed on my mind through experience behind the cemetery in the field of a multitude of dead Russian partisans whose bodies were buried shallowly and came to view after a heavy rain. While I was tending the cattle with Stanislaw Baszuro, we saw wolves dragging arms and legs of those dead into the forest. In the heat of summer two weeks after the Russian and German engagement we found one dead Russian in a potato row by the skirt of woods already in the process of decomposition, for its stench led us to it. A German soldier threw his boots at my feet and demanded I wash them. Being terrified of the dead body and its foul odor I refused. At that, he put his gun to my head and told me, "If you do not pick up these boots now, I will shoot you." So I carried the boots down to the spring, and I had to use my hands as he ordered to pull some skin off and a toe stuck to the leather because of the scorching sun. Then I washed them with gravel and finally with soap to the German's satisfaction.

After this most terrifying experience, I could not eat my food over three days, because no matter how many times I washed my hands I could not stop smelling that dead man. However, on the third day my father told me that the smell of the dead man was in my mind and not on my hands.

The battle of divisions from the territory of Nowogrodek and Wilno persisted from July 7 – 13, 1944, and Wilno was liberated from German occupation. General A. Krzyzanowski ("Wilk"), Colonel T. Cotys ("Slaw") and the commander of A.K. were arrested in Wilno by NKVD on July 17 in the two-story villa with pillars of General Czerniachowski at 16 Kosciuszko Street.

My father participated in the Nowogrodek division, but in the Wilno division my uncle Boleslaw Lojko persevered from September 1939 until the end of World War II. However, in 1944 the Nowogrodek division was attached to Naliboki's unit of Major Eugenjusz Klimowicz. On account of elimination of the Polish leaders in Wilno by the Soviet notorious tactics, those of Katyn forest, near Smolensk, the Polish underground forces commenced advancing toward Warsaw in conformity with "Premier's Plan" in expectation of being combined with the Polish leaders and their armed forces from abroad. This endeavor was the last and foremost sacrifice of human lives to redeem Poland from oppression and restore the Free State of Poland, notwithstanding the fact that Premier Wladyslaw Sikorski met his tragic death in an airplane crash at Gibraltar on July 4, 1943.

Subsequent to this tragedy it was revealed to the public that Winston Churchill had obtained the services of a Czechoslovakian pilot in England to assassinate Premier Wladyslaw Sikorski, the top Polish national figure. The enraged Czech, motivated by fanaticism, assumed a chance to revenge for the Teschen district appropriated by Poland in 1938. Apparently Premier Sikorski with his "plan" to liberate Poland from oppression and or despotism of the USSR and German socialism, was impeding Winston Churchill's strategy established with Joseph Stalin set on closing the invasion of the Europe, which indeed succeeded, but regrettably with an outcome of incessant cold war of the world.

Since there is nothing new under the sun, it is generally understood and recurrently quoted that history repeats itself. Just as it in the case of Marshal Jozef Pilsudski, the same occurred in the circumstance of Premier Sikorski. In both instances, however, the prime factor to terminate their goal was death. It stands to reason that their unique goals designed to achieve worldly peace and security happened to be in direct collision with a god of this system of things. The devil knows he has a short period of time; therefore, having great anger, he walks about like a roaring lion, hunting to devour many by means of his scheming hoax, and so it must proceed under his dominion until the appointed time when the nations will say, "Now, at last, we have peace and security!" Then sudden destruction is to be instantly upon them, just as the pang of distress upon a pregnant woman, and they will by no means escape. The fall of Babylon the Great will be mourned by her companions in fornication, the kings of the earth, and also by the merchants and shippers who dealt with her in supplying luxurious commodities and gorgeous fineries. While these political and commercial representatives survive her desolation, notably no religious representatives are depicted as still on the scene to share in mourning her downfall. Then the "land of Magog" will occur in the "time of end, "the final attack of world powers upon the Kingdom of God, the land of Magog representing "the world as hostile to God's people and kingdom." God's people will stand and see the mighty hand of Jehovah, as in the day of Moses at the Red Sea, when God drowned Pharaoh and his military forces who came in pursuit.

Such a great day of God the Almighty in a minute sense is portrayed by "The Last Day of Naliboki." The people here suffered endless tyranny, persecution, injustice and brutality inflicted by evildoers, until once again Poland was restored and Naliboki experienced zestfully "peace and prosperity;" then came sudden destruction. The church of St. Bartholomew was desecrated, the Pillar of St. John was destroyed and eventually the church was burned to the ground. The priests at first were scattered, and subsequently they were all murdered. All the local stores became obsolete, and proprietors complained because of not being able to maintain an existence. The political elements of Communism and German socialism prevailed to crush the innocent people of Naliboki, but God intervened and rescued them from the final attack of these evil powers and placed them in a new land of freedom to worship the one true God who brought them out of the house of thralldom.

Beginning on July 19, 1943, German military forces penetrated a vast territory even farther beyond the Wilderness of Naliboki. They burned many homes with the families alive. They also burned the entire village known as "Natyn" with all its inhabitants. The abducted a great number of young girls and boys from all localities in the neighborhood to hard labor camps in Germany. They were quickly capturing Russian partisans and transporting them by army trucks to the close railway station, and on to Germany for hard labor in order to win the war. At the same time, they were working progressively on the utter destruction of our identities and all the records in archives located throughout the country in order to conceal the Nazis' war crimes.

The Nazis' atrocious genocide and deeds of holocaust, as well as the millions murdered by the People's Commissariat of Internal Affairs of the Soviet Union, by now had reached its climax, not only in the vicinity of Naliboki but worldwide, because Satan and the wicked spirit forces were misleading the entire inhabited earth. From the heavenly defeat Satan has only a short period of time, during which he makes war with the remaining ones of (the woman's) seed, who observe the commandments of God and have the work of bearing witness to Jesus. In his efforts to devour the remaining ones of the woman's seed, he is called "the dragon," inasmuch as he is a "swallower or crusher." That is why it is written: This is what Jehovah of armies has said. For then there will be great tribulation such as has not occurred since the world's beginning until now, no, nor will occur again. In fact unless those days were cut short, no flesh would be saved, but on account of the chosen ones "the woman's seed" those days will be cut short. (Mt. 24:21,22)

Then, it will be in those days that ten men out of all the languages of the nations will take hold; yes, they will actually take hold of the skirt of a man who is a Jew, saying: We will go with you people, for we have heard that God is with you people. (Zec. 8:23)

On July 31 mother decided to go to Maczylin to examine the fields of growing wheat and rye to see if the grain was fully developed for harvest since this year we had a lot of crop to gather but not enough help at hand. I remember vividly that we had an uninterrupted period of dry weather, when mother came back said, "All our grain in Maczylin is ripe and ready to gather, so tomorrow we shall start to do our best." In that case I gathered all the implements necessary for the job and placed them on the wagon in the yard, ready to go next day.

On August 1, 1943, at daybreak while we were still asleep, a Polish-speaking German soldier knocked at our door, and when mother opened it, he told her, "All householders must appear at the square in town, at once."

At that very moment, mother, in a hurry, grabbed hold of her tucker and run out. Within ten minutes she leapt over to the house hysterically and uttered in a screaming voice, "We must pack and be gone in one hour, or the Germans will shoot us!"

Naturally, in extreme panic mother did not know what to grasp, as she was utterly disoriented and terrified. What a horrifying, unforgettable flash it was. Mother got hold of her sewing machine and put it on the wagon, thinking that it was her livelihood, and as she was grabbing other things, she was worried about the bread, since we had exhausted our supply. In such sudden, unexpected, overpowering dread, when one's very soul faints out of fear, I just ran outside, took an axe, jumped in a pen and hit the swine once between its ears, killing it. I tied its back feet and used the horse to drag some 300 pounds of pig onto the wagon with help of a sliding board. At the same time I was interrupted by our neighbor, Mania Baszuro, who saw me doing this and asked me to kill her pig also, since they were not in a habit of slaughtering animals. Not to waste any time of this one hour of life and death, I jumped over the fence with my axe and did the same in their pen. Of course, then I quickly harnessed our horse, Maszka, and mother, Krystina and Antoni drove away from our residence southward to Stolpce, but I chased the cattle behind because the Germans told us that we would need them.

Before we reached Derewno, looking back we saw an immense fire and black smoke extending up to the heavens as the Germans set on fire everything from sheaf to standing grain, the orchards and the buildings. It seemed just like an end of the world for us. By the time we were passing through Jankowicze under German escort, the local people there were telling us, "The Germans seized us the same as Jews, and we will all be killed just like them." And then they said, "That is why you do not need to carry your luggage."

Unfortunately for the people of Jankowicze, they did not know that the same fate was in store for them. However, we had seen a lot of people dropping their suitcases, trunks, and so on and so forth, but

The last day of Naliboki on August 1, 1943.

my mother was thinking only of today, and therefore she suggested to me, "When the Germans withdraw, try then, Mietek, to separate our young bull from the herd and lead him to some farm in exchange for bread."

After we passed the night at a halfway point on our to journey to Stolpce in some valley through which a stream flowed from the south northward with an eastern post-Deluge neverending hummock similar to "Garb Oszmianski," the following day our convoy was stretched out and the German escort withdrew for a while. Then, in most tiring way, I somehow succeeded at keeping this young bull from the herd and chasing him to a farm, and there I locked the gate on him. The folks there looked at me, but I said to them, "You can have this bull for a few loafs of bread because we have none since we were seized in an awkward time."

They called me inside the house, gave me breakfast—hot mashed potatoes with sourmilk—and offered me the last half a loaf of bread they had, unfortunately, for they also ran out of it. It must have been 11 a.m. I took the bread, thanked them for their kindness and began running along the course of the convoy to overtake our wagon. After an hour, winded, I told mother, "We are just having bad luck concerning bread, because you see, Mom, that is all they had, only this piece of bread."

Since the previous day Mother was still working on the pig, cutting it up, separating meat from bacon, salting and sewing it up in linen for the preservation and easy handling. Before the sun set on the following day, August 2, we arrived in Stolpce. The German so-called "super race" piled us up at the railway tracks and ordered everybody to submit their cattle by placing them immediately in a compound, and also all horses and wagons were to be surrendered in another compound so that all people's livestock was confiscated for German public use.

As we left with our neighbor Baszuro, we persisted being together throughout the journey. Mania Baszuro told my mother that since our cows were accustomed grazing as one herd with theirs, she would take ours as well to the German trap. Of course, Mother was glad because she was with the baby, Krystina, but I, after unloading the wagon, drove to submit our horse, Maszka. Being as a matter of fact scared for the first time in such a city, about which I had heard so much and was overwhelmed with wonder, but now in wartime it was overridden by the German army. I was riding through a street crowded with German soldiers when some boy my age unexpectedly packed in on my wagon and told me to give the reins to him. He said, "I will drive to my home, because the Germans will kill your horse for meat anyway."

Being scared of so many Germans, I replied, "I am sorry. I cannot do this because too many soldiers are here. If they detect, they will kill me."

Then the boy led me into another street where there were no soldiers and he said, "See, no Germans."

At that moment I descended from the wagon and traced my way back to my mother, as they all were sitting on the baggage.

Mania came and said, "It was heartbreaking to see so many cows piled up in one place with nothing to eat or drink. The animals were making deep mournful sounds and they were licking the surface of the ground. The scene was horrible."

As she was speaking of the loss of all the cattle, her husband Witold forfeited the horse and wagon. I told mother softly that I did not surrender Maszka to the Germans like Witold, but that I passed our horse on to some local Polish boy. Soon, however, this boy came with his father into our crowd and found me. I told him, "This is my mother."

His father approached and spoke with my mother. He asked her if she needed anything. When she explained to him about our bread deficiency, he sent his son at once home, and in no time he brought for us a several loafs of bread. Then his father said he would keep our horse safe for us until we returned. Unfortunately, we had no idea that we were destined for Germany on a goods trains, which was only apparent the following day. Yet, one thing for certain, we knew that we had to pass another night beneath the expanse of the heavens in care of tutelary genius, the only one true God who guides us throughout life.

The German army had no power to show mercy or compassion over the unfortunate ones in Naliboki. Those who were unable to move due to sickness or because of old age were killed instantly in the style of execution, and many people were burned alive at their homes just because they procrastinated their abandonment. They destroyed the entire town by fire and all the fields of grain. The church of St. Bartholomew and the entire parsonage were burned to the ground, whereas only the brick wall structure of the unfinished church was left standing because the fire could not consume it. The Germans murdered Prelate Jozef Bajko, Priest Baradyn, Priest Dadis and the priest of the army.

Hence, the last day of Naliboki, embraced by the perimeter of Tartarus, annihilated a much more extensive area in its circumference set in the ancient fork of Satan between two great rivers, Niemen and Wilia. And these environs are as follows: Chotow, Cielechowszczyzna, Jankowicze, Kleciszcze, Kosliki, Niescierowicze, Ogrodniki, Prudy and Rudnia, and so this entire neighborhood remains in extinction.

Prelate Jozef Bajko (pictured), Priest Baradyn, Priest Dadis and the priest of the army were murdered by the German army on August 1, 1943.

However, other environs sustained loss but not entirely, such as: Szczorcy, Lipniki, Derewno, Sioboda, Bakszty, Rakow, Kamieh, Rubiezewicze and Pieszczyce.

Within the perimeter of Tartarus was actually "Golgotha," or "Skull Place," also called "Calvary" from the Latin Calvaria ("a bare skull"). In this skull-like place before the end, twenty-two German SS had been ambushed and killed on the eastern side of the cemetery and also over five hundred Jews had been systematically exterminated by the German SS. Over two thousand Soviet partisans and two Germans had been killed in combat on the cemetery and the western side of it. Some ten Soviet partisans flogged to death by German SS, and forty-four Nalibokians were executed on the ground of Majatek next to the cemetery. In the borough Baszuro was killed by a German, and Kozuszko and a Russian were hung by Chief Sawinola. Behind the cemetery in Pozarecze more than one hundred Soviet partisans had been killed in their assault on a single house by one man, Jozef Lojko. In defeat of Naliboki, over one hundred Soviet partisans had been killed on the bridge by the cemetery by Jan Radziwill. More than two hundred Soviets ere killed north of the cemetery in Kamionka by Mr. Hodyl and his two sons, and more than five hundred Nalibokians had been massacred by the Soviet partisans.

Not to mention the thousands of people seized to Siberia, or those who were tortured to death by NKVD, and many people were burned alive by the Soviet partisans and Germans as well. Before the first homicide had occurred in Naliboki, the old man from Terebejno had foretold the last day of Naliboki at the start of August 1937, saying, "A state of great distress will persist until the final end comes within the devil's number." Thus August 1, 1943 marked six years. In the first year, six months passed to the vision in school, and again six months passed to another vision in Maczylin in August 1938. As he said, "Naliboki shall become a capital place of corpses (GOLGOTHA), and all these things which must come to pass shall be executed in the range of the devil's number, which comes into view the number 666."

Yet many survivors thought thus far that it was a mysterious occurrence containing something unknown because it had not been fully revealed. Nonetheless, it was not beyond the power of perception—just because we cannot behold an evil spirit, it would be not wise to ignore its existence; on the contrary, we have felt its effect, which has manifested its own presence by performance of such an incredible series of events, which had been foretold and took place on or around the cemetery over a period of six years. At this ancient cemetery throughout generations the people were terrified by gleamy pillars rising up from under the ground and setting themselves in motion to the four cardinal points. But in our terminal generation, at the same cemetery people were fainting out of fear to bear witness to such a great killing of human beings. Why, one may ask, did the great slaughter have to take place particularly at this prehistoric cemetery and nowhere else? Or, who is accountable for such a massacre and holocaust? Of course, none other than Satan the devil with his tripod.

Indeed, what an amazing, thunderstruck prophesy was told in Naliboki by the 105-year-old Jazeb Byczkiewicz from Terebejno, whose name was even concealed from cognition of people who respected his age and, of course, his demonstrative power of dedication to the Roman Catholic Church. One may wonder, therefore, who can really foretell events in such a minute detail, unless one is assured beyond question that Jazeb Byczkiewicz was inspired by God.

Since Jazeb Byczkiewicz was in fact inspired by God, it is most essential to establish by which God he was moved to this particular idea. His introductory concept of the prophesy was based on the appearance of two signs, which occurred sequentially six months apart. The first vision of Virgin Mary appeared in the third class at school, and the second vision of Virgin Mary turned up in Maczylin, but those who claimed they had a good sight of it perished within fulfillment of his prophesy, so that such a vision to them was not a blessing or protection but rather curse or damnation. Besides, when God moved his servants to tell the people of coming destruction, he also provided a remedy of escape from disaster at every occasion of God's prophesy. Over a period of a hundred years Noah expounded upon the Deluge to all the people, even demonstrated to them how they ought to build an ark. Again, when Jesus foretold of the coming destruction of Jerusalem, he also told his followers, "When you catch sight of the disgusting thing that causes desolation, as spoken of through Daniel the prophet, standing in a holy place, then let those in Judaa begin fleeing into the mountains." However, there was no remedy of escape provided in Byczkiewicz's prophesy, nor was it granted by the Holy Virgin Mary, and since this divine inspiration of the events was merciless, barbarous, and inhuman, it did not originate from the true God.

I was present at those two occasions, and in Maczylin even with my family, and it was lucky for us that we did not see the Virgin Mary. Yet, if our Heavenly Father did not intervene, we would certainly not have survived, including the great number of all other families, on account of the fact that sooner or later the Soviets aimed to exterminate all the people in Naliboki to the extent that nothing would be left to extricate or to uproot the family tree from this ancient city of fallen angels.

In the fork of river Niemen and Wilia, the land that resembles Mesopotamia between the Tigris and Euphrates Rivers, here a multitude was possessed by the demons. The people were known to be manifesting various supernatural powers. Some controlled by evil spirits possessed the power of healing the sick. Others were a fortune tellers who were in this land, mainly the Gypsies who used to call upon every home persistently. Again, many were mentally deranged; some of course were walking about freely, like Arszula from Terebejno, but others, being serious and austere in disposition, were locked up at Naliboki's police station temporarily, or timeless in an asylum elsewhere, like the Jewish woman in Lubcz.

This Jewish woman, possessed by a legion of demons, with superhuman power crossed the wilderness in the nude with an invisible force that repelled predatory animal life, and passed through haunted Kroman, pronouncing a message, "Ere Mene Na Robilo," that no one could discern. In Kroman she ran over many graves of Russian soldiers killed during World War I, showing an apparent tendency that similar killing was about to happen in the near future.

As a consequence of this phenomenon, Naliboki disappeared in one day, and soon after, in mid-August, 1943, "Okon" at Kroman defeated the German army, and thus all demons were expelled from dead bodies and descended to their original condition at the bottom of the haunted Lake Kroman.

In a like manner, one cannot underestimate the power of demons exercised in the vicinity of Maczylin. Here, Mr. Kanawal's sister possessed the power to heal the sick. Jazeb Byczkiewicz possessed the power to prophesy. The Virgin Mary in tears appeared in Maczylin and was perceived by many. As a consequence of such phenomena, Szabunia, being a devil's instrument, desecrated the church, demolished St. John's Pillar, and many people were tortured to death; plus, thousands were seized to Siberia. Jazeb Byczkiewicz disappeared without a trace. Szabunia mysteriously expired. Mr. Kanawal's sons met tragic deaths in Maczylin, and on the very spot of the manifestation of the vision, the three German monsters possessed by triad devils Labartu, Labasu and Akhkhazu were tortured to death. It is therefore no doubt that the evil spirits terminated possessed dead bodies and lowered themselves to the original condition Tartarus, to pits of dense darkness to be reserved for judgment of the great day.

The correlative phenomenon bechanced at lastingly haunted Kamionka, Pazarecze and, of course, the central cemetery plot of the Parish of Naliboki. Here at the cemetery, in the progress of a relentless bloody battle, a German breaks into Uncle Michal Lojko's house, naturally armed, aims, ready to shoot, and says, "You have been shooting at us!"

This scares Michal Lojko to death, literally, a man who claimed to be fearless and correspondingly disciplined his children not to fear gleamy pillars or any ghosts at this cemetery they lived by. How ironic that his brother Jozef Lojko was trapped in the single house, surrounded by 150 Soviet partisans, and alone fought his way out, but subsequently was not in any way affected by shock and finally death. Also comparable to Jozef Lojko was Benedikt Klimowicz, whose death did not disturb him playing his favorite last piece of music "Bokalis," nor did the shock of dying paralyze his fingers. What really shocked Michal Lojko to death was not a German with the gun, but another entity in his figure that my uncle never expected to behold, and that was indubitably the devil with his tripod.

This unfortunate ordeal of Naliboki being destroyed by fire is worthy of comparison to my father's episode, which narrates about a student who had a ride given by a Byelorussian peasant in the direction to his destination, at which time this boor educated him concerning three essential factors, namely "Czystadom," "Krasido," and "Wysado," which depicted a cat, a burning element, and an elevated place. However, in Naliboki's disaster Czystadom coincides with the devil, Krasido complies with his burning affliction, and lastly Wysado matches an elevated Naliboki based on Tartarus. Considering the fact that the household of a peasant is the victims who perished in Naliboki, and indeed the predicament of the student represents all those who survived this dreadful ordeal.

Long ago in the beginning, the devil with his godless race, Nephilim, known same as "Gibborim," the mighty ones who were men of note in days of old, came and took up new lodgings in the land of Nowogrodek, "Nowogrodczyzna," by the River Niemen, into which falls larger affluents, Szczara, Berezyna, Gawja, Dzitwa, Serwecz, and Usza. In this amazingly prolific land those hybrid giants had their fixed abode with the true God and his patience after 120 years. Subsequently 131 years passed, until 2239 B.C.E., the building of the tower of Babel, one of the first cities to be built after the Flood. The Supreme Being had scattered the population from there over all the surface of the earth. Those people dedicated to false, man-made religion came to this prolific land to build new cities and to worship the triad of the devils. Those inspired by the evil spirits polluted the land with moral defilement until the day of their extinction, when the cities became legendary haunted lakes, which throughout the ages diversified the landscape of Nowogrodek with the lakes Switez, Koidyczewskie, Kroman, and of course a great number of smaller lakes. After a swift devastation of drowned cities, the disturbed demons enticed a new adherent people from the plain of Babylonia, who came here after the city's fall to the Meds and Persians, the Fourth World Power in 539 B.C.E. These heathenish idol-worshipers raised pagan temples in Nowogrodek, Naliboki, and in other regional places. Undoubtedly, Naliboki acquired its prominence due to the Wilderness of Naliboki since the temple was dedicated to a goddess of animals.

When the sense of human life was embodied in a tragic drama, Jerusalem and its temple were destroyed by the Romans in 70 A.D.. The Jewish fate disseminated them throughout the world, and then many of them settled in the land of Wilenszczyzna and Nowogrodczyzna in the midst of a population of heathens. Satan became extremely vivacious, and in his ignoble manner enticed Christianity to corruption. The conception of Poland came about by means of a pagan, Mieszko (Miecislas I), 960 A.D., which was the reason the nation became Roman Catholic. From 1390 A.D. the Spanish Inquisition for the ultimate purpose of enforcing orthodoxy killed indiscriminately in great numbers Jews in ghettos, which finally were abolished in 1820 A.D. The Spanish Inquisition compelled the Jews to flee from death, and thus more Jews came to live in the land of Nowogrodek and Wilno. In the meantime, a royal hunt for the human life of noble warriors in the Wilderness of Naliboki laid a curse on Naliboki. Here then, magnificent swords were manufactured, by which the blood of many was spilled. An endurance of cruelty and ruthlessness bent people to repentance and to undertake a strict zeal in the performance of religious duties. They were noted to be humble, meek, and lowly in heart, always with a form of greeting, "Praised be Jesus Christ!" And with closing words of salutation, "For the ages of ages, Amen."

After short lasting peace and prosperity in Naliboki, enraged Satan with his demons seized many God-fearing people to a godless land, in Siberia, and began the savage, indiscriminate killing of human beings as an act of persecution and revenge. Consequently the entire Jewish national group in this triangle of Minsk, Nowogrodek, and Wilno was systematically exterminated by the German SS. In this monstrous, strikingly wrong way, Naliboki near Nowogrodek was made to be Skull Place, that is to say, Golgotha.

In the nick of time, God the Almighty intervened within the confines of this wicked land, prolixly infested by demons, on behalf of the innocent and removed the rest of the people perpetually by placing them in a free western part of the world where they all would have opportunities to hear "the chosen ones" preach, whom God has sent forth. An opportunity to hear the angel cry out with a strong voice, saying:

She has fallen! Babylon the great has fallen, the world empire of false religion, and she has become a dwelling place of demons and a lurking place of every unclean exhalation, and a lurking place of every unclean and hated bird! And to hear another voice out heaven say: Get out of her my people, if you do not want to share with her in her sins, and if you do not want to receive part of her plagues. (Rev. 18:2, 4)

We, the ones left behind after annihilation and extirpation in Naliboki under German occupation, still prolong to live in the last days under critical times, hard to deal with, that are here. Also, we are living during Jesus's presence in Kingdom power, and therefore in God's borrowing time before the end of this system of things, since the "Appointed Times of the Nations" have ended. The fulfillment of Jesus's prophesy accommodates the whole human species with global wars, food shortages, earthquakes and pestilences. During such a time as this, his disciples will be hated and killed. False prophets will arise and mislead many. Lawlessness will increase and the love of the great number will cool off. At the same time, the good news of God's Kingdom will be preached as a witness to all the nations.

Admonishing those disciples who would be alive during the momentous last days, Jesus says: Pay attention to yourselves that your hearts never become weighed down with overeating and heavy drinking and anxieties of life, and suddenly that day be instantly upon you as a snare. For it will come in upon all those dwelling upon the face of all the earth. Keep awake then, all the time making supplication that you may succeed in escaping all these things that are destined to occur, and in standing before the Son of man. (Lu. 21:34, 36)

Chapter X

THE ULTIMATE DESTINY

On the day Hitler invaded the USSR, Prime Minister Winston Churchill promised Britain's full support to Stalin and the Soviet people. Subsequently at the last meeting in Moscow, Churchill shook hands with Stalin and positively declared, "The next time we shall be shaking hands, it will be in Berlin." Thus, after a secret arrangement was made as to how to invade and divide Europe, Stalin and Churchill knew that the Polish struggle for independence, the Free State of Poland, would end in vain. This, of course, was the initial will of Satan.

Under the circumstances, God the Almighty intervened and punctually removed all the people westward, entirely away from the Soviet Union and its godless race. Because these people were ensnared by the forces of darkness too long, God closed that ancient wicked land, secured it with an authoritative seal, and made it impossible for anyone who was born and lived there to return. Miraculously, also all the victims subjected to suffering and death in Siberia were set free. It became clear to the victims that without a miracle no one would remain to know whether God cares or not. That is why, before destroying this wicked system, God allowed the opportunity for people to demonstrate whether they really wanted to live in harmony with his righteous laws or not. At his appointed time, he will without fail destroy the wicked.

During our last day in Naliboki was indeed the most terrifying anticipation of evil and great danger. Yet, insight into my very soul caused me to be fearless and somewhat glad, knowing that my father and sister Waclawa would have a chance to live and that four of us at least got away from the two Russian killers. Except the fact that we did not know what the future held for any of us, since we had no idea what the Germans were going to do with us because it seemed like we had been taken by them in the exact threatening and severe manner as the Jews. After passing the night in Stolpce at the railway, the following day, August 3, the German soldiers began to load us like cattle into a goods train. Involuntarily from the start, however, we stuck with our neighbors, the Baszuro family, and with them were their relatives—another Baszuro, Grygorcewicz and Dubicki family—and in this way we all filled up one train's wagon. As soon as the train was fully packed with people, it proceeded westward until we arrived to Bialystok. In this city we were ordered to leave the train, and the German soldiers quickly placed us in some large building. Inside they set males and females into separate groups and demanded of us to divest of clothes. Then they moved us into a shower room, at which time many thought that we all had reached the final destination, because here we all supposedly would be subjected to death by gas, as we had heard the Germans gassed the Jews. But surprisingly enough, instead of gas we actually received a bath, and after the Germans fumigated us and ordered us to dress, they eventually led us back to the same goods train, which had a scheduled route to Germany.

We passed through Warsaw, and then, for the last time in our country, the train stopped in Poznan. In this city the Germans provided us with boiled, unpeeled potatoes and they gave one liter of vodka per wagon. Yet, we still felt the Germans most likely aimed to destroy us, and because of such fear and uncertainty, while the train was delayed for some reason the mothers let their children be scattered into different directions in Poznan. In our wagon Witold Baszuro's sister let her son go, and he was her only child, seven years old.

On August 5 our train reached its final destination in Germany. Here the people from the train were loaded onto trucks and each wagon of people was dispersed throughout Germany. Our group landed in Ludenscheid, Westfalen, and was subjected to hard labor camp, in the production of ammunition at the "Paulmann und Krone" factory. Now, as we all had been stripped of our possessions, our land, and the country, we felt as if we were flayed alive in a manner of St. Bartholomew, Naliboki's patron, and in Germany on August 24 we celebrated his feast day, but thank God, not crucified as he was in Armenia. A few perished in the concentration camps. Some were killed during an air raid and others died from starvation. The lives of the majority, however, had been spared, perhaps, some were saying, for God's own purpose.

Over many years I did ponder and was inquisitive as to why the church contained a "votive offering" that was Gk. anathema, and why this church in Naliboki was suitably dedicated to the martyr St. Bartholomew, and above all why, since four generations had passed, a startling calamity embraced all the people in the Parish of Naliboki? Then one day I stumbled upon the written Word that says: God merciful and gracious, slow to anger and abundant in loving-kindness and truth, preserving loving-kindness for thousands, pardoning error and transgression and sin, but by no means will he give exemption from punishment, bringing punishment for the error of fathers upon sons and upon grandsons, upon the third generation and upon the fourth generation. (Ex 34:6, 7)

In Germany we were confined to hard labor camps, constrained unnaturally in the production of ammunition and subjected to inhumane starvation. Under these conditions by attendant circumstances, we supplied the German armed forces with bullets to slaughter our own people in the country as well as abroad. Although under duress, consequently we aided the Germans in killing fifteen thousand of our compatriots at Monte-Casino, thousands in Tobruk and many thousands in Poland and its capital's insurrection in 1944. It was unthinkable even to imagine that my own hands produced by fabrication bullets that penetrated the hearts of my fellow citizens. How awful and wicked it must have been for Naliboki willfully to manufacture expensive swords that pierced the hearts of the nation, inasmuch as it was no different from those legendary drowned cities when the beating hearts were sacrificed to the triad of devils, namely Labartu, Labasu and Akhkhazu.

A poor was the Polish soldier who became destined to defend and protect in vain the Free State of Poland in the midst of global forces of darkness, an indigent indeed, was my uncle, Eugenjusz Klimowicz, who desired to be a doctor like his father but instead was drafted for service in the armed forces. In war he escaped his destiny from the Katin massacre, and since had struggled against the odds of two enemies, sometimes successfully and sometimes unsuccessfully. Several times he was wounded and taken captive and again escaped his death. Subsequently with his unit he joined A.K. Then, in the rank of major, in spite of the premier being removed out of existence, A.K. advanced to Warsaw as planned with the expectation that the Polish armed forces from abroad would facilitate for the organized resistance to establish a government. Consequently, when the German front drew near Warsaw, the Polish insurrection commenced, and at that point in time the USSR front withdrew in order to make it possible for the Germans to squash an open revolt against the oppressor, and at the same time the Polish armed forces abroad did not stir a finger. After the Germans annihilated our capital city, the Soviet army pursued the Germans up to Berlin; thus Poland, together with all the contiguous countries, was absorbed by the godless regime, the king of the north. That is why it is written in the prophecy concerning two kings closing a deal: And as regards these two kings, their heart will be inclined to doing what is bad, and at one table a lie is what they will keep speaking. But nothing will succeed, because the end is yet for the time appointed. (Da. 11:27)

Eventually, on August 1, Naliboki was destroyed similarly to ancient Babylon, ultimately at the time of displacement of all the people from the region. Some, however, were left behind, and in particular those who lived in remote dispersed places. For example, among those left behind was Jozef Lojko's wife and five children. Albeit a small group of people, nonetheless it was trapped indefinitely in the land that presently appeared to be the Soviet Union.

Unluckily the uprising from July to October led by Lieutenant General Tadeusz Komarowski in opposition to control of Poland by the USSR ended tragically. The successor of Premier Sikorski, Stanislaw Mikolajczyk, resigned on November 7, 1944. At the Yalta Crimea Conference of the "Big Three," the United States, Great Britain and the Soviet Union, February 4 – 11, 1945, it was agreed that the "Curzon Line" should be the eastern boundary of Poland, and thus our homeland became the land of the Soviet Union. On May 5, two days before the surrender of Germany and the end of the war in Europe, sixteen Polish underground leaders were arrested. Finally, on June 23, the Communist government established at Lublin assimilated Poland—Boleslaw Bierut was president and Edward Csubka-Morowski prime minister. It was recognized by Great Britain and the United States on July 5 and 6, 1945, and admitted to the United Nations. The occupation of former German territory to the Oder River, including Szczecin, as a provisional line was permitted. The devastation of war and human losses had left Poland in a state of collapse. Migrations from Russia to Poland and from Poland to Germany involved about one fifth of the total population. Assistance from U.N.R.R.A. virtually saved Poland from starvation and death.

The domination of the Soviet Union in Poland caused the eradication of the most prestigious literature that conferred glory in domain of the Free State of Poland, and in harmony with Communism the royal crown from the white eagle was removed; thus the mark of sovereign power throughout eight centuries was dishonored.

After a tragic end in Warsaw, the surviving patriots scattered throughout the country and disguised themselves to be unrecognizable before the brainwashed national Communists. All Nalibokians were persuaded to take such a course of action since their lives were at stake. Our kinsmen, Eugenjusz Klimowicz, Jozef Lojko, Boleslaw Lojko, Alfons K. Lojko and my father, Wilhelm Klimowicz, dispersed in the newly received country that started at the Curzon Line on the eastern boundary and finished at the Oder River of the former German territory. Here in such a predicament as they actually were including the great number of others found a temporary refuge until many of them were exposed, they stood trial and were imprisoned. Eugenjusz Klimowicz acquired his sojourn in Slupsk, Boleslaw Lojko in Szczecin, and father and Alfons Lojko settled down near Jelenia Gora, but Jozef Lojko came to live in Czestochowa. Eugenjusz Klimowicz was promptly discovered by the Communists, was arrested and tried, and the judgment formally was pronounced imposing the punishment to be inflicted as death. Jozef Lojko was also found, arrested and sentenced to life imprisonment. Boleslaw Lojko remained unfound; he completed his law course and was employed as a prosecuting attorney. My father remained unfound and was employed on the railway.

However, in spite of some infrequent exceptions, all the members of A.K. were subjected to persecution and deprivation from employment to time indefinite, that is if they happened to be known as such by the Communistic regime. Surviving a cruel war for the rest of their natural lives, virtually they withered as a plant when trampled down or deprived of moisture, because there was no place for them in this kind of country for which they so vigorously and bravely fought.

So, whether man strives for freedom and peace or prominence and power, it really is vanity. Solomon in his God-given wisdom called it "striving after the wind."

If this life is all there is, there is nothing important. This life is like a candle burning that soon burns out and is no more. It is a fleeting shadow, a fading flower, a blade of grass to be cut and soon withered ... We are so soon gone we might as well have never come, one of billions to come and go, with so few ever knowing that we were here in existence. This view is not cynical or sedate or morose or unwholesome. It is truth, a fact to face, a practical view, if this life is all there is.

One main purpose that Solomon repeatedly raised was that servants of the true God should find joy in their activities before him. "I have come to know that there is nothing better for them than to rejoice and to do good during one's life, and also that every man should eat and indeed drink and see good for all his hard work. It is the gift of God." (Ecclesiastes 3:12)

In contrast with the situation in Poland, Germany for the liberated Nalibokian victims was incomparable with the Soviet Union camouflaged paradise. Here, suddenly after almost two years of inhumane deadly force, starvation, hard labor and daily bombardment, everyone felt like a drowned man who was rescued from his dying condition. New houses were given to all the persecuted victims, those of the German people. Surely, everyone was grateful for the "One" who cut short these days; otherwise no flesh would be saved. And as a result we are also free at last, but not at liberty to go back to our homeland in any possible or conceivable way.

Now being classified as displaced persons in D.P. camps in Germany under the provisions of United Nations Relief and the Sehabilitation Administration, we were hopeful, but in vain, that soon the western world power would disarm the Soviet Union and abolish its Communism; then we would be able to return home to the free country. Of course, following such a notion we had been listening to the radio broadcasts in Polish from New York and London (Tu Mowi Londyn), which undoubtedly encouraged us to wait on account of confidence in the great General Joseph Raymond McCarthy, whose supporters praised him for a patriotic effort to expose Communist subversion.

Soviet diplomats came to D.P. camps with their propaganda to persuade the Polish nation to go home where the land (they declared) was flowing with milk and honey, where the children would obtain a free of the highest standard education, and where there would be no fear of unemployment for their parents. Naturally, some people from the western part of Poland without hesitation and based on no experience or actual participation within the Communist regime went blindfoldedly home, but we from behind the Curzon Line, a bearing west of Lvov, declined to go back.

When the question of the reconstitution of Poland arose at the Teheran Conference in 1943, the Curzon Line was accepted as the basis for discussion, although Roosevelt and Eden strongly urged the Line B version, which would keep Lvov in Polish hands. Churchill, despite the bitter objections of the London Polish government-in-exile, reluctantly yielded to Stalin's position, and all parties to the Yalta agreement in 1945 officially concurred that the Curzon Line should become Poland's eastern border.

Under such conditions of a most incredible political outcome, Naliboki's people were barred from going home and thus were ultimately destined to seek new dwelling places elsewhere in the western part of the world, in non-Communist countries. On this account, not only we the people from the Wilderness of Naliboki, but all the others from behind the Curzon Line—that is to say, from Lvov to Bialystok Polish majority on the west including Lithuanian, Byelorussian, and Ukrainian majority on the east—refused to go back to their country, and hence all became refugees.

During the first days in May 1945, after a several days of U.S. military cannon fire over our heads, the German soldiers stationed next to our labor camp fled toward the east away from the American invasion. Seeing the fact that the German army had long gone, I got to their "Kaserne" looking for some food, and there I found a storeroom packed with all sorts of provisions. Immediately I grabbed a sack of flour and carried it out through the window facing the camp. At that moment, when the starved people saw me with a sack on my back, they all moved impetuously there to get anything they could lay their hands on. In the meantime, the cannon firing ceased and some Germans came back and saw our people stealing their food. Lucky for me, since I was quite a distance from the Kaserne, I jumped the fence and soon was in the woods upon a hill when I saw the Germans coming back. They at once rounded up all men in the camp ready for execution, but the German neighbors came and pleaded with the officers to spare these people, "for by killing them, you will kill us also," they deplored. "You see, soon American soldiers will be here, and when they see these Polish people dead, they surely kill us too out of revenge. Please, be considerate," they begged.

As I watched this dramatic scene from the hill, I saw the Germans move out in the direction of Llidenscheid without killing anybody. Then I came back to the camp and my mother began to cook some pancakes, which we were eating with mother's admonition. Because of our debilitated state of health, a sudden overindulgence of eating could be oftentimes be fatal, which mother knew from her experience during a starvation period in World War I.

Momentarily an American reconnaissance in heavily armored combat vehicles passed through to town; they moved fast on a rubber wheels, and after a short while they drove hack. Then immediately U.S. soldiers walked into our camp speaking Polish and telling us, "Now you have been set free from the German bondage and confinement."

Freedom at last, after six blood-thirsty, evil years of war. What a relief and joy! Like the poets used to say: How much such a freedom as this can be valued, only the one will ever know who has lost it.

Within the first year in the hard labor camp, my great uncle Jozef Wolan, the clockmaker, was able to furnish me with pocket and wrist watches that were useless before he had them restored to a sound condition. So, in order to find suitable customers, I had first to disguise myself as a "Deutsche junger," a German youth, and sneak out from the camp to town, Ludenscheid, and there I had a chance to meet some so called "Volks-deutscher," ethnic Germans of Polish descent. These people from the Polish-German border were voluntarily employed here under full benefits of the German National Socialism provisions, and additionally they had been receiving parcels from Poland. I traded with them my watches in exchange for bread and butter coupons and tobacco leaves, which usually were rolled up in a cylindrical form at a weight of five grams each. In this black-market business I accumulated a considerable sum of money, which I spent only in the bakery and in transactions with these customers of mine. (The Deutsche Mark were useless in the possession of a foreigner, Auslander.) My supply of tobacco leaves in the camp was highly appreciated, which I was selling for twenty-five marks a roll at to our own people, and afterwards the proceeds I shared with my great uncle. So, in order to survive under the German National Socialism inhumane conditions, I had to use my wits and adopt the tactics of Jozef Kosciukiewicz, who was married to my father's first cousin, Gabryjela Klimowicz, since he was the only one in Naliboki who had fooled the Russian Communists within the time of his disastrous fate that saved his life.

In the state of being disguised as a German youth, I illegally unsewed the blue patch with a yellow letter P, which was imperative for nobody to recognize that I was a Pole. Despite everything, I was in grave danger by undertaking such a risk; nonetheless, I was quite successful and helpful to our people until the year 1944. During this year the German national economy rapidly deteriorated to the point that when I managed to obtain German coupons, it was impossible to buy bread or butter in the stores or bakeries since they all were empty. Consequently, I acquired a great deal of money, but it became just worthless paper, for there was no food from any source obtainable. Hence, it began to be a time period when we suffered from severe hunger that became preposterous to endure. During this starvation period my beloved great uncle, the brother of my grandmother Elizabet, was taken ill, and soon after he passed away.

The day we arrived to Ludenscheid, the Germans located us in a small old barrack. The men were separated from their families and placed in another camp with the Russian men. At the age of fourteen, classified as a minor, I was left with my mother, sister and brother. Most women dived eagerly to work in the kitchen that provided food for all of the foreigners employed in the factory, but my mother and I, as well as the other boys my age, toiled at the same establishment, "Paulmann und Krone," for the manufacturing of ammunition twelve hours per day, six days in a week. Since we came from the east of Poland, the Germans considered us as Russians and gave us an OST to wear, a mark of distinction like all the people from the Soviet Union. When our group of people acknowledged the fact that we were all Roman Catholics and of Polish nationality, the German authority refused to recognize, and therefore ignored this vehement dispute.

Sunday was our day of rest, and on this day men were allowed to come and stay with the family. Here our camp, as all others in Germany, was under control of the "Lagerfuhrer" camp leader. In the beginning our first Lagerfuhrer was an old man of mild temper, and he was in charge over us just a few months before another came who was of a brutal disposition. As time went by it manifested itself. When some women quarrelled at the stove in the morning to feed the children as to whom was supposed to be the first using it, he came with a whip and flogged them.

When Baszuro and his brother-in-law, Grygorcewicz, complained on account of jealousy against Teresa Baszuro, Witold's sister, that she had been so lucky to stay in the barracks doing nothing instead of working in the factory, they began to pass remarks saying, "She is extremely beautiful, without a husband, who probably was killed by the Soviets. She abandoned her only child in Poznah. Now being single, she is free to have a love affair," which also implicated the Lagerfuhrer. Of course, unknown at the time was that her husband, a policeman in Stolpce, escaped through Hungary and was in the Polish forces abroad fighting the Germans. He eventually survived the war. He also had relatives in Poznah, to whom Teresa sent her son to be taken care of.

It came about that as soon as the malicious gossip concerning Teresa got to the ears of Lagerfuhrer, he grabbed hold of his gun and drove Baszuro and Grygorcewicz outside into the yard, and there he was ready to shoot them. But all the women and children approached entreatingly and began weeping and begging, "Please do not kill my daddy. Please do not shoot my husband."

This softened the rage of the German, himself united in matrimony, and he let go of his gun and tremblingly in absence of mind walked into his office. Subsequently, he arranged that these two relatives of Teresa Baszuro be sent to the Russian front to dig trenches for the German soldiers, with a notion that there they would have a slight chance to survive anyway.

In the meantime about six months passed in Germany, and surprisingly we received a letter from our father written in Russian, which I read to my mother. The letter was opened and stamped with a German censorship; obviously it has passed an official examination. It conveyed a message that father and Waclawa were both alright and in good health, except that every day he was in combat against the Russians.

A new idea entered my head to use father's letter as leverage in order to acquire better conditions from the Germans. Immediately, I laid a plan and started to rehearse in German how to present my complaint before the chief, the Paulmann und Krone. When I became ready, I approached the engineer that was in charge of our section and told him that it was most important I speak to our chief. Always seen walking fast around the factory in a white coat like a doctor, he told me to keep on working and wait. However, several days later this engineer came straight to me, turned around and moved his finger as usual, meaning to follow him. So I followed him closely and he led me into the most luxurious office I could ever imagine. Here, behind a huge table, was sitting the proprietor in person. A master and nobleman of extremely dark complexion, he had long scar across his cheek, exactly the same as those three Germans murdered in Macsylin, as I remembered. The engineer exchanged a few words with his boss and quickly left. At that moment I was left standing alone before the chief. He looked at me with his dark, piercing eyes and said, "Yes! What can I do for you?"

Being frightened inwardly I endeavored to maintain composure and thus boldly said, "Herr Chief, my name is Mieczyslaw Klimowicz. My grandmother's maiden name was Wolan of German descent; my uncle Metro Majer is a Berliner and my father Wilhelm Klimowicz is in the German army fighting the Russians. I am working here twelve hours per day almost nine months without pay, and when I finish working I go to the barracks to rest and sleep, but the roof leaks whenever it rains. Also, we are Poles.

Why do we wear an OST?"

After the chief heard what I said, he said, "Do you have any proof that your father is in the German army?"

I replied, "Herr Chief, I have only this letter from my father written in the Russian language."

At once, he rung for a German interpreter who was the factory's timekeeper and spoke fluent Russian. As soon as he arrived, he took my letter and translated it to the chief. In addition, the interpreter made a comment and said, "This boy's father without any doubt is in the German army on the Russian front."

At that point the chief told me to go back to work.

A few weeks before while still wearing an OST, I was working together with a bunch of Russian youths who were seized in their homeland for labor in Germany. Naturally among ourselves we used the Russian language exclusively. A truckload of young Polish girls arrived from the district of Poznah to Paulmann und Krone factory. The Russians looked through the window and saw a full truck of girls in the yard. Being in the state of astonishment, they appealed loudly by saying, "Look! Polish girls."

At that moment, full of enthusiasm, I said, "Hey, I am Polish too!"

Then one Russian said to all others. "This fool thinks he is a Pole ... ha, ha, ha."

Suddenly I became doleful and regretted being blended together in their company.

The day after seeing the chief my engineer came and nodded to follow him outside the factory. There was a truck and a man standing by, and the engineer said to me, "Go with this gentleman."

The German drove westward outside the Ludenscheid and stopped by the Kaserne on the right side of the road. Here, parallel with an existing barracks of wooden construction in sound condition, he began to measure a foundation for the new brick building with my assistance. By the time this German construction engineer laid a base and the first few tiers of bricks, my help was no longer needed and I was sent back to work in the factory.

Now I was thinking something good was coming from the courage I had expressing my feelings of dissatisfaction to the Paulmann und Krone. Yet I was not sure if this new place was meant to be for us. Since no ruling was made in regard to my complaint, one can only observe the oncoming developments, whether it be good or bad, and form an opinion concerning the situation by its outcome.

Several weeks went by until unexpectedly we were moved from the Ludenscheid old barracks to a new place by the Kaserne outside town. Our group from Naliboki consisted of six families, and another family soon after was added. Mr. and Mrs. Sliwinski and their five children derived from the Ukraine territory. Our people were located at the wooden barracks by the road and the Polish girls from the district of Poznah were placed in a large room at the newly built brick dwelling. Next to the large room was Lagerfuhrer's quarters, and opposite across the corridor the living room was granted to us. At the entrance of this building on the Lagerfuhrer's side was a large room with victuals he provided once a week for everyone in the camp, and on our side of similar space was a bathroom.

Our weekly nourishment per person comprised of a tablespoon of marmalade, five grams of margarine, two thick slices of solid black German bread and ten grams of cheese. This weekly ration, however, one could eat as a single meal and wait for another the following week. Besides this weekly ration, the factory provided all workers once daily with liquid food made by boiling some horse meat, potatoes, and turnips or cabbages. This soup was always watery thin, deficient in substance of vegetable and meat. Still, there was perpetually a great deal of salt on the table since abundantly it was obtained from the ground nearby, so it could be taken with soup excessively. It helped to drink much water to reduce the discomfort caused by lack of food.

Throughout the period of nine months in Ludenscheid barracks, almost every night the Lagerfuhrer was driving us out to the woods during air raids, until I got so sick and tired because of exhaustion that I hid myself in the camp to sleep despite danger. Now in the new place at least we were undisturbed during the nightly air raids we watched from the distance; only the throng of hunger was greater each day. We were granted a "P" to wear and the men from the Russian camp were permitted to live with their families. After nine months I was also enrolled on payroll and began receiving five marks per month as one who is below full legal age. During many nights, when once I used to secretly sleep, now I was determined to hunt for food by sneaking out through the window and searching throughout the German dustbins, where mainly I could find some potato peelings, which I pushed inside my shirt since the Germans themselves were under depression of a severe decline in food resources. Mother used to wash these peelings from children's excrement and fry them on the stove for us to eat, and stretch it out to last us through many days. While we were walking to the factory to work in the dark at five in the morning, many of us used to collide into a lamppost because of blindness caused by lack of vitamin A, essential to the prevention of atrophy of epithelial tissue.

Shortly after we were liberated by the U.S. armed forces, we were moved from this new camp in Ludenscheid to a larger camp in Bucholtz that previously was occupied by the foreigners, who were severely maltreated and many killed and buried in the mass grave nearby. This camp upon the hill was badly infested with bugs, and these crawling insects at night in bed were sucking the blood of people asleep. Since virtually it was impossible to sleep, we used to be very busy at night burning these bugs in the cracks of wooden beds. A large crowd of Polish people at this camp immediately commenced to receive American rations delivered by the army, even including cigarettes, and of course soon everyone was revived from the German starvation.

Man's plight in the time of war habitually is an ideal tutor; it instructs how to survive when one is exposed to gunfire or famish. For example, during starvation in the hard labor camp I had ventured to be a black marketer in order to gain as much food as possible. I used to convert four rolls of tobacco into five simply by spreading the leaves, dampening them and assembling them to five rolls at the exact weight of five grams each. Naturally then, I placed some bad leaves inside and covered them with good ones to look presentable externally, just as any butcher displays his pork chops in a packet. Of course, many ideas like these were popping out freely from the mind and instinctively without external factor because I wanted to live and to diminish the bearing of pain. Since at the Bucholtz camp I was ineligible to receive cigarettes because of being sixteen years of age, I was impelled to alter my year of birth on the German document (Arbeits Buch) from 1929 to 1927; thus I was eligible at eighteen years of age to receive my cigarettes. After all, the Germans had destroyed all our records of birth in Poland, and no one would ever be wiser whether I was sixteen or eighteen. Except my mother two weeks later expressed feelings of dissatisfaction when I was drafted for service in the armed forces because I had caused myself to be eighteen years of age.

Just a short time before the actual partition of Germany, the Americans had mobilized Polish men from the ages of thirteen to thirty-five in the territory occupied by the U.S. armed forces. From Westphalia (Ger. Westfalen) at the end of May we were transported by army trucks to Bonn. Here in the huge German Kaserne, the following day exactly twenty-five men were placed in each goods- wagon, comprising one trainload of a thousand men. The train's destination was Verdon, France. But unfortunately the train traveling on a single railway track collided before reaching the Belgian border, and on the verge of surviving the war, this tragedy resulted in five hundred casualties. However, I was among the five hundred lucky ones, and arrived to Verdon in company with my school colleague, Mieczyslaw Dubicki. After completion of proper training we were employed in the U.S. army as Polish guards over 27,000 German prisoners of war. Subsequently, the dropping of the atom bombs on Hiroshima and Nagasaki on August 6 and 8, 1945, was the immediate cause of the cessation of hostilities on August 14, and the unconditional surrender was signed September 2, 1945. Thus World War II was ended.

After being discharged from the U.S. service in France, Mieczyslaw Dubicki and I came back to Germany and joined our families at D.P. camp Kosciuszko in Menden. Upon the hillock overlooking this town the newly built German residence came to be occupied by the Polish people. The displaced persons in Kosciuszko camp as well as in all other D.P. camps in Germany were taken care of by the United Nations Relief and Rehabitation Administration, and in addition, on account of lost schooling due to war, the Polish youths were sponsored educational opportunities of one's own free will. Necessary German educational centers were appropriated for Polish use, and thus the progress of enlightenment and culture was set up for the benefit of Polish youth in Germany.

Among a few Nalibokians from camp Kosciuszko, I also took advantage of this astounding opportunity and entered the school at Lippstadt - Consular Department of the Polish Army Mission by Expedient Control in Germany. Then I went to school near Hamburg, and finally at Moringen-Soiling, the Central Commission of Professional Association.

At Kosciuszko camp in Meaden there was a considerable number of people from Naliboki, and among those was my mother's cousin Lojko and her two little girls, Mr. Sienkiewicz and his family, including an adopted Russian little girl, and also Arkadjusz Makarewicz. My godmother, Marylka Wolan, her three children and Teresa Baszuro from this camp emigrated to England to join their husbands, who were there stationed in the Polish army. Mr. Baszuro and Mr. Grygorcewicz survived the Russian front and came back to Germany to join their families at the camp Kosciuszko in Menden.

The life in general in the camp was well adjusted for the reason that everyone was happy, well fed and entertained. Here the people had the Roman Catholic Church with Polish priests, a doctor clinic, an elementary school, a dance hall, and the cinema. Yet, in spite of such a comfortable life, we were all anxious to return to our homeland, Naliboki, the Free State of Poland. At this point in time I wondered what source of power actually was holding us back. Why were we not permitted to go home to rebuild the place? The war had ended and yet we were not quite free. Who had the true answers to these questions?

Over a year had passed since the war ended and not till then did we receive our father's letter in Mendea from Jeleaia Gora, the retrieved new land of Poland. This was indeed unexpected news to us, knowing that he and Waclawa survived the war and came to live in the western part of Poland. Soon after we also received a letter from our cousin Czestaw Lojko from England. He wrote about how miraculously he, his mother and father were rescued from Siberia and brought to convalescence in Uganda, Africa, an independent member of the Commonwealth of Nations. Unfortunately, Heniek, his little brother, died in Siberian enslavement. Czeslaw, however, after training in Africa became a navigator and was assigned to England for the bombardment of Germany, and as usual his missions were carried out at night. But now after the war, he still remained with his parents in England.

Just before the educational centers were established there was nothing much to do to arise my curiosity in the camp, and besides, it happened to be most convenient to travel by train in Germany. So I took a tour for inspection of the D.P. camps in order to see if I could find some relatives who outlived the war. As I visited quite a number of scattered D.P. camps in the British Zone, I was lucky to find my three cousins, Boniutek, Gienek and Michal Klimowicz, with their mother Genefa. I also found my great-aunt Wolan, who was an extraordinary loving person and extremely hospitable to me since my childhood. She used to call me inside her house and feed me when I was playing near their home. Her kind generosity left a good impression on my mind to remember her genuine love for the little children. Presently in the D.P. camp she was left with two grandchildren (girls) and a daughter-in-law, the wife of her son Edward, who was killed in Naliboki's massacre in May 1943. My poor great-aunt was overwhelmed by grief because her last son, Kazimerz, was seized by the Gestapo to a concentration camp and tortured to death together with other men from Naliboki. Among those victims there was my school colleague Szarzanowicz, who claimed he saw the vision of Virgin Mary in our classroom when it happened back in 1938; likewise Edward and Kazimerz beheld the same six months later in Maczylin.

As I returned to camp Kosciuszko my baby Krystina was received into the church by confirmation and brother Antoni began his elementary school, which he completed in the duration of just two years due to a speedy process of education that was honored on account of the war impeding and with respect to excellent pupils.

Periodically all displaced persons were interrogated by the British authorities, who were determined to know why the Polish people did not want to go back to their homeland. Of course, those from the Curzon Line A on the west side of Poland were gradually going home. However, those people like ourselves from the eastern part of Curzon Line A categorically refused to go back on the ground of Communistic disposition and Soviet Union occupation. So from this point of view it was generally understood and commonly recognized that the people from Naliboki had no country to go to, and correspondingly it was entered into the record of each individual that stated, "I refuse to go back to my country because of the Communistic disposition in Poland." Thus in actual sense or fact, legally each one of us declared to be an enemy of the Soviet Union. Therefore, henceforth it became clear to us that in a conceivable outcome of the USSR invasion on Great Britain, we the people with such a record became the first in line for extermination by the Communistic regime, as it occurred during Bolshevik's revolution or Stalin's collectivization when millions of people were killed. Nevertheless, it did not come to pass because God intervened and his appointed time had not yet arrived for the annihilation of impious peoples.

Before destroying this wicked system, God is allowing an opportunity for the people to demonstrate whether they really want to live in harmony with his righteous laws or not. At God's appointed time, he will without fail destroy the wicked. Thus God put off the destruction of the wicked so as to allow time to select people whom he would glorify with Christ as members of the heavenly Kingdom. It is part of God's arrangement for blessing people of all sorts who will be favored with the opportunity to live forever on a paradise earth. (Psalm 37:10, 11) All the earth will be transformed into a paradise under the rule of Christ as king because in the days of those kings the God of heaven will set up a Kingdom that will never be brought to ruin. And the Kingdom itself will not be passed on to any other people, it will crush and put an end to all these kingdoms, and it itself will stand to time indefinite. The earthly resurrection will follow, all those in the memorial tombs will hear the voice of Jesus and come out. The persons remembered by God will be resurrected with the opportunity to live forever.

And then it will be just as Apostle John wrote on Patmos 96 A.D. And I saw a new heaven and a new earth, for the former heaven and the former earth had passed away, and the sea is no more. I saw also the holy city, New Jerusalem, coming down out of Heaven from God and prepared as a bride adorned for her husband. With that I heard a loud voice from the throne say. Look! The tent of God is with mankind, and he will reside with them and they will be his peoples. And God himself will be with them. And he will wipe out every tear from their eyes, and death will be no more, neither will mourning nor outcry nor pain be any more. The former things have passed away. And the one seated on the throne said. Look! I am making all things new. Also, he says. Write, because these words are faithful and true. (Da. 2:44; Re. 21:5)

Looking way back upon this sad prose literature that embraces Naliboki, the ancient city of fallen angels, it conveys nothing else than the ultimate destiny of devastation by repeated tragedies that became legendary events of that period. However, in order to be fully convinced about these factual past occurrences one must go back in time to antiquity to imagine and see how the earth was filled with violence. And look! It was ruined because all flesh had ruined its way on the earth. Then from that point, as one goes forward some centuries, one can see how a giant's footprint washed away by the Deluge, and other generations built new wicked cities about the place. Further in time one can see how these chronic, fatal cities had been plunged beneath the waters without power to show mercy or compassion, and thus became haunted lakes ever since. See how anew the pagan temples of Perkuna were raised and consecrated to the worship of the goddess of animals in the Wilderness of Naliboki. See how these temples were consumed in a direction toward eternal ruin. See how the savage hunt of noble warriors began in the Wilderness of Naliboki until the time when King Sigismund Augustus realized he had almost lost his life. See how this last king of the dynasty of Jagellon constructed a Chapel of Rome in Naliboki on the ruins of Perkuna temple and performed in fulfillment of a vow his salvation by setting apart the votive offerings as sacred in this chapel so that an ancient curse may be revived in this archaic city of fallen angels. See how the Radziwill principality that resided in the castles of Nowogrodek came to Naliboki and raised the church of St. Bartholomew on the elated ground of demons where the king's chapel was and consigned his votive offerings for future use of condemnation. See how additionally, in order to excite to anger our loving heavenly Father, the people in Naliboki manufactured magnificent swords with hilts from the polished stone, which spilled the blood of many fellow citizens until the curse took its toll in effect that Poland underwent the act of partition and ceased to exist. Thus the Polish kingdom, despite 835 years of reign, become extinct, and there was left only the time and space for poets to pine after. See how unpleasant and spiteful tyranny persisted over the period of 123 years, but finally, owing to a phenomenal man who derived from Wilenszczyzna, Jozef Pilsudski, a twinkling independence of Poland was proclaimed and it was recognized by the Treaty of Versailles. Such a laconic independence only deceived penitent people who in the form of daily greeting spoke loud the Lord Jesus Christ. And in this pompous freedom of peace and security the last Radziwill in Naliboki was a dreamer to fall in love with a gorgeous Wierka Klimowicz. See how Radziwill's subsequent sense of human life was embodied in a tragic drama by the arch-opposer of both God and man, and as a widower with two children in painful sorrow he finalized his hymeneal remembrance in a composition of poems. And finally see the last day of Naliboki prepared by Satan, but God took a decisive role, and the multitude of family trees on that precise day he uprooted from the city of fallen angels and planted afresh in the free countries of Europe and the Western Hemisphere. After that, Jehovah shut the door behind them just like an ark door in Noah's day, thus making sure that no one was able to go back before the great day of God the Almighty.

Because of the undeserved kindness of God we were rescued from the cursed homeland, and his free gift with the undeserved kindness by the one man Jesus Christ abounded much more to many, and that is why we will not need to fight anymore, but take our position, stand still and see the salvation of Jehovah in our behalf.

She is to become an uninhabited desolation and a haunt of wild creatures for generation after generation, as Jehovah sweeps Babylon with the broom of annihilation. No name, no remnant, no progeny, no posterity are to remain! These are the words that were written two hundred years in advance by Isaiah pronouncing Babylon's doom. It is also a remarkable concurrence of calamity in comparison to that of Naliboki, including its proximity, which just over a half of century ago was swept with the broom of annihilation. So that there is no name, except those of the dead, no remnant left of any relatives; thus no progeny, no posterity are there to remain. That is why the Wilderness of Naliboki became an uninhabited desolation and a haunt of wild beasts until the time of the end of this system of things.

The supernatural event of the last day of Naliboki actually happened to be a miniature portrayal of the great tribulation in reference to unclean inspired expressions that come out of the mouth of the dragon and out of the mouth of the wild beast and out of the mouth of the false prophet. They are, in fact, expressions inspired by demons and perform signs, and they go forth to the kings of the entire inhabited earth, to gather them together to the war of the great day of God the Almighty. (Rev. 16:13) Yes, in Naliboki there was peace, prosperity and security; then befell a sudden destruction that took its toll in the three particular stages: Stage 1. Desecration of the church. Stage 2. Collapse of commercial practices. Stage 3. Satan's final attack on God's remaining fearing people. But his assault set off Jehovah's rage, which brought terrible defeat and destruction upon his crowd, by means of which defenseless people from Naliboki had been set free.

Because of uninhabited desolation, the pavements and cobblestone streets, where once during the massacre blood of many flowed in the gutters just like water after a heavy rain fall, now are covered with a blanket of dirt, a fragmentary material deposited by air from one to two feet thick. The landscape of Naliboki is fashioned no different than the ruins in the area of Ishtar Gate of ancient Babylon, except for skeleton structures. There are none, since the dwellings were mainly constructed of wood and thus were utterly consumed by fire. A few relatives from the remote places, like Jozef Lojko's wife with five children, for some reason failed to abandon their homestead in time. Later, however, they were detained by the Soviet Union, and it was impossible for them to obtain release for Poland, but eventually they

The brick structure of the church in Naliboki from 1936 was klmpleted and consecrated to the Virgin Mary July 5, 1994.

were all set free after Stalin's death in 1953. Some new settlers from godless Communist Russia came to Naliboki, and a small insignificant group of Polish people chose to live there from encirclement. These Polish Roman Catholic people built a barracks upon the ashes of the church of St. Bartholomew for use as a house of worship and school for their children. Recently, however, this small group of Polish people received a donation from Nalibokian folks residing abroad and in Poland for the completion of the unfinished brick structure church, which was finally consecrated to the Virgin Mary on July 5, 1994, by the metropolitan Minsk-Mohylew archbishop Kazimierz Swiatek.

My uncle Jozef Lojko was released from Polish prison and lived with his mistress in Czenstochowa. Subsequently his wife and five children were set free from the Soviet Union, but she declined to live with him. Jozef Lojko made a living from apiculture and passed away in 1983.

My father's cousin, Alfons Lojko resides near Jelenia Gora with his mistress. His wife with daughter survived in the Soviet Union, and a long time after World War II they were released and came to Poland. She also refused to live with her husband Alfons on the grounds of betrayal.

My uncle Eugenjusz Klimowicz had his death sentence reversed because of Stalin's death, and after ten years imprisonment he was released, but Janka, his wife, was living with another man. He married again and resided in Slupsk. He died at age seventy-two on February 13, 1988, in the rank of major, and his name was placed on the marble tablet among Polish heros in Warsaw.

My father Wilhelm Klimowicz passed away in February 1955 in Jelenia Gora. Our grandfather Franciszek Lojko was in care of my sister Waclawa, and he passed away in Jelenia Gora. His wife, Orszula Lojko, our grandmother, previously died in Poland from starvation. Her son Boleslaw Lojko, employed as a public prosecutor, died in Szczecin at the age of eighty-one on September 24, 1992, and was succeeded by his wife, son and two daughters.

Orszula Lojko, the wife of Michai Lojko, came to live in Szczecin with her three children, Marysia, Lucjan and Helena. Their mother passed away in Szczecin.

All other displaced persons from Naliboki and its vicinity who were disseminated in Germany, the part occupied by USSR, were involuntarily trapped in Poland. However, the most fortunate ones were found in American and British Zones and became refugees, and from Germany subsequently they emigrated to the countries of democracy of their own choice, such as Great Britain, Canada, the United States of America and Australia.

In 1948 I emigrated to England with the anticipation of meeting my uncle Waclaw Lojko, but when I got there they had already left for United States and settled down in Hartford, Connecticut with my aunt's relatives, permanent residents. Aunt Mania Lojko passed away in 1970, and Uncle Waclaw died in 1985 and is buried with his wife in Hartford. Their son Czeslaw Lojko while in England married a Scottish girl, and from England they emigrated to Australia. Czeslaw, an ex-navigator in World War II, was employed as a surveyor and died in 1987, succeeded by his wife and two children.

My mother, Jozefe Klimowicz, sister Krystina and brother Antoni consequently made their homestead in Angola, New York. Mother passed away in Angola in 1984. Antoni's oldest son bears the name of our father, Wilhelm Klimowicz, or William Anthony Klimowicz; he has been awarded the degree of Bachelor of Chemical Engineering at the University of Dayton and was appointed second lieutenant, reserve commissioned officer in the United States Army in 1985. Subsequently, he achieved a master's degree and married General Robson's daughter Catherine, but unfortunately William's dearly beloved wife passed away at the age of twenty-three. Her funeral was accompanied by all members of the Pentagon at Arlington Cemetery. Presently my nephew William Klimowicz holds the rank of major and is ambitiously pursuing his remarkable career to become a general.

Mieczyslaw Klimowicz

KATHERINE

I once knew a yellow rose
which I always loved to see;
We waited for each other,
as happy as can be:

Her eyes were bright as diamonds,
they sparkled like the dew:
Her color was the sweetest,
a fellow ever knew:

But then the weather changed,
turning very cold:
That beautiful yellow rose,
began to wither and fold:
The days came very quickly,
I soon was left to know:
The rose that once stood boldly,
no longer shined and glowed:

Now the site of yellow roses,
brings tears to my eyes:
She'll always live on forever,
for I keep her in my heart:

All of our memories,
and all of our joys:
Are standing in Arlington Cemetery,
where she'll always live on and be heard.

by David Klimowicz

The ultimate destiny of our small group of people in Ludenscheid was to be scattered throughout the world just like any other group of Nalibokians in Germany. Jozef Dubicki and his wife, son Mieczyslaw and daughter Jadwiga emigrated to Australia. Witold Baszuro with his wife Mania, son Stanislaw and two daughters, Teresa and Jadwiga, emigrated to Minnesota in the USA. (Witold is deceased.) Karol Grygorcewicz and his wife and four children emigrated to Buffalo, N.Y. Karol, his wife and daughter Lonia passed away in Buffalo. My godmother Marylka Wolan, her three children and Baszuro Witold's sister joined their husbands in England. Of course, Baszuro, who was on the Russian front with Karol, emigrated with his wife and children to Australia, and with them also emigrated Mr. Sliwinski and his wife and four children, who were with us in Ludenscheid from Galicia.

My father's dear friend Antoni Szarzanowicz and his wife, two sons and daughter were also sponsored by U.S. citizens in Buffalo. Antoni, his wife and two sons are deceased, succeeded by only daughter Wala. She is married with children, and her daughter, after she completed her college studies, became employed in the White House in Washington, D.C.

My uncle Jan Radziwill with two children, Jurek and Danusia, emigrated to the USA. Jan's avocation was destined to write some symbolic poetry pertaining to his painful memories of a tragic life with Wierka, about which he always ejaculated to his acquaintance until his death in 1977 in Indianapolis, Indiana. Jurek Radziwill, married with three children, and also Danusia, married with three children, both reside in Indianapolis, Indiana. Jan Radziwill was sponsored by the Catholic Church in Indianapolis, where he was also permanently employed. He is buried at Holy Cross and St. Joseph Cemeteries, Catholic Cemeteries Association.

My father's cousin Gabryjela and her husband, Jozef Kosciukiewicz, and two daughters emigrated to the USA. Jozef, who once fooled NKVD in Naliboki, here was nicknamed "Happy Joe." He died as such in South Bend, Indiana. Also Gabryjela passed away recently.

Orszula Klimowicz, sister of Benedikt Klimowicz, with her niece Regina Klimowicz, whose mother was Alzusia Klimowicz, emigrated from Germany to the USA and lived in Chicago, Illinois. Orszula met a tragic death by fire and Regina passed away in 1970.

Gabryjela's nephews Bonifacy Klimowicz, Eugenjusz and Michal, along with their mother Genefa Klimowicz, they emigrated from Germany to Hamilton, Canada, and in this way they were devoted neighbors to my immediate family in Buffalo. Bonifacy, Michal and Genefa passed away and are succeeded by Eugenjusz Klimowicz.

My aunt Bronislawa Klimowicz married Antoni Kiczuia from Galicia in Germany. They emigrated to the USA in 1951 and lived in Baltimore, Maryland. My great aunt Wolari emigrated with her daughter-in-law and two grandchildren, whose father Edward Wolan died in Naliboki's massacre, to Massachusetts. These two Wolan young girls on their vacation from school frequently visited Bronislawa Kiczuia in Baltimore before they both became nurses. Aunt Bronislawa passed away in my

The memorial tombs of Eugenjusz Klimowicz and Jan Radziwill, one in Poland and the other in the USA.

arms on March 5, 1975, and according to her wishes I buried her with her dearly beloved husband Antoni Kiczula in a Baltimore cemetery.

Undoubtedly in like manner a hodomania and necromania was such an ultimate destiny of all others, the great number of people from Naliboki, Terebejno, Prudy, Jankowicze, Kleciszcze, Szemioty, Niescierowicze, Clelechowszczyzna, Ogrodniki, Kozliki, Rudnia, and Chotow.

Since the whole world is lying in the power of the wicked one, what can we expect of the wicked one, Satan? Satan brought his untimely death to many during World War II and threatened to destroy Jehovah's institution of marriage, and thus he brought an end to our peaceful family life. We as little children had even never dreamed to be completely deprived from our parents and not ever see them during their natural lifetimes. As a consequence of the satanic war, most of the survivors from the region of Naliboki became disunited, when once they were all happy family units. Subsequently, being also scattered worldwide, most of them already passed away and remain in memorial tombs with regard to the earthly resurrection to be a subjects of God's Messianic kingdom after the end of this system. Then the kingdom of God takes up full power; this would be because his Deputy King, his son, would now enter into a special, more extensive phase of ruling, and the "kingdom of the world would became the kingdom of our Lord and of his Christ, and he will rule as king forever and ever." The arrival of this time would mean Jesus Christ now taking all necessary measures to clean out opposition to God's sovereignty both in heaven and on earth.

There will be no more gleamy pillars at the cemetery in Naliboki that caused harm to so many and no more haunting by demons at Lake Kroman. Then, the archenemy, Satan the devil himself, will be seized and completely put out of operation for a thousand years, during which all the effects of his vile influence will be completely removed and the earth will be transformed into Paradise. After that, Satan will be released for a short period of time to test restored mankind. All humans that choose to follow him will be annihilated, together with Satan and his demons.

At last, what a wonderful aspect it will be when all the families are united in their own homeland, Naliboki, into one genealogical tree. When the earth will be transformed into Paradise, the wolf and the lamb themselves will feed as one, and the lion will eat straw just like the bull. They will do no harm nor cause any ruin in all Jehovah's holy mountain.

The provision of a resurrection for humankind is indeed an undeserved kindness of Jehovah God, for he was not obligated to provide a resurrection. Love for the world of mankind moved him to give his only begotten son so that millions, yes, even thousands of millions who have died without a real knowledge of God might have the opportunity to know and love him, and so that those who love and serve him can have this hope and encouragement to faithful endurance, even as far as death.

Conditions then prevailing on earth will be refreshingly different from anything that the old world has ever produced. Through application of the benefits of Christ's sacrifice and by means of education in the will of God, obedient ones, including those resurrected from the dead, will be freed from every trace of sin and will be helped to progress physically, mentally, emotionally and spiritually until they attain perfection. The earth's produce will be used to supply generously the needs of all mankind. Life will take on greater richness of meaning than ever before as mankind works together to fulfill the Creator's original purpose for this earth and its inhabitants.

In joyful anticipation of all of this, God's spirit and the bride of Christ now extend an earnest invitation to people everywhere and to those from the region of Naliboki who had been miraculously rescued, saying: "Come!" And let anyone hearing say: "Come!" And let anyone thirsting come; let anyone that wishes take life's water free. (Revelation 22;17)

Now, therefore, is no time simply to wait until the countdown to Jehovah's great day reaches its zero hour at the great tribulation in which this last generation foretold by Jesus will not pass away, for some people although very old will still remain alive to see it. So, hope in Jehovah and keep his way, and he will exalt you to take possession of the earth. When the wicked ones are cut off, you will see it. (Psalm 37:34)

Having accepted the gracious invitation to "take life's water free," you now have the privilege to extend that invitation to others. It is a time for zealous activity on the part of all whose eager desire is to be survivors into God's splendid "new earth."

This mysterious triangle of poltergeists throughout the centuries turned out to be the greatest casualty location in Europe that exists within the geographical fork of river Niemen and Wilia, or for that matter a symbolic fork of Satan. Here, from the rise of the People's Commissariat of Internal Affairs in 1935, and a subsequent despot of Nazis, over a million innocent people had been massacred by the end of World War II. Who can calculate then the number of people, particularly those who were killed during World War I and all those in the previous centuries, and even people of those centuries who are stretching up to other civilized nations of antiquity?

Satan had a grip on all mankind through sin, and even succeeded in having Jesus put to death. First getting control of one of his apostles, then using the Jewish leaders and the Roman world power to execute Jesus in a painful and ignominious manner. Here Satan acted as "the one having the means to cause death, that is, the Devil. But in this Satan failed to promote his cause, he only unwillingly fulfilled prophecy, which required that Jesus had to die as a sacrifice. The death of Jesus in blamelessness provided the ransom price for humankind, and by his death and subsequent resurrection by God Jesus could now help sinful humankind to escape from the grip of Satan, for, as it is written, Jesus became blood and flesh, that through his death he might bring to nothing the one having the means to cause death, that is, the Devil, and that he might emancipate all those who for fear of death were subject to slavery all through their lives." (Heb. 2:14, 15)

CONCLUSION

Notwithstanding the fact that we were born and lived in that archaic city of fallen angels under a cursed ordeal beyond man's imagination, and since those who sustained such a trial continue to exist by haunting tune of nightmares, for this reason I hereby respectfully dedicate this authentic untold story to the memory of all the victims who originated in the region of Naliboki. To the foresters and their families who perished in Siberia from cold and hunger, and their survivors. To the police and social workers who were tortured to death by NKVD and murdered by Byelorussian people. To all the Hebrew people who underwent barbarous, genocidal death by the hands of German SS in the Nowogrodek, Minsk and Wilno triangle, to the forty-four victims, men, women and children, massacred in a mass grave by Wehrmach at the little valley between two skirts of wood. To the more than five hundred men and boys massacred in the streets of Naliboki by the Soviet partisans and to all those families burned alive and murdered previously by the Byelorussian and Ukrainian bandits. To all the people and priests whom Wehrmach butchered on the last day of Naliboki. To all those who perished in the hard labor camps and concentration camps in Germany, and to all those thousands who survived and live in Poland, and to all those thousands of refugees who enjoy freedom pertaining to the principles of democracy abroad in the distant countries of the world.

It is also my privilege and honor to dedicate this story to the prominent Dr. Kevin Reid, to whom God without niggardliness enhanced the skill that recurrently saved my life. As a consequence of revealing divine truth concerning God in his relations to man, the great adversary of God and tempter of mankind, Lucifer became displeased and thus made an attempt to terminate my work. Nevertheless, Jehovah God has granted time and guided me in the process of connecting all the scattered pieces together into one combined unit so that you, the reader, may know the machination of the devil and see the mighty hand of Jehovah, so that he may exalt you in due tine.

Seek Jehovah, all you meek ones of the earth, who have practiced His own judicial decision. Seek righteousness, seek meekness. Probably you may be concealed in the day of Jehovah's anger. (Zep. 2:3)

The progeny of Edward Wolan.
Two daughters, Stefania and Anna Wolan in Germany. Their father Edward Nolan died in Naliboki's massacre on May 23, 1943. Subsequently in the USA both Stefania and Anna were granted a diploma by an educational institution.

Left: In Germany, on the left standing with two other girls from Naliboki, Krystyna Klimowicz at her first holy communion. Right: In Buffalo, N.Y., Krystyna is kneeling in front of her mother and brother Antoni Klimowicz. On the left is Wala Szarzanowicz and standing next to my mother on the right is Mrs Szarzanowicz and her husband, Antoni Szarzanowicz, my father's closest neighbor and loyal friend. His son Michael Szarzanowicz, a mere youth, died in Naliboki's massacre.

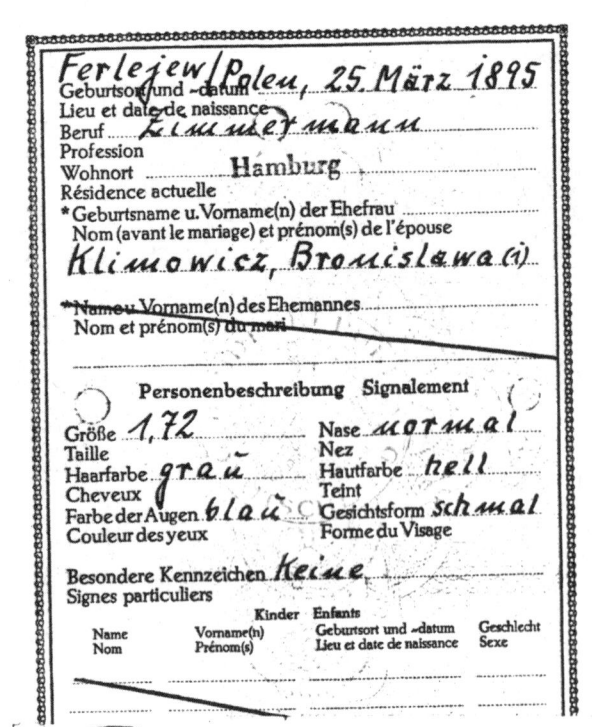

Ferlejew/Polen, 25. März 1895
Geburtsort und -datum
Lieu et date de naissance
Beruf Zimmermann
Profession
Wohnort Hamburg
Résidence actuelle
*Geburtsname u. Vorname(n) der Ehefrau
Nom (avant le mariage) et prénom(s) de l'épouse
Klimowicz, Bronislawa (i)
*Name u. Vorname(n) des Ehemannes
Nom et prénom(s) du mari

Personenbeschreibung Signalement
Größe 1,72   Nase normal
Taille   Nez
Haarfarbe grau   Hautfarbe hell
Cheveux   Teint
Farbe der Augen blau Gesichtsform schmal
Couleur des yeux   Forme du Visage

Besondere Kennzeichen Keine
Signes particuliers

Kinder Enfants
Name Vorname(n) Geburtsort und -datum Geschlecht
Nom   Prénom(s)   Lieu et date de naissance Sexe

F 2

Heiratsurkunde

amt Glücksburg ———————— Nr. 51/1948)

Der Zimmermann Antin Kiczula, katholisch ————
———————, wohnhaft Glücksburg, Ukrainerlager Meierwik

geboren am 25. März 1895 in Firlejów, Kreis Rohatyn, Polen

(Standesamt ———————————— Nr. ————————), und

die Bronislawa Klimowicz, Köchin, katholisch ————
———————, wohnhaft Glücksburg, Polenlager Meierwik

geboren am 2. Oktober 1893 in Naliboki, Polen

(Standesamt ———————————— Nr. ————————)

haben am 27. April 1948 ————

Glücksburg ————————

Heiratsurkunde (ohne Elternangabe).
Lager-Nr. St. B 10. — F. Johannsens Buchdruckerei, Johs. Ibbeken, Schleswig

A 8214888   I 1087175
(REGISTRATION NO.) THIS IS TO CERTIFY THAT
BRONISLAWA
KICZULA
WAS ADMITTED TO THE UNITED STATES
ON 011152 AT 0300
   MONTH DAY YEAR   DISTRICT PORT
AS A DP QUOTA IMMIGRANT UNDER 555 OF THE
    TYPE   SECTION
IMMIGRATION ACT OF 1924 AND HAS BEEN REGISTERED
UNDER THE ALIEN REGISTRATION ACT OF 1940.
DATE OF BIRTH   SEX
100293 F
MONTH DAY YEAR
COMMISSIONER OF IMMIGRATION AND NATURALIZATION

About the Author

Author photograph by Janusz Skowron.

MIECZYSLAW KLIMOWICZ was liberated from the German hard labor camp that served as his home for two years on May 10, 1945. He was immediately mobilized to the U.S. Army, and after passing military training was assigned to guard German prisoners of war in Verdon, France. After Japanese capitulation on September 2, 1945, Mieczyslaw was voluntarily discharged and returned to Germany to be with his family. He eventually finished his elementary education and passed an entry exam to the agricultural school in Lippstadt. After earning a certificate of completion there, he completed a course with the Young Men's and Women's Christian Association in Hamburg and received accreditation as a YMCA Leader. In this capacity he was assigned to the YMCA & YWCA summer camp in Izerlon. He subsequently received a certificate for completing the regional farming school of breeding faculty in Moringen-Solling. Having now completed his education, he relocated to England in July 1948. Throughout his professional career he spent time employed as an interpreter, a constructional engineer, and finally as a businessman. Presently retired, Mieczyslaw enjoys drawing and painting.